Henry Hart Milman

History of Latin Christianity

Including that of the Popes to the Pontificate of Nicolas V.

Henry Hart Milman

History of Latin Christianity
Including that of the Popes to the Pontificate of Nicolas V.

ISBN/EAN: 9783741183799

Manufactured in Europe, USA, Canada, Australia, Japa

Cover: Foto ©Thomas Meinert / pixelio.de

Manufactured and distributed by brebook publishing software
(www.brebook.com)

Henry Hart Milman

History of Latin Christianity

HISTORY

OF

LATIN CHRISTIANITY;

INCLUDING THAT OF

THE POPES TO THE PONTIFICATE OF NICOLAS V.

By HENRY HART MILMAN, D.D.,

DEAN OF ST. PAUL'S.

IN NINE VOLUMES.—Vol. IX.

FOURTH AND REVISED EDITION.

LONDON:
JOHN MURRAY, ALBEMARLE STREET.
1867.

CONTENTS

OF

THE NINTH VOLUME.

BOOK XIV.

CHAPTER I

SURVEY.

a 2

CHAPTER II.

BELIEF OF LATIN CHRISTIANITY.

CHAPTER III.

LATIN LETTERS.

CHAPTER IV.

CHRISTIAN LATIN POETRY.—HISTORY.

CHAPTER V.

CHRISTIAN LETTERS IN THE NEW LANGUAGES OF EUROPE.

CHAPTER VI.

CHAPTER VII.

TEUTONIC LANGUAGES.

CHAPTER VIII.

CHRISTIAN ARCHITECTURE.

CHAPTER IX.

CHRISTIAN SCULPTURE.

CHAPTER X.

CHRISTIAN PAINTING.

HISTORY

OF

LATIN CHRISTIANITY.

BOOK XIV.

CHAPTER I.

Survey.

FROM the reign of Nicolas V. and the close of our history, as from a high vantage-ground, we must survey the whole realm of Latin Christendom—the political and social state, as far as the relation of Latin Christianity to the great mass of mankind; the popular religion, with its mythology; the mental development in philosophy, letters, arts.

Eight centuries and a half had elapsed since the Pontificate of Gregory the Great—the epoch of the supreme dominion of Latin Christianity in the West. The great division of mankind, which at that time had become complete and absolute, into the Clergy (including the Monks, in later days the Friars) and the rest of mankind, still subsisted in all its rigorous force. They were two castes, separate and standing apart as by the irrepealable law of God. They were distinct, adverse, even antagonistic, in their theory of life, in their laws, in their corporate property, in their rights, in their immunities. In the aim and object of their existence, in their social duties and position, they were set asunder by a broad,

deep, impassable line. But the ecclesiastical caste being
bound, at least by its law, to celibacy, in general could
not perpetuate its race in the ordinary course of nature;
it was renewed by drawing forth from the laity men
either endowed with or supposed to be trained to a
peculiar mental turn, those in whom the intellectual
capacity predominated over the physical force. Religion,
which drove many out of the world within the sacred
circle, might be a sentiment, a passion, an unthinking
and unreasoning impulse of the inward being; holy ignorance might be the ambition, the boast of some monks,
and of the lower friars; but in general the commission
to teach the religion implied (though itself an infused
gift or grace, and the inseparable consequence of legitimate consecration to the office) some superiority of
mind. At all events the body was to be neglected,
sacrificed, subdued, in order that the inner being might
ripen to perfection. The occupations of the clergy were
to be in general sedentary, peaceful, quiescent. Their
discipline tended still further to sift, as it were, this
more intellectual class: the dull and negligent sunk
into the lower offices, or, if belonging by their aristocratic descent to the higher, they obtained place and influence only by their race and connexions, wealth and
rank by unclerical powers of body and of mind. These
were ecclesiastics by profession, temporal princes, even
soldiers, by character and life. But this, according to
the strict theory of the clerical privilege, was an abuse,
an usurpation. Almost all minds which were gifted with
or conscious of great intellectual capacity, unless kings,
or nobles, or knights, whose talents might lead to military distinction, appeared predestined for, were irre-
sistibly drawn into, or were dedicated by their prescient
parents or guardians to the Church. The younger sons,

especially the illegitimate sons, even of kings, far more
of princes and nobles, were devoted, as the Church became wealthy and powerful, to this career as a provision.
But even with this there either was, or according to
general opinion there ought to have been, some vocation
and some preparation : many of these were among the
ablest, some even among the most austere and pious of
churchmen. The worst, if they did not bring the more
fitting qualifications, brought connexion, famous names
(in feudal times of great importance), and thus welded
together, as it were, the Church with the State.

Education, such as it was (and in many cases for the
times it was a high education), had become, *Education.*
with rare exceptions, their exclusive privilege.
Whoever had great capacities or strong thirst for knowledge could neither obtain nor employ it but· in the
peaceful retirement, under the sacred character, with
the special advantages of the churchman, or in the
cloister. The whole domain of the human intellect was
their possession. The universities, the schools, were
theirs, and theirs only. There the one strife was between
the secular clergy and the regulars—the monks, or the
friars the disciples of S. Dominic and S. Francis. They
were the canon lawyers, and for some centuries, as far
as it was known or in use, the teachers and professors of
the civil law. They were the historians, the poets, the
philosophers. It was the first omen of their endangered
supremacy that the civil lawyers in France rose against
them in bold rivalry. When in the Empire the study
of the old Roman law developed principles of greater
antiquity, therefore, it was asserted, of greater authority
than the canon law, it was at once a sign and a proof
that their absolute dominion was drawing towards its
close—that human intellect was finding another road to

distinction and power. Physical science alone, in general, though with some famous exceptions, they unwisely declined: they would not risk the popular suspicion of magical and forbidden arts—a superstition which themselves indulged and encouraged. The profound study of the human body was thought inconsistent with the fastidious modesty of their profession.* The perfection of medicine and of all cognate inquiries, indeed in general of natural philosophy itself, was left to Jews and Arabs: the great schools of medicine, Montpellier and Salerno, as they derived their chief wisdom from these sources, so they freely admitted untonsured, perhaps unbaptised, students. It is difficult to calculate the extent of this medical influence, which must have worked, if in secret, still with great power. The jealousy and hatred with which Jews or supposed unbelievers are seen at the courts of kings is a secret witness to that influence. At length we find the king's physician, as under Louis XI., the rival in authority of the king's confessor. In this alone the hierarchical caste does not maintain its almost exclusive dominion over all civil as well as ecclesiastical transactions.

For it is not only from their sacred character, but from their intellectual superiority, that they are in the courts, in the councils, of kings; that they are the negotiators, the ambassadors of sovereigns; they alone can read and draw up state papers, compacts, treaties, or frame laws. Writing is almost their special mystery; the notaries, if not tonsured, as they mostly were, are directed, ordered by the Clergy: they are in general the servants and agents of ecclesiastics. In every king-

---

* The observant Chaucer gives the converse. Physicians were even then under the evil fame of irreligion. "His studie was but littel on the Bible." Prologue on the Doctor o' Physique.

dom of Europe the Clergy form one of the estates, balance or blindly lead the nobles; and this too not merely as churchmen and enrolled in the higher service of God, but from their felt and acknowledged pre-eminence in the administration of temporal affairs.

To this recognised intellectual superiority — arising out of the power of selecting the recruits for their army according to their mental stature, their sole possession of the discipline necessary to train such men for their loftier position, and the right of choosing, as it were, their officers out of this chosen few—must be added their spiritual authority, their indefeasible power of pre-declaring the eternal destiny of every living layman. To doubt the sentence of that eternal destiny was now an effort of daring as rare as it was abhorrent to the common sense of men. Those who had no religion had superstition; those who believed not trembled and were silent; the speculative unbeliever, if there were such, shrouded himself in secrecy from mankind, even from himself: the unuttered lawless thought lay deep in his own heart. Those who openly doubted the unlimited power of the clergy to absolve were sects, outcasts of society, proscribed not only by the detestation of the clergy, but by the popular hatred. The keys of heaven and hell were absolutely in the hands of the priesthood —even more, in this life they were not without influence. In the events of war, in the distribution of earthly misery or blessing, abundance or famine, health or pestilence, they were the intercessors with the saints, as the saints were intercessors with heaven. They were invested in a kind of omniscience. Confession, since the decree of the Lateran Council under Innocent III., an universal, obligatory, indispensable duty, laid open the whole heart of every one, from the Emperor to the peasant, before the priesthood; the entire moral being of man, undistinguishable from his religious being, was under their supervision and control, asserted on one side, acknowledged on the other. No act was beyond their cognisance, no act, hardly any thought, was secret. They were at once a government and a police, to which every one was bound to inform against himself, to be the agent of the most rigid self-delation, to endure the closest scrutiny, to be denied the least evasion or equivocation, to be submitted to the moral torture of menaced, of dreaded damnation if he concealed or disguised the truth, to undergo the most crushing, humiliating penance. Absolution, after which the soul thirsted with insatiable thirst, might be delayed, held in suspense, refused; if granted it was of inestimable price. The sacraments, absolutely necessary to spiritual life, were at their disposal. Baptism to the infant would hardly be refused; but the Eucharist, Christ himself offered on the altar, God made by consecrated hands, God materialised down to the rudest apprehension, could be granted or withheld according to the arbitrary, irresponsible judgement of the priest. The body, after death, might repose in consecrated ground with the saints, or be cast out, to be within the domain, the uncontested prey of devils. The Excommunication cut the man off, whatever his rank or station, from the Church, beyond whose pale was utter impossibility of salvation. No one could presume to have hope for a man who died under excommunication. Such were the inculcated, by most recognised, at least apprehended, doctrines. The Interdict, the special prerogative of the Pope, as the antagonist, the controller of Sovereigns, smote a kingdom with spiritual desolation, during which the niggardly and imperfect rites, the baptism sparingly administered, the rest of the life without any religious ceremony, the extreme unction or the last sacrament coldly vouchsafed to the chosen few, the churchyard closed against the dead, seemed to consign a whole nation, a whole generation, to irrevocable perdition.

Thus throughout the world no man could stand alone; the priest was the universal lord of the universal human conscience. The inward assurance of faith, of rectitude, of virtue, of love of man or love of God, without the ratification of the confessor; the witness of the spirit within, unless confirmed, avouched by the priest, was nothing. Without the passport to everlasting life, everlasting life must recede from the hopes, from the attainment of man. And by a strange yet perhaps unavoidable anomaly, the sacredness of the priest was inalienable, indelible, altogether irrespective of his life, his habits, his personal holiness or unholiness. There might be secret murmurs at the avarice, pride, licentiousness of the priest; public opinion might even in some cases boldly hold him up to shame and obloquy, he was still priest, bishop, pope; his sacraments lost not their efficacy, his verdict of condemnation or absolution was equally valid; all the acts of John XXIII., till his deposal, were the acts of the successor of St. Peter. And if this triumph over the latent moral indignation of mankind was the manifestation of its strength, so its oppugnancy to that indignation was its fall; it was the premonition, the proclamation of its silent abrogation in the hearts of men. The historian has to state the fact, rather than curiously and judicially to balance the good and evil (for good there undoubtedly was, vast good in such ages of class tyrannising over class, of unintermitting war on a wide or a narrow scale, of violence, lawlessness, brutality) in this universal sacerdotal domination.

It is impossible to estimate the fluctuating proportion

between these two castes of the Christian population to

Monks and Friars. each other. The number of the Secular Clergy was of course, to a certain extent, limited by the spiritual wants of the community and the means of maintenance. But it comprehended within the sacred circle of immunity and privilege a vast host of unenrolled and subordinate retainers, those who had received for some purpose of their own, some who in the ruder ages had been compelled to take the simple tonsure, some admitted to what were called the lower orders, and who in all large churches, as subdeacons, acolytes, singers, were very numerous, down to those who held more menial offices, sacristans, beadles, servants of all classes. But there was absolutely nothing to limit the number of Monks, still less that of the Friars in their four Orders, especially the disciples of S. Dominic and S. Francis. No one was too poor or too low to become a privileged and sacred Mendicant. No qualification was necessary but piety or its semblance, and that might too easily be imitated. While these Orders in the Universities boasted of the most erudite and subtle, and all-accomplished of the Schoolmen, they could not disdain or altogether reject those who in the spirit, at least of one of their Founders, maintained the superiority of holy ignorance. Instead of being amazed that the Friars swarmed in such hordes over Christendom, it is rather wonderful that the whole abject and wretched peasantry, rather than be trampled to the earth, or maddened to Flagellantism, Jacquerie, or Communism, did not all turn ablebodied religious Beggars, so the strong English sense of Wycliffe designates the great mass of the lower Franciscans in England. The Orders themselves, as was natural when they became wealthy and powerful, must have repressed rather than encouraged the enrolment of such persons; instead of prompting to the utmost, they must have made it a distinction, a difficulty, a privilege, to be allowed to enter upon the enjoyment of their comparatively easy, roving, not by all accounts too severe, life. To the serf inured to the scanty fare and not unfrequent famine, the rude toil and miserable lodging; and to the peasant with his skin hard to callousness and his weather-beaten frame, the fast, the maceration, even the flagellation of the Friar, if really religious (and to the religious these self-inflicted miseries were not without their gratification), must have been no very rigorous exchange; while the freedom to the serf, the power of wandering from the soil to which he was bound down, the being his own property, not that of another, must have been a strong temptation. The door must have been closed with some care; some stern examination, probation, or inquiry, must have preceded the initiation and the adoption of brethren into the fraternity, or the still enlarging houses had been too narrow; they would have multiplied into unmanageable numbers. Yet, if more cold and repulsive in the admission of those humbler votaries, the protests of the Universities, and other proofs, show that the more promising and higher youth were sought with ardent proselytism.[b]

The property, especially the territorial and landed property of the Hierarchy and the Monastic Orders, it is equally impossible to estimate. It varied, of course, in different ages, and in every kingdom in Christendom.

---

[b] On the degenerate state of the Friars the serious prose and the satirical poetry are full of details. Read too the Supplication of Beggars (a later production, temp. Henry VIII.), and the inimitable Colloquies of Erasmus. One of the reasons alleged at the Council of Trent against submitting the regulars to episcopal discip'ine was their " numero eccessivo."—Sarpi, lii. p. 158. Ed. Helmstadt.

Nor if we knew at any one time the proportionate extent
of Church lands to that not under mortmain, would it
be any measure, or any sure criterion, of their relative
value. This property, instead of standing secure in its
theoretic inalienability, was in a constant fluctuation:
the Papal territory itself was frequently during the
darker centuries usurped, recovered, granted away,
resumed. Throughout Christendom the legal inalienability of Church lands was perpetually assailed in earlier
times by bold depredators, and baffled by ingenious
devices of granting away the usufruct. We have heard
perpetual complaints against these kinds of endowments
of their sons or descendants by the married clergy; the
unmarried yet dissolute or extravagant beneficiaries,
were no doubt as regardless of the sanctity of ecclesiastical property, and as subtle in conveying away its
value to their kinsmen, or for their own immediate advantage. Besides all these estates, held in absolute
property, was the tithe of the produce of all other lands.[*]
The whole sacerdotal system of Latin Christianity, first
from analogy, afterwards as direct procedent, assumed
all the privileges, powers, rights, endowments of the
Levitical priesthood; and thus arraying itself in the irrefragable authority of God's older Word, of which it did
not acknowledge the abrogation where its interests were
so nearly concerned, claimed the tithe as of inherent,
perpetual, divine law. From an early period Christians
had been urged to devote this proportion of their wealth
to religious uses; a proportion so easy and natural that
it had prevailed, and had obtained a prescriptive autho-

---

[*] Hallam has summed up (Middle Ages, c. vii.) with his usual judge-ment and accuracy what is most im-portant on this subject, in Father Paul, Muratori, Giannone, Fleury, and Schmidt.

rity, as the rule of sacred oblation to the temples among
the customs of many Heathen nations.[d]   The perpetual
claim to tithes was urged by Councils and by Popes in
the sixth century.   Charlemagne throughout his empire,
King Ethelwolf, and, later, Edward the Confessor in
England, either overawed by the declared authority of
the Old Testament, or thinking it but a fair contribution
to the maintenance of public worship and for other
religious uses, gave the force of civil law to this presumed sacred obligation.   During several centuries it
was urged by the preachers, not merely as an indispensable part of Christian duty, but as a test of Christian
perfection.[e]

Tithe was first received by the Bishop, and distributed
by him in three or in four portions; to himself, to the
clergy, for the fabric of the churches, for the poor. But
all kinds of irregularities crept into the simple and stately
uniformity of this universal tax and its administration.
It was retained by the Bishop; the impoverished clergy
murmured at their meagre and disproportionate share.
As the parochial divisions became slowly and irregularly
distinct and settled, it was in many cases, but by no
means universally, attached to the cure of souls.   The
share of the fabric became uncertain and fluctuating,
till at length other means were found for the erection
and the maintenance of the Church buildings.   The
more splendid Prelates and Chapters, aided by the piety
of Kings, Barons, and rich men, disdained this fund, so

---

[d] In the controversy which arose on
the publication of Selden's book on
Tithes, the High Church writers, Mon-
tagne and Tildesley, were diffuse and
triumphant in their quotations from
Heathen writers, as though, by showing the concurrence of universal religion with the Mosaic Institutes, to
make out tithes to be a part of Natural
Religion. See abstract of their arguments in Collier.

[e] Paolo Sarpi, quoted by Mr. Hallam.

insufficient for their magnificent designs; the building
of churches was exacted from the devotion or the superstition of the laity in general, conjointly with the munificence of the ecclesiastics. So, too, the right of the
poor to their portion became a free-will contribution,
measured by the generosity or the wealth of the Clergy;
here a splendid, ever-flowing largess; there a parsimonious, hardly-extracted dole.

The tithe suffered the fate of other Church property;
it was at times seized, alienated, appropriated by violence or by fraud. It was retained by the Bishops or
wealthy clergy, who assigned a miserable stipend to a
poor Vicar; it fell into the hands of lay impropriators,
who had either seized it, or, on pretence of farming it,
provided in the cheapest manner for the performance of
the service; the Monasteries got possession of it in
large portions, and served the cures from their Abbey or
Cloister. In England it was largely received by foreign
Beneficiaries, who never saw the land from which they
received this tribute.

Still, however levied, however expended, however
invaded by what were by some held to be sacrilegious
hands, much the larger part of this tenth of all the
produce of the land throughout Christendom, with no
deduction, except the moderate expense of collection,
remained in the hands of the Hierarchy. It was
gradually extended from the produce of land to all other
produce, cattle, poultry, even fish.

The High Aristocracy of the Church, from the Pope
to the member of the capitular body, might not disdain
to participate in this, which ought to have been the
exclusive patrimony of the parochial and labouring
clergy; but their estates, which were Lordships, Baron-
ages, Princedoms, in the Pope a kingdom, were what

placed them on a level with, or superior to, the Knights,
Barons, Princes, Kings of the world.

These possessions throughout Latin Christendom, both
of the Seculars and of the Monasteries, if only calculated
from their less clerical expenditure, on their personal
pomp and luxury, on their wars, on their palaces, and
from their more honourable prodigality on their cathedrals, churches, monastic buildings, must have been
enormous; and for some period were absolutely exempt
from contribution to the burthens of the State.[f] We
have seen the first throes and struggles of Papal nepotism; we have seen bold attempts to quarter the kinsmen
of Popes on the territories of the Papacy, to create noble
patrimonies, or even principalities, in their favour; but
there is no Papal family of the time preceding Nicolas V.
which boasts its hereditary opulence or magnificent
palace, like the Riarios, Farneses, Barberinis, Corsinis,
of later times. The Orsinis and Colonnas were Princes
created Popes, not descendants of Popes. The vast
wealth of the Archbishopric of Milan has shone before
us; an Archbishop was the founder of the Ducal House
of Visconti. In Italy, however, in general, the Prelates
either never possessed or were despoiled of the vast
wealth which distinguished the Ultramontane Prelates.
Romagna had become the Papal domain; Ravenna had
been compelled to yield up her rival territory. The
Crusades had not thrown the lands into their hands by
the desertion of their lords. In the commercial wealth
of Venice, Genoa, Pisa, Florence, they had no share.
At Constance, as it has appeared, the Ultramontanes
feared that the poverty of the Italian Bishops would

---

[f] Some estates of the Church were held on the tenure of military service,
most in Francalmoigne.—Hallam.

place them at the command of the Pope. In Germany
the Prince-Archbishops, the Electors, were not scrupulous in extending the wide pale of their ecclesiastical
principalities. The grant of estates, of territories, was
too common a bribe or a reward from a doubtful aspi-
rant to the Imperial throne. How many fiefs held by
Mentz, by Trèves, and by Cologne, dated from the eve
of, or from the coronation of an Emperor, raised to the
throne after a severe contest! Among the other Prince-
Prelates of the Empire, distracted as Germany was for
centuries by wars between the Popes and the Emperors,
wars between the Emperor and his refractory subjects,
their power was perpetually increasing their wealth,
their wealth aggrandising their power. They were too
useful allies not to be subsidised by the contending
parties; and those subsidies, being mostly in grants of
lands, enhanced the value of their alliance.

In France, the prodigality of the weaker Kings of
each race, and each race successively, from the fainéant
Merovingians, seemed to dwindle down into inevitable
weakness, had vied with each other in heaping estates
upon the clergy, and in founding and endowing monasteries. If the later Kings, less under strong religious
impulses, and under heavier financial embarrassments,
were less prodigal,—if the mass of secular ecclesiastical
property is of earlier date,*—few reigns passed without

---

* The Abbé Maury, in the debate
on the confiscation of church property,
asserted that the tenure of some of
their estates was older than Clovis.
(Lamartine, Les Constituants, iii. p.
113.) In the debates on the confiscation of church property in the National
Assembly in 1789, 1790, M. Talleyrand estimated the income of the
clergy from tithes at eighty millions
of francs, from the lands at seventy
millions; total one hundred and fifty
millions. This, I presume, did not
include the lands, at least not the
houses of the monasteries. (Buchon
et Roux, Hist. Parlementaire de la
Rév. Française, iii. p. 156.) In the
proposal for the suppression of the

the foundation of some religious houses. The Mendicant Orders had their spacious and splendid convents in
Paris,[h] and in the other great cities of France.[i]

In England the Statute of Mortmain had been the
National Protest against the perpetual encroachment of
the Church on the landed property of the realm. At
length the subtlety of the Lawyers baffled the subtlety
of the Churchmen; the strong, stern Law could be
neither infringed nor eluded. But it left the Church in
possession of all which had been heaped at her feet by
the prodigal Anglo-Saxon Kings, and the Normans
hardly less prodigal. If it had not passed down absolutely undiminished, it had probably on the whole been
constantly enlarging its borders; if usurped, or its usufruct, if not the fee, fraudulently made away,[k] it had in
many cases widely extended itself by purchase, as well
as by donation and bequest.[l]

There are four periods at which public documents

religious houses, M. Treilhard declared
that four hundred millions might be
produced by the sale of the monastic
houses, which might be secularised.
Those in Paris alone might be sold for
one hundred and fifty millions. A
calculation was produced, made in
1775, that at 150 livres the toise,
they would yield 217,309,000 livres.
In another report it was stated that
the clergy held one-fifth of the net
revenue from land in France, amount-
ing to two hundred millions, exclusive
of the tithe. (T. v. p. 328.)

[h] See Dulaure, Hist. de Paris, a
book with much valuable information,
but hostile to the clergy.

[i] At the Revolution six Orders had
three houses in Paris, some others two.
They must have amounted to between
forty and fifty.

[k] Churches were leased to laymen,
and without doubt became their actual
property; as such were bought and sold.

[l] The Church bought largely. The
statute "Quis Emptores" shows abundantly that the possessions of the
Church were greatly increased by purchase as well as by donation and
bequest. It was a very common practice to purchase an estate in reversion,
or to purchase and grant the estate
to the former Lord for his life: on his
death (si obire contigerit) it fell to
the Church. Few rich men entered
a monastery without bringing some
estate or provision with them, which
became the inalienable property of the
Community. See instances in Taylor's
Index Monasticus.

seem at first sight to throw a steady and distinct light
on the extent and value of church property in England,
its actual if not its relative value. Yet on examination
the result of the inquiry becomes dim, confused, and
contradictory. It offers no more than a very rude and
uncertain approximation to positive conclusions.

I. Doomsday-Book gives the lands in the possession
of ecclesiastics, as well as lay holders, those of bishops,
chapters, churches, monasteries. The first inspection of
Doomsday may seem to present startling facts. In the
whole County of Kent, besides the King (with whom the
Churches of St. Martin in Dover and the Church of
Canterbury share those towns), appear as landowners:—
1. The Archbishop of Canterbury; 2. His Monks (Christchurch); 3. The Bishop of Rochester; 4. The Bishop of
Bayeux;[m] 5. The Abbey of Battle; 6. St. Augustine's;
7. Abbey of St. Peter's, Ghent. Only four knights, and
Albert the Chaplain. In Middlesex are the King, the
Archbishop, the Bishop of London, his Canons (of St.
Paul's), the Abbot of Westminster, the Abbot of the
Holy Trinity in Rouen, the Abbot of Barking, with
eighteen others, barons and knights. In Worcestershire
the King, the Church of Worcester, the Bishop of Here-
ford, the Church of St. Denys near Paris, the Church of
Cormelies, the Abbeys of Westminster, Pershore, Evesham; the Bishop of Bayeux, the Church of St. Guthlac,
the Clerks of Wrehampton, with fifteen laymen. In
Berkshire, among sixty-three holders, are the King, five
Bishops, among them Durham and Coutances, ten Abbots and Abbesses. In Devonshire, of fifty-three, are
the King, two Bishops, Exeter and Coutances, ten abbeys,

---

[m] Odo, Bishop of Bayeux, held lands in sixteen counties.—Sir H. Ellis, Introduction.

among them Rouen, Mont St. Michael, St. Stephen and Holy Trinity at Caen. During the reign of our Norman sovereigns these transmarine monasteries held their lands in England. They were either cells or dependent priories which sent their revenues across the sea. As England and France became hostile powers they were gradually seized, till at length, in the time of Henry V., they were confiscated by the strong hand of the law, and vested by Act of Parliament in the Crown.[n] Our history has dwelt, on more than one occasion, on the estates and benefices held by foreign prelates, chiefly Italians.

II. The valuation made in the reign of Edward I., by order of Pope Nicolas IV. The whole ecclesiastical property was assessed at rather more than 200,000*l.*, a valuation much higher than had been admitted before; the tenth levied was above 20,000*l.*[o]

III. The remarkable petition of the Commons to Henry IV.,[p] for the confiscation of the whole Church property and its appropriation to the maintenance of a nobility, knighthood, squirehood, burghership, and alms-houses, retaining only a priesthood of 15,000, without distinction of Orders, and on the annual stipend of seven marks each. This wild revolutionary scheme estimated the temporalities of the Church at 322,000 marks a year.[q] They were thrown together in large masses, each of 20,000, as—1. The see of Canterbury, with the abbeys of Christchurch, St. Augustine, Shrewsbury, Coggleshal, St. Osyth. 2. York (not including Fontaines, Rivaux,

[n] Ellis, Introduction to Doomsday. Collier, I. p. 650.

[o] See vol. vii. p. 54, and note, for the details, A.D. 1292.

[p] Walsingham, p. 379. Introd. Fox, ii. p. 725. A.D. 1410.

[q] That is (calculating the mark at two-thirds of a pound, 13*s.* 4*d.*), nearly the same as the Papal valuation.

and some other abbeys). 3. Six of the larger abbeys, Dover, Battle, Lewes, Coventry, Daventry, and Tournay (Thorney ?) make up another 20,000.[f] The total estimate of the Church property may seem to have been based on the valuation of Pope Nicolas, the established cataster which had been acted upon for above a century. It is curious, however, as setting down the annual income necessary to maintain the state of an Earl at 3000 marks; of a Knight at 100, with four plough-lands; an Esquire 40, with two plough-lands. How the poor Priest was to live on his seven marks, unless by the bounty and hospitality of his parishioners—certainly with no hospitality or almsgiving of his own—these early levellers seem not to have thought.[g] About this period, according to another statement, there were in England 46,822 churches, 52,285 villæ, 53,225 military fiefs, of which the ecclesiastics and religious held 28,000. Thus they were in possession of above one-half of the knights' fees in the realm.[h]

---

[f] Walsingham seems to say that they were set to prove this vast wealth of the clergy, and failed: "Sed cum alterentur ostenders de quibus locis tam grandes summæ levari possent, unde præmissi dotarentur vel ditarentur, defecerunt scrutantes scrutinio et dum diligunt vanitatem quærivere mendacium."

[g] This concurrence, which is at least approximate, may appear to be of higher authority than the calculation drawn from a passage of Knighton, which would more than double the amount of church property. In the year 1337 two Cardinal Legates came to England. They received for their expenses 50 marks a day, which was raised by four pennies from every bene-

fice, exempt or not exempt. The revenue of the Church would thus amount to 2000 marks a day; multiplied by 365, 730,000 marks; nearly 500,000l. Macpherson's Annals of Commerce, i. 519; Hallam. But the Valor of Pope Nicolas was framed by those who wished as much as possible to elude or lighten their taxation.

[h] This rests on a passage in the Appendix to Hearne's Avebury. Mr. Sharon Turner, v. 186, quotes it. Mr. Hallam appears to accept its results, Middle Ages, ii. p. 506. Other authorities, quoted in Taylor, p. xxlii., make 60,215 knights' fees; those held by the clergy, 23,115. Spelman brings down the proportion to a third; so too Sir W. Temple.

IV. The valuation of the whole church property, immediately before the suppression of the larger monasteries,[a] as compared with that of Nicolas IV., might be expected to furnish at once a positive and a relative estimate of the Church possessions. In the Act for the suppression of the smaller monasteries,[a] those with an income under 200*l.* a year, it was supposed that about 380 communities would be dissolved (about 100 then escaped or eluded dissolution), and that the Crown would derive 32,000*l.* of yearly revenue from the confiscation, with 100,000*l.* in plate, jewels, money, and other valuables. After the suppression of the larger monasteries,[f] the amount of the whole revenue escheated to the Crown was calculated at 161,000*l.*[a] A little before this period the revenue of England from lands and possessions had been calculated at 4,000,000*l.*:[a] the monastic property, therefore, was not more than a twentieth part of the national property. To this must be added the whole Church property that remained, that of the Bishops, Chapters, Colleges, and Parochial Clergy.[b] The

---

[a] Ann. Hen. VIII. 26, A.D. 1534, published by the Record Commission, to be compared with Speed's Catalogue of Religious Houses, Basilicas, &c. On the revenues of the monasteries, see Dugdale and Stevens, Mr. Nasmith's excellent edition of Tanner's Notitia. No book is more instructive than the Index Monasticus of the diocese of Norwich, by Mr. Richd. Taylor, London, 1821.

[a] Burnet, 192, 222. Rymer, xiv. 574. Stevens, Appendix to Dugdale. Lingard, c. iv. Burnet gives 131,607*l.* 6*s.* 4*d.* for the larger monasteries, but adds, " it was at least ten times the sum in true value."

[f] Lord Herbert; Speed; Hume, c. 31.

[a] It is singular that these two sums amount to near 200,000*l.* The whole property of the Church, according to the valuation of Nicolas IV., stood at about 204,000*l.*, so that the value of Monastic property was then near that of the whole Church property under Edward I.

[a] This is stated by Hume, and on such a subject Hume was likely to be accurate, but he does not give his authority, Vol. i. p. 485; ii. p. 106.

[b] One insulated point of comparison has offered itself. According to the Valor of Nicolas, Christ Church, Can-

Valor Ecclesiasticus of Henry VIII. offers no sum total;
but, according to Speed, the whole value was 320,150*l.*
10*s.* If of this, 186,512*l.* 8*s.* 11½*d.* was the gross value
of that of the monasteries (the sum escheated to the
King, 161,000*l.*), the secular property was about half of
the whole. Together the two sums would amount to a
tenth of the revenue of the kingdom as estimated by
Hume.[c]

But this estimate is very fallacious,[d] both as to the
extent and the actual value[e] of the Church property.
As to the extent, in London and the neighbouring
counties of Middlesex, Surrey, Essex, the Church lands,
or at least the lands in which the Church had some
tenure, must have been enormous. Hardly a parish in
Middlesex did not belong, certainly so far as manorial
rights, to the Bishop of London, the Dean and Chapter

---

terbury, was assessed at 353*l.* 19*s.* 2*d.*,
under Henry VIII. at 3,349*l.* 8*s.* 5*d.*,
an increase of about seven times.

[c] When, by Bishop Burnet's advice
(Burnet's Own Times, edit. Oxford, v.
p. 116), the First Fruits and Tenths
were made over to the Board, called
Queen Anne's Bounty, the tenths were
reckoned at 11,000*l.*, which has now
remained unaltered, according to the
valuation of Henry VIII. This would
make the property 111,000*l.* Speed
gives 111,207*l.* 14*s.* 2*d.*, bit n certain
portion had been appropriated to the
new Bishops and Chapters, which makes
up the total.

[d] Some of the richer monasteries
had sunk to a small oligarchy. Chert-
sey, with 14 monks, had 740*l.* a year;
Furness, with 30, 960*l.* It is curious
to compare Hume and Lingard. Both
select Furness as their example (Hume

puts Furness in Lincolnshire). Hume
gives the small number of monks as
compared with the great income; on
the signal iniquity of the mode in
which the suppression was enforced he
is silent. Lingard is coldly eloquent,
as is his wont, on the iniquity—of the
small number of monks not a word.

[e] On the important question of the
relative value of money at that time
and the present, taking in the joint
consideration of weight of silver and
price of provisions, Mr. Taylor, in
1821, would multiply by 15 times.
Land in Norfolk let from 1*s.* 6*d.* to
2*s.* 6*d.* an acre; wages for a hay-
maker were, during Henry VII. and
Henry VIII., 1*d.* to 1½*d.* a day. The
whole ecclesiastical revenues in the
diocese of Norwich would be worth
510,000*l.* a year.

of St. Paul's, the Abbot and monks of Westminster, and other religious houses—the Carthusians, St. John's Clerkenwell (the Hospitallers), Sion, and many smaller foundations. The Chapter of St. Paul's swept in a broad belt round the north of London till they met the Church of Westminster at Hampstead and Paddington.[f] The Abbot of Westminster was almost a prince of Westminster.[g]

On the other hand, the estates and manors of the Church and of the monasteries, though, as probably having been the longest under cultivation, the best cultivated, in productive value were far below their imagined wealth. The Church was by usage, perhaps from interest, an indulgent landlord. Of the estates, a large part had become copyhold, and paid only a moderate quit-rent, and a small fixed fine on renewal. Of those on which the Church reserved the full fee, the fines on renewals, whether on lives or for terms of years, were no doubt extremely moderate. They had become hereditary in families, and acquired the certainty of actual possession. The rents were paid in money, usually of small amount, in services to the landlord (the Prebendary or the Church), in the cultivation of their lands, and to a considerable extent in kind. Probably the latter contribution was not taken into the account of their value. But not only had each monastery its common refectory, each Chapter had its common establishment, its common table, its horses, and other conveniences, largely supplied

[f] Archdeacon Hale has printed (for the Camden Society) what he calls the Domesday of St. Paul; the Visitation of the manors of the Dean and Chapter (not the separate estates of the prebendaries). It throws great light on this point, as well as on the tenure and condition of the Church property.

[g] At the Dissolution Westminster was the most wealthy monastery—it was estimated at 3977*l*.; St. John's, Clerkenwell, the richest of the military orders, 2385*l*.; Sion, the richest nunnery, 1944*l*.—Speed.

by the growers; hay and straw, beasts, poultry furnished at specified times by the tenants. Each had its mill, its brewhouse, its bakery; and no doubt the annual expenses of the House, or Domus, were to a large extent supplied from these unreckoned sources.[h] Yet on the whole the tenants, no doubt, of the Church shared a full portion of the wealth of the Church, so secure and easy was their tenure; and it was not uncommon for ecclesiastics to take beneficiary leases of the lands of their own Church, which they bequeathed as property to their kindred or heirs, not unfrequently to their children. Besides this, over all their property the Church had a host of officers and retainers, stewards of their courts, receivers, proctors, lawyers, and other dependents, numberless in name and function.

But of the wealth of the Clergy, the landed property, even with the tithe, was by no means the whole; and, invaded as it was by aggression, by dilapidation, by alienation through fraud or violence, limited in its productiveness by usage, by burthens, by generosity, by maladministration, it may be questioned whether it was the largest part. The vast treasures accumulated by the Avignonese Pontiffs when the Papal territories were

---

[h] All this throws light on a very curious state of things at St. Paul's; no doubt not peculiar to St. Paul's. The Chapter consisted of 30 Prebendaries, each with his separate estate, and originally his right to share in the common fund, on condition of performing certain services in the Church. The Prebendaries withdrew each to the care and enjoyment of his Prebend, or, if a Pluralist, of many Prebends, leaving the duties to be performed by certain Residentiaries; so when the daily mass, the perpetual office, was imposed as a burthen, it was difficult to keep up the number of Residentiaries. In process of time the Common Fund grew larger, the emoluments and advantages from oblations, obits, and other sources increased in value; there was then a strife and a press to become a Residentiary. It was necessary (the exhausted fund was the plea) to obtain Papal or Archiepiscopal decrees to limit the number of Residentiaries.

occupied by enemies or adventurers, and could have yielded but scanty revenues, testify to the voluntary or compulsory tribute paid by Western Christendom to her Supreme Court of Appeal. If the Bishops mainly depended on their endowments, to the Clergy, to the monastic churches, oblations (in many cases now from free gifts hardened into rightful demands) were pouring in, and had long been pouring in, with incalculable profusion. Not only might not the altars, hardly any part of the church might be approached, without a votive gift. The whole life, the death of every Christian was bound up with the ceremonial of the Church; for almost every office, was received from the rich and generous the ampler donation, from the poorer or more parsimonious was exacted the hard-wrung fee. Above all, there were the masses, which might lighten the sufferings of the soul in purgatory; there was the prodigal gift of the dying man out of selfish love for himself;[i] the more generous and no less prodigal gift of the bereaved, out of holy charity for others. The dying man, from the King to the peasant, when he had no further use for his worldly riches, would devote them to this end;[k] the living, out of profound respect or deep affection for the beloved husband, parent, brother, kinsman, friend, would be, and actually was, not less bountiful and munificent.[m]

[i] I am able to illustrate this from the records of St. Paul's, which have been investigated with singular industry and accuracy by my friend Archdeacon Hale, to whom I am indebted for much valuable information.

[k] There is another curious illustration of the wealth of the Clergy. The inventory of the effects of Richard Gravesend, Bishop of London, from 1290 to 1303. It measures 28 feet in length; it gives in detail all his possessions, his chapel (plate of the chapel), jewels, robes, books, horses, the grain and stock on each of his manors, with the value of each. The total amounts to 2871l. 7s. 10¼d. Corn was then 4s. per quarter.

[m] We have in St. Paul's an account of the obits or anniversaries of the deaths of certain persons, for the celebration of which bequests had been

Add to all this the oblations at the crosses of the Redeemer, or the shrines of popular and famous saints, for their intercessory prayers to avert the imminent calamity, to assuage the sorrow, or to grant success to the schemes, it might be, of ambition, avarice, or any other passion, to obtain pardon for sin, to bring down blessing: crosses and shrines, many of them supposed to be endowed with miraculous powers, constantly working miracles.[n] To most of these were made perpetual processions, led by the Clergy in their rich attire. From the basins of gold or the bright florins of the King to the mite of the beggar, all fell into the deep, insatiable box, which unlocked its treasures to the Clergy.[o]

----

made in the fourteenth century. The number was 111. The payments made amounted in the whole to 2678s. 5½d., of which the Dean and Canons Residentiary (present) received 1461s., about 73l.; multiply by 15, to bring to present value, 1075l.

[n] E. g., Richard Preston, citizen and grocer, gave to the shrine of St. Erkenwald his best sapphire stone, for curing of infirmities of the eyes, appointing that proclamation should be made of its virtues.—Dugdale, p. 21.

[o] We have an account of the money found in the box under the great Cross on the entrance of the Cathedral (Recepta de pixide Crucis Borealis). In one month (May, A.D. 1344) it yielded no less than 50l. (præter argentum fractum). This was more than an average profit, but taken as an average it gives 600l. per annum. Multiply this by 15 to bring it to the present value of money, 9000l. This, by an order of the Pope's Commissary, A.D. 1410 (Dugdale, p. 20), was di-

vided among the Dean and Canons Residentiary. But this was by no means the only box of offerings—perhaps not the richest. There was one at the magnificent shrine of St. Erkenwald; another at that of the Virgin, before which the offerings of wax tapers alone were so valuable, that the Dean and Chapter would no longer leave them to the vergers and servants of the Church. They were extinguished, carried to a room behind the chapter-house, and melted, for the use of the said Dean and Canons. Archbishop Arundel assigned to the same Dean and Canons, and to their successors for ever, the whole profits of the oblation box. Dugdale recounts gifts by King John of France, especially to the shrine of St. Erkenwald. The shrine of St. Thomas at Canterbury received in one year 812l. 11s. 3d.; in another, 954l. 6s. 3d.—Burnet, Hist. Reformat. vol. i. See Taylor, Index for our Lady of Walsingham. Our Chauntry accounts are full and well

Besides all these estates, tithes, oblations, bequests to the Clergy and the monasteries, reckon the subsidies in kind to the Mendicants in their four Orders—Dominicans, Franciscans, Augustinians, Carmelites. In every country of Latin Christendom, of these swarms of Friars, the lowest obtained sustenance: the higher means to build and to maintain splendid churches, cloisters, houses. All of these, according to their proper theory, ought to have lived on the daily dole from the charitable, bestowed at the gate of the palace or castle, of the cottage or hovel. But that which was once an act of charity had become an obligation. Who would dare to repel a holy Mendicant? The wealth of the Mendicants was now an object of bitter jealousy to the Clergy and to the older monastic Orders. They were a vast standing army, far more vast than any maintained by any kingdom in Christendom, at once levying subsidies to an enormous amount, and living at free quarters throughout the land. How onerous, how odious they had become in England, may be seen in the prose of Wycliffe and in the poetry of Piers Ploughman.[p]

The Clergy, including the Monks and Friars, were one throughout Latin Christendom; and through them, to a great extent, the Latin Church was one. *Unity of the clergy.* Whatever antagonism, feud, hatred, estrangement, might rise between rival Prelates, rival Priests, rival Orders—whatever irreconcileable jealousy there might be between the Seculars and Regulars—yet the

---

preserved, and would furnish a very curious illustration of the office and income of the Mass Priest.

[p] Later, Speed, from the Supplication of Beggars, asserts, as demonstrated, that, reckoning that every householder paid the five Orders five-pence a year only, the sum of 43,000*l*. 6*s*. 8*d*. was paid them by the year, besides the revenues of their own lands.

Caste seldom, and but on rare occasions, betrayed the
interest of the Caste. The high-minded Churchman,
who regarded his country more than the Church, was
not common; the renegade, who pursued his private
interests by sacrificing those of his Order, might be
more so; but he stood alone, a hated and despised apos-
tate. There might be many traitors from passion,
ignorance, obstinacy, blindness to its interests — few
premeditated and deliberate deserters of its cause. The
Clergy in general (there were noble exceptions) were
first the subjects of the Pope, then the subjects of the
temporal Sovereign. The Papal Legate, the Proconsul
of the Pope, the co-Ruler with the King, was not
dependant on the reception of a cold perhaps or hostile
Court; he could almost command, rarely did not
receive, the unlimited homage of the Clergy: to him
was due their first obedience. The Pope claimed and
long maintained the sole right of taxation of ecclesiastical property; only under his authority could that
property be assessed by the State. This general taxation by the Pope began during the Crusades, for that
holy purpose; it was continued for all other Crusades
which he might command, and was extended to his
general uses; he condescended from time to time to
throw some part, in his bounty, to the temporal Sovereign;[a] but, in theory, the right was in him and in him
alone. It was asserted over the whole of Christendom,
and made him, as the guardian, so in some respects the
Suzerain of Church property throughout the world.
The allegiance of the hierarchy to the Church was at
'once compulsory and voluntary; the Pope's awful

---

[a] It is curious to see the words " caritativum subsidium " creep into the
more weak demands of the Popes during the schism.—MS. B. M. passim at that
period.

powers held in check the constant inevitable tendency
to rebellion and contumacy, which was usually that of
individual Prelates or small factions. Among themselves the Clergy could not but at times split into
parties on temporal or religious subjects; but if the
Papal or hierarchical authority lost ground by their
turbulence or their divisions, they were soon driven
back to an unanimity of dependance on the Papal
power by the encroachments of the State, or to settle
their own disputes. They fled from ruder tyrants to
the throne of St. Peter. The Pope was at least a more
impartial judge than their rival or antagonist—mostly
than the civil ruler. On the whole the Order of the
Clergy was one from the utmost East to the farther
West, from the North to the South.

The universal fraternity of the Monastic Orders and
of the Friars was even more intimate. Everywhere,
from the Scottish islands to the Spanish frontier of
Christendom, the Benedictine, the Clugniac, the Cister-
cian, might find a home; the abbey of his brethren
opened to him its hospitable doors. This was of less
importance to the elder and more sedentary Orders
(they, too, travelled, a few in search of learning—most
who did leave their homes, as pilgrims to Rome, to
other famous shrines, or to the East): but to the
wandering Friars, who spread all over Europe, of what
incalculable advantage to find everywhere brethren
connected with them by a closer, as they thought a
holier tie, than that of kindred or consanguinity;
a ready auditory prepared by the tertiaries of the
Order; allies in their invasion on the parishes of
the secular priests; a crowd of admirers of their learning, which added fame and so strength to their Order,
and of their zeal or eloquence, which brought in new

proselytes; abettors and maintainers of their influence, which was still wringing further wealth for the Order from the timid living or the remorseful dying man. This all-comprehending fraternisation had the power, and some of the mystery, without the suspicion and hatred which attaches to secret societies. It was a perpetual campaign, set in motion and still moving on with simultaneous impulse from one or from several centres, but with a single aim and object, the aggrandisement of the Society, with all its results for evil or for good.

The Clergy had their common language throughout Western Christendom. In their intercourse with each other they needed no interpreter. This was far more than their bond; it was among the most lasting guarantees of their power. It was not from their intellectual superiority alone, but from their almost exclusive possession of the universal European language, that they held and retained the administration of public affairs. No royal Embassy was without its Prelate, even if the Ambassadors were not all Prelates, for they only could converse freely together without mutual misunderstanding of their barbarous jargon, or the precarious aid of an interpreter. The Latin alone was as yet sufficiently precise and definite in its terms to form binding treaties; it was the one language current throughout Europe; it was of necessity that of all negotiations between distant kingdoms.

Hence, too, in some respects, the Churchman was of all countries. His knowledge, at least the knowledge of the Churchman who moved beyond the bounds of his narrow parish, of the universal Latin—the ability (in theory possessed by all) to officiate in the unchangeable service of the Church—was the only indispensable

qualification for any dignity or benefice throughout
Christendom. Latin Christianity had invaded the East,
and planted Latin Bishops to celebrate Latin services
almost throughout the Byzantine Empire. German
Popes, French Popes, one English Pope, a Portuguese,
a Greek or Calabrese Antipope, have occupied or have
aspired to the throne of St. Peter: none of them were
foreigners in tongue. All Christendom, especially
England, saw their richest benefices held by strangers,[r]
ignorant of the native language, and these did not
always hold their remote cures as honours and appen-
dages to their Italian dignities, but visited them at
least occasionally, and had no difficulty in going
through the routine of religious service.[s] There might
be bitter complaints of the imperfect fulfilment of duty:
conscientious men might refuse preferment among a
people of strange language; but there was no legal or
canonical disqualification; all that could be absolutely
demanded was the ability to recite or chant the Latin
breviary; no clergyman was a stranger or foreigner
among the Clergy in any European kingdom.

That ubiquity of the Clergy, as belonging to one
Order, under one head, under one law and discipline,
speaking a common language, to a certain extent with
common habits of life, was of inestimable importance,
as holding together the great commonwealth of European nations, in antagonism to the Eastern races,
aggregated into one horde by the common bond of the
Koran. Had the Christian kingdoms grown up sepa-

---

[r] I have noticed (vol. vi. p. 84)
the pluralist who held the archdeaconry
of Thessalonica with benefices in Norfolk.

[s] Michael Scott is a rare instance of

scrupulousness in refusing the Archbishopric of Cashel, on account of his
ignorance of Irish. The objection does
not seem to have occurred to his patron
the Pope.

rate, isolated, adverse, even if each with its independeht national hierarchy, still with hardly any communication but by the war of neighbouring States with neighbouring States, and with commerce restricted, precarious, unenterprising, there must have been either one vast Asiatic despotism, founded by some mighty conqueror —a Charlemagne, without his sagacious religious as well as civil organisation—or a disruption into hard repulsive masses, a shifting and conflicting aggregate of savage tribes. There could have been no confederacy to oppose the mighty invading league of Mohammedanism. Christendom could only have a religious Capital, and that Capital in all the early period was Rome. To Rome there was a constant ebb and flow from the remotest borders of Europe, and this chiefly of the Clergy; through them, knowledge, arts, whatsoever remained of the older civilisation, circulated to the extremities. The Legate, the Nuncio, if he came to bow kings and nations to an imperious yoke and to levy tribute, brought with him the peaceful pomp, the courtly manners, the knowledge, the refinement of the South: his inalienable character was that of an emissary of peace; he had no armed retainers; he found his retainers, except the few who accompanied him, in the land which he visited—the Clergy. He might, as he too often did, belie his character of the Angel of Peace;[1] he might inflame civil wars, he might even set up rebellious sons against fathers, but his ostensible office was always moderation: his progress through interjacent realms, where he passed safe, respected, honoured by the deferential veneration of all the hier-

---

[1] This is the title perpetually introduced into the instructions and powers given to the Cardinal or other Legates.

archy, was an homage to the representative of one
whose office at least was to promote peace; it was an
universal recognition of the blessings, the sanctity of
peace. However the acts of Popes, of worldly or martial Prelates, or of a rude or fierce Clergy, might be at
issue with the primal principles of the faith, yet, at the
same time that they practised this wide apostasy, they
condemned their own apostasy; their language could
not entirely throw off, far from throwing off, it dwelt
ostentatiously, though against themselves, on the true
and proper aim of their interference. Where war was
the universal occupation, though swept away by the
torrent, they were constantly lifting up their voice
against war, at least against war of Christian against
Christian; they would divert the whole martial impulses of Christendom against the Mohammedan. Thus
for centuries, through the length and breadth of Latin
Christendom, was propagated and maintained, even by
those who were constantly violating and weakening
their own precepts, a sympathy for better and more
Christian tenets—a faint yet undying echo of the
angelic annunciation of Christianity, appealing to the
whole Christian priesthood, and through the priesthood
to universal man; "peace on earth, good will to men."
Through the Hierarchy Christian Europe was one; and
Christian Europe was at least brooding over the seeds
of a richer harvest; it was preparing for a generous
rivalry in laws, letters, arts, even in religion.

Another result of the ubiquitous Hierarchical influence, though not so much a result of its   Effects on
ubiquity as of its inalienable character, must   social rank.
not be passed by. It was not only a bond which held
together the Christian nations, of different races and of
different tongues, but in every nation of the Christian

commonwealth the Clergy, and the Clergy alone, held
together the different ranks and classes. The old
Roman prejudice of the ineffaceable distinction between
the free man and the slave lurked in the minds of the
aristocratic Hierarchy of the South. The Clergy could
not but be deeply impregnated with the feudal respect
for high birth,* but they could not efface from the
record of the faith, from the older traditions, to do
them justice they never lost sight of, the saying of the
Saviour, that the poor were their especial charge;
poverty was, as it were, consecrated by the humble
lives of the Lord and his Apostles. Many Popes have
been seen rising from the meanest parentage to the Pontifical throne. In every kingdom some of the highest
examples of Christian piety and ability, canonised
Saints, were constantly drawn up from the humblest

---

* In the Papal dispensations we constantly find " nobilitas generis " spoken
of with " scientia et honestas ;" as a
justification of the permission to hold
benefices in plurality.—MS. B. M.
passim.

I select one illustration as in every
way remarkable, not the less as pro-
ceeding from Nicolas V. It is an
answer to a petition from George
Neville, Canon of York, son of his
beloved son Richard Earl of Salisbury.
" The nobility of his descent (he was
even, as he said, of royal lineage) induced the Pope to grant him a dispen-
sation (he being fourteen years old) to
hold a canonry in the Church of Salisbury, with one in York. Moreover,
the gracious favour of the Pope (' tu-
orum intuitu meritorum '), the merit of
a boy of fourteen! allowed him to
hold three or any other two incompa-
tible benefices, with or without cure of

souls; even Parish Churches, or any
dignities, below the highest; to hold
them together, or to exchange them at
his will during his whole life (' quoad
vixeris '). The provision must be added,
that the benefices were to be properly
served, and the cure of souls not neglected."—Rome, A.D. 1447, July 7.

At twenty-three years old the same
George Neville was appointed Bishop
of Exeter; as he could not be consecrated for four years, he had a Bull to
receive the profits.—Collier, i. 674.
He was afterwards Archbishop of York.
See Collier, 682. I would add on
pluralities that, though not noble,
Wykeham, before he was Bishop, held
the archdeaconry of Buckingham, the
Provostship of Wells, twelve other
prebends or canonries, " sacerdotiusque
cum cura plus quam satis."—Godwin.
p. 280.

of mankind. Once a Churchman, the hallowed man
took his position from his ecclesiastical rank, not from
his birth or descent; that higher nobility had cancelled
all the want of noble ancestry. There might be at
some periods a closer brotherhood—a kind of separate
corporate spirit—between ecclesiastics of high or generous lineage, but it rarely dared to be exclusive; other
qualities, either worldly or religious, were allowed to
dress the balance. The Bishop with royal blood in his
veins was no more a Bishop than he who had sprung
from the dregs of the people; he wore the same dress;
according to his possessions, might display the same
pomp; was often not less proud in the cathedral; not
only in the cathedral, even in the royal Council he
occupied the same seat; had almost as fair a chance of
canonisation. The power of overleaping the line, which
lay so broad and deep, between the high and low, the
noble and the peasant, the lord and the serf, must have
been a perpetual consolation and hope in the conscious
abasement of the poor man and of the serf—a drop of
sweetness in his bitter cup.

This, indeed, could be but the lot of few; and there
might in the lower orders be much envy and jealousy
of those who rose from their ranks to the height of
Churchmanly dignity, as well as pride and emulation to
vie with their success. Men do not always love and
honour those who have outstripped them in the race of
fortune or distinction; but, whether objects of envy or
of encouragement, these were but rare: and most, no
doubt, of the humbler classes who were admitted into
the Hierarchy rose no higher than the meanest functions, or the privilege of becoming Holy Mendicants.
But, in the darkest periods, when all other Christian
virtues were nearly extinct, charity, in its form of

almsgiving, survived, and was strong; and, indeed, in
institutions for the poor, hospitals, leper-houses, charity
was not only recognised as a duty especially incumbent
on Churchmen; it was a duty ostentatiously discharged.
The haughtiest Pope condescended to imitate the Lord
in washing the feet of poor men. Many of the most
worldly Prelates were the most munificent; perhaps
satisfied their consciences in the acquisition of un-
apostolic pomp and wealth by applying it to apostolic
uses. The donation, the bequest, prodigally bestowed
or ungraciously yielded by the remorseful sinner to the
Priest or Bishop, as it was made to God and his Poor,
however much of it might linger in the hands of the
Clergy, and be applied to less hallowed purposes, never-
theless did not all lose its way; part of it strayed to its
proper object—the assuagement of human indigence
and misery. This was especially the case with the
monastic establishments: it has been said that they
were the poor-houses of the middle ages; but if poor-
houses, like our own by no means wisely or providently
administered, still they had those twofold blessings of
acts of mercy—some softening of the heart of him who
gave, some consolation to the victim, in those days
probably more often of the hard times than of his own
improvidence. Latin Christianity may point to still
surviving Foundations for the good—the temporal, the
intellectual good—of mankind; her Hospitals and her
Brotherhoods, her Universities and her Schools, her
Churches and her Missions, in large part owing to the
munificence or the active agency of her universal Hierarchy; and may thus calmly and securely appeal to
the sentence of the most enlightened Christianity
which will ever, as it may be hoped, prevail in the
world.

And if the Hierarchy drew too imperiously, too sternly, too deeply the line of demarcation between the hallowed and unhallowed castes of mankind, it *Equality of mankind.* had the inestimable merit of asserting the absolute spiritual equality of all not in sacred orders. On the floor of the Church, before the Priest, before God (however there might be some and not always unwise distinction in place and in the homage to rank), the King and the Serf, in all essential points, stood on the same level. The same Sacraments were the common right of all. They were baptised in the same font, heard the same masses, might listen to the same sermons, were married by the same rites, knelt at the same altar, before the throne of the same Saint, received the body and blood of the same Redeemer, were even buried (though with very different pomp of funeral) in ground equally consecrated. The only distinction was excommunication or non-excommunication. The only outlaw was, it was believed, self-outlawed by wandering beyond the pale of the Church. The faithful were one people. Who shall estimate the value, the influence, the blessing of this perpetual assertion, this visible manifestation, of the only true Christian doctrine of equality—equality before God?

One subject we would willingly decline, but the historian must not shrink from truth, however repulsive. Celibacy, which was the vital energy of the Clergy, was at the same time their fatal, irremediable weakness. One-half, at least a large portion, of human kind could not cease to be human kind. The universal voice, which arraigns the state of morals, as regards sexual intercourse, among the Clergy, is not that of their enemies only, it is their own. Century after century we have heard throughout our history the eternal protest of the

severer Churchmen, of Popes, of Legates, of Councils.
The marriage, or, as it was termed, the concubinage, of
the Clergy was the least evil. The example set in high
places (to deny the dissoluteness of the Papal Court at
Avignon, would be to discard all historical evidence)
could not be without frightful influence. The Avignonese Legates bore with them the morals of Avignon.
The last strong effort to break the bonds of celibacy at
the council of Basle warned but warned in vain. It is
the solemn attestation to the state of Germany and the
northern kingdoms.[1] Even in his own age, no doubt,
Henry Bishop of Liège was a monster of depravity. The
frightful revelation of his life is from an admonitory
letter of the wise and good Pope Gregory X. His lust
was promiscuous. He kept as his concubine a Benedictine Abbess. He had boasted in a public banquet
that in twenty-two months he had had fourteen children
born. This was not the worst—there was foul incest,
and with nuns. But the most extraordinary part of the
whole is that in the letter the Pope seems to contemplate only the repentance of the Prelate, which he urges
with the most fervent solemnity. Henry's own prayers,
and the intercessory prayers of the virtuous—some such,
no doubt, there must be in Liège—are to work the
change ; and then he is to administer his Pontifical
office, so as to be a model of holiness, as he had been of
vice, to his subjects. As to suspension, degradation,
deposition, there is not a word. The Pope's lenity may
have been meant to lure him to the Council of Lyons,

---

[1] Look back to vol. viii. p. 457. Be-
fore the Council of Trent, the Elector of
Bavaria declared in a public document,
that of 50 Clergy very few were not
concubinarii.—Sarpi, viii. 7, p. 414.
See for Italy references to Justiniani,
Patriarch of Venice ; S. Antoninus,
Archbishop of Florence ; Weissenburg,
Kirchen Versammlungen, ii. p. 229 ;
again for Germany, ii. p. 228.

where he was persuaded to abdicate his See.[7] Hardly
less repulsive, in some respects more so, as it embraces
the Clergy and some of the convents of a whole province, is the disclosure, as undeniable and authentic, of
sacerdotal morals, in the Register of the Visitations
of Eudes Rigaud, Archbishop of Rouen, from 1248 to
1269.[8] We must suppose that only the Clergy of notorious and detected incontinence were presented at the
Visitation. The number is sufficiently appalling : probably it comprehends, without much distinction, the
married and concubinarian, as well as looser Clergy.
There is one convent of females, which might almost
have put Boccaccio to the blush. I am bound to confess that the Records of the Visitations from St. Paul's,
some of which have been published not without reserve,
too fully vindicate the truth of Langland, Chaucer, and
the Satirists against the English Clergy and Friars in
the fourteenth century.[9] And these Visitations, which
take note only of those publicly accused, hardly reached,
if they did reach, the lowest and the loosest. Only
some of the Monks, none of the Wandering Friars, were
amenable to Episcopal or Archidiaconal jurisdiction.

---

[7] "Circa divinum quoque et ponti-
ficale officium sic te sedulum et devo-
tum exhibere " "Subditi." Henry of
Liège was of princely race, of the house
of Gueldres, Consio-German to the
Priest-Emperor, William of Holland ;
he became Bishop when a mere boy.
Concilia sub ann. 1274. Hocsemius,
Vit. Episcop. Leodens., p. 209.

[8] Registrum Archep. Rotomagen-
sium, published by M. Bonnin, Rouen,
1846. It is full of other curious and
less unedifying matter.

[9] Praecedents in Criminal Causes

edited by Archdeacon Hale, London,
1847. There is enough in these, the
Visitations themselves make matters
worse. It is curious that much earlier
under the reign of K. Stephen, the Dean
Ralph de Diceto speaks of the "forn-
ria " of the canons. Mr. Froude has
published from the Records (in Fra-
ser's Magazine, Feb. 1857) the visitation of a later time, of Archbishop
Morton. The great Abbey of St.
Alban's was in a state which hardly
bears description.

Whether we call it by the holier name of marriage, or the more odious one of concubinage, this, the weakness or the sin of the Clergy, could not be committed by the Monks and Friars. They, mostly with less education and less discipline, spread abroad through the world, had far greater temptations, more fatal opportunities. Though they had, no doubt, their Saints, not only Saints, but numberless nameless recluses of admirable piety, unimpeachable holiness, fervent love of God and of man, yet of the profound corruption of this class there can be no doubt. But Latin, Roman Christianity, would not, could not, surrender this palladium of her power.[b]

Time and the vicissitudes in political affairs had made a great difference in the power of the Clergy in the principal kingdoms of Europe. In Italy, in his double character of Italian potentate and as the Pontiff of Christendom, the Pope, after the discomfiture of the Council of Basle, had resumed in great measure his ascendancy. He now aspired to reign supreme over Letters and Arts. But from this time, or from the close of this century, the Italian Potentate, as has been said, began to predominate over the Pope. The successor of St. Peter was either chosen from one of the great Italian families, or aspired to found a great family. Nepotism became at once the strength and the infirmity, the glory and the shame, of the Papacy: the strength,

---

[b] The Roman view is thus given in an argument before the Pope by the Cardinal de Carpi :—" Dal matrimonio de' Preti ne seguirà che avendo casa, moglie, e figli, non dipenderanno dal Papa, ma dal suo Principe, e la carità della prole gli farà condescendere ad ogni pregiudizio della Chiesa ; cercaranno anco di far i benefici ereditari, ed in brevissimo spazio la Sede Apostolica si ristringerà a Roma. Innanzi che fosse instituito il celibato non cavava frutto alcuno la Sede Romana dell' altre città e regioni ; per quello e fatta padrona di tanti benefizi, de' quali il matrimonio la priverebbe in breve tempo."—Sarpi, L. v. Opere, v. ii. p. 77.

as converting the Popes into the highest rank of Italian
princes; the weakness, as inducing them to sacrifice
the interests of the Holy See to the promotion of their
own kindred: the glory, as seeing their descendants
holding the highest offices, occupying splendid palaces,
possessors of vast estates, sovereigns of principalities;
the shame, as showing too often a feeble fondness for
unworthy relatives, and entailing on themselves some
complicity in the guilt, the profligacy or wickedness of
their favoured kindred.

While the Pope thus rose, the higher Prelates of
Italy seemed to sink, with no loss, perhaps, of
real dignity, into their proper sphere.   The   Italy.
Archbishops of Milan, Florence, Genoa, Ravenna, are
obscured before the Viscontis and Sforzas, the Medicis
and Dorias, the hereditary Sovereigns, the princely
Condottieri, the republican Podestàs, or the Dukes.
Venice adhered to her ancient jealous policy; she
would have no ambitious, certainly no foreign, Prelate
within her lagunes.   She was for some time content to
belong to the province of an Archbishop hardly within
her territory; and that Archbishop, if not a stranger
within her walls, had no share in Venetian power or
wealth.   The single Bishop in Venice was Bishop of one
of the small islands, Castello.   Venice was first erected,
and submitted to be erected, into a patriarchate by
Nicolas V.[e]   When she admitted a Bishop or a Patriarch
(perhaps because no one of inferior dignity must appear
in St. Mark's), that Bishop received his investiture of
his temporal possessions, his ring and pastoral staff, from
the Doge.   No Synods could be held without permission
of the Council.   It was not till after her humiliation by

---

[e] Ughelli, Italia Sacra.

the League of Cambray that Venice would admit the
collation of Bishops to sees within her territories; even
then they must be native Venetians. The Superiors of
the Monasteries and Orders were Venetians. Even
Papal vacancies were presented to by the Venetian Cardinals. The Republic maintained and exercised the
right of censure on Venetian Bishops and on Cardinals.
If they were absent or contumacious their offences were
visited on their families; they were exiled, degraded,
banished. The parish priests were nominated by the
proprietors in the parish. There was a distinct, severe,
inflexible prohibition to the Clergy of all Orders to in-
termeddle in political affairs. Thus did Venice insulate
herself in her haughty independence of Papal as of all
other powers.[a] Paolo Sarpi could write, without fear of
the fulminations of Rome: he had only to guard against
the dagger of the papalising fanatic. There was a complete, universal toleration for foreign rites; Greek,
Armenian, and Mohammedan were under protection.
Prosecutions for heresy were discouraged.

Ravenna had long ceased to be the rival of Rome;
the Malatestas, not the Archbishop, were her Lords.
The younger branches of the great princely families,
those who were disposed to ease, lettered affluence, and
more peaceful pomp, by no means disdained the lofty
titles, the dignity, the splendid and wealthy palaces of
the Prelature: some aspired to the Popedom. Those
too, and they were by no means wanting, who were possessed with a profound sense of religion, rose, from better motives and with the noblest results, to the honours
of the Church. The Roman Colonnas, the Venetian

---

[a] Daru, Hist. de Venise, L. xxviii. c. xi. The saying—" Siamo Venetiani,
poi Christiani "—was their boast or their reproach.

Contarinis, the Lombard Borromeos, some of the holiest men, were of famous or Papal houses. The Medicis gave two Popes, Leo X. and Clement VII., princes rather than Saints, to the throne of St. Peter. Few Prelates, however, if any, excepting Popes, founded princely families. The Republics, the Tyrants who overthrew or undermined the Republics, the great Trans-alpine powers which warred for the mastery of Italy, warred by temporal arms alone. No Prelates took the field or plunged into politics, except the Pope and his Cardinals; even from them excommunications had lost their power. They warred with the ordinary instru-ments of war, soldiers, lances, and artillery. Every other Prelate was content if he could enjoy his revenues and administer his diocese in peace. In general, even the least religious had learned the wisdom or necessity of decency; the more accomplished indulged in the patronage of letters and arts, often letters and arts Pagan rather than Christian; the truly religious rarely wrought their religion to fanaticism; they shone with the light of the milder virtues, and spent their super-fluous wealth on churches and on ecclesiastical objects. Christian Art had its papal, its prelatical, its monastic impulses.

In France the Pragmatic Sanction, not repealed till the reign of Francis I., left the disposal of the great preferments in the power of the Crown. France. But, as has been said, the Pragmatic Sanction was no bold assertion of religious freedom, no generous effort for the emancipation of the universal Church. The Gallican liberties were throughout a narrow, national claim to a special and peculiar exemption from that which was acknowledged to be elsewhere an unlimited autocracy. The claim rested on its own grounds, was

more endeared to France because it was distinctive; it
was a perpetual appeal to the national vanity, the vindication of a privilege of which men are more fond than
of a common right. As an exceptional case, though in
direct contradiction with its first principle, it affirmed in
all other countries the plenary indispensable power of
the Pope.[e]

The civil wars of the Armagnacs and the Burgundians, the wars with England, threw the hierarchy of
France, as it were, into the shade; more violent impulses agitated the realm than struggles for power between the Church and State.[f] The Churchmen were
divided in these fatal quarrels: like the nobles of
France, there were Orleanist and Burgundian Bishops.
The King of England named Bishops, he had Bishops
for his unscrupulous partisans, in the conquered provinces of France. It was the Bishop of Beauvais—with
the Inquisitors of France—who condemned Joan of Arc
as a witch, and burned her at the stake. In this
wicked, contemptible, and hateful process the Church
must share the guilt with England. High feudal names
during all this period are found in the hierarchy of
France, but the rich prelacies and abbacies had not yet
become to such an extent as hereafter the appanages of
the younger branches of the noble families. So long as
the King possessed the inappreciable prerogative of rewarding the faithful, or purchasing the wavering loyalty

---

[e] Gioberti has somewhere declared
the Gallican Liberties a standing Antipope.

[f] The Parliament of Poitiers compelled Charles VII. to renounce an
ordinance, Feb. 14, 1424, which they
refused to register, restoring to the
Pope the nomination to the Benefices.
This weak concession had been obtained
from the King by the Queen of Sicily.
The Parliament declared the ordinance
surreptitious, and contrary to the rights
of the Bishops.—Ordonnances des Rois,
Préface, t. xiii. Sismondi, Hist. des
Français, xiii. 54.

of those dangerous, once almost coequal, subjects by the bestowal of benefices, this power had no inconsiderable influence on the growth of the royal authority. At all events, the Church offered no resistance to the consolidation of the kingly power; the ecclesiastical nobles were mostly the obsequious partisans of the Crown.

In Spain the Church had not begun to rule her Kings with absolute sway, or rather her Kings had not yet become in mind and heart Churchmen. *Spain.* The Crusade still continued against the Mohammedan, who was slowly and stubbornly receding before the separate kingdoms, Castile, Arragon, Portugal. Spain had not yet begun—might seem unlikely to begin—her crusade against the rising religious liberties of Europe. She aspired not to be the Champion, and, as the Champion, the Sovereign of Latin Christendom; she had given to the Church St. Dominic, she had yet to give Ximenes, Philip II., Torquemada, Loyola.

In Germany the strife of the Papacy and the Empire seemed altogether worn out; the Emperor was content to be a German Sovereign, the *Germany.* Pope to leave the German sovereignty to the German Electors. The Concordat and the Articles of Aschaffenburg had established a truce which might settle down into peace. If the Pope had been satisfied to receive, Germany would hardly have been unwilling to pay, the stipulated, before long the customary, tribute. The Bishop-Electors no longer took the lead, or dictated to the Prince-Electors. In general they were quietly magnificent, rather than turbulent or aggressive Prelates. Still the possession of three out of the seven suffrages for the Empire maintained at once the dignity of the Church, and made these prizes objects of ambition to

the princely houses of Germany.[f] Nor did these arch-
bishoprics stand alone. Metropolitans like those of
Saltzburg, Prague, Olmutz, Magdeburg; Bishops in the
flourishing cities of the Rhine, Worms, Spiers, Strasburg, or in its neighbourhood, Wurtzburg, Bamberg,
Passau, Ratisbon, were, in their domains, privileges,
feudal rights, and seignoralties, principalities. Yet all
was apparent submission, harmony, mutual respect; perhaps the terrors of the Turkish invasion, equally formidable to Pope and Emperor, aided in keeping the
peace. The balance of power was rather that of the
Prince-Electors and Princes of the Empire against the
Emperor and the Pope, than of Emperor against Pope.[h]
The estrangement from the Papal dominion, the once
clamorous demand for the reformation of the Church,
the yearning after Teutonic independence, had sunk
into the depths of the national mind, into which it could
not be followed by the most sagacious political or religious seer. The deep, silent, popular religious movement, from Master Eckhart, from the author of the
Book on the Imitation of Christ, and from Tauler,
above all, from the author of the German Theology and
his disciples, might seem as if it was amassing strength
upon the foundation of Latin Christianity and the
hierarchical system; while these writers were the moni-
tory signs, and as far as showing the uncongeniality
of the Latin and Teutonic mind, the harbingers of the
coming revolution.

---

[f] In the fifteenth century, indeed, the Bishoprics began to be commonly bestowed on the younger sons of Sovereign Princes; the Court of Rome favoured this practice, from the conviction that the Chapters could only be kept in order by the strong hand and the authority of Sovereign power, &c.—Ranke's Germany, Mrs. Austin's Translation, i. p. 68.

[h] Compare the Introduction of Ranke.

England had long ceased to be the richest and most
obedient tributary province of the Holy See. The Statutes of Mortmain, Provisors, Præmunire, had become
the law of the land. Peers and Commons had united
in the same jealousy of the exorbitant power and influence of the Pope. The remonstrances of the Popes
against these laws had broken and scattered like foam
upon the rocks of English pride and English justice.[1]
The Clergy, as one of the estates of the realm, hold their
separate Parliament, grant their subsidies or benevo-
lences; but they now take a humbler tone, meekly
deprecate rather than fulminate anathemas against those
who invade their privileges and immunities. Trembling
for their own power, they care not to vindicate with
offensive haughtiness that of the Pope. The hierarchy,
awed by the spreading opinion of the Lollards, had
thrown themselves for protection under the usurping
house of Lancaster, and had been accepted as faithful
allies of the 'Crown under Henry IV. Though the
Archbishop of York is at the head of the great Northern insurrection, on Henry's side are the successive Pri-
mates of Canterbury, Arundel, and Courtenay. It might
seem that the Pope and the Crown, by advancing Eng-
lishmen of the noble houses to the Primacy, had deliberately determined on a league with the Lords against
the civil and spiritual democracy—on one side of Wat
Tyler and Jack Straw, on the other of the extreme followers of Wycliffe. The first act of this tacit league was

---

[1] Under Henry IV., the Parliament
resolves that "the Pope's collector,
though he had the Pope's Bull for this
purpose, hath no jurisdiction within
this realm."—1 Henry IV. The Præmunire is confirmed against unlawful
communication with Rome, at the
same time that the Act against heresy
is passed; and this Act is not a Canon
of the Church, but a Statute of the
Realm.—Parliamentary History.

to establish the throne of Henry Bolingbroke and put in execution the burning statute against heretics. It cannot be doubted that Archbishop Chichely, in his support of the French war, sought less to propitiate the royal favour than to discharge on France some of the perilous turbulence which was fermenting in England. At the commencement of Henry VI. the Cardinal Beaufort of Winchester is striving for supreme power with the Duke of Gloucester; but Beaufort is a Prince of the blood, uncle of the King, as well as Bishop and Cardinal.[k] In the French wars, and in the civil wars, the Bishops seem to have shrunk into their proper and more peaceful sphere. Chichely was content with blowing the trumpet in the Parliament in London; he did not follow the King with the armed retainers of Canterbury. The high places of the Church—though so many of the younger as well as the elder sons of the nobility found more congenial occupation in the fields of France—

A.D. 1443. were rarely left to men of humbler birth. Stafford, who succeeded Chichely, was of the house of the Counts of Stafford, Bourchier of the Earls of

A.D. 1454. Essex.[m] Neville, brother of the Earl of Warwick, was Archbishop of York.[n] In the wars of the Roses, the Nobles, the Somersets, Buckinghams,

---

[k] Among the Ambassadors of England to Basle were the Bishops of London, Lisieux, Rochester, Bayeux, and Aix, and other English and Norman divines.—See Commission, Fuller's Church History, p. 178.

[m] Chichely was said to be the son of a tailor.—Fuller, p. 182. His biographer rather confirms this, speaking respectfully of it as a reputable trade, p. 3.

[n] The Pope still maintained the form of the appointment to the Primacy. As in a case cited above of York, the Monks of Canterbury elected Chichely (no doubt under royal influence). The Pope refused the nomination, but himself appointed Chichely by a Papal provision. Chichely would not accept the Primacy till authorised by the King. Stafford's successor, Kemp, was in like manner elected by the Monks, refused, and then nominated of his own authority by the Pope.—

Warwicks, Cliffords—not the Canterburies, Yorks, or
Londons—are at the head of the conflicting parties.
The banners of Bishops and Abbots wave not over the
fields of Barnet, Towton, Wakefield, St. Alban's, Tewkes-
bury. It is not till the war is over that they resume
their seat or authority in the Parliament or Council
board. They acknowledge and do homage to the conqueror, York or Lancastrian, or, like Henry VII.,[*]
blending the two titles. From that time the Archbishop is the first subject in the realm, but in every
respect a subject. Some of the great English Prelates,
from Wykeham to Wolsey, seem to have been more
prescient than those in other kingdoms of the coming
change. It is shown in their consecration of large
masses of ecclesiastical wealth and landed property for
the foundation of colleges rather than monasteries, by
Wykeham, Wainfleet, Fox, Wolsey. It can hardly be
doubted that some wise Churchman suggested the noble
design of Henry VI. in the endowment of King's at
Cambridge and of Eton. Wolsey's more magnificent
projects seem, as it were, to be arming the Church
for some imminent contest; they reveal a sagacious
foreknowledge that the Church must take new ground
if she will maintain her rule over the mind of
man.

Still on the whole throughout Christendom the vast

Godwin, in Chichely and Kemp. The
Pope confirmed the election of Bourchier.—Godwin, in Bourchier. The
Pope was thus content with a specious
maintenance of his right, the more
practical English with the possession of
the real power.

[*] "This king's reign afforded little
Church storie," says Fuller. He fills

it up with an account of an enormous
banquet given by Neville, Archbishop
of York. Neville could not help being
a politician. When Edward, afterwards
the IVth, was a prisoner, he was in
the custody of Neville, who does not
seem to have watched him too carefully. Neville was seized and sent
prisoner to Calais by Edward IV.

fabric of the hierarchy stood unshaken. In England alone there was suppressed insurrection among the fol-

Power of hierarchy unshaken. lowers of Wycliffe, now obscure and depressed by persecution; and in Bohemia. There the irresistible armies of Ziska and Procopius had not only threatened to found an anti-hierarchical State; but for the mutual antipathy between the Sclavonian and Teutonic races, they might have drawn Germany into the revolt. But Bohemia, again bowed under hierarchical supremacy, was brooding in sullen sorrow over her lost independence. In no other land, except in individual minds or small despised sects, was there any thought, any yearning for the abrogation of the sacerdotal authority. The belief was universal, it was a part of the common Christianity, that a mysterious power dwelt in the hierarchy, irrespective of the sanctity of their own lives, and not dependant on their greater knowledge, through study, of Divine revelation, which made their mediation absolutely necessary to escape eternal perdition and to attain eternal life. The keys were in their hands, not to unlock the hidden treasures of Divine wisdom in the Gospels, or solely to bind and loose by the administration of the great Sacraments; but the keys absolutely of Heaven or Hell. Not, indeed, that death withdrew the soul from the power of the Priest; not even after it departed from the body was it left to the unerring judgement, to the inexhaustible mercy of the one All-seeing Judge. In Purgatory the Priest still held in his hands the doom of the dead man. This doom, in the depths of the other world, was hardly a secret. The torments of Purgatory (and the precincts of purgatory were widened infinitely—very few were so holy as to escape, few so desperately lost as not to be admitted to purgatorial probation) might be mitigated

by the expiatory masses, masses purchased by the
wealthy at the price dictated by the Priest, and which
rarely could be gained without some sacrifice by the
brokenhearted relative or friend. They were more
often lavishly provided for by the dying sinner in his
will, when wealth, clung to with such desperate tenacity
in life, is thrown away with as desperate recklessness.
This religion, in which man ceased to be the guardian
of his own soul—with all its unspeakable terrors, with
all its unspeakable consolations (for what weak mind—
and whose mind on such points was not weak?—would
not hold as inestimable the certain distinct priestly
absolution, or the prayers of the Church for the dead),
—this vicarious religion was as much part of the ordinary faith, as much an article of Latin Christianity, as
the retributive judgement of God, as the redemption
through Christ.

It is difficult (however vain it may be) not to specu-
late how far the conservative reformation in the Pope
and in the Hierarchy, urged so earnestly and eloquently
by Gerson and D'Ailly, more vehemently and therefore
more alarmingly, by the Council of Basle, might have
averted or delayed the more revolutionary reform of the
next century. Had not the Papacy, had not the Hierarchy, with almost judicial blindness, thrown itself
across the awakening moral sense of man; had it not,
by the invidious possession, the more invidious accumulation, of power and wealth, with all the inevitable
abuses in the acquisition, in the employment, of that
power and wealth, aggravated rather than mitigated
their despotic yoke; had they not by such reckless
defiance as the lavish preaching of Indulgences by profligate and insolent men, insulted the rising impatience,
and shown too glaringly the wide disruption and dis-

tance between the moral and the ritual elements of religion ; had not this flagrant incongruity of asserting the Divine power of Christ to be vested in men, to so great an extent utterly unchristian, compelled reflection, doubt, disbelief—at length indignant reprobation—would the crisis have come when it came ? Who would have had the courage to assume the responsibility for his own soul ? Who would have renounced the privilege of absolution ? Who would have thrown himself on the vaguer, less material, less palpable, less, may it be said, audible mercy of God in Christ, and in Christ alone ? Who would have withdrawn from what at least seemed to be, what was asserted and believed to be, the visible Church, in which the signs and tokens of Divine grace and favour were all definite, distinct, cognisable by the senses ; were seen, heard, felt, and not alone by the inward consciousness ? Who would have contented himself with being of that Invisible Church, of which the only sign was the answer of the good conscience within, faith and hope unguaranteed by any earthly mediator, unassured by any authoritative form of words or outward ceremony ? Who would have rested in trembling hope on the witness of the Spirit of God, concurrent with the testimony of the spirit within ? We may imagine a more noiseless, peaceful, alas, we must add, bloodless change ! We may imagine the Gospel, now newly revealed, as it were, in its original language (the older Testament in its native Hebrew), and illustrated by the earlier Greek Fathers, translated into all living languages, and by the new art of Printing become of general and familiar use, gradually dispersing all the clouds of wild allegoric interpretation, of mythology, and materialism, which had been gathering over it for centuries, and thus returning to its few majestic primal

truths in the Apostolic Creed. We may even imagine
the Hierarchy receding into their older sphere, in-
structors, examples in their families as in themselves,
of all the virtues and charities; the religious adminis-
trators of simpler rites. Yet who that calmly, philo-
sophically, it may almost be said religiously, surveys
the power and strength of the Latin religion, the religion
of centuries, the religion of a continent—its extraordinary and felicitous adaptation to all the wants and
necessities of man—its sympathy with some of the
dominant faculties of our being, those especially developed at certain periods of civilisation—its unity—its
magisterial authority—the depth to which it had sunk
in the human heart—the feelings, affections, passions,
fears, hopes, which it commanded: who that surveys it
in its vast standing army of the Clergy, and Monks and
Friars, which had so long taken service in its defence,
with its immense material strength of Churches, Monasteries, Established Laws, Rank; in its Letters, and in
its Arts; in its charitable, educational, Institutions:
who will not rather wonder at its dissolution, its aboli-
tion in so large a part of Christendom, than at its duration? It is not so marvellous that it resisted, and
resisted with success; that it threw back in some
kingdoms, for a time, the inevitable change; that
it postponed in some until a more remote, more terrible and fatal rebellion some centuries after, the de-
trusion from its autocratic, despotic throne. Who shall
be astonished that Latin Christianity so long maintained a large part of the world at least in nominal
subjection; or finally, that it still maintains the contest
with its rival Teutonic Christianity without, and the
more dangerous, because unavowed, revolt within its
own pale—the revolt of those who, in appearance

E 2

its subjects, either altogether disdain its control, and,
not able to accept its belief and discipline, compromise by a hollow acquiescence, or an unregarded, un-
punished neglect of all discipline, for total inward
rejection of belief?

CHAPTER II.

· Belief of Latin Christianity.

LATIN Christendom, or rather universal Christendom, was one (excepting those who were self-out-   Unity of   lawed, or outlawed by the dominant authority   creed.   from the Christian monarchy), not only in the organisation of the all-ruling Hierarchy and the admission of Monkhood, it was one in the great system of Belief. With the exception of the single article of the procession of the Holy Ghost, the Nicene formulary had been undisturbed, and had ruled with undisputed sway   Procession   of the Holy   for centuries. The procession of the Holy   Ghost.   Ghost from the Son as well as the Father was undoubtedly the doctrine of the early Latin writers; but this tenet stole noiselessly—it is not quite certain at what time—into the Creed. That Creed, framed at the great Council of Nicæa, had been received with equal unanimity by the Greek and Latin Churches. Both Churches had subscribed to the anathemas pronounced by the second Council of Constantinople, and ratified by the first Council of Ephesus, against any Church which should presume to add one word or letter to that Creed. Public documents in Rome showed that Pope Leo III. had inscribed on a silver tablet the Creed of Rome without the words "from the Son," as the authorised faith of the Latin Church. In the great quarrel with Photius, the Greeks discovered, and charged against the Latins, this audacious violation of the

decrees of the Councils, this unauthorised impious addition to the unalterable Creed of Nicæa. The Patriarch
of Constantinople charged it, justly or unjustly, against
his own enemy, Nicolas I.[*] In the strife with Michael
Cerularius, at the final disruption between the two
Churches, this was one of the inexpiable
offences of the Latin Church. The admission
of the obnoxious article by the Greeks at the Council
of Florence was indignantly repudiated, on the return
of the Legates from the Council, by the Greek Church.
But the whole of Latin Christendom disdained to give
ear to the protest of the Greeks; the article remained,
with no remonstrance whatever from the West, in the
general Latin Creed.

A.D. 1053.

But the Creeds—that of the Apostles, that of Nicæa,
or even that ascribed to St. Athanasius, and
chanted in every church of the West—formed
but a small part of the belief of Latin Christendom.
That whole world was one in the popular religion. The
same vast mythology commanded the general consent;
the same angelology, demonology; the same worship of
the Virgin and the Saints, the same reverence for pilgrimages and reliques, the same notions of the life to
come, of Hell, Purgatory, Heaven. In general, as
springing out of like tendencies and prepossessions of
mind, prevailed the like or kindred traditions; the
world was one in the same vulgar superstitions. Already,
as has been seen, at the close of the sixth century,
during the Pontificate of Gregory the Great, the Christianisation not only of the speculative belief of man, of

Unity of popular religion.

---

[*] I know no more brief or better
summary of the controversy than the
common one in Pearson on the Creed.
I have some doubts whether the accu- | sation of Photius, as to its introduction,
is personal against Pope Nicolas or
against the Roman Church.

that also which may justly be called the religion of man,
was complete: but no less complete was the Christianisation, if it may be so said, of the lingering Paganism.
Man had divinised all those objects of awe and veneration, which rose up in new forms out of his old religion,
and which were intermediate between the Soul and God,
—"God," that is, in "Christ," as revealed in the Gospels.
Tradition claimed equal authority with the New Testament. There was supposed to be a perpetual power in
the Church, and in the Hierarchy the Ruler and Teacher
of the Church, of infinitely expanding and multiplying
the objects of faith; at length, of gradually authorising
and superinducing as integral parts of Christianity the
whole imaginative belief of the Middle Ages. Even
where such belief had not been canonically enacted by
Pope or Council, the tacit acceptance by the general
practice of Priest as well as of people was not less authoritative; popular adoration invested its own objects in
uncontested sanctity. Already the angelic Hierarchy,
if not in its full organisation, had taken its place between mankind and God; already the Virgin Mary was
rising, or had fully risen, into Deity; already prayers
rarely ascended directly to the throne of grace through
the One Intercessor, a crowd of mediate agencies was
almost necessary to speed the orison upward, and to
commend its acceptance, as it might thwart its blessing.
Places, things, had assumed an inalienable holiness, with
a concentered and emanative power of imparting or
withholding spiritual influences. Great prolific principles had been laid down, and had only to work in the
congenial soil of the human mind. Now, by the in-
fusion of the Barbaric or Teutonic element, as well as
by the religious movement which had stirred to its
depths the old Roman society, mankind might seem

renewing its youth, its spring-time of life, with all its
imaginative creativeness, and its unceasing surrender to
whatever appeared to satisfy the yearnings of its hardly
satisfied faith.

There was unity in the infinite diversity of the popular
worship. Though each nation, province, parish, shrine,
had its peculiar and tutelar Saint, none was without a
Saint, and none denied the influence of the Saints of
others. Christianity was one in this materialistic intercommunion between the world of man and the extra-
mundane; that ulterior sphere, in its purer corporeity,
yet still, in its corporeity, was perpetually becoming
cognisable to the senses of man. It was one in the
impersonation of all the agencies of nature, in that universal Anthropomorphism, which, if it left something of
vague and indefinite majesty to the Primal Parental
Godhead, this was not from any high intellectual or
mental conception of the incongruity of the human and
divine; not from dread of the disparagement of the
Absolute and the Infinite; from no predilection for
the true sublimity of higher Spiritualism; but simply
because its worship, content to rest on a lower sphere,
humanised all which it actually adored, without scruple,
without limit; and this not in language only, but in its
highest conception of its real existence.

All below the Godhead was materialised to the
thought. Even within the great Triune Deity the Son
still wore the actual flesh which he had assumed on
earth; the Holy Ghost became a Dove, not as a symbol,
but as a constantly indwelt form. All beyond this
supercelestial sphere, into which, however controversial
zeal might trespass, awful reverence yet left in it some
majestic indistinctness, and some confessed mysterious
transcendentalism; all lower, nearer to the world of

man, angels, and devils, the spirits of the condemned and the beatified Saints, were in form, in substance however subtilised, in active only enlarged powers, in affections, hatred or attachment, in passions, nothing more than other races of human beings.

There was the world of Angels and of Devils. The earlier faith, that of Gregory the Great, had contented itself with the notions of Angels as dimly revealed in the Scriptures. It may be doubted if any names of angels, except those in the Sacred Writings, Michael, Gabriel, Raphael, or any acts not imagined according to the type and precedent of the angelic visitations in the Old and New Testament, will be found in the earlier Fathers. But by degrees the Hierarchy of Heaven was disclosed to the ready faith of mankind, at once the glorious type and with all the regular gradations and ranks of the Hierarchy upon Earth. There was a great celestial Church above, not of the beatified Saints, but of those higher than human Beings whom St. Paul had given some ground to distinguish by different titles, titles which seemed to imply different ranks and powers.

Latin Christendom did not give birth to the writer who, in this and in another department, influenced most powerfully the Latin mind. The author of those extraordinary treatises which, from their obscure and doubtful parentage, now perhaps hardly maintain their fame for imaginative richness, for the occasional beauty of their language, and their deep piety—those treatises which, widely popular in the West, almost created the angel-worship of the popular creed, and were also the parents of Mystic Theology and of the higher Scholasticism—this Poet-Theologian was a Greek. The writings which bear the venerable name of Dionysius the Areopagite, the proselyte of St. Paul, first appear

Dionysius the Areopagite. under a suspicious and suspected form, as authorities cited by the heterodox Severians in a conference at Constantinople.[b] The orthodox stood aghast: how was it that writings of the holy Convert of St. Paul had never been heard of before? that Cyril of Alexandria, that Athanasius himself, were ignorant of their existence? But these writings were in themselves of too great power, too captivating, too congenial to the monastic mind, not to find bold defenders.[c] Bearing this venerable name in their front, and leaving behind them, in the East, if at first a doubtful, a growing faith in their authenticity,[d] they appeared in the West as a precious gift from the Byzantine Emperor to the Emperor Louis the Pious. France in that age was not likely to throw cold and jealous doubts on writings which bore the hallowed name of that great Saint, whom she had already boasted to have left his primal bishopric of Athens to convert her forefathers, whom Paris already held to be her tutelar Patron, the rich and powerful Abbey of St. Denys to be her founder. There was living in the West, by happy coincidence, the one man who at that period, by his knowledge of Greek, by the congenial speculativeness of his mind, by the vigour and richness of his imagination, was qualified to trans-

---

[b] Concilia sub ann. 533. Compare the Preface to the edition of Corderius.

[c] Photius, in the first article in his Bibliotheca, describes the work of a monk, Theodorus, who had answered four out of the unanswerable arguments against their authenticity, as the writings of the Areopagite; but about the answers of Theodorus, and his own impression of the authority and value of the books, Photius is silent.—Photii Biblioth. p. 1, ed. Bekker.

[d] There is a quotation from them in a Homily of Gregory the Great, Lib. ii. Hom. 34, Oper. i. p. 1607. Gregory probably picked it up during his controversy in Constantinople.—(See vol. i. p. 435.) There is no other trace of an earlier version, or of their earlier influence in the West.

late into Latin the mysterious doctrines of the Areopagito, both as to the angelic world and the subtile theology. John Erigena hastened to make known in the West the "Celestial Hierarchy," the treatise "on the Name of God," and the brief chapters on the "Mystic Philosophy." These later works were more tardy in their acceptance, but perhaps more enduring in their influence. Traced downwards through Erigena himself, the St. Victors, Bonaventura, to Eckhart and Tauler in Germany, and throughout the unfailing succession of Mystics, they will encounter us hereafter.[*]

The "Celestial Hierarchy" would command at once, and did command, universal respect for its authority, and universal reverence for its doctrines. The "Hierarchy" threw upward the Primal Deity, the whole Trinity, into the most awful, unapproachable, incomprehensible distance; but it filled the widening intermediate space with a regular succession of superhuman Agents, an ascending and descending scale of Beings, each with his rank, title, office, function, superior or subordinate. The vague incidental notices in the Old and New Testament and in St. Paul (and to St. Paul doubtless Jewish tradition lent the names), were wrought out into regular Orders, who have each, as it were, a feudal relation, pay their feudal service (here it struck in with the Western as well as with the Hierarchical mind) to the Supreme, and have feudal superiority or subjection to each other. This theory ere long became almost the authorised Theology; it

(marginal note: The Celestial Hierarchy.)

---

* The Preface of Corderius (Observat. xi.) briefly shows the connexion of the pseudo-Dionysius with Scholasticism, especially with Thomas Aquinas. Observat. xii. shows the innumerable references of Aquinas to those works; yet Aquinas was far less mystic than other schoolmen.

became, as far as such transcendent subjects could be familiarised to the mind, the vulgar belief. The Arts hereafter, when mature enough to venture on such vast and unmanageable subjects, accepted this as the tradition of the Church. Painting presumed to represent the individual forms, and even, in Milton's phrase, "the numbers without number" of this host of heaven.

The Primal Godhead, the Trinity in Unity, was alone Absolute, Ineffable, Inconceivable; alone Essential Purity, Light, Knowledge, Truth, Beauty, Goodness.[f] These qualities were communicated in larger measure in proportion to their closer approximation to itself, to the three descending Triads which formed the Celestial Hierarchy:—I. The Seraphim, Cherubim, and Thrones. II. The Dominations, Virtues, Powers. III. Principalities, Archangels, Angels. This Celestial Hierarchy formed, as it were, concentric circles around the unapproachable Trinity. The nearest, and as nearest partaking most fully of the Divine Essence, was the place of honour. The Thrones, Seraphim, and Cherubim approximated most closely, with nothing intermediate, and were more immediately and eternally conformed to the Godhead. The two latter of these were endowed, in the language of the Scripture, with countless eyes and countless wings.[g] The second Triad, of less marked and definite attributes, was that of the

---

[f] The writer strives to get beyond Greek copiousness of expression, in order to shroud the Godhead in its utter unapproachableness. He is the Goodness beyond Goodness, ὑπεράγαθος ἀγαθότης, the Super-Essential Essence, οὐσία ὑπερούσια, Godhead of Godhead, ὑπέρθεος θεότης.

[g] Πρωτὴν μὲν εἶναι φησι, τὴν περὶ θεὸν οὖσαν ἀεὶ καὶ πρὸ τῶν ἄλλων ἀμέσως ἱδρῶσθαι παραδεδομένην, τούς τε γὰρ ἁγιωτάτους θρόνους καὶ τὰ πολυόμματα καὶ πολύπτερα τάγματα Χερουβὶμ, Ἑβραίων φωνῇ, καὶ Σεραφὶμ ὀνομάσμενα.—C. vi.

Powers, Dominations, Virtues.[b] The third, as more
closely approximating to the world of man, if it may be
so said, more often visited the atmosphere of earth, and
were the immediate ministers of the Divine purposes.
Yet the, so-called, Areopagite laboriously interprets into
a spiritual meaning all the forms and attributes assigned
in the sacred writings to the Celestial Messengers, to
Angels and Archangels. They are of fiery nature. Fire
possesses most properties of the Divinity, permeating
everything, yet itself pure and unmingled: all mani-
festing, yet undiscernible till it has found matter to
enkindle ; irresistible, invisible, subduing everything
to itself; vivifying, enlightening, renewing, and moving
and keeping everything in motion ; and so through a
long list of qualities, classed and distinguished with
exquisite Greek perspicuity. He proceeds to their
human form, allegorising as he goes on, the members of
the human body, their wings, their partial nakedness,
their bright or their priestly raiment, their girdles, their
wands, their spears, their axes, their measuring-cords,
the winds, the clouds, the brass and tin, the choirs and
hallelujahs, the hues of the different precious stones;
the animal forms of the lion, the ox, the eagle, the
horse ; the colours of the symbolic horses; the streams,
the chariots, the wheels, and finally, even the joy of the
Angels.[i] All this, which to the wise and more reflective
seemed to interpret and to bestow a lofty significance
on these images, taken in its letter—and so far only
it reached the vulgar ear—gave reality, gave a kind
of authority and conventional certainty to the whole
Angelic Host as represented and described for the popu-

---

[b] All this was said to be derived
from St. Paul. Gregory the Great
(Lib. ii. Moralis) has another distribution, probably from some other
source.
[i] Ch. xv.

lar worship. The existence of this regular Celestial Hierarchy became an admitted fact in the higher and more learned Theology; the Schoolmen reason upon it as on the Godhead itself: in its more distinct and material outline it became the vulgar belief. The separate and occasionally discernible Being and Nature of Seraphim and Cherubim, of Archangel and Angel, in that dim confusion of what was thought revealed in the Scripture, and what was sanctioned by the Church—of image and reality; this Oriental, half Magian, half Talmudic, but now Christianised theory, took its place, if with less positive authority, with hardly less questioned credibility, amid the rest of the faith.

But this, the proper, if it may be so said, most heavenly, was not the only Celestial Hierarchy. There was a Hierarchy below, reflecting that above; a mortal, a material Hierarchy: corporeal, as communicating divine light, purity, knowledge to corporeal Beings. The triple earthly Sacerdotal Order had its type in heaven, the Celestial Orders their antitype on earth. The triple and novene division ran throughout, and connected, assimilated, almost identified the mundane and supermundane Church. As there were three degrees of attainment, Light, Purity, Knowledge (or the divine vision), so there were three Orders of the Earthly Hierarchy, Bishops, Priests, and Deacons; three Sacraments, Baptism, the Eucharist, the Holy Chrism; three classes, the Baptised, the Communicants, the Monks. How sublime, how exalting, how welcome to the Sacerdotalism of the West this lofty doctrine! The Celestial Hierarchy were as themselves; themselves were formed and organised after the pattern of the great Orders in heaven. The whole worship of Man, in which they administered, was an echo of that above;

Celestial Hierarchy.

it represented, as in a mirror, the angelic or super-angelic worship in the Empyrean. All its splendour, its lights, its incense, were but the material symbols; adumbrations of the immaterial, condescending to human thought, embodying in things cognisable to the senses of man the adoration of the Beings close to the throne of God.[k]

The unanswerable proof, were other wanting, of the Greek origin of the Celestial Hierarchy is, that in the Hierarchical system there is no place for the Pope, nor even—this perhaps might seem more extraordinary to the Gallic Clergy—for the Metropolitan. It recognises only the triple rank of Bishops, Priests, and Deacons. Jesus to the earthly Hierarchy is as the higher Primal Godhead, as the Trinity, to the Celestial Hierarchy. He is the Thearchic Intelligence, the super-substantial Being.[m] From him are communicated, through the Hierarchy, Purity, Light, Knowledge. He is the Primal Hierarch, that imparts his gifts to men; from him and through him men become partakers in the Divinity. The Sacraments are the channels through which these graces, Purification, Illumination, Perfection, are distributed to the chosen. Each Hierarchical Order has its special function, its special gifts. Baptism is by the Deacon, the Eucharist by the Priest, the Holy Chrism by the Bishop. What the Celestial Hierarchy are to the whole material universe the Hierarchy of the Clergy are to the souls of men; the trans-

---

[k] 'Επεὶ μηδὲ δυνατὸν ἐστιν τῷ καθ' ἡμᾶς νοῖ, πρὸς τὴν ἄθλον ἐκείνην ἀνετίθηται τῶν οὐρανίων 'Ιεραρχιῶν μίμησίν τε καὶ θεωρίαν, εἰ μὴ τῇ κατ' αὐτὸν ὑλαίᾳ χειραγωγίᾳ χρήσαιτο τὰ μὲν φαινόμενα κάλλη τῆς ἀφανοῦς εὐπρεπείας ἀπεικονίσματα λογιζόμενοι, καὶ τὰς αἰσθητὰς εὐωδίας ἐκτυπώματα τῆς νοητῆς διαδόσεως, καὶ τῆς αὔλου φωτοδοσίας εἰκόνα τὰ ὑλικὰ φῶτα.—Lib. i. c. i. p. 3.

[m] Θεαρχικώτατος νοῦς, ὑπερούσιος.

mittants, the sole transmittants, of those graces and blessings which emanate from Christ as their primal fountain.

Still, however, as of old,[a] angelic apparitions were *Demonology.* rare and unfrequent in comparison with the demoniacal possessions, the demoniacal temptations and interferences. Fear was more quick, sensitive, ever-awake, than wonder, devotion, or love. Men might in their profound meditations imagine this orderly and disciplined Hierarchy far up in the remote Heavens. The visitations to earth might be of higher or lower ministers, according to the dignity of the occasion or the holiness of the Saint. The Seraphim might flash light on the eye, or touch with fire the lip of the Seer; the Cherubim might make their celestial harmonics heard; the Archangel might sweep down on his terrible wings on God's mission of wrath; the Angel descend on his more noiseless mission of love. The air might teem with these watchful Beings, brooding with their protecting care over the Saints, the Virgins, the meek and lowly Christians.[c] They might be in perpetual contest for the souls of men with their eternal antagonists the Devils. But the Angelology was but dim and indistinct to the dreadful ever-present Demonology; their name, the Spirits of Air, might seem as if the atmosphere immediately around this world was their inalienable, almost exclusive domain.

So long as Paganism was the antagonist of Christianity, the Devil, or rather the Devils, took the names of Heathen Deities: to St. Martin of Tours, they were Jove, Mercury, Venus, or Minerva. They wore the form

---

[a] Compare vol. ii. p. 152.

[c] Spenser's beautiful and well-known lines express the common feeling.

and the attributes of those rejected and degraded Gods,
no doubt familiar to most by their statues, perhaps by
heathen poetry—the statues not yet destroyed by neglect or by Christian Iconoclasm, the poetry, which yet
sounded to the Christian ear profane, idolatrous, hateful.[p] At a later period the Heathen Deities have sunk
into the obscure protectors of certain odious vices.
Among the charges against Pope Boniface VIII. is the
invocation of Venus and other Pagan demons, for success in gambling and other licentious occupations. So,
too, in the conversion of the Germans, the Teutonic
Gods became Demons. The usual form of recantation
of heathenism was, "Dost thou renounce the Devils?
Dost thou renounce Thonar, Woden, Saxnote?"[q] "Odin
take you," is still the equivalent in some Northern
tongues to "the Devil take you."[r]

But neither did the Greek Mythology, nor did that of
the Germans, offer any conception like that of the later
Jewish and the Christian Antagonist of God. Satan
had no prototype in either. The German Teufel (Devil)
is no more than the Greek Diabolus. The word is used
by Ulphilas; and in that primitive translation Satan
retains his proper name.[s] But as in Greek and Roman

[p] "Nam interdum in Joris personam,
plerumque Mercurii, persæpe etiam se
Veneris ac Minervæ transfiguratum
vultibus offerebat."—Sulp. Sever. Vit.
S. Mat. cxxiii. Martin was endowed
with a singular faculty of discerning
the Devil. "Diabolum vero tam con-
spicabilem et subjectum oculis habebat,
ut sive se in propriâ substantiâ contineret, sive in diversas figuras spiri-
tualesque nequitiæ transtulisset, quali-
lot ab eo sub imagine videretur."
Once Martin promised the Devil the

Divine forgiveness at the Day of
Judgement, on his ceasing to persecute,
and his repentance of his sins. "Ego
tibi vero confisus in Domino, Christi
misericordiam polliceor." The heterodox clarity of St. Martin did not meet
the same aversion as the heterodox
theology of Origen.

[q] See vol. lii. p. 267.
[r] Grimm. Mythologie, p. 569.
[s] Mark lll. 23. John xiii. 27.
Edit. Zahn.

heathenism the infernal Deities were perhaps earlier,
certainly were more universally, than the deities of
Olympus, darkened into the Demons, Fiends, Devils
of the Christian belief; so from the Northern mythology, Lok and Hela, before and in a greater degree than
Odin or the more beneficent and warlike Gods, were
relegated into Devils. Pluto was already black enough,
terribly hideous enough, cruel and unrelenting enough;
he ruled in Tartarus, which was, of course, identified
with Hell: so Lok, with his consummate wickedness,
and consummate wiliness, as the enemy of all good,
lent and received much of the power and attributes of
Satan.

The reverent withdrawal not only of the Primal
Parental Godhead, the Father, but likewise of the two
coeternal Persons of the Trinity into their unapproachable solitude, partly perhaps the strong aversion to
Manicheism, kept down, as it were, the antagonism
between Good and Evil into a lower sphere. The Satan
of Latin Christianity was no Eastern, almost coeval,
coequal Power with Christ; he was the fallen Archangel, one it might be of the highest, in that thrice-
triple Hierarchy of Angelic Beings. His mortal enemy
is not God, but St. Michael. How completely this was
the popular belief may appear from one illustration, the
Chester Mystery of the Fall of Lucifer.[1] This drama,
performed by the guilds in a provincial city in England,
solves the insoluble problem of the origin of Evil
through the intense pride of Lucifer. God himself is
present on the scene; the nine Orders remonstrate

---

[1] Thus speaks Lucifer to the Celestial Hierarchy :

Devtres, I commaunde you for to cesse,
And see the bewtye that I beare,
All Heaven shines through my brightnes,
For God himself shines not so clear.—*Chester Mysteries*, p. 13.

against the overweening haughtiness of Lucifer, who, with his Devils, is cast down into the dark dungeon prepared for them.

But in general the sublimity even of this view of the Antagonist Power of Evil mingles not with the popular conception. It remained for later Poetry: it was, indeed, reserved for Milton to raise his image of Satan to appalling grandeur; and Milton, true to tradition, to reverential feeling, to the solemn serene grandeur of the Saviour in the Gospel, leaves the contest, the war with Satan, to the subordinate Angels and to Michael, the Prince of the Angels. The Son, as coequal in Godhead, sits aloof in his inviolate majesty.[*]

The Devil, the Devils of the dark ages, are in the vulgar notion something far below the Lucifer, the fallen Son of the Morning. They are   Devils.
merely hideous, hateful, repulsive—often, to show the power of the Saint, contemptible. The strife for the mastery of the world is not through terrible outbursts of power. The mighty destructive agencies which war on mankind are the visitations of God, not the spontaneous, inevitable, or even permitted devastations of Satan. It ·
is not through the loftier passions of man, it is mostly

---

* Remark Milton's wonderful sublimity, not merely in his central figure of him, who had not "lost all his original brightness," who was "not less than archangel ruined," but in his creation, it may also be said, out of Selden's book, and the few allusions in the Old Testament, of a new Demonology. He throws aside the old Patristic Hierarchy of Devils, the gods of Greece and Rome, whom the revival of classical literature had now reinstated in their majesty and beauty, as seen in the Poets. He raises up in their stead the biblical adversaries of the Godhead of the Old Testament; the Deities of the nations, Canaan and Syria, circumjacent and hostile to the Jews. Before Milton, if Moloch, Belial, Mammon, were not absolutely unknown to poetry, they had no proper and distinct poetic existence. I owe the germ of this observation, perhaps more than the germ, to my friend Mr. Macaulay.

by petty tricks and small annoyances, that the Evil One
endeavours to mislead or molest the Saint. Even when
he offers temptations on a larger scale, there is in
general something cowardly or despicable; his very
tricks are often out-tricked. The form which he assumed, the attributes of the form, the horns, the tail,
the cloven foot, are vulgar and ludicrous. The stench
which betrays his presence, his howlings and screech-
ings are but coarse and grovelling. At first, indeed, he
was hardly permitted to assume the human form:[*] his
was a monstrous combination of all that was most ugly
and hateful in the animal shape. If Devils at times
assumed beautiful forms, as of wanton women to tempt
the Saints, or entered into and possessed women of
attractive loveliness, it was only for a time; they withdrew and shrunk back to their own proper and native
hideousness.

Even Dante's Devils have but a low and menial
malignity; they are base and cruel executioners, torturers, with a fierce but dastardly delight in the pains
they inflict. The awful and the terrible is in the human
victims: their passions, their pride, ambition, cruelty,
avarice, treachery, revenge, alone have anything of
the majesty of guilt: it is the diabolic in man, not the
Devils acting upon men and through men, which makes
the moral grandeur of his Inferno.

The symbol under which the Devil, Satan as Lucifer,
as well as his subordinate fiends, are represented

---

[*] " Alors qu'aux yeux du vulgaire
celui-ci fut devenu un être hideux,
incohérent assemblage des formes les
plus animales, et les plus effrayantes;
un personnage grotesque à force d'être
laid." — Maury, Légendes Pieuses,

p. 193.

M. Maury says that the most
ancient representation of the Devil in
human form is in an ivory diptych of
the time of Charles the Bald, p. 136,
note. See also text.

throughout this period, the Serpent, was sometimes terrific, often sunk to the low and the ludicrous. This universal emblem of the Antagonist Power of evil runs through all religions[7] (though here and there the Serpent is the type of the Beneficent Deity, or, coiled into a circular ring, of eternity).[8] The whole was centered in the fearful image of the great Dragon in the Apocalypse. St. Michael slaying the Dragon is among the earliest emblems of the triumph of Good over Evil. From an emblem it became a religious historical fact. And hence, doubtless, to a great extent, the Dragon of Romance; St. George is but another St. Michael of human descent. The enmity of the serpent to the race of man, as expressed and seemingly countenanced by the Book of Genesis, adds wiliness to the simply terrible and destructive monster. Almost every legend teems with serpent demons. Serpents are the most dire torturers in hell. The worm that never dieth (Dante's great Worm) is not alone; snakes with diabolic instincts, or snakes actually devils, and rioting in the luxury of preying on the vital and sensitive parts of the undying damned, are everywhere the dreadful instruments of everlasting retribution.

Closely connected with these demoniac influences was the belief in magic, witchcraft, spells, talismans, conjurations. These were all the actual delusions or operations of obedient or assistant Evil Spirits. The Legislature of the Church and of the State, from Con-

---

[7] The connexion of the Dragon, Serpent, and Worm with the Devil in its countless forms is traced with inexhaustible learning by M. Maury, in his Légendes Pieuses, pp. 131, 154. So too the growth of each demoniac beast out of other notions, the lion, the wolf, the swine. It would be impossible to enter in such a work as this into the endless detail.

[8] The ample references of M. Maury on this subject might be enlarged. See too the work of Mr. Deane on the Worship of the Serpent.

stantine down to a late period, the post-Papal period of
Christianity ; Roman, Barbarian, even modern Codes
recognised as real facts all these wild hallucinations of
our nature, and by arraying them in the dignity of
heretical, impious, and capital offences, impressed more
deeply and perpetuated the vulgar belief. They have
now almost, but by no means altogether, vanished
before the light of reason and of science. The most
obstinate fanaticism only ventures to murmur, that in
things so universally believed, condemned by Popes and
Councils, and confirmed by the terrible testimony of
the excommunication and the execution of thousands of
miserable human beings, there must have been something more than our incredulous age will acknowledge.[*]
Wisdom and humanity may look with patience, with
indulgence, with sympathy, on many points of Christian
superstition, as bringing home to hearts which would
otherwise have been untouched, unsoftened, unconsoled,
the blessed influences and peace of religion ; but on
this sad chapter, extending far beyond the dark ages,
it will look with melancholy, indeed, but unmitigated
reprobation. The whole tendency was to degrade and
brutalise human nature : to degrade by encouraging
the belief in such monstrous follies ; to brutalise by the
pomp of public executions, conducted with the solemnity
of civil and religious state.

All this external world-environing world of Beings
possessed the three great attributes, ubiquity, incessant
activity with motion in unappreciable time, personality.
God was not more omnipresent, more all-knowing, more
cognisant of the inmost secrets of the human heart than

---

* See Görres, Christliche Mystik, that strange erudite rhapsody, which,
with all its fervour, fails to convince us that the author was in earnest.

were these angelic or demon hosts. These divine attributes might be delegated, derivative, permitted for
special purposes ; but human fear and hope lost sight
of this distinction, and invested every one of the countless preternatural agents in independent, self-existent,
self-willed life. They had, too, the power of assuming
any forms; of endless and instantaneous transmutation.

But the angels were not the only guardians and protectors of the faithful against the swarming, busy, indefatigable malignant spirits, which claimed the world of
man as their own. It might seem as if human weakness required something less impalpable, more sensibly
real, more akin to itself, than beings of light and air,
which encircled the throne of God. Those
Beings, in their essence immaterial, or of a   The Saints.
finer and more ethereal matter, might stoop to earth,
or might be constantly hovering between earth and
heaven; but besides them, as it were of more distinct
cognisance by man, were those who, having worn the
human form, retained it, or reassumed it, as it were
clothing over their spiritualised being. The Saints,
having been human, were more easily, more naturally
conceived as still endowed with human sympathies ;
intermediate between God and man, but with an imperishable ineffaceable manhood more closely bound up
with man. The doctrine of the Church, the Communion
of Saints, implied the Church militant and the Church
triumphant. The Christians yet on earth, the Christians
already in heaven, formed but one polity ; and if there
was this kindred, if it may be so said, religious consanguinity, it might seem disparagement to their glory
and to their union with Christ to banish the Saints to a
cold unconscious indifference, and abase them to ignorance of the concerns of their brethren still in the flesh.

Each Saint partook, therefore, of the instinctive omniscience of Christ. While unabsorbed in the general
beatified community, he kept up his special interest and
attachment to the places, the companions, the fraterni-
ties of his earthly sojourn; he exercised, according to
his will, at least by intercession, a beneficent influence;
he was tutelar within his sphere, and therefore within
that sphere an object of devout adoration. And so, as
ages went on, saints were multiplied and deified. I am
almost unwilling to write it; yet assuredly, hardly less,
if less than Divine power and Divine will was assigned
by the popular sentiment to the Virgin and the Saints.
They intercepted the worship of the Almighty Father,
the worship of the Divine Son. To them, rather than
through them, prayer was addressed; their shrines
received the more costly oblations; they were the
rulers, the actual disposing Providence on earth: God
might seem to have abandoned the Sovereignty of the
world to those subordinate yet all-powerful agencies.

High above all this innumerable Host of Saints and
Martyrs, if not within the Trinity (it were not easy, if
we make not large allowance for the wild language of
rapturous adoration, to draw any distinction), hardly
below, was seated the Queen of Heaven.[b] The worship
of the Virgin, since the epoch of Gregory the Great,
had been constantly on the ascendant; the whole progress of Christian thought and feeling converged towards this end.[c] The passionate adoration of the Virgin

---

[b] "At qualis currus, cujus aurigæ sunt im-
mortales Spiritus!
Qualis Illa quæ accredit, et cui Deus fit
obvius!
Hæc est Regina naturæ, et pæne gratiæ.
Toll prompt excipiendam eat quæ Deum
exceperat.
Adsurge, anima, die aliquid sublimius.
Ante adventum Mariæ regnabant in cælo
tres persona.

Nec regnabant tres Reges,
Alterum thronum adddidit homo Deus;
Adveniante Maria tertius thronus est
additus.
Et nunc triplex in cælo regnum est, ubi
erat unicum.
Sedet proxima Deo mater Dei."
Lable in Elogiis.—Comp. August. v. iii. p. 55.

[c] Compare on the earlier period

was among the causes of the discomfiture of Nestorianism—the discomfiture of Nestorianism deepened the
passion. The title "Mother of God" had been the
watchword of the feud; it became the cry of victory.
Perhaps as the Teutonic awe tended to throw back into
more remote incomprehensibility the spiritual Godhead,
and therefore the more distinct human image became
more welcome to the soul; so perhaps the purer and
loftier Teutonic respect for the female sex was more
prone to the adoration of the Virgin Mother. Iconoclasm, as the images of the Virgin Mother, then perhaps
usually with the Child, were more frequent and regarded
with stronger attachment, would seem a war specially
directed against the blessed Mary; her images, when
they rose again, or, as was common, smiled again on the
walls, would be the objects of still more devout wonder
and love. She would vindicate her exalted dignity by
more countless miracles, and miracles would be multiplied at once by the frantic zeal and by the more easy
credulity of her triumphant worshippers; she would
glorify herself, and be glorified without measure. It
was the same in the East and in the West. The East
had early adopted in the popular creed the groundwork,
at least, of the Gospel of the Infancy and of the other
spurious Gospels, which added so prodigally to the
brief allusions to the Mother in the genuine Gospels.[4]
The Emperor Heraclius, it has been seen, had the Virgin
on his banner of war; to the tutelar protection of the
Virgin Constantinople looked against the Saracen and

Beugnot, Destruction du Paganisme,
ii. 267. The whole subject of the
progress of the worship of the Virgin,
in Augusti, Denkwürdigkeiten, iii.
pp. 1 et seqq., with ample illustrations.

[4] Perhaps the reception of these
into the Koran as part of the universal
Christian belief is the most striking
proof of this.

the Turk. Chivalry above all would seem, as it were,
to array the Christian world as the Church militant of
the Virgin.[*] Every knight was the sworn servant of
our Lady; to her he looked for success in battle—
strange as it may sound, for success in softer enter-
prises.[f] Poetry took even more irreverent licence; its
adoration in its intensity became revoltingly profane.
Instead of hallowing human passion, it brought human
passion into the sphere of adoration, from which it
might have been expected to shrink with instinctive
modesty. Yet it must be known in its utmost phrensy
to be judged rightly.[g]

So completely was this worship the worship of Christendom, that every cathedral, almost every spacious
church, had its Chapel of our Lady. In the hymns to
the Virgin, in every breviary, more especially in her
own "Hours" (the great universal book of devotion) not
merely is the whole world and the celestial world put
under contribution for poetic images, not only is all the
luxuriance and copiousness of language exhausted, a
new vocabulary is invented to express the yet inex-
pressible homage; pages follow pages of glowing simili-
tudes, rising one above another. In the Psalter of the

---

* On the chivalrous worship of the
Virgin, Le Grand d'Aussy, Fabliaux,
v. 27.

f The poetry of the Troubadours
is full of this.

g "C'est ainsi que le même Gautier
(de Coron,) conçut pour la Vierge
Marie un amour véritable, qui l'en-
flamma, le dévora toute sa vie. Elle
était pour lui ce qu'est une amante
pour le plus passionné des hommes. Il
réunissait pour elle toutes les beautés
qu'il apercevait dans les religieuses

d'un couvent qu'il dirigeait; lui adres-
sait chaque jour des vers pleins
d'amour, d'érotiques chansons; il la
voyait dans ses rêves, et quelquefois
même quand il veillait, sous les formes
les plus voluptueuses, et la croyait
l'héroïne des mille aventures, que,
dans son délire, il inventait, et puis ra-
contait en vers innumérables."—Hist.
Littéraire de la France, xix. p. 843.

To purify son imagination from this,
let the reader turn to Petrarch's noble
ode " Vergine bella, che di sol vestita."

Virgin almost all the incommunicable attributes of the
Godhead are assigned to her; she sits between Cherubim
and Seraphim; she commands, by her maternal influences, if not by authority, her Eternal Son.[h] To the
Festivals of the Annunciation and the Purification (or
the Presentation of Christ in the Temple) was added
that of the Assumption of the Virgin.[i] A rich and
copious legend revealed the whole history of her birth
and life, of which the Sacred Scriptures were altogether
silent, but of which the spurious Gospels furnished
many incidents,[k] thus, as it were, taking their rank as
authorities with the Apostolic four. And all this was
ere long to be embodied in Poetry, and, it might seem,
more imperishably in Art. The latest question raised
about the Virgin—her absolute immunity from the sin
of Adam—is the best illustration of the strength and
vitality of the belief. Pious men could endure the
discussion. Though St. Bernard, in distinct words which
cannot be explained away, had repudiated the Immaculate Conception of the Virgin [m]—though it was rejected
by Thomas Aquinas,[n] that Conception without any taint
of hereditary sin, grew up under the authority of the
rival of Aquinas. It became the subject of contention
and controversy, from which the calmer Christian shrinks
with intuitive repugnance. It divided the Dominicans

---

[h] " Excelsus super Cherubim Thronus
ejus, et sedes ejus super cardines cœli."
— Ps. cxlii. " Domina Angelorum,
regina Mundi !"— Ps. xxxix. " Quod
Deus imperio, tu prece, Virgo, facis—
Jure matris impera filio !"

[i] Titian's Assumption of the Virgin
at Venice, to omit the Murillos, and
those of countless inferior artists.

[k] See three Gospels in Thilo, Codex
Apocryphus.

[m] " Mariam in peccato conceptam,
cum et ipsa vulgari modo per libidinem
maris et fœminæ concepta est." One is
almost unwilling to quote in Latin
what St. Bernard wrote. Ad canon.
Lugdun. It is true St. Bernard made
a vague submission on this, as on
other points, to the judgement of the
Church.

[n] Summa Theologiæ, iii. 27, and in
course terms.

and Franciscans into hostile camps, and was agitated
with all the wrath and fury of a question in which was
involved the whole moral and religious welfare of mankind.° None doubted[p] that it was within the lawful
sphere of theology.[q] Wonderful as it may seem, a
doctrine rejected at the end of the twelfth century by
the last Father of the Latin Church, has been asserted
by a Pope of the nineteenth, and a Council is now
sitting in grave debate in Rome on the Immaculate
Conception.[r]

The worship of the Saints might seem to be endan
gered by their multiplicity, by their infinity. The
crowded calendar knew not what day it could assign to
the new Saint without clashing with, or dispossessing,
an old one; it was forced to bear an endless accumulation on some favoured days. The East and the West
vied with each other in their fertility. The Greek
Menologies are not only as copious, in the puerility

° When the stranger travelling in
Spain arrived at midnight at a convent-
gate, and uttered his "Santissima
Virgen," he knew by the answer,
either "Sin pecado concebida," or by
the silence with which the door opened,
whether it was a Franciscan or a
Dominican.

[p] Singular it may seem, the doctrine
was first authorised by the reforming
(heterodox?) Council of Basle, A.D.
1439. Session xxv. vi.

[q] Even such a writer as Augustin
Theiner was, can write such pages as
appear in the Vie de Clément XIV.,
t. p. 341.

[r] Is there not wisdom enough in the
Church, which has never been thought
wanting in wisdom, to consider whether
it is wise to inflame a passionate

paroxysm of devotion in a very few;
and to throw back, by an inevitable
revulsion, and by so fatal an argument
placed in their hands, multitudes into
utter unbelief and contempt of all
religion?—So had I written in 1854:
the Council has passed its decree; by
all who own its authority the Immaculate Conception is admitted, or, what
is very different, not denied to be an
Article of the Christian creed. But
is not the utter and total apathy with
which it has been received (one day's
Spectacle at Rome, and nearly silent
indifference throughout Christendom)
the most remarkable sign of the times
—the most unanswerable proof of the
prostration of the strength of the
Roman Church? There is not life
enough for a schism on this vital point.

and trivialness of their wonders they even surpass the
Western Hagiologies. But of the countless Saints of
the East, few comparatively were received in the West.
The East as disdainfully rejected many of the most
famous, whom the West worshipped with the most
earnest devotion; they were ignorant even of their
names. It may be doubted if an Oriental ever uttered
a prayer in the name of St. Thomas of Canterbury.
Still that multiplicity of Saints, as it bore unanswerable
witness to the vigour of its belief, so also to its vitality.
It was constantly renewing its youth by the elevation
of more favourite and recent objects of adoration.
Every faculty, every feeling, every passion, every affection, every interest was for centuries in a state of perpetual excitement to quicken, keep alive, and make
more intense this wonder-fed and wonder-seeking worship. The imagination, the generous admiration of
transcendent goodness, of transcendent learning, or,
what was esteemed even more Christian, transcendent
austerity; rivalry of Church with Church, of town with
town, of kingdom with kingdom, of Order with Order;
sordid interest in the Priesthood who possessed, and the
people who were permitted to worship, and shared in
the fame, even in the profit, from the concourse of worshippers to the shrine of a celebrated Saint; gratitude
for blessings imputed to his prayers, the fruitful harvest,
protection in war, escape in pestilence; fear lest the
offended Saint should turn away his face; the strange
notion that Saints were under an obligation to befriend
their worshippers; the still bolder Brahminical notion
that Saints might be compelled by the force of prayer,
or even by the lavish oblation, to interpose their reluctant influence;—against all this stood one faculty of
man alone, and that with difficulty roused out of its

long lethargy, rebuked, cowed, proscribed, shuddering
at what might be, which was sure to be, branded as
impiety—the Reason.   Already in the earliest period to
doubt the wild wonders related of St. Martin of Tours
is to doubt the miracles of the Gospel.[*] Popular admiration for some time enjoyed, unchecked, the privilege of canonisation.   A Saint was a Saint, as
it were, by acclamation ; and this acclamation
might have been uttered in the rudest times, as during
the Merovingian rule in France ; or within a very
limited sphere, as among our Anglo-Saxon ancestors, so
many of whose Saints were contemptuously rejected by
the Norman Conqueror.   Saints at length multiplying
thus beyond measure, the Pope assumed the prerogative
of advancing to the successive ranks of Beatitude and
Sanctity.   If this checked the deification of such per-
plexing multitudes, it gave still higher authority to those
who had been recognised by more general consent, or
who were thus more sparingly admitted to the honours
of Beatification and Sanctification (those steps, as it
were, of spiritual promotion were gradually introduced).
The Saints ceased to be local divinities; they were
proclaimed to Christendom, in the irrefragable Bull, as
worthy of general worship.[+]

    There were some, of course, the universal Saints of

---

[*] " Quanquam minimè mirum sit si
in operibus Martini infirmitas humana
dubitaverit, cum multos hodieque vide-
amus, nec Evangelicis quidem credi-
disse."—Sulp. Sever., Dial. ii. 15.
Sulpicius almost closes the life of
St. Martin with these words : " De
cetero si quis infideliter legerit, ipse
peccabit."

[+] Canonisation has been distributed
into three periods.   Down to the tenth
century the Saint was exalted by the
popular voice, the suffrage of the people
with the Bishops.   In the intermediate
period the sanction of the Pope was
required, but the Bishops retained
their right of initiation.   Alexander III.
seized into the hands of the Pope alone
this great and abused Prerogative.—
Mabillon, Act. S. Benedict. V. in Praef.

Christendom, the Apostles, the early martyrs; some of
Latin Christendom, the four great Fathers of the Latin
Church; some few, like St. Thomas of Canterbury, the
martyr of the ecclesiastical Order, would be held up
by the whole Hierarchy as the pattern and model of
sanctity; St. Benedict, in all the Benedictine monasteries, the founders or reformers of the Monastic Institutes, St. Odo, St. Stephen Harding, St. Bernard, St.
Romuald, St. Norbert. At a later period, and, above all,
wherever there were Mendicant Friars (and where were
there not?), St. Dominic and St. Francis would have
their images raised, their legends read and promulgated
with the utmost activity, and their shrines heaped with
offerings. Each Order was bound especially to hold up
the Saints of the Order; it was the duty of all who
wore the garb to spread their fame with special assi-
duity.* The Dominicans and Franciscans could boast
others besides their founders: the Dominicans the
murdered Inquisitor Peter the Martyr, and St. Thomas
Aquinas; the Franciscans St. Antony of Padua, and
San Bonaventura. Their portraits, their miracles, were
painted in the churches, in the cloisters of the Friars;

---

* The great authority for the Lives
of the Saints, of course with strong
predilection for the Saints of the West,
is the vast Collection of the Bollandists, even in the present day pro-
ceeding towards its termination. On
the origin and the writers of. this
Collection, consult Pitra, Etudes sur la
Collection des Actes des Saints par les
Jésuites Bollandistes. To me the
whole beauty and value is in the
original contemporary form (as some,
for instance, are read in Pertz, Monumenta Germaniæ). In the Bollandists,
or even in the Golden Legend of
Jacob a Voragine, they become cold
and controversial; the original documents are overlaid with dissertation.
Later writers, like Alban Butler, are
apologetic, cautious, always endeavouring to make the incredible credible.
In the recent Lives of the English
Saints, some of them admirably told,
there is a sort of chilly psychological
justification of belief utterly irreconcileable with belief; the writers urge
that we ought to believe, what they
themselves almost confess that they
can only believe, or fancy they believe,
out of duty, not of faith.

hymns in their name, or sentences, were chanted in
the services. All these were world-wide Saints: their
shrines arose in all lands, their churches or chapels
sprung up in all quarters. Others had a more limited
fame, though within the pale of that fame their worship
was performed with loyal fidelity; their legend read,
their acts and miracles commemorated by architecture,
sculpture, painting. As under the later Jewish belief
each Empire had its guardian Angel, so each kingdom
of Christendom had its tutelar Saint. France had three,
who had each his sacred city, each, as it were, succeeded to, without dispossessing, the other. St. Martin
of Tours was the older ; St. Remi, who baptised Clovis
into the Catholic Church, had an especial claim on all
of Frankish descent. But, as Paris rose above Tours
and Rheims, so rose St. Denys, by degrees, to be the
leading Saint of France. St. Louis was the Saint of the
royal race.[a] St. Jago of Compostella, the Apostle St.
James, had often led the conquering Spaniard against
the Mussulman. The more peaceful Boniface, with
others of the older missionaries, was honoured by a
better title in Germany. Some of the patron Saints,
however, of the great Western kingdoms are of a later
period, and sprung probably out of romance, perhaps
were first inscribed on the banners to distinguish the
several nations during the Crusades. For the dignity
of most of these Saints there is sufficient legendary
reason : as of St. Denys in France, St. James in Spain,
St. Andrew in Scotland (there was a legend of the

---

[a] Charlemagne was a Saint (Baro-
nius, sub ann. 814). He was unfortunately canonised by a Pseudo-Pope
(Paschal). He was worshipped at Aix-
la-Chapelle, Hildesheim, Osnaburg,
Minden, Halberstadt—thus a German
rather than a French Saint. See the
Hymn to him, Daniel, i. p. 305, from
the Halberstadt Breviary.

Apostle's conversion of Scotland), St. Patrick in Ireland.
England, however, instead of one of the old Roman or
Saxon Saints, St. Alban, or St. Augustine, placed herself
under the tutelar guardianship of a Saint of very doubtful origin, St. George.[r] In Germany alone, notwithstanding some general reverence for St. Boniface, each
kingdom or principality, even every city, town, or
village had its own Saint. The history of Latin Christianity may be traced in its more favoured Saints, first
Martyrs, then Bishops, then Fathers, Jerome, Augustine,
Gregory, then Monks (the type St. Benedict). As the
Church grew in wealth, Kings or Nobles, magnificent
donors, were the Saints; as it grew in power, rose
Hierarchical Saints, like Becket. St. Louis was the Saint
of the Crusades and Chivalry; St. Thomas Aquinas
and Bonaventura of Scholasticism. Female prophets
might seem chosen to vie with those of the Fraticelli
and of the Heretics; St. Catherine of Sienna, St. Bridget,[s]
those Brides of Christ, who had constant personal intercourse with the Saints, with the Virgin, with our
Lord himself. In later days Christian charity, as well
as Mysticism, had its Saints, St. Vincent de Paul, with
St. Teresa, and St. Francis de Sales.

---

[r] Dr. Milner (the Roman Catholic)
wrote an Essay against Gibbon's assertion that "the infamous George of
Cappadocia became the patron Saint of
England." He was, I think, so far
successful; but it is much more easy
to say who St. George was not than
who he was.

[s] St. Bridget was beatified by Boniface IX., canonized by John XXIII. at
the Council of Constance, confirmed
by St. Martin. The Swedes were
earnest for their Saint (and she had
had the merit of urging the return of

the Popes from Avignon). But Gerson
threw some rationalising doubts on the
visions of St. Bridget, and on the
whole bevy of female saints, which he
more than obviously hinted might be
the dupes or accomplices of artful
Confessors. The strange wild rhap-
sodies, the visions of St. Bridget, under
the authority of Turrecremata, were
avouched by the Council of Basle.
See Gerson's Tracts, especially de pro-
batione spirituum, de distinctione
verarum visionum a falsia.—Helyot,
iv. p. 25. Shroek, xxxiii. p. 189, &c.

To assert, to propagate the fame, the miracles, of his proper Saint was the duty of every King, of every burgher, of every parishioner, more especially of the Priesthood in the Church dedicated to his memory, which usually boasted of his body buried under the high altar, or of reliques of that body. Most churches had a commemorative Anniversary of the Saint, on which his wonders were the subjects of inexhaustible sermons. It was the great day of pomp, procession, rejoicing, feasting, sometimes rendered more attractive by some new miracle, by some marvellous cure, some devil ejected, something which vied with or outdid the wonders of every neighbouring Saint. Of old, the Saint-worshippers were more ambitious. In the days of St. Martin, Sulpicius Severus urges on his friend Posthumianus to publish everywhere, in his distant travel or on his return from the East, the fame of St. Martin.[*] " Pass not Campania ; make him known to the holy Paulinus, through him it will be published in Rome, in Italy, and in Illyricum. If you travel to the right, let it be heard in Carthage, where he may rival Cyprian ; if to the left, in Corinth, who will esteem him wiser than Plato, more patient than Socrates. Let Egypt, let Asia hear the fame of the Gaulish Saint." That, however, was when Saints were rare. More restricted commerce, and the pre-occupation of every land, every city, every church with its own patron Saint, confined within the province, city, or hamlet, all who had not some universal claim to respect, or some wide-spread fraternity to promulgate their name. Yet though there might be jealousy or rivalry in the worship of distant or . neighbouring Saints ; as the heathens denied not the

---

[*] " Dum recurris diversasque regiones, loca, portus, insulas, urbesque præter legis, Martini nomen et gloriam sparge per populos."—V. S. Martini, Dialog. iii. p. 583.

gods of other nations, even hostile nations, whom themselves did not worship as gods; so none would question
the saintship, the intercessory powers, the marvels of
another Saint.

Thus throughout Christendom was there to every
community and every individual man an Intercessor with the one Great Intercessor between   Legends.
God and man, some intermediate being, less awful, more
humble, whose office, whose charge, almost whose duty
it was to speed, or who, if offended, might withhold the
suppliant orison. Every one of these Saints had his life
of wonder, the legend of his virtues, his miracles, perhaps
his martyrdom, his shrines, his reliques. The legend
was to his votaries a sort of secondary Gospel, wrought
into the belief by the constant iteration of its names and
events. The legend, in truth, was the dominant, universal poetry of the times. Unless it had been poetry
it had not ruled the mind of man; but, having been
poetry, it must submit to remain poetry. It is the
mythic literature of Christendom,[b] interminable in its
extent; but, as its whole life is in its particularity, it
suffers and withers into dulness by being brought into a

---

[b] M. Maury's work, "Les Légendes
Pieuses," has exhausted the subject.
The more cautious readers must be
warned that M. Maury carries up his
system, where few Christians will
follow him, with hardly less audacity
than Strauss himself, into the Scriptural narratives. But while we admit
that the desire of conformity with the
Life of the Saviour suggested a great
part of the incidents, and that the
Gospel miracles suggested the miracles
of the later Saints—the originality,
the truth, the unapproachable dignity

of the Gospel type is not only unim-
paired, but to me becomes only more
distinct and real. There is an intimate
harmony, nowhere else found, between
the moral and the supernatural. The
line appears in my judgement broad and
clear; and those who, like the modern
advocates for the belief of the middle
ages, resolve the whole into the attainment of a proper frame of mind to
receive legend as truth, seem to me to
cut up altogether all belief in miracle.
Compare some good observations of
M. Ampère, Leçon XIV.

more compendious form; and so it is that Hagiography
has withdrawn into its proper domain, and left the
province of human affairs to history, which is not dis-
dainful, of course, of the incidental information or illustration of events, manners, characters, which transpire
through the cloud of marvels. Even the philosophy of
history endeavours only to divine how men believed, or
believed that they believed, this perpetual suspension or
abrogation of the laws of nature; how that which was
then averred on the authority of experience has now
fallen into neglect as contrary to all experience : so that
even the most vigorous attempt to reinstate them is
received as a desperate, hardly serious, effort of para-
doxical ingenuity, falls dead on the general mind, hardly
provokes scorn or ridicule, and, in fact, is transcended
in interest by every transitory folly or new hallucination
which seems to be the indispensable aliment required
by some part of mankind in the highest as in the lowest
social or intellectual state.

The legend was perpetually confirmed, illustrated,
kept alive by the substantial, if somewhat dimly and
mysteriously shown, reliques which were either
in the church, under the altar, or upon the
altar; the treasure of the community, or tho property,
the talisman of the prelate, the noble, or the king. The
reliquary was the most precious ornament in the lady's
chamber, in the knight's armoury, in the king's hall of
state, as well as in that of the Bishop or the Pope. Our
history has perhaps dwelt on reliques with sufficient
frequency. Augustine, in the earlier times, had reproved
the wandering monks who made a trade of selling
martyrs' limbs, "if indeed they are the limbs of martyrs."[c]

Reliques.

---

[c] De oper. Monachorum, c. 8.

The Theodosian Code had prohibited the violation
of the tombs of the martyrs, and the removal and
sale of their bodies.[d]   Gregory the Great had reproved the Greek practice of irreverently disinterring
and sending about the bodies of Saints: he refused to
the Empress of Constantinople reliques of St. Paul.[e]
We have seen with what jealous parsimony he distributed
the filings of the chains of St. Peter.[f]   But, as the world
darkened, these laws fell into desuetude: the first reverential feeling died away.   In truth, to the multiplication, dissemination, veneration of reliques conspired all
the weaknesses, passions, innate and seemingly unex-
tinguishable propensities, of mankind; the fondness for
cherishing memorials of the beloved, in human affection
so excusable, so amiable, how much more so of objects
of holy love, the Saints, the Blessed Virgin, the Saviour
himself! the pride of possessing what is rare; the desire
to keep alive religious associations and religious thoughts;
the ignorance of the priesthood, the pious fraud of the
priesthood, admitted to be Christian virtue in order to
promote devotion and so the spiritual welfare of man.
Add to all this the inherent indefeasible power ascribed
to reliques to work miracles.   No wonder that, with the
whole Christian world deeming it meritorious and holy
to believe, dangerous, impious to doubt, there should be
no end or limit to belief; that the wood of the true Cross
should grow into a forest; that wild fictions, the romance
of the Wise Men of the East transmuted into kings, the
Eleven Thousand Virgins, should be worshipped in the
rich commercial cities on the Rhine; that delicacy and
even reverence should not take offence, as at the milk

[d] "Humanum corpus nemo ad alterum locum transferat, nemo mar-
tyrem detrahat, nemo m-rostur."

[e] Ad Imperat. Constant.—Compare
Act. Ordinis S. Benedicti II. Præf. xxx.
[f] Vol. ii. p. 153.

of the Blessed Virgin ; that the most perishable things
should become imperishable, the garments of the Saviour
and the Saints. Not even the fiercest feuds could detect
imposture. Tours and Poitiers quarrelled for the body
of St. Martin ; St. Benedict was stolen away from Italy :
we have seen the rejoicing at his arrival in France ; and
the expedition sent by Eginhard to Italy in search of
pious plunder. There were constant wars between monastery and monastery ; marauding campaigns were
carried on against some neighbouring treasure-house.
France was smitten with famine, because Clotaire II.
cut off and stole an arm of St. Denys, under the instigation of the Devil.[g] It was virtue in St. Ouen to steal
the head of St. Marculph. But as to disputing the
genuineness, unless of rival reliques, or questioning their
wonder-working power, it never entered into the profane
thought of man. How the Crusades immeasurably increased the wealth of Western Christendom in reliques,
how they opened an important branch of traffic, needs
no further illustration. To the very verge of our historic
period the worship of reliques is in its unshaken authority.
At the close of the fourteenth century the Duke of Berry
obtains a piece of the head of St. Hilary of Poitiers as a
most splendid present for the city of Poitiers from the
Abbey of St. Denys ;[h] he had already obtained the chin.

---

[g] Annales Dagobert. Herman Corner
gives the price of some reliques.
Egilmund, Archbishop of Canterbury,
bought for his Church (A.D. MXXI.) an
arm of St. Augustine, at Paris, for
100 talents of pure silver and one of
gold.

[h] " Particulam quandam capitis ejus
sancti, a parte posteriori versus aurem
dextram ad modum trianguli, in longi-

tudine et latitudine spacium trium digi-
torum."—Rel. de St. Denys. xiv. 16.
The mutilation seems not to have been
thought irreverent. See also the pious
theft of reliques at Rome, recorded by
the legend to the glory of St. Patrick.
Todd's St. Patrick, p. 481. The good
Hugh of Lincoln (see his Life recently
printed (1864) among the Rolls Publications) was a great worshipper of

The exhibition of the Holy Coat of Treves—a treasure possessed by more than one other Church, and more than one avouched by Papal authority—may show how deep-rooted in human nature is this strange form of religiousness. One of the most remarkable illustrations of relique-worship occurs after the close of our history, during the pontificate of Æneas Sylvius, Pius II. The head of St. Andrew (Amalfi boasted the immemorial possession of the body) had been worshipped for centuries at Patras. As the Turks advanced in the Morea, the fugitive Despot would not leave this precious treasure exposed to the profane insults of the unbelievers. He carried it with him in his flight. Kings vied for the purchase; vast sums were offered. The Pope urged upon the Despot that he could not permit such a relique to repose anywhere but at Rome. The head of St. Andrew should rest by that of his brother St. Peter; the Saint himself would resist any other arrangement. The Despot arrived at Ancona with his freight. It was respected by the stormy seas. A Cardinal of the most blameless life was chosen to receive and inspect the relique; by what signs he judged the head to be that of St. Andrew we know not. But Romagna was in too dangerous a state to allow it at once to be transported to Rome; the fierce Piccinino or the atheist Malatesta would not have scrupled to have seized it for their own use, worshipped it, or sold it at an exorbitant price. It was conveyed for security to the strong fortress of Narni. When Piccinino's forces were dispersed, and peace restored, it was brought in stately procession to Rome. It was intended that the most glorious heads of St. Peter

reliques, and not always above the temptation of purloining. See especially his biting off a chip of a bone of S. | Mary Magdalene at Fecamp, to the great indignation of the Monks, p. 317.

and St. Paul should go forth to meet that of their brother
Apostle. But the vast mass of gold which enshrined,
the cumbrous iron which protected, these reliques were
too heavy to be moved: so without them the Pope, the
Cardinals, the whole population of Rome thronged forth
to the meadows near the Milvian Bridge. The Pope
made an eloquent address to the head; a hymn was
sung, entreating the Saint's aid in the discomfiture of
the Turks. It rested that day on the altar of St. Maria
del Popolo, was then conveyed through the city, decorated with all splendour (the Jubilee under Nicolas V.
saw not Rome more crowded), to St. Peter's. Cardinal
Bessarion preached a sermon; the head was deposited
with those of his brother Apostles under the high altar.[1]

Throughout the middle ages the world after death
continued to reveal more and more fully its awful
secrets. Hell, Purgatory, Heaven became more distinct,
if it may be so said, more visible. Their site, their topo-
graphy, their torments, their trials, their enjoyments,
became more conceivable, almost more palpable to sense:
till Dante summed up the whole of this traditional lore,
or at least, with a Poet's intuitive sagacity, seized on all
which was most imposing, effective, real, and condensed
it in his three co-ordinate poems. That Hell

Hell.

had a local existence, that immaterial spirits
suffered bodily and material torments, none, or scarcely
one hardly speculative mind, presumed to doubt.[2] Hell .

---

[1] Commentarii Pii II.

[2] Scotus Erigena, perhaps alone,
dared to question the locality of Hell,
and the material tortures of the
damned. " Diversas suppliciorum for-
mas non localiter in quadam parte,
veluti toto hujus visibilis creaturæ, et
ut simpliciter dicam neque intra di-

remitatem totius naturæ a Deo conditæ
futuras esse credimus; et neque nunc
esse, et nunquam et nunquam." The
punishment in which Erigena believed
was terrible remorse of conscience, the
sense of impossible repentance or
pardon. At the final absorption of all
things (that genuine Indian absorption,

had admitted, according to legend, more than one visitant
from this upper world, who returned to relate his fearful
journey to wondering man: St. Fiercy,[m] St. Vettin,[n] a
layman, Bernilo.[o] But all these early descents interest
us only as they may be supposed or appear to have been
faint types of the great Italian Poet. Dante is the one
authorised topographer of the mediæval Hell.[p] His
originality is no more called in question by these mere
signs and manifestations of the popular belief than by
the existence and reality of those objects or scenes in
external nature which he describes with such unrivalled
truth.[q] In Dante meet unreconciled (who thought of or
cared for their reconciliation?) those strange contradic-
tions, immaterial souls subject to material torments:
spirits which had put off the mortal body, cognisable by
the corporeal sense.[r] The mediæval Hell had gathered

derived from his master the Pseudo-
Dionysius), evil and sin would be
destroyed for ever, not evil ones and
sinners. Erigena boldly cites Origen,
and extorts from other authorities an
opinion to the same effect, of the final
salvation, the return unto the Deity, of
the Devil himself. There is nothing
eternal but God. "Omne quod æter-
num in Deo solummodo intelligi; nec
ulla æternitas extra eum qui solus est
æternus et æternitas." He thus gets
rid of all relating to eternal fire. Read
the remarkable passage in the 5th
book de Natura, from the xxvth. at
least to xxxviith. chapters.

[m] Bede, iii. 19. Mabillon, Acta S.
Benedicti, iii. 307. The Bollandists,
Jan. ii. p. 44.

[n] Mabillon, iv. 272.

[o] Flodoard, iii. 3.

[p] See Damiani's Hell and Heaven,

iv. Ep. xiv. viii. 2. Consult also
Cædmon.

[q] There is a strange book, written at
the beginning of the seventeenth century, "De Inferno," by Antonio Rusca
(Milan, 1621). It is dedicated with
fearful simplicity to our Saviour. It
settles gravely, logically, as it would
be supposed, authoritatively, and not
without erudition, every question relating to Hell and its Inhabitants, its
place, extent, divisions, torments.

[r] This was embarrassing to the
philosophic heathen. "Tantum valuit
error, ut corpora cremata cum acirent,
tamen ea fieri apud Inferos fingerent,
quæ sine corporibus nec fieri possunt
nec intelligi. Animos enim per seipsos
viventes non poterant mente complecti,
formam aliquam figuramque quære-
bant."—Cicer. Tusc. i. c. 16. Busæ
lays it down as the Catholic doctrine,

from all ages, all lands, all races, its imagery, its denizens, its site, its access, its commingling horrors; from the old Jewish traditions, perhaps from regions beyond the sphere of the Old Testament; from the Pagan poets, with their black rivers, their Cerberus, their boatman and his crazy vessel; perhaps from the Teutonic Hela, through some of the earlier visions. Then came the great Poet, and reduced all this wild chaos to a kind of order, moulded it up with the cosmical notions of the times, and made it, as it were, one with the prevalent mundane system. Above all, he brought it to the very borders of our world; he made the life beyond the grave one with our present life; he mingled in close and intimate relation the present and the future. Hell, Purgatory, Heaven, were but an immediate expansion and extension of the present world. And this is among the wonderful causes of Dante's power, the realising the unreal by the admixture of the real: even as in his imagery the actual, homely, everyday language or similitude mingles with and heightens the fantastic, the vague, the transmundane. What effect had Hell produced, if peopled by ancient, almost immemorial objects of human detestation, Nimrod or Iscariot, or Julian or Mohammed? It was when Popes all but living, Kings but now on their thrones, Guelfs who had hardly ceased to walk the streets of Florence, Ghibellines almost yet in exile, revealed their awful doom—this it was which, as it expressed the passions and the fears of mankind of an instant, immediate, actual, bodily, comprehensible place of torment:

"Docet tamen Catholica veritas, infernum malorum carcerem esse locum quendam materialem et corporeum." l. c. xxiii. The more enlightened Peter Lombard speaks of "non corporalem, sed corpori similem." Souls were borne bodily to Heaven by visible Angels, fought for by visible Devils. See the battle for the Soul of King Dagobert. Maury, p. 80.

so, wherever it was read, it deepened that notion, and
made it more distinct and natural. This was the Hell,
conterminous to the earth, but separate, as it were, by a
gulph passed by almost instantaneous transition, of which
the Priesthood held the keys. These keys the audacious
Poet had wrenched from their hands, and dared to turn
on many of themselves, speaking even against Popes the
sentence of condemnation. Of that which Hell, Purgatory, Heaven, were in popular opinion during the Middle
Ages, Dante was but the full, deep, concentered expression; what he embodied in verse all men believed, feared,
hoped.

Purgatory had now its intermediate place between
Heaven and Hell, as unquestioned, as undis-
turbed by doubt; its existence was as much   *Purgatory.*
an article of uncontested popular belief as Heaven or
Hell. It were as unjust and unphilosophical to attribute
all the legendary lore which realised Purgatory, to the
sordid invention of the Churchman or the Monk, as it
would be unhistorical to deny the use which was made
of this superstition to exact tribute from the fears or
the fondness of mankind. But the abuse grew out of
the belief; the belief was not slowly, subtly, deliberately
instilled into the mind for the sake of the abuse.
Purgatory, possible with St. Augustine,* probable with
Gregory the Great, grew up, I am persuaded (its
growth is singularly indistinct and untraceable), out of
the mercy and modesty of the Priesthood. To the
eternity of Hell torments there is and ever must be—
notwithstanding the peremptory decrees of dogmatic
theology and the reverential dread in so many religious
minds of tampering with what seems the language of

---

* De fide et oper., c. 16. On Gregory, see note, vol. II. p. 157.

the New Testament—a tacit repugnance. But when
the doom of every man rested on the lips of the Priest,
on his absolution or refusal of absolution, that Priest
might well tremble with some natural awe—awe not
confessed to himself—at dismissing the soul to an irrevocable, unrepealable, unchangeable destiny. He would
not be averse to pronounce a more mitigated, a re-
versible sentence. The keys of Heaven and of Hell
were a fearful trust, a terrible responsibility; the key
of Purgatory might be used with far less presumption,
with less trembling confidence. Then came naturally,
as it might seem, the strengthening and exaltation of
the efficacy of prayer, of the efficacy of the religious
ceremonials, of the efficacy of the sacrifice of the altar,
and the efficacy of the intercession of the Saints: and
these all within the province, within the power of the
Sacerdotal Order. Their authority, their influence,
their intervention, closed not with the grave. The
departed soul was still to a certain degree dependent
upon the Priest. They had yet a mission, it might be
of mercy; they had still some power of saving the soul
after it had departed from the body. Their faithful
love, their inexhaustible interest might yet rescue the
sinner; for he had not reached those gates—over which
alone was written, "There is no Hope"—the gates of
Hell. That which was a mercy, a consolation, became
a trade, an inexhaustible source of wealth. Praying-
souls out of Purgatory by Masses said on their behalf,

Masses.   became an ordinary office, an office which
deserved, which could demand, which did demand, the most prodigal remuneration. It was later

Indulgences.   that the Indulgence, originally the remission
of so much penance, of so many days, weeks,
months, years; or of that which was the commutation

for penance, so much almsgiving or munificence to
churches or Churchmen, in sound at least extended
(and mankind, the high and low vulgar of mankind, are
governed by sound) its significance: it was literally
understood, as the remission of so many years, sometimes centuries, of Purgatory.[1]

If there were living men to whom it had been vouchsafed to visit and to return and to reveal the secrets of
remote and terrible Hell, there were those too who
were admitted in vision, or in actual life to more accessible Purgatory, and brought back intelligence of its
real local existence, and of the state of souls within
its penitential circles. There is a legend of St. Paul
himself; of the French monk St. Farcy; of Drithelm,
related by Bede; of the Emperor Charles the Fat, by
William of Malmesbury. Matthew Paris relates two or
three journeys of the Monk of Evesham, of Thurkill, an
Essex peasant, very wild and fantastic. The Purgatory
of St. Patrick, the Purgatory of Owen Miles, the vision
of Alberic of Monte Casino, were among the most
popular and wide-spread legends of the ages preceding
Dante; and as in Hell, so in Purgatory, Dante sums up
in his noble verses the whole theory, the whole popular
belief as to this intermediate sphere.[a]

---

[1] " Unde quibusdam in locis concele-
bantur tandem expresse Indulgentiæ a
pœná et a culpd, licet quidam summi
Pontifices absurdum censuisse videntur
aliquas indulgentias a pœuâ et a culpâ
rese nominandas, cum a solo Deo culpa
deleatur; et indulgentia est remissio
pœnæ temporalis. . . . Unde quidam
concessiones hujusmodi magis descrip-
tiones quam indulgentiarum concessiones interpretantes cum eas intentu

lucri temporalis fieri judicabant, dicere
non timebant; anima nostra nauseat
super cibo levissimo."—Gobelinus Per-
sonn, p. 320. This was in Germany
during the Schism, above a century
before Luther.

[a] Vincent of Beauvais. See the
curious volume of Mr. Wright, St.
Patrick's Purgatory, on Tundale, p. 32.
&c. On Patrick's Purgatory in all
its forms, as sanctioned by Popes, and

If Hell and Purgatory thus dimly divulged their gloomy mysteries, if they had been visited by those who returned to actual life, Heaven was unapproached, unapproachable. To be rapt to the higher Heaven remained the privilege of the Apostle; the popular conception was content to rest in modest ignorance. Though the Saints might descend on beneficent missions to the world of man; of the site of their beatitude, of the state of the Blest, of the joys of the supernal world, they brought but vague and indefinite tidings. In truth, the notion of Heaven was inextricably mingled up with the astronomical and cosmogonical as well as with the theological notions of the age. Dante's Paradise blends the Ptolemaic system with the nine angelic circles of the Pseudo Dionysius; the material heavens in their nine circles; above and beyond them, in the invisible heavens, the nine Hierarchies; and yet higher than the highest heavens the dwelling of the Ineffable Trinity. The Beatific Vision, whether immediate or to await the Last Day, had been eluded rather than determined, till the rash and presumptuous theology of Pope John XXII. compelled a declaration from the Church. But yet this ascent to the Heaven of Heavens would seem from Dante, the best interpreter of the dominant conceptions, to have

---

by the Bollandist writers, as it appears in Calderon's poetry, and as it is kept up by Irish popular superstition and priestcraft, Mr. Wright has collected many wild details. Papal authority, as shown by an Inscription in the cloister of S. Andrea and S. Gregorio in Rome, testifies to the fact, which, I suspect, would have startled S. Gregory himself, that he got a monk out of Purgatory at the expense of thirty masses.

D. O. M.

Clemens Papa X.
Cultum Clementium VIII. et VIII.
imitatus . .
In hoc S. Gregorii Templum.
Ubi xxx missis animam monachi
Ea igne purgatorio liberavit, &c.

Copied by an accomplished friend of the author.

been an especial privilege, if it may be so said, of the
most Blessed of the Blessed, the Saint of Saints. There
is a manifest gradation in Beatitude and Sanctity.
According to the universal cosmical theory, the Earth,
the round and level earth, was the centre of the whole
system.* It was usually supposed to be encircled by
the vast, circumambient, endless ocean; but beyond
that ocean (with a dim reminiscence, it should seem, of
the Elysian Fields of the poets) was placed a Paradise,
where the souls of men hereafter to be blest, awaited
the final resurrection. Dante takes the other theory:

* The Eastern notions may be
gathered from the curious Treatise of
Cosmas Indicopleustes, printed by
Montfaucon, in his Collectio Nova.
Cosmas wrote about A.D. 535. He is
perhaps the earliest type of those who
call themselves Scriptural Philosophers;
with all the positiveness and contemp-
tuousness of ignorance, he proves that
the heavens are a vault, from Isaiah xi.
22; from Job, according to the LXX.,
and St. Paul's image of a Tabernacle.
The second Prologue is to refute the
notion that the earth is a sphere—the
antipodes, which at first were not so
disdainfully denied, are now termed
γραώδεις μῦθοι: men would fall in
opposite directions. Paradise is beyond
the circumfluent Ocean; souls are
received in Paradise till the last day
(p. 315). He afterwards asserts the
absolute incompatibility of the spherical
notion of the earth with the resurrection. He gives several opinions, all of
which, in his opinion, are equally wrong.
Οἱ μὲν ἐξ αὐτῶν τὰς ψυχὰς μόνας
μετὰ θάνατον, περιπολεύειν σὺν τῇ
σφαίρᾳ, καὶ ὁρᾶν ἤτοι γιγνώσκειν

πάντα λέγουσι· οἱ δὲ καὶ μετενσω-
μάτωσιν βούλωνται, καὶ προβιοτὴν
ἀσπάζουσι, οἷς καὶ ἕπεται λέγειν
ἐξ ἀπολουθίας καταλύεσθαι τὴν
σφαῖραν. The Heavens are indis-
soluble, and all spiritualised bodies are
to ascend to heaven. He gets rid of
the strong passages about the heavens
passing away, as metaphors (this in
others he treated as absurd or impious).
He denies the authenticity of the
Catholic Epistles.
It is remarkable that what I presume to call the Angelology of this
Treatise shows it to be earlier than the
Pseudo-Dionysius; that work cannot
have been known to Cosmas. One
office of the Angels is to move—they
are the perpetual movers of, the Sun,
Moon, and Stars. After the Last day,
the stars, sun, and moon being no more
wanted, the Angels will be released
from their duty, p. 154. The Angels
carry the rain up from heaven into the
clouds, and so manage the stars as to
cause Eclipses. These are guardian
Angels. The Angels do not ascend
above the stars, p. 315.

he peoples the nine material heavens—that is, the
cycle of the Moon, Venus, Mercury, the Sun, Mars,
Jupiter, Saturn, the fixed stars, and the firmament
above, or the Primum Mobile—with those who are
admitted to a progressively advancing state of glory
and blessedness. All this, it should seem, is below the
ascending circles of the Celestial Hierarchies, that immediate vestibule or fore-court of the Holy of Holies,
the Heaven of Heavens, into which the most perfect of
the Saints are admitted. They are commingled with,
yet unabsorbed by, the Redeemer, in mystic union;
yet the mysticism still reverently endeavours to maintain some distinction in regard to this Light, which, as
it has descended upon earth, is drawn up again to the
highest Heavens, and has a kind of communion with
the yet Incommunicable Deity. That in all the Paradise of Dante there should be a dazzling sameness, a
mystic indistinctness, an inseparable blending of the
real and the unreal, is not wonderful, if we consider the
nature of the subject, and the still more incoherent and
incongruous popular conceptions which he had to represent and to harmonise. It is more wonderful that, with
these few elements, Light, Music, and Mysticism, he
should, by his singular talent of embodying the purely
abstract and metaphysical thought in the liveliest
imagery, represent such things with the most objective
truth, yet without disturbing their fine spiritualism.
The subtlest scholasticism is not more subtle than
Dante. It is perhaps a bold assertion, but what is
there on these transcendent subjects, in the vast theology of Aquinas, of which the essence and sum is not in
the Paradise of Dante? Dante, perhaps, though expressing to a great extent the popular conception of

Heaven, is as much by his innate sublimity above it, as St. Thomas himself.[f]

---

[f] Read the Anglo-Saxon description of Paradise, from the De Phœnice, ascribed to Lactantius, in the Easter book by Thorpe, p. 197.

I am disposed to cite a description of Paradise according to its ordinary conception, almost the only possible conception—life without any of its evils —from a Poet older than Chaucer :—

There is lyf withoute ony deth,
And ther is youthe withoute ony elde,
And ther is alle maner welth to welde :
And ther is reste withoute ony travaille—
And ther is pees without ony strife,
And ther is alle manner lykynge of life—
And ther is bright somer ever to be :
And ther is nevere wynter in that contree :
And ther is more worshipe and honour,
Than ever hadde kynge other emperour.
And ther is greter melodee of aungelles songes,
And ther is preysing him amonge.
And ther is alle maner friendshipe that may be,
And ther is evere parfyt love and charitie ;
And ther is wisdom withoute folye :
And ther is honeste without vilenage.
All these a man may joyes of Hevene call,
As yitte the most sovereign joye of alle
Is the sight of Goddes bright face,
In whom remaineth alle manere grace.
Richard of Hampole, quoted from MSS. by Turner, Hist. of England, v. 233.

This poem, the 'Pricke of Conscience,' by Richard Rolle de Hampole, has been printed (1863) by the Philological Society.

CHAPTER III.

Latin Letters.

LATIN CHRISTIANITY might seem to prolong, to perpetuate, the reign of Latin letters over the
Latin letters. mind of man. Without Christianity, the language of Cicero, of Virgil, and of Tacitus, might have
expired with the empire of Julius, of Augustus, and of
Trajan. At the German invasion it must have broken
up into barbarous and shifting dialects, as the world
into barbarous and conflicting kingdoms. But as the
language of religion, it continued to be the language of
letters, for letters were almost entirely confined to
those who alone could write books or read books, religious men. Through the clergy, the secretaries as it
were of mankind, it was still the language of business,
of law, of public affairs, of international treaties and
private compacts, because it was the only common language, and because the ecclesiastics, the masters of that
language, were from this and from causes already traced,
the ministers of kings, the compilers of codes of law,
mostly the notaries of all more important transactions.
It only broke down gradually ; it never, though defaced
by barbarisms and foreign terms and forms of speech,
Maintained by changing grammar and by the introduction
by Christ-
ianity. of new words, fell into desuetude. Even just
before its abrogation, it revived in something approaching to purity, and resumed within its own, and that no
narrow sphere, its old established authority. The period

at which Latin ceased to be the spoken language, at
which the preacher addressed his flock, the magistrate
the commonalty, the demagogue the populace, was of
course different in different countries, especially in the
Romance and Teutonic divisions of mankind.   This
may hereafter be the subject of very difficult, obscure,
it must be feared, unsatisfactory inquiry.

But if Latin was the language of public affairs, it was
even more exclusively so that of letters.   Not only all
theologians, for a time all poets (at least those whose
poetry was written), still longer all historians, to the
end all philosophers, wrote in Latin.   Christian literature however arose, not only when Latin letters had
passed their meridian, but after their short day of glory
and strength had sunk into exhaustion.   The universal
empire of Rome had been fatal to her letters.   Few,
indeed, of her best early writers had been Roman by ·
birth; but they were Italians, and submitted to the
spell of Roman ascendancy.   Even under the Emperors,
Gaul and Spain began to furnish Latin poets and
writers: for a short time Rome subdued them to the
rules of her own grammar and the purer usages of her
speech.   But in the next century Latin letters, excepting only among the great jurisprudents, seem
almost to have given place to Greek.   They awoke
again profoundly corrupt; the barbarising Augustan
historians sink into the barbarous Ammianus Mar-
cellinus.   Africa becomes a prolific but dissonant school
of heathen and of Christian writers; from some of the
Panegyrists, who were Gallic rhetoricians, low enough
in style, the fall is rapid and extreme to Hilary of
Poitiers.   Yet even in this respect Latin owes its
vitality, and almost its Latinity, to Christian writers.
Augustine and Jerome, though their Latin is very dif-

H 2

ferent from that of Livy or of Cicero, have a kind
of dexterous management, a vigorous mastery, and
a copiousness of language, unrivalled in their days.
Sulpicius Severus surpasses in style any later historical
work; Salvian is better than the Panegyrists. The
Octavius of Minucius Felix has more of the older
grace and correctness than any treatise of the day.
Heathenism, or Indifferentism, strangely enough, kept
up the Pagan supremacy in poetry alone; Claudian,
and even the few lines of Merobaudes, stand higher in
purity, as in the life, of poetry, than all the Christian
hexametrists.

Latin letters, therefore, having become the absolute
exclusive property of the clergy, theology, of course,
took the first place, and almost absorbed into itself
every other branch of literature. Oratory was that of
the pulpit, philosophy was divinity in another form.
Even poetry taught theology, or, at its highest, celebrated the holy exploits of hermits or monks, of saints
and martyrs; and so it was through centuries, Theology
once having assumed, held its unshaken supremacy
over letters.

But at the time of Nicolas V. became manifest the
great revolution within Latin Christianity itself, which
was eventually to be fatal, at least to its universal
dominion. The great system of scholastic
theology, the last development of that exclusive Hierarchical science, which had swallowed up all
other sciences, of which philosophy was but a subject
province, and dialectics an humble instrument, found
itself, instead of the highest knowledge and the sole
consummate dictatorial learning of the world, no more
than the retired and self-exiled study of a still decreasing few, the professional occupation of a small

section of the reading and inquiring world. Its empire
had visibly passed away—its authority was shaken. In
its origin, in its objects, in its style, in its immeasurable
dimensions, in its scholasticism in short, this all-ruling
Theology had been monastic ; it had grown up in cloisters
and in schools. There, men of few wants, and
those wants supplied by rich endowments, in the dignity
which belonged to the acknowledged leading intellects
of the age, could devote to such avocations their whole
undisturbed, undivided lives—lives, at least, in which
nothing interfered with the quiet, monotonous, un-
distracting religious services. But Theology, before it
would give up its tenacious hold on letters, must
become secular ; it must emancipate itself from scholasticism, from monasticism.' It was not till after that
first revolution that the emancipation of letters from
theology was to come.

Our history, before it closes, must survey the immense, and, notwithstanding its infinite variety and
complexity of detail, the harmonious edifice of Latin
theology.* We must behold its strife, at times successful, always obstinate, with philosophy—its active
and skilful employment of the weapons of philosophy,
of dialectics, against their master—its constant effort to
be at once philosophy and theology ; the irruption of

---

* That survey must of necessity be
rapid, and, as rapid, imperfect; nor
can I boast any extensive or profound
acquaintance with these ponderous
tomes. The two best guides which I
have been able to find (both have read,
studied, profited by their laborious
predecessors) are Ritter, in the volumes
of his Christliche Philosophie, which
embrace this part of his history ; and
an excellent Treatise by M. Hauréau,

de la Philosophie Scolastique. Mémoire Couronné par l'Académie, 2
tomes, Paris, 1850.

In England we have no guide. Dr.
Hampden, who, from his article in the
Encyclopædia Metropolitana, on Thomas
Aquinas, promised to be the English
historian of this remarkable chapter in
the history of the human mind, has
sunk into a quiet Bishop.

Aristotelism and of the Arabic philosophy, of which the
Church did not at first apprehend all the perilous
results, and in her pride supposed that she might bind
them to her own service; the culmination of the whole
system in the five great schoolmen, Albert the Great,
Thomas Aquinas, Bonaventura, Duns Scotus, William
of Ockham. All this scholasticism was purely Latin—
no Teutonic element entered into the controversies of
the philosophising theologians. In England, in Germany, the schools and the monasteries were Latin; the
disputants spoke no other tongue. The theology which
aspired to be philosophy would not condescend to,
could not indeed as yet have found expression in, the
undeveloped vulgar languages.[b]

Our history has already touched on the remoter ancestors of the Scholastic theology, on the solitary Scotus
Erigena, who stands as a lonely beacon in his dark and
turbulent times, and left none, or but remote, followers.
The philosophy of Erigena was what the empire of
Charlemagne had been, a vast organisation, out of the
wreck of which rose later schools. He was by anticipation or tradition (from him Berengar, as has been
shown, drew his rationalising Eucharistic system), by
his genius, by his Greek or Oriental acquirements, by
his translation of the Pseudo-Dionysius, a Platonist, or
more than a Platonist; at length by his own fearless
fathoming onwards into unknown depths, a Pantheist.
We have dwelt on Anselm, in our judgement the real
parent of mediæval theology—of that theology, which
at the same time that it lets loose the reason, reins it in
with a strong hand; on the intellectual insurrection,

ᵇ " Die Philosophie des Mittelalters gehört nicht der Zeiten an wo das
Deutsche Element die Herrschaft hatte, sie ist vorherschend Romanische Natur."
—Ritter p. 37.

too, under Abélard, and its suppression.   Anselm's
lofty enterprise, the reconciliation of divinity and philosophy, had been premature; it had ended in failure.[e]
Abélard had been compelled to submit his rebellious
philosophy at the feet of authority.   His fate for a
time, to outward appearance at least, crushed the bold
truths which lay hid in his system.   Throughout the
subsequent period theology and philosophy are contesting occasionally the bounds of their separate domains—bounds which it was impossible to mark with
rigour and precision.   Metaphysics soared into the
realm of Theology; Theology when it came to Onto-
logy, to reason on the being of God, could not but be
metaphysical.   At the same time, or only a few years
later than Abélard, a writer, by some placed on a level,
or even raised to superiority, as a philosophical thinker
over Abélard, Gilbert de la Porée, through the abstruse-
ness, perhaps obscurity of his teaching, the dignity of
his position as Bishop, and his blameless character, was
enabled to tread this border ground, if not without censure, without persecution.

But below that transcendental region, in which the
mind treated of Being in the abstract, of the primary
elements of thought, of the very first conception of
God, Theology, in her proper sphere, would not endure
the presence of her dangerous rival.   Theology, rightly
so called, professed to be primarily grounded on the
Scriptures, but on the Scriptures interpreted, commented on, supplemented by a succession of writers
(the Fathers), by decrees of Councils, and what was
called the authority of the Church.   The ecclesiastical

e " L'entreprise de S. Anselme avait échoué; personne n'avait pu concilier la
philosophie et la théologie."—Haureau, i. p. 318.

law had now taken the abbreviated form of a code,
rather a manual, under Ivo of Chartres. So Theology
was to be cast into short authoritative sentences, which
might be at once the subject and the rule of controversy, the war-law of the schools. If Philosophy presumed to lay its profane hands on these subjects, it was
warned off as trespassing on the manor of the Church.
Logic might lend its humble ministrations to prove in
syllogistic form those canonised truths; if it proceeded
further, it became a perilous and proscribed weapon.

Peter the Lombard was, as it were, the Euclid of this
science. His sentences were to be the irrefragable
axioms and definitions from which were to be deduced
all the higher and more remote truths of divinity; on
them the great theological mathematicians built what
appeared their infallible demonstrations.

Peter the Lombard was born near Novara, the native
Peter the
Lombard. place of Lanfranc and of Anselm. He was
Bishop of Paris in 1159. His famous book
of the Sentences was intended to be, and became to a
great extent, the Manual of the Schools. Peter knew
not, or disdainfully threw aside, the philosophical cultivation of his day. He adhered rigidly to all which
passed for Scripture, and was the authorised interpretation of the Scripture, to all which had become the
creed in the traditions, and law in the decretals, of
the Church. He seems to have no apprehension
of doubt in his stern dogmatism; he will not recognise
any of the difficulties suggested by philosophy; he
cannot, or will not, perceive the weak points of his own
system. He has the great merit that, opposed as he
was to the prevailing Platonism, throughout the Sentences the ethical principle predominates; his excellence
is perspicuity, simplicity, definiteness of moral purpose.

His distinctions are endless, subtle, idle ; but he wrote
from conflicting authorities to reconcile writers at war
with each other, at war with themselves. Their quarrels had been wrought to intentional or unintentional
antagonism in the "Sic et Non" of Abélard. That
philosopher, whether Pyrrhonist or more than Pyrrhonist, had left them in all the confusion of strife ; he
had set Fathers against Fathers, each Father against
himself, the Church against the Church, tradition
against tradition, law against law. The Lombard announced himself and was accepted as the mediator, the
final arbiter in this endless litigation ; he would sternly
fix the positive, proscribe the negative or sceptical view,
in all these questions. The litigation might still go on,
but within the limits which he had rigidly established ;
he had determined those ultimate results against which
there was no appeal. The mode of proof might be
interminably contested in the schools ; the conclusion
was already irrefragably fixed. On the sacramental
system Peter the Lombard is loftily, severely hierarchical. Yet he is moderate on the power of the
keys : he holds only a declaratory power of binding
and loosing—of showing how the souls of men were to
be bound and loosed.[4]

From the hard and arid system of Peter the Lombard
the profound devotion of the Middle Ages took refuge
in Mysticism. But it is an error to suppose Mysticism
as the perpetual antagonist of Scholasticism ; the Mystics
were often severe Logicians ; some Scholastics had all

---

[4] " Non autem hoc sacerdotibus con-
cessit, quibus tamen tribuit potestatem
solvendi et ligandi, i.e. ostendendi
homines ligatos vel solutos." Quoted by
Ritter, p. 499. Ritter's account of
the Lombard appears to me, as compared with the Book of Sentences, so
just and sagacious, that I have adopted
implicitly his conclusions, to a certain
extent his words.

the passion of Mystics. Nor were the Scholastics always
Aristotelians and Nominalists, or the Mystics, Realists
and Platonists. The logic was often that of Aristotle,
the philosophy that of Plato. Hugo and Richard de
St. Victor (the Abbey of St. Victor at Paris) were the
great Mystics of this period. The mysticism of Hugo
de St. Victor withdrew the contemplator altogether •
from the outward to the inner world—from God in the
works of nature to God in his workings on the soul of
man. This contemplation of God, the consummate perfection of man, is immediate, not mediate. Through
the Angels and the Celestial Hierarchy of the Areopagite it aspires to one God, not in his Theophany, but
in his inmost essence. All ideas and forms of things
are latent in the human soul as in God, only they are
manifested to the soul by its own activity, its meditative
power. Yet St. Victor is not exempt from the grosser
phraseology of the Mystic—the tasting God, and other
degrading images from the senses of men. The ethical

Hugo de St. Victor. system of Hugo de St. Victor is that of the
Church, more free and lofty than the dry and
barren discipline of Peter Lombard:* it looks to the end
and object, not merely to the punctilious performance

Richard de St. Victor. of Church works. Richard de St. Victor was
at once more logical and more devout, raising
higher at once the unassisted power of man, yet with
even more supernatural interference—less ecclesiastical,
more religious.† Thus the silent, solemn Cloister was
as it were constantly balancing the noisy and pugnacious
School. The system of the St. Victors is the contem-

---

* "Contemplatio est illa vivacitas
intelligentiæ, quæ cuncta palam Patris
manifestâ visione comprehendit."—M.
In Eccles. 1. p. 55, quoted by Ritter,
p. 538.

† Ritter has drawn the distinction
between these two writers with great
skill and nicety.

plative philosophy of deep-thinking minds in their profound seclusion, not of intellectual gladiators : it is that
of men following out the train of their own thoughts,
not perpetually crossed by the objections of subtle rival
disputants. Its end is not victory, but the inward satisfaction of the soul. It is not so much conscious of ecclesiastical restraint, it is rather self-restrained by its inborn
reverence ; it has no doubt, therefore no fear ; it is bold
from the inward consciousness of its orthodoxy.

John of Salisbury, though he professed to be of the
school of the St. Victors, had something of the
practical English character. He was far less
of a Monk, more of an observant man of the world. The
Mystic was lost in the high Churchman. He was the
right hand and counsellor of Becket, though, like Becket,
he says hard things of the Pope and of Rome ; he was
the inflexible asserter of the rights of the Church. John
has the fullest faith in the theological articles of the
Church, with some academic scepticism on the philosophic questions. John was neither of the cloister nor
of the school : he has something of the statesman, even
something of the natural philosopher.

Scholastic philosophy has no great name during the
last quarter of the twelfth to the middle of the thirteenth
century. But during this barren and mute period came
gradually and silently stealing in, from an unobserved
unsuspected quarter, new views of knowledge, new
metaphysical modes of thought, which went up into the
primal principles of theology ; dialectic processes, if not
new, more perfect. Greek books, as yet unknown, are
now in the hands of the studious ; works of Aristotle,
either entirely lost for centuries, or imperfectly known
in the abstracts of Augustine, of Boethius, and Marti-
anus Capella. It was from the Arabic language, from

the godless and accursed Mohammedans, that Christendom received these inauspicious gifts.

This Mohammedan, or Græco-Mohammedan philosophy, was as far removed from the old stern inflexible Unitarianism of the Korân as the Korân from the Gospel. Philosophy was in truth more implacably oppugnant, a more flagrant heresy to Islam than to mediæval Christianity. Islam, like Christianity, the Latin hierarchical Christianity, had its Motakhelim, its high churchmen ; its Sufis, its mystic monks; its Mootizali, its heretics or dissidents : its philosophers, properly so called, its Aristotelians. But the philosophic schools of Islam were as much or more foreign to the general Mohammedan mind than the scholastic oligarchy of Christendom to that of Western Europe. In the general estimation they were half or more than half heretical, the intellectual luxuries of splendid Courts and Caliphs, who were, at least, no longer rigid Islamists.[f] It was not, as in Europe, the philosophy of a great hierarchy.

Of all curious chapters in the history of the human
Arabic
Philosophy.
mind, none is more singular than the growth, progress, and influence of the Arabo-Aristotelian philosophy.[h] Even in the second century after the Hegira, or more fully in the third, this science found its way among the Mohammedans of Syria. After having made its circuit, five or six centuries later it came out again in Spain, and from the schools of Cordova entered

[f] Mahomet is made to prophesy in as stern language as the fiercest Catholic. " Mon église sera divisée en plus de soixante-dix sectes : il n'y a qu'une qui sera sauvée, les autres iront à l'enfer ; or ce qu'il a prédit, est arrivé."—Schmolders, p. 89.

[h] " On ne pourra parler d'une philo- sophie Arabe dans le sens strict du mot . . . . On n'entend dire autre chose que la Philosophie Grecque, telle que les Arabes la cultivaient."—Schmolders, Essai sur les Ecoles Philosophiques des Arabes, p. 41.

Again,

" Græcia capta ferum victorem cepit."

into the Universities of France and Italy. In both cases it
was under the same escort, that of medicine, that it subju-
gated in turn Islam and Christianity. Physicians were its
teachers in Damascus and Bagdad, in Paris and Auxerre.

The Arabians in their own country, in their free wild
life, breathing the desert air, ever on horseback, had
few diseases or only diseases peculiar to their habits.
With the luxuries, the repose, the indolence, the residence in great cities, the richer diet of civilisation, they
could not avoid the maladies of civilisation. They were
obliged to call in native science to their aid. As in their
buildings, their coinage, and most handicraft works, they
employed Greek or Syrian art, so medicine was introduced and cultivated among them by Syrians, Greeks,
and Jews. They received those useful strangers not only
with tolerant respect, but with high and grateful honour.
The strangers brought with them not only their medical
treatises, the works of Hippocrates and Galen, and besides these the Alexandrian astronomy, which developed
itself in the general Asiatic mind into astrology;[1] but
at length also and by degrees the whole Greek philosophy, the Neo-Platonism of Alexandria and the Aristotelian dialectics of Greece. The asserters of the one Book,
the destroyers as they are said to have been of all books
but that one, became authors so prolific, not in poetry
alone, their old pride and delight, but in the infinite
variety and enormous mass of their philosophic treatises,

" Diese Ansicht der Dinge welche
das Geschehen auf der Erde mit den
Bewegungen des Himmels in einen
physichen Zusammenhang bringt, ist
ein characteristiches Zug welche durch
alle Lehre der Arabischen Aristotelischer
hindurch geht. Wenn auch schon vor
ihnen Astrologische Lehren auf der
Philosophie einen Influss geübt hatten,
so bildeten doch sie zuerst die Astrologie
zu einem philosophischen Systeme aus."
Ritter, viii. p. 161. The Astrology of
the Middle Ages no doubt owes much
to and is a sign of the prevalence of
the Arabic philosophy.

as to equal if not surpass the vast and almost incalculable volumes of Scholastic divinity.[1]

As in Syria of old, so now in France and other parts of Christendom, Philosophy stole in under the protection of medicine. It was as physicians that the famous Arabian philosophers, as well as some Jews, acquired unsuspected fame and authority. There is not a philosopher who has not some connexion with medicine, nor a physician who has not some connexion with philosophy. The translators of the most famous philosophers, of Averrhoes and Avicenna, were physicians; metaphysics only followed in the train of physical science.[m]

The Græco-Arabic philosophy worked into the system of the schools in two different modes:—I. The introduction of works of Aristotle, either unknown or now communicated in a more perfect form. II. The Arabic philosophy, which had now grown to its height under the Abbasside Caliphs in the East, Almanzor, Haroun al Raschid, Motakem,[n] and under the Ommiades in Spain. The Eastern school, after Alghazil and Fakhreddin Rhazis, had culminated in Avicenna, the Western in Averrhoes. Schools had arisen in Cordova, Seville, Toledo, Grenada, Xativa, Valencia, Murcia, Almeria. Averrhoes had an endless race of successors.

Profound, it might seem almost impenetrable darkness, covered the slow, silent interpenetration of both these influences into the Christian schools.

Aristotelian Philosophy.

How, through what channels, did Aristotle rise to his

---

[1] " La masse des pretendus Philosophes est si grande, leurs ouvrages sont numériquement si prodigieux, que toute la Scholastique est bien pauvre en comparaison des Arabes."—Schmolders. Has this learned author calculated or weighed the volumes of the Schoolmen?

[m] Ritter, p. 676.

[n] The Nestorian Churches in Persia and Khorasan were instrumental to the progress of philosophising Islamism.

ascendancy? to what extent were the Schoolmen acquainted with the works of the Arabian philosophers? The first at least of these questions has found a satisfactory solution.[o] During all the earlier period, from Anselm and Abélard to the time of Albert the Great, from the eleventh to the thirteenth century, the name of Aristotle was great and authoritative in the West, but it was only as the teacher of logic, as the master of Dialectics. Even this logic, which may be traced in the darkest times, was chiefly known in a secondary form, through Augustine, Boethius,[p] and the Isagoge of Porphyry; at the utmost, the Treatises which form the Organon, and not the whole of these, were known in the Church. It was as dangerously proficient in the Aristotelian logic, as daring to submit theology to the rules of Dialectics, that Abélard excited the jealous apprehensions of St. Bernard.[q] Throughout the intermediate period, to Gilbert de la Porée, to the St. Victors, to John of Salisbury, to Alain de Lille, to Adelard of Bath, Aristotle was the logician and no more.[r] Of his

---

[o] This question has been, if I may so say, judicially determined by M. Jourdain, Recherches Critiques sur l'Age et l'Origine des Traductions Latines d'Aristote, new edition, revised by his son, Paris, 1843. These are the general conclusions of M. Jourdain: 1. That the only works of Aristotle known in the West until the twelfth century were the Treatises on Logic, which compose the Organon. (The Analytics, Topics, and Sophistic Refutations are more rarely cited.) II. That from the date of the following century, the other parts of his philosophy were translated into Latin. III. That of those Translations some were from a Greek, some from an Arabic text. M. Jourdain fairly examines and states the names of former writers on the subject,—Brucker, Tiedemann, Buhle, Tenneman, Heeren.

[p] On the books translated by Boethius and the earlier Translations, Jourdain, pp. 30, 52, &c.

[q] See vol. iii. B. viii. c. 5. Compare Jourdain, p. 24. Abélard confesses his ignorance of the Physics and Metaphysics. "Quæ quidem opera ipsius nullus adhuc translata linguæ Latinæ apparuit: ideoque minus natura eorum nobis est cognita."—Abelard. Oper. Ined. p. 200.

[r] The name of Aristotle is not to be found in Peter the Lombard.—Jourdain, 29.

Morals, his Metaphysics, his Physics, his Natural History, there is no knowledge whatever. His fame as a great, universal philosopher hardly lived, or lived only in obscure and doubtful tradition.

On a sudden, at the beginning of the thirteenth century, there is a cry of terror from the Church, in the centre of the most profound theological learning of the Church, the University of Paris, and the cry is the irrefragable witness to the influence of what was vaguely denounced as the philosophy of Aristotle. It is not now presumptuous Dialectics, which would submit theological truth to logical system, but philosophical theories, directly opposed to the doctrines of the Church; the clamour is loud against certain fatal books[a] but newly brought into the schools.[b] Simon of Tournay,[c] accused of utter infidelity, may have employed the perilous weapons of Dialectics to perplex his hearers and confute his adversaries; but he was also arraigned as having been led into his presumptuous tenets by the study of the Physics and Metaphysics of Aristotle. The heresies of Amaury de Bene, and of David of Dinant, were traced by the theologians of Paris to the same fertile source

---

[a] These books are said by the continuator of Rigord, William the Breton, to have contained the Metaphysics of Aristotle; and in two other writers of the period, in Cæsar of Heisterbach, and Hugh the Continuator of the Chronicle of Auxerre, to have been the Physics. The Decree for burning the books (see below) determines the point.

[b] Crevier, t. i. p. 338, or rather Du Boulay, asserted that these books had been brought from Constantinople about 1167, and translated into Latin. M. Jourdain, Note, p. 46, has shown the inaccuracy of this statement.

[c] Simon of Tournay delivered with wonderful applause a Lecture, in which he explained or proved all the great Mysteries of religion by the Aristotelic process. "Stay," he closed his Lecture; "to-morrow I will utterly confute all that I have proved to-day by stronger arguments." He was struck on that morrow with apoplexy, and lost his speech.—Crevier, i. p. 309. It should seem that Simon de Tournay was rather an expert dialectician than an inquiring philosopher.

of evil.   An exhumation of the remains of Amaury de
Bene, who, though suspected, had been buried in consecrated ground, was followed by a condemnation of his
followers, the teachers of these dreaded opinions.   Some
were degraded and made over to the secular arm (to
the State), some to perpetual imprisonment.   There was
a solemn prohibition against the reading and copying of
these books; all the books which could be seized were
burned.[x]   Six years after, Robert de Courçon, the Papal
Legate, interdicted the reading of the Physics and Metaphysics of Aristotle in the schools of Paris.[y]   A milder
decree of Gregory IX. ordered that they should not be
used till they had been corrected by the theologians of
the Church; yet two years before this Gregory had ful-
minated a violent Bull against the presumption of those
who taught the Christian doctrine rather according to
the rules of Aristotle than the traditions of the Fathers,[z]
against the profane usage of mingling up philosophy with
Divine revelation.   But the secret of all this terror and
perplexity of the Church was not that the pure and more
rational philosophy of Aristotle was revealed in the
schools; the evil and the danger more clearly denounced
were in the Arabian Comment, which, inseparable from

---

[x] All kinds of incongruous charges
were heaped on the memory of Amaury
de Bene: he was an Albigensian,
believed in the Everlasting Gospel.

[y] See the Decree of the Archbishop
of Sens and the Council, unknown to
Launoi and earlier authors, Martene,
Nov. Thes. Anec. iv. 166.   "Corpus
Magistri Amaurici extrahatur a ceme-
terio et projiciatur in terram non
benedictam et idem excommunicetur
per omnes ecclesias totius provinciæ." A
list of names follows, "isti degradentur,

penitus sæculari curiæ relinquendi;"
another list, "perpetuo carceri manci-
pandi."   The Books of David de Dinant
are to be burned, "nec libri Aristotelis
de Naturali Philosophia, nec Commenta
legantur Parisiis publice vel secreto."

[z] "Non legantur libri Aristotelis de
Metaphysicâ et Naturali Philosophiâ,
nec summa de eisdem, aut de doctrinâ
Mag. David de Dinant, aut Almerici
heretici, aut Mauritii Hispan."—Stat.
Univ. Par.

the Arabo-Latin translation, had formed a system fruitful of abuse and error.[a]

The heresy of Amaury de Bene, and that of David de Dinant, was Pantheism.[b] The Creator and the Creation were but one; all flowed from God, all was to be reabsorbed in God—a doctrine not less irreconcileable with genuine Aristotelism than with the doctrine of the Church.[c] But the greater Schoolmen of the next period aspired, with what success it may be doubted, to the nobler triumph of subjugating Aristotelism to the science of Theology, not the logical science only, but the whole range of the Stagirite's philosophy.[d] It was to be an obsequious and humble, though honoured ally, not a daring rival; they would set free, yet at the same time bind its stubborn spirit in their firm grasp, to more than amity, to perfect harmony.

Albert the Great, in his unbounded range of knowledge, comprehends the whole metaphysical, moral, physical, as well as logical system of Aristotle.[e] He had read all, or, with but few unimportant exceptions, his whole works. He had read them in Latin, some translated directly from the Greek, some from the Arabic; some few had been translated from the Arabic into Hebrew, and from the Hebrew into the Latin. Those which came through the Arabic retain distinct

---

[a] "On voit dans ces trois condamnations une diminution successive de sévérité. La première est la plus rigoureuse, les autres s'en vont s'adoucissant." Crevier blames this mildness, p. 312.

[b] "Roger Bacon nous apprend que l'on s'oppose long temps à Paris à la philosophie naturelle et à la metaphysique d'Aristote exposées par Avicenne et Averroès; ceux qui s'en servaient furent excommuniés."—P. 194. See the following quotation from Roger Bacon, and the whole passage.

[c] See the sources of their doctrines, Jourdain, p. 196.

[d] See in Jourdain the works cited by William Bishop of Paris, who died 1248.—P. 31.

[e] Works quoted by Albert the Great also, p. 32.

and undeniable marks of their transmission — Arabic
words, especially words untranslated, Arabic idioms,
and undeniable vestiges of the Arabic vowel system.[f]
These versions from the Arabic came: I. From Spain
and from Spanish scholars in the South of France, at
Marseilles, Montpellier, Toulouse. II. From Sicily,
where Frederic II. had fostered Arabic learning, and
had encouraged translations from that tongue. Under
his auspices the famous Michael Scott had translated, at
least, the books of Natural History.[g] Besides these
some had come through the Hebrew; the great age of
Jewish philosophy, that of Aben-Esra, Maimonides, and
Kimchi, had been contemporaneous with the later
Spanish school of Arabic philosophy. There had been
an intercommunion or rivalry in the cultivation of the
whole range of philosophy. The translations from the
Greek were as yet few, imperfect, inaccurate.[h] The
greater Thomas Aquinas has the merit of having encouraged and obtained a complete translation of the
works of Aristotle directly from the Greek.[i] The culti-

---

[f] "Jamais une version dérivée d'un
texte Arabe ne présenta, fidèlement
orthographié, un mot qui aura passé
par l'intermédiaire de l'Arabe, langue
où la prononciation n'est réglée que
par les points diacritiques qui sont
rarement bien placés. Souvent aussi
les traducteurs ne connaissant pas la
valeur d'un terme l'ont laissé en Arabe."
—Jourdain, p. 19. See the whole
passage, and also p. 37.

[g] On the translation by M. Scott,
from the Arabic, not through the
Hebrew, Jourdain, p. 124, et seqq.,
and Herman Alemannus, with whom
the older Hermann Contractus (the
Lame) has been confounded.—Jourdain, p. 93.

[h] Among the earliest Translations
from the Greek was the Nicomachean
Ethics, by no less a man than Robert
Grostête, Bishop of Lincoln. M.
Jourdain satisfactorily proves this re-
markable fact.—P. 59, et seqq.

[i] "Scripsit etiam super philosophiam
naturalem et moralem et super meta-
physicam, quorum librorum procuravit
ut fieret nova translatio quæ sententiæ
Aristotelis contineret clarius veritatem."
—Tocco, Vit. C. Th. Aquin. Act.
SS. March. "On sait que ce fut par les
conseils et les soins de S. Thomas
d'Aquin que fut faite une traduction
Latine d'Aristote."—Tenneman, Manuel, French Translation.

I 2

vation of Greek had never entirely ceased in the West.
After Scotus Erigena and Adelard of Bath travelled in
the East, these casual and interrupted communications
grew into more regular and constant intercourse.　But
now the Latin conquest of Constantinople had made
Eastern and Western Christendom one.　If the conquering army, the sovereign and the territorial lords,
did not condescend to acquire much of the language of
their subjects, the conquering Church was more wise
and enterprising.　Innocent III. proposed to the University of Paris to send a colony of scholars to learn the
tongue of the people, among whom the Latin clergy
was to administer the rites of the Church ;[k] a school for
youths from Constantinople was to be opened at Paris.[m]
No doubt many Byzantine exiles, men of peace and
learning, found their way to the West.　The Mendicant
Orders, spreading over the world, made it their duty
and their boast to acquire foreign tongues; and now
especially the Dominicans aspired to the highest places
in learning and knowledge.　Thus the complete and
genuine Aristotle was divulged.　Towards the end of
the thirteenth century the philosophers of Greece and
Rome were as well known, as in our own days; the
schools rung with their names,[a] with the explanation of
their writings.　A scholastic Doctor was not thought
worthy of his name who had not publicly commented
on their writings.[o]　It was not alone as a servile translator of the Greek, as the inert and
uninventive disciple of the Western philosophy, which it

Arabian
Philosophy.

---

[k] Epistolæ Innocent. III. Brequigny
et Du Theil, il. 712, 723.

[m] Bulæus, iii. iv.

[a] The earlier Western students, who
travelled before the twelfth century,

Constantine the Monk, the famous
Gerbert, Adelard of Bath, sought rather
mathematical or astronomical science.

[o] Jourdain, p. 2.

was to restore to its forgotten honours in the West, that
Arabian Philosophy aspired, if not to rule, to influence
the mind of Christendom.[9] The four great Arabic
authors, Avicenna, Aven Pace, Avicebron, Averrhoes,
with David the Jew, and others of less fame,[4] introduced
chiefly perhaps through the Jews of Andalusia, Marseilles, and Montpellier (those Dragomen of Mediæval
Science), are not only known to the later Schoolmen ;
but even the suspicion, the jealousy, the awe, has fallen
away. They are treated with courtesy and respect,
allowed fair hearing; that which at the beginning of
the century appeared so perilous, so formidable, is no
longer the forbidden lore of heretics, of unbelievers, of
atheists. The Arabians are entertained as grave philosophers ; their theories are examined, their arguments
discussed. Their authority, as representatives of a lofty
and commanding philosophy, which has a right to respectful attention, is fully acknowledged.[r] Avicenna
and Averrhoes are placed by Dante among the philosophers who wanted only baptism to be saved; and

---

[9] See Jourdain on the Translations
from the Arabic, by Dominic and John
the Jew, in the twelfth century.

[4] "Ajoutons que les philosophes
Arabes, Avicenne, Averroes, Aven
Pace, etc., oubliés maintenant, jouis-
saient alors d'une grande réputation."
— *Ibid.* Avicebron turns out to be
the famous Hebrew poet, Solomon
Ibn Gebirol. See the abstract and
extracts from his 'Fons Vitæ,' in
Munk. Mélanges de Philosophie Juive
et Arabe. Paris, 1859. There is
much on Arabian philosophy of
great value in this work, and other
writings of M. Munk. On Averrens,
see the masterly treatise of Ernest

Renan — Averroes et l'Averroïsm.
Paris, 1861.

[r] M. Schmolders is of opinion that
the Schoolmen were much more indebted to the Græco-Arabic philosophy
than is generally supposed. "L'influence exercée par eux sur le Scolastique est beaucoup plus grande qu'on
ne la suppose ordinairement. Non
seulement les Scolastiques semblent
en convenir eux-mêmes à cause de leurs
nombreuses citations, mais il n'est pas
difficile de prouver qu'ils sont rede-
vables aux Arabes d'une foule d'idées,
qu'on leur a jusqu'à présent attri-
buées."—P. 104.

Dante no doubt learned his respect for their names from his master S. Thomas.[*]

The extent to which Latin Christianity, in its highest scholasticism, admitted, either avowedly or tacitly, consciously or imperceptibly, the influence of the philosophy of Bagdad or Cordova, how far reached this fusion of refined Islamism and Christianity, our History wants space, the Historian knowledge of the yet unfathomed depths of Arabian learning, to determine.[a]

Now came the great age of the Schoolmen. Latin Christianity raised up those vast monuments of Theology which amaze and appal the mind with the enormous accumulation of intellectual industry, ingenuity, and toil;[a] but of which the sole result to posterity is this barren amazement. The tomes of Scholastic Divinity may be compared with the pyramids of Egypt, which stand in that rude majesty, which is commanding from the display of immense human power, yet oppressive from the sense of the waste of that power for no discoverable use. Whoever penetrates within, finds himself bewildered and lost in a labyrinth

Great era of scholasticism.

---

[*] Inferno, iv. This shows at once their fame, and that Arabic philosophers were not popularly rejected as impious and godless.

[a] I almost presume, as far as my own reading extends, to doubt whether there are sufficient grounds as yet for deciding this question. It requires a profound knowledge of Oriental and of Mediæval lore in one person. M. Schmölders possesses the first, M. Ritter perhaps a large proportion of both. M. Hauréau, the great Master of Scholasticism, rather declines, at least does not fully enter into, the discussion.

[a] The study of Arabic, which had been fostered by Frederick II., carried to high perfection by Michael Scott and others, was not discouraged in the Universities. Honorius IV. proposed an endowment for this study in the University of Paris. The ostensible object was the education of Missionaries to propagate the Gospel among the Islamites. The foundation did not take place till the Council of Vienna. —Crevier, ii. 112. At an early period, perhaps, it might rather have promoted the invasion of Christianity by the Arabic philosophy.

of small, dark, intricate passages and chambers, devoid
of grandeur, devoid of solemnity : he may wander without end, and find nothing! It was not indeed the enforced labour of a slave population : it was rather voluntary slavery, submitting in its intellectual ambition and
its religious patience to monastic discipline : it was the
work of a small intellectual oligarchy, monks, of necessity, in mind and habits; for it imperiously required
absolute seclusion either in the monastery or in the
University, a long life under monastic rule. No Schoolman could be a great man but as a Schoolman. William
of Ockham alone was a powerful demagogue—scholastic
even in his political writings, but still a demagogue. It
is singular to see every kingdom in Latin Christendom,
every Order in the social State, furnishing the great
men, not merely to the successive lines of Doctors, who
assumed the splendid titles of the Angelical, the
Seraphic, the Irrefragable, the most Profound, the most
Subtle, the Invincible, even the Perspicuous,[*] but to
what may be called the supreme Pentarchy of Scho
lasticism. Italy sent Thomas of Aquino and Five Great
Bonaventura ; Germany Albert the Great; Schoolmen.
the British Isles (they boasted also of Alexander Hales
and Bradwardine) Duns Scotus and William of Ockham ; France alone must content herself with names
somewhat inferior (she had already given Abélard,
Gilbert de la Porée, Amaury de Bene, and other famous
or suspected names), now William of Auvergne, at a
later time Durandus. Albert and Aquinas were of
noble Houses, the Counts of Bollstadt and Aquino ;
Bonaventura of good parentage at Fidenza ; of Scotus

---

[*] Aquinas, Bonaventura, Alexander Hales, Ægidius de Colonna, Ockham,
Walter Burley.

the birth was so obscure as to be untraceable. Ockham was of humble parents in the village of that name in Surrey. But France may boast that the University of Paris was the great scene of their studies, their labours, their instruction. The University of Paris was the acknowledged awarder of the fame and authority obtained by the highest Schoolmen. It is no less remarkable that the new Mendicant Orders sent forth these five Patriarchs, in dignity, of the science. Albert and Aquinas were Dominicans, Bonaventura, Duns Scotus, Ockham, Franciscans. It might have been supposed that the popularising of religious teaching, which was the express and avowed object of the Friar Preachers and of the Minorites, would have left the higher places of abstruse and learned Theology to the older Orders, or to the more dignified Secular Ecclesiastics. Content with being the vigorous antagonists of heresy in all quarters, they would not aspire also to become the aristocracy of theologic erudition. But the dominant religious impulse of the times could not but seize on all the fervent and powerful minds which sought satisfaction for their devout yearnings. No one who had strong religious ambition could be anything but a Dominican or a Franciscan; to be less was to be below the highest standard. Hence on one hand the Orders aspired to rule the Universities, contested the supremacy with all the great established authorities in the schools; and having already drawn into their vortex almost all who united powerful abilities with a devotional temperament, never wanted men who could enter into this dreary but highly rewarding service,—men who could rule the Schools, as others of their brethren had begun to rule the Councils and the minds of Kings. It may be strange to contrast the popular simple preaching,

All Mendicants.

for such must have been that of S. Dominic and
S. Francis, such that of their followers, in order to contend with success against the plain and austere Sermons of the heretics, with the Sum of Theology of
Aquinas, which of itself (and it is but one volume in
the works of Thomas) would, as it might seem, occupy
a whole life of the most secluded study to write, almost
to read. The unlearned, unreasoning, only profoundly,
passionately loving and dreaming S. Francis, is still
more oppugnant to the intensely subtle and dry Duns
Scotus, at one time carried by his severe logic into
Pelagianism; or to William of Ockham, perhaps the
hardest and severest intellectualist of all; a political
fanatic, not like his visionary brethren, who brooded
over the Apocalypse and their own prophets, but for the
Imperial against the Papal Sovereignty.

As then in these five men culminates the age of
genuine Scholasticism, the rest may be left to be designated and described to posterity by the names assigned
to them by their own wondering disciples.

We would change, according to our notion, the
titles which discriminated this distinguished pentarchy.
Albert the Great would be the Philosopher, Aquinas
the Theologian, Bonaventura the Mystic, Duns Scotus
the Dialectician, Ockham the Politician. It may be
said of Scholasticism, as a whole, that whoever takes
delight in what may be called gymnastic exercises of
the reason or the reasoning powers, efforts which never
had, and hardly cared to have, any bearing on the life,
or even on the sentiments and opinions of mankind, may
study these works, the crowning effort of Latin, of
Sacerdotal, and Monastic Christianity, and may acquire
something like respect for these forgotten athletes in
the intellectual games of antiquity. They are not of so

much moment in the history of religion, for their theology was long before rooted in the veneration and awe
of Christendom ; nor in that of philosophy, for except
as to what may be called mythological subtleties, questions relating to the world of angels and spirits, of
which, according to them, we might suppose the revelation to man as full and perfect, as that of God or of the
Redeemer, there is hardly a question which has not
been examined in other language and in less dry and
syllogistic form. There is no acute observation on the
workings of the human mind, no bringing to bear extraordinary facts on the mental, or mingled mental and
corporeal, constitution of our being. With all their
researches into the unfathomable they have fathomed
nothing : with all their vast logical apparatus they have
proved nothing to the satisfaction of the inquisitive
mind. Not only have they not solved any of the insoluble problems of our mental being, our primary conceptions, our relations to God, to the Infinite, neither
have they (a more possible task) shown them to be
insoluble.[1]

Albert the Great was born at Lauingen in Swabia, of
the ancient house of the Counts of Bollstadt.
He studied at Paris and in Padua. In Padua,
Jordan the Saxon, the head of the Dominicans, laid on
him the spell of his own master-mind and that of his
Order ; he became a Dominican. He returned
to Cologne, and taught in the schools of that
city. In 1228 he was called to fill the chair of his

Albert the
Great.
A.D. 1193.

1211.

---

[1] "Il est donc bien difficile aux philosophes d'avouer que la philosophie con-
siste plutôt à reconnaître la limite
naturelle de l' intelligence humaine
qu'à faire de puérils efforts pour re-
culer cette limite."—Hauréau, ii. p. 45,
quoting Locke, whose whole, wise, but
strangely misrepresented, work is a
comment on that great axiom.

Order in the Jacobin convent at Paris. There, though
his text-book was the rigid, stone-cold Sentences of
Peter the Lombard, his bold originality, the confidence
with which he rushed on ground yet untrodden, at once
threw back all his competitors into obscurity, and
seemed to summon reason, it might be to the aid, it
might be as a perilous rival to religion. This, by his
admirers, was held as hardly less than divine inspiration,
but provoked his adversaries and his enemies. "God,"
it was said, "had never divulged so many of his secrets
to one of his creatures." Others murmured, "He must
be possessed by an evil spirit:" already the fame, the
suspicion of a magician had begun to gather round his
name. After three years of glory, perhaps of some
danger, in Paris, he settled among his Dominican
brethren at Cologne. At Cologne he was visited by
the Emperor William of Holland, who bowed down in
wonder before the extraordinary man. As Provincial
of Germany, commissioned by the Diet of Worms, he
visited all the monasteries of his jurisdiction. He
severely reproved the Monks, almost universally sunk
in ignorance and idleness; he rescued many precious
manuscripts which in their ignorance they had left
buried in dust, or in their fanaticism cast aside as profane. He was summoned to Rome, and named   ' 1260.
Grand Master of the Palace—the great dignity   1265.
usually held by his Order—by Pope Alexander IV.
He laid down his dignity, and retired to his school at
Cologne. He was compelled to accept the Bishopric of
Ratisbon. After three years of able administration he
resigned to Urban IV. the unwelcome great-   Died in 1280.
ness, and again retired to his seclusion, his
studies, and public instruction at Cologne. Such was

the public life, such the honours paid to the most illustrious of the Schoolmen.[a]

Albert the Great at once awed by his immense erudition and appalled his age. His name, the Universal
Doctor, was the homage to his all-embracing knowledge.
He quotes, as equally familiar, Latin, Greek, Arabic,
Jewish philosophers.[a] He was the first Schoolman who
lectured on Aristotle himself, on Aristotle from Græco-
Latin or Arabo-Latin copies. The whole range of the
Stagirite's physical and metaphysical philosophy was
within the scope of Albert's teaching.[b] In later days
he was called the Ape of Aristotle; he had dared to
introduce Aristotle into the Sanctuary itself.[c] One of
his Treatises is a refutation of the Arabian Averrhoes.
Nor is it Aristotle and Averrhoes alone that come within

[a] Haureau, t. II. p. 1, et seqq. I
owe most of what follows, with references to the original works, to the
two Chapters on Albert the Great in
Ritter, Christliche Philosophie, viii. p.
181, and M. Haureau, De la Philosophie Scolastique, II. p. 1. I think the
German has an unusual advantage
over the Frenchman in the order, and
therefore in the perspicuity, with
which he has developed the system of
Albert the Great. In his sharp, precise language the Frenchman resumes
his superiority; and it must be remembered that the object of M.
Haureau's work is the Scholastic Philosophy. I have also read M. Rousselot,
Études, and some of the older writers.

[a] " Et in hanc sententiam convene-
runt multi Theologi diversarum reli-
gionum tam scilicet Saracenorum quam
Judæorum, quam Christianorum."—
Lib. viii. Physic. c. vi., quoted by

[a] M. Haureau, ii. p. 54. Alexander
Hales (about 1222) had illustrated
Christian Theology from Aristotle and
Avicenna.—Ritter, 181. Also Wil-
liam of Auvergne. See Haureau,
p. 31.

[b] The only Treatises which the
Scholastic Philosopher might seem to
disdain were the popular and practical
ones, the Rhetoric, Poetics, and the
Politics.—Ritter, p. 188.

[c] See quotation from Thomasius in
Haureau, and M. Haureau's refutation. "An andern Orten giebt er zu
erkennen, er wollte hier nur die Mei-
nung der Peripatetiker wiedergeben;
wie dieselbe mit der Katholischen Lehre
ausgeglichen werden könne, lässt er
dahin gestellt seyn." Ritter, however,
does full justice to his religion, p. 191.
De unitate intellectus contra Aver-
rhoem. His works fill twenty-one
volumes folio.

the pale of Albert's erudition; the commentators and
glossators of Aristotle, the whole circle of the Arabians,
are quoted, their opinions, their reasonings, even their
words, with the utmost familiarity. But with Albert
Theology was still the master-science. The Bishop of
Ratisbon was of unimpeached orthodoxy; the vulgar
only, in his wonderful knowledge of the secrets of
Nature, in his studies of Natural History, could not
but see something of the magician. Albert had the
ambition of reconciling Plato and Aristotle, and of
reconciling this harmonised Aristotelian and Platonic
philosophy with Christian Divinity. He thus, in some
degree, misrepresented or misconceived both the Greeks;
he hardened Plato into Aristotelism, expanded Aristotelism into Platonism; and his Christianity, though
Albert was a devout man, while it constantly subordi-
nates, in strong and fervent language, knowledge to
faith and love, became less a religion than a philosophy.
Albert has little of, he might seem to soar above the
peculiar and dominant doctrines of Christianity; he
dwells on the nature of God rather than on the Trinity,
on the immortality of the soul rather than the redemption; on sin, on original sin, he is almost silent. According to the established Christian theology, Creation and
Redemption were simultaneously in the counsels of God.
In the new system, Grace was a gift for the advancement of Man's indefeasible intellectual nature. But
though Albert thus dwells on the high, as it were
philosophic, Godhead, he reserves religiously for God a
sole primary existence; he rejects with indignation his
master Aristotle's tenet of the co-eternity of matter and
the eternity of the world;[d] but he rests not in the

---

[d] "Gott wurde bedürftig sein, wenn   setze. . . . . Dass die Materie nicht
sein Werken eine Materie voraus-   ewig sein könne, wird aber auch

sublime simplicity of the Mosaic creation by the Word
of God out of nothing.   Since St. Augustine, the Platonic doctrine of the pre-existence of the forms, or the
ideas, of all things in the mind of God, had been almost
the accredited doctrine of the Church.   Even Matter
was in God, but before it became material, only in its
form and possibility.   Man, indeed, seems to be doomed,
if he can soar above the corporeal anthropomorphism
which arrayed the Deity in human form (the anthropomorphism of the poets, the sculptors, and the painters),
to admit an intellectual anthropomorphism ; to endeavour to comprehend and define the laws and the
capacities of the Divine Intelligence according to his
own.*   Yet when Albert thus accepted a kind of Platonic emanation theory of all things from the Godhead,'
he repudiated as detestable, as blasphemous, the absolute unity of the Divine Intelligence with the intelligence of man.   This doctrine of Averrhoes destroyed the
personality of man, if not of God.   He recoils from
Pantheism with religious horror.   His perpetual object

darans erschlossen, dass Gott, die ewige
Form, und die Materie nicht mit
einander gemein haben können, also
auch nicht die Ewigkeit.   Hier ge-
braucht Albert diesen Satz des Aristoteles gegen den Aristoteles selbst."—
Ritter, pp. 201-2.

* "Le Dieu des philosophes, c'est à
dire des Théologiens éclairés, ne fut
pas, il est vrai, celui des sculpteurs et
des peintres ; mais Il eut bien avec lui,
pour ne rien celer, quelques traits
de ressemblance.   Pour représenter la
figure de Dieu, l'artiste avait choisi
dans la nature, avec les yeux du corps,
les formes qui lui avaient semblé ré-
pondre le mieux au concept idéal de la

beauté parfaite, et il s'était efforcé de
les reproduire sur le bois ou sur la
pierre.   Pour représenter Dieu comme
l'intelligence parfaite, la philosophe
procéda suivant la même méthode ;
arrivant au dernier terme de l'abstraction, il trouva dans l'entendement
humain, les idées générales, et il ne
sut alors mieux faire, que de définir
l'intelligence de Dieu le lieu primordial
de ces idées."—Hauréau, p. 84.   Compare the whole passage, as just as it is
brilliant.

' "Primum principium est indefi-
nienter fluens, quo intellectus univer-
saliter agens indesinenter est intelligen-
tias emittens "—Apud Ritter, p. 199.

is to draw the distinction between the Eternal and the Temporal, the Infinite and the Finite; how knowledge is attained, how the knowledge of God differs from the enthusiastic contemplation of God. God, though not to be comprehended, may be known, and that not only by grace, but by natural means. God is as the Light, everywhere seen, but everywhere escaping the comprehension of the vision. God is omnipresent, all-working yet limited by the capacities of existing things.

God the Creator (and Creation was an eternal, inalienable attribute of the God) was conceived, as having primarily called into being four coeval things of everlasting duration,—the primal Matter, Time, Heaven, the Everlasting Intelligence.[e] But Matter, and Time, it should seem, were properly neither Matter nor Time. Matter has no proper existence, it is only privative; it is something by which and in which works Intelligence.[b] The Heavens exist (and in the Heavens, though this is something, as it were, apart from his theory, Albert admits the whole established order and succession of the Angels from Dionysius the Areopagite)[i] and Intelligence, which subsists, though oppressed and bowed

---

[e] " Ille enim maxime intelligibilis est et omnis intellectus et intelligibilis causa et in omni intelligibili attingitur, sicut lumen quod est actus vialidium, attingitur in omni visibili per visum. Sicut tamen lumen secundum immensitatem, quam habet in rota solis et secundum immensitatem potestatis, qua omnia visibilia comprehendere potest, non potest capi vel comprehendi a visu, ita nec intellectus divinus, secundum excellentiam, quâ excellit in se ipso, et secundum potestatem quâ illustrare potest super omnia, etiam super infinita intelligibilia, capi vel comprehendi potest ab intellectu creato." Summa Theolog., quoted in Ritter, p. 198. The finite cannot comprehend the Infinite. But Albert always pre-supposes the moral as well as the Christian preparative for knowledge, virtue, and faith.

[b] Ritter, p. 205.

[i] The whole Universe was a progressive descendant development, and ascendant movement, towards perfection.

down, even in lifeless things. But between the higher, imperishable intelligence of man and the intelligence of God there is nothing intermediate;[k] and yet there is eternal, irreconcileable difference. The Unity of God must develope itself in multiplicity. Man's Intelligence is a continual efflux from God, an operation of God, but yet not divine. As God it has its own Free Will.[m]

And so Albert goes on, and so went on Albert's successors, and so go on Albert's interpreters, with these exquisitely subtle distinctions of words, which they refuse to see are but words, making matter immaterial,[n] forms actual beings or substances; making God himself, with perfect free-will, act under a kind of necessity; making thoughts things, subtilising things to thoughts; beguiling themselves and beguiling mankind with the notion that they are passing the impassable barriers of human knowledge; approaching boldly, then suddenly recoiling from the most fatal conclusions. In the pride and in the delight of conscious power, in the exercise of the reason, and its wonderful instrument Logic, these profound and hardy thinkers are still reproducing the same eternal problems; detaching the immaterial part of man, as it were, from his humanity, and blending him with the Godhead; bringing the Godhead down into the world, till the distinction is lost; and then perceiving

---

[k] On the great mediæval question Albert would be at once a Realist, a Conceptualist, and a Nominalist. There were three kinds of Universals, one abstract, self-existing, one in the object, one in the mind.—Ritter, p. 219. Haureau, p. 14. M. Haureau treats this part at length.

[m] Yet he does not deny, he asserts in other places, that which Christianity and Islam, Latin, Greek, and Arabian,

equally admitted, the operation of God in the soul of man through Angels.

[n] "Daher ist das Sein an einem jeden Geschöpfe verschieden von dem, was es ist."—Ritter, p. 211. The matter is only the outward vehicle, as it were,—the Form gives the Being. This is the theory of Averrhoes. See on this subject the just and sensible observation of M. Haureau, from p. 34.

and crying out in indignation against what seems their own blasphemy. The close of all Albert the Great's intense labours, of his enormous assemblage of the opinions of the philosophers of all ages, and his efforts to harmonize them with the high Christian Theology, is a kind of Eclecticism, an unreconciled Realism, Conceptualism, Nominalism, with many of the difficulties of each. The intelligence of God was but an archetype of the intelligence of man, the intelligence of man a type of that of God; each peopled with the same ideas, representatives of things, conceptional entities, even words; existing in God before all existing things, before time, and to exist after time; in man existing after existing things, born in time, yet to share in the immortality of the intelligence. Thus religion, the Christian religion, by throwing upward God into his unapproachable, ineffable, inconceivable Mystery, is perhaps, in its own province, more philosophical than philosophy. Albert, in admitting the title of the Aristotelian or Greek, or Arabian philosophy, to scrutinize, to make comprehensible the Divine Intelligence; in attempting, however glorious the attempt, the Impossible, and affixing no limits to the power of human reason and logic, while he disturbed, to some extent unintentionally deposed, Theology, substituted no high and coherent Philosophy. Safe in his own deep religiousness, and his doctrinal orthodoxy, he saw not how with his philosophic speculations he undermined the foundations of his theology.

But this view of Albert the Great is still imperfect and unjust. His title to fame is not that he introduced and interpreted to the world, the Metaphysics and Physics of Aristotle, and the works of the Arabian philosophers on these abstruse subjects but because he

opened the field of true philosophic observation to mankind. In natural history he unfolded the more precious
treasures of the Aristotelian philosophy, he revealed all
the secrets of ancient science, and added large con-
tributions of his own on every branch of it; in mathe-
matics he commented on and explained Euclid; in
chymistry, he was a subtle investigator; in astronomy,
a bold speculator. Had he not been premature—had
not philosophy been seized and again enslaved to theology, mysticism, and worldly politics—he might have
been more immediately and successfully followed by the
first, if not by the second, Bacon.[a]

　　Of all the schoolmen Thomas Aquinas[b] has left the
Thomas Aquinas. greatest name. He was a son of the Count of
Aquino, a rich fief in the Kingdom of Naples.
His mother, Theodora, was of the line of the old Norman
Kings; his brothers, Reginald and Landolph, held high
rank in the Imperial armies. His family was connected
by marriage with the Hohenstaufens; they had Swabian
blood in their veins, and so the great schoolman was
of the race of Frederick II. Monasticism seized on
Thomas in his early youth; he became an inmate of
Monte Casino; at sixteen years of age he caught the
more fiery and vigorous enthusiasm of the Dominicans.
By them he was sent—no unwilling proselyte and pupil—
to France. He was seized by his worldly brothers, and

---

[a] "Nous n'avons interrogé que le
philosophe; nous n'avons parcouru que
trois ou quatre de ses vingt-un volumes
in-folio, œuvre prodigieuse, presqu'
surhumaine, à laquelle aucune autre
ne saurait être comparée: que nous
auraient appris, si nous avions eu le
loisir de les consulter, le théologien
formé à l'école des Pères, le scrupu-
leux investigateur des mystères de la
nature, le chimiste subtil, l'audacieux
astronome, l'habile interprète des théo-
rèmes d'Euclide. Le resultat des tra-
vaux d'Albert n'a été rien moins qu'une
veritable révolution! Cela résume
tous ses titres à la gloire."—Haureau,
li. p. 103. He perhaps rather fore-
boded than wrought this revolution.

[b] Born about 1227.

sent back to Naples; he was imprisoned in one of the
family castles, but resisted even the fond entreaties of
his mother and his sisters. He persisted in his pious
disobedience, his holy hardness of heart; he was released
after two years' imprisonment—it might seem strange—
at the command of the Emperor Frederick II. The
godless Emperor, as he was called, gave Thomas to the
Church. Aquinas took the irrevocable vow of a Friar
Preacher. He became a scholar of Albert the Great at
Cologne and at Paris. He was dark, silent, unapproachable even by his brethren, perpetually wrapt in profound meditation. He was called, in mockery, Cologne,
the great dumb ox of Sicily. Albert ques- 1244, 1245.
tioned the mute disciple on the most deep and knotty
points of theology; he found, as he confessed, his equal,
his superior. "That dumb ox will make the world
resound with his doctrines." With Albert the faithful
disciple returned to Cologne. Again he went back to
Paris, received his academic degrees, and taught with
universal wonder. Under Alexander IV. he stood up in
Rome in defence of his Order against the eloquent
William de St. Amour; he repudiated for his Order, and
condemned by his authority, the prophecies of the Abbot
Joachim. He taught at Cologne with Albert the Great;
also at Paris, at Rome, at Orvieto, at Viterbo, at Perugia.
Where he taught, the world listened in respectful silence.
He was acknowledged by two Popes, Urban IV. and
Clement IV., as the first theologian of the age. He
refused the Archbishopric of Naples. He was expected
at the Council of Lyons, as the authority March 2.
before whom all Christendom might be ex- 1274.
pected to bow down. He died ere he had passed the
borders of Naples at the Abbey of Rossa Nuova, near
Terracina, at the age of forty-eight. Dark tales were

told of his death;[a] only the wickedness of man could
deprive the world so early of such a wonder. The University of Paris claimed, but in vain, the treasure of his mortal remains.[b] He was canonised
by John XXII.

Thomas Aquinas is throughout, above all, the Theologian. God and the soul of man are the only objects
truly worthy of his philosophic investigation. This is
the function of the Angelic Doctor, the mission of the
Angel of the schools. In his works, or rather in his one
great work, is the final result of all which has been
decided by Pope or Council, taught by the Fathers,
accepted by tradition, argued in the schools, inculcated
in the Confessional. The Sum of Theology is the
authentic, authoritative, acknowledged code of Latin
Christianity. We cannot but contrast this vast work
with the original Gospel: to this bulk has grown the
New Testament, or rather the doctrinal and moral part
of the New Testament.[c] But Aquinas is an intellectual
theologian: he approaches more nearly than most philosophers, certainly than most divines, to pure embodied
intellect. He is perfectly passionless; he has no polemic

---

[a] See vol. vi. p. 406, with the
quotation from Dante. One story was
that Charles of Anjou had attempted
violence on a niece of S. Thomas, and
that the Saint had determined to de-
nounce the crime before the Council of
Lyons; others said that Charles re-
sented the free if not king-killing doctrines of the treatise of S. Thomas, de
Regimine Principum. But there is a
full account of the calm, pious death
of S. Thomas. He was ill more than
a month, with every sign of natural
decay.

[b] Read the remarkable letter of the

University in the Life in the Bollandists.

[c] My copy of the Summa of Aquinas
has above twelve hundred of the very
closest printed folio pages in double
columns, without the indexes. I pretend not to have read it; but whoever is curious to know, as it were,
the ultimate decisions of the Latin
Church on most theological or ethical
points will consult it; and will see
the range and scope of that theology,
and the groundwork of all the later
casuistry.

indignation, nothing of the Churchman's jealousy and
suspicion; he has no fear of the result of any investigation; he hates nothing, hardly heresy; loves nothing,
unless perhaps naked, abstract truth.   In his serene
confidence that all must end in good, he moves the most
startling and even perilous questions, as if they were the
most indifferent, the very Being of God.   God must be
revealed by syllogistic process.   Himself inwardly conscious of the absolute harmony of his own intellectual
and moral being, he places sin not so much in the will
as in the understanding.   The perfection of man is
the perfection of his intelligence.   He examines with the
same perfect self-command, it might almost be said
apathy, the converse as well as the proof of the most
vital religious truths.   He is nearly as consummate a
sceptic, almost atheist, as he is a divine and theologian.
Secure, as it should seem, in impenetrable armour, he
has not only no apprehension, but seems not to suppose
the possibility of danger; he has nothing of the boast-
fulness of self-confidence, but in calm assurance of victory, gives every advantage to his adversary.   On both
sides of every question he casts the argument into one
of his clear, distinct syllogisms, and calmly places himself as Arbiter, and passes judgement in one or a series
of still more unanswerable syllogisms.   He has assigned
its unassailable province to Church authority, to tradition or the Fathers, faith and works; but beyond,
within the proper sphere of philosophy, he asserts full
freedom.   There is no Father, even St. Augustine, who
may not be examined by the fearless intellect.

Thomas Aquinas has nothing like the boundless range
of Albert the Great; he disdains or fears Natural Philosophy.   Within their common sphere he is the faithful
disciple of the Master, but far surpasses him in clear-

ness, distinctness, precision, conclusiveness. He had some works of Plato, unknown to Albert, acquired perhaps in his native Magna Græcia; but, with Albert, he rejects the co-eternal ideas subsistent without and beyond the Deity. With Albert in that controversy he is a high Aristotelian, but repudiates as decisively the eternity of matter, the imperishability of the Universe.

Aquinas has, as it were, three distinct and unmingling worlds: the world of God, the world of the immaterial angels and demons, the world of mingled matter and intelligence,—that of man. God is alone, the One absolute, infinite, self-subsistent, whose essence it is "to be." No Eastern anti-materialist ever guarded the primal Godhead more zealously from any intrusive debasement. God is his own unique form: proceeds from no antecedent form, communicates with no inferior form. The Godhead is in itself, by itself, all that is. It is pre-existent to matter, eternally separate from matter.[1] But Thomas must never lose the Christian theologian in the philosopher. All this abstract, un-mingling, solitary Deity, is not merely to be endowed with his eternal, immutable attributes, Omnipresence, Omniscience, Providence, but reconciled with the mysterious doctrine of the Trinity. Thomas has not merely to avoid the errors of Plato and Aristotle, but of Arius and Sabellius; and on the Trinity he is almost as diffuse, even more minute, than on the sole original Godhead. The most microscopic eye can hardly trace his exquisite and subtle distinctions, the thin and shadowy differences of words which he creates or seizes. Yet he himself seems to walk unbewildered in his own labyrinth; he walks apparently as calmly and firmly as if he were in

[1] Compare Hauréau, p. 155.

open day; leaves nothing unquestioned, unaccounted for; defines the undefinable, distinguishes the undistinguishable; and lays down his conclusions as if they were mathematical truths.

Aquinas' world of Angels and Demons comprehended the whole mystic Hierarchy of the Areopagite. Matter is not their substance; they are immaterial. They are not self-subsistent; being is not their essence." They are, on one side, finite; on the other, infinite: upwards, finite; for they are limited by the stern line which · divides them from the Godhead: infinite, downwards; for they seek no inferior subject. But as that which diversifies, multiplies, and individualises, is matter, and divisibility is the essential property of matter, all the Angels, thence, logically, would be but one Angel, as there is but one pure spirituality. In this point, and about the whole subject of Angels, Thomas, instead of being embarrassed, seems to delight and revel; his luxury of distinction and definition, if it be not a contradiction, his imaginative logic, is inexhaustible. He is absolutely wanton in the questions which he starts, and answers with all the grave satisfaction as on solemn questions of life and death.[x]

The third world is that of matter and of man. The world was created by God according to forms (or ideas) existent, not without but within the Deity; for God must have known what he would create. These forms, these ideas, these types of existing things, are part of God's infinite knowledge; they are the essence of God;

" "Esse Angeli non est essentia sed accidens."—Summa, i. quæst. iii. Art. 4. They owe their being to a free act of the divine will. Compare Haureau, p. 155.

[x] E. g. "Utrum in Angelis sit cognitio matutina et vespertina." "Whether angels reason by logic" had been discussed before.

they are God. Man is inseparable from matter; matter
cannot exist without form.[y] The soul, the intelligence
of man, constitutes the third world. It shares, in some
degree, the immateriality of the two higher orders. It
is self-subsistent; but it needs the material body, as its
organ, its instrument. It is not, however, pre-existent.
Origen was a name of ill repute in the Church; his
doctrine therefore, by some subtle logical effort, must
be rejected. Each separate soul is not created ere it is
infused into the human body; this creation is simultaneous; nothing uncreate is presupposed.[*] But if not
self-subsistent, not possibly pre-existent, before their
union with the body, how, according to the orthodox
doctrine, can souls be self-subsistent after the dissolution
of the union? St. Thomas takes refuge in the Angelic
world. This, too, was created; and the souls, retaining
the individuality, which they had acquired in their con-
junction with matter, withdraw as it were into this separate immaterial and unmingling world.

It is obvious that our space only permits us to touch,
and, we fear, with inevitable obscurity, some of the
characteristic views of St. Thomas. St. Thomas, like
his predecessor, Albert, on the great question of universals, is Eclectic; neither absolutely Realist, Conceptualist, nor Nominalist. Universals are real only in
God, and but seemingly, in potentiality rather than
actuality; they are subjective in the intelligence of
man; they result objectively in things. St. Thomas

---

[y] God cannot create matter without
form; this is a necessary limit of his
omnipotence. It would be a contradiction.—Summa.

[*] "Cum anima sine corpore existens
non habeat suæ naturæ perfectionem,
nec Deus ab imperfectis suum opus in-
choaret, simpliciter fatendum est animas
simul cum corporibus creari et infundi."
—Summa, I. quæst. xviii. 3.   "Cre-
atio est productio alicujus rei secundum
suam totam substantiam nullo præsup-
posito quod sit vel incrementum, vel ab
aliquo creatum."—Quæst. lxv. 3.

rejects the Democritean effluxes of outward things, by
which the atomistic philosophy accounted for our perceptions : he admits images of things reflected and received by the senses as by a mirror, and so brought
under the cognisance of the intelligence. The intelligence has, as it were, only the power, a dormant faculty
of knowledge, till the object is presented, through the
image. But the conception by the senses is confused,
indeterminate ; till abstracted, analysed, at once univer-
salised and individualised by the intelligence.[a]

Yet Thomas ruled not in uncontested supremacy even
in his intellectual realm : he was encountered
by an antagonist as severely intellectual as   *Franciscans.*
himself. No doubt the jealousy of the rival orders, the
Dominican and the Franciscan, had much to do with
the war of the Scotists and the Thomists, which divided
the very narrow world which understood, or thought
they understood, the points in dispute, and the wider
world who took either side, on account of the habit,
Franciscan or Dominican, of the champion. It is singular to trace, even in their Scholasticism, the ruling
characters, so oppugnant to each other, of the two Orders.

---

[a] "Cognitio indistincta. Ainsi la
sensation est antérieure à l'intellection,
c'est convenu ; mais toute sensation est
indéterminée, universellement confuse,
avant d'être achevée, avant d'être acte
qui la termine, c'est-à-dire l'idée indivi-
duelle de la chose-sentie, le fantôme ; de
même l'intellection n'est devenue cette
idée claire, positive, absolument distincte
de toute autre, qui répond au mot humanité, qu'après un travail de l'esprit qui
distrait tout le propre de l'humanité de
la notion antérieure et confuse de l'ani-
malité. On ne s'attendait peut-être
pas à ce travail, chez un docteur du

treizième siècle, cette savante critique
de la faculté de connaître."—Haureau,
p. 203. I have made this extract, not
merely because it contains an important illustration of the philosophy of
Aquinas, but because it is such a remarkable indication of the penetrative
good sense, which, notwithstanding all
his scholastic subtlety, appears, as far
as my narrow acquaintance with his
works, to set Aquinas above all Schoolmen. I have read the splendid quarto
volume of M. Carle, ' Histoire de la
Vie et des Écrits de S. Thomas d'Aquin,'
of which I much admire the—type.

In Albert the Great, and in St. Thomas, there is something staid, robust, muscular, the calmness of conscious strength; their reasoning is more sedate, if to such a subject the term may be applied, more practical. The intelligence of man is to be trained by severe discipline to the height of knowledge; and knowledge is its high ultimate reward. With the Franciscans there is still

Bonaventura.   passion: in Bonaventura, the mild passion of Mysticism; in Duns Scotus, if it may be so said, Logic itself is become a passion. Duns is, by nature, habit, training, use, a polemic. In Ockham it is a revolutionary passion in philosophy as in politics. The true opposite, indeed rival he may be called, of Thomas, was his contemporary, his friend Bonaventura. These two men were to have met at the Council of Lyons. One died on the road, the other just lived to receive his Cardinal's hat, with the full applause of that great Œcumenic Synod: a Pope, an Emperor, and a King, attended his magnificent funeral. In Bonaventura the philosopher *recedes;* religious edification is his mission. A much smaller proportion of his voluminous works is pure Scholasticism: he is teaching by the Life of his Holy Founder, St. Francis, and by what may be called a new Gospel, a legendary Life of the Saviour, which seems to claim, with all its wild traditions, equal right to the belief with that of the Evangelists. Bonaventura himself seems to deliver it as his own unquestioning faith. Bonaventura, if not ignorant of, feared or disdained to know much of Aristotle or the Arabians: he philosophises only because in his age he could not avoid philosophy. The philosophy of Bonaventura rests on the theological doctrine of Original Sin: the soul, exiled from God, must return to God. The most popular work of Bonaventura, with his mystic admirers, was

the Itinerary of the Soul to God. The love of God,
and the knowledge of God, proceed harmoniously together, through four degrees or kinds of light. The external light, by which we learn the mechanic arts: the
inferior light, which shines through the senses, by these
we comprehend individuals or things: the internal light,
the reason, which by reflection raises the soul to intellectual things, to universals in conception: the superior
light of grace, which reveals to us the sanctifying virtues, shows us universals, in their reality, in God.

Bonaventura rests not below this highest light.[b] Philosophy pretends that it may soar to the utmost heights,
and behold the Invisible; it presumes to aver that
thought, by dwelling on God, may behold him in spirit
and in truth. Against this doctrine Bonaventura protests with all his energy. Reason may reach the ultimate bounds of nature: would it trespass farther, it is
dazzled, blinded by excess of light. Is faith in the
intellect or in the affections? it enlightens the intellect, it rules over the affections. Which has the greater
certitude, knowledge or faith? There must be a distinction. There is a knowledge which is confined to
human things. There is a knowledge which is the
actual vision of God. This ultimate knowledge, though
of faith, is superior to faith; it is its absolute perfection.
There is a certainty of speculation, a certainty of adhesion. The certainty of adhesion is the certainty of
faith; for this men have died. What Geometer ever
died to vindicate the certainty of geometry?[a] All this

---

b From Haureau, p. 224.

a " Est enim certitudo speculationis
et est certitudo adhæsionis; et prima
quidem respicit intellectum, secunda
vero respicit ipsum affectum. . . .

Sic major est certitudo in ipsa fide
quam sit in habitu scientiæ, pro eo quod
vera fides magis facit adhærere ipsum
credentem veritati creditæ, quam ali-
qua scientia alicujus rei sentæ. Videmus

lower knowledge ought to be disdainfully thrown aside
for the knowledge of God. All sensible appearances,
all intellectual operations, should be dismissed; the
whole weight of the affections be fixed and centred on
the one absolute essence in God. The faithful Christian,
if he might know the whole of physical science, would,
in his loyal adhesion to his belief, lose all that science
rather than abandon or deny one article of the faith.
The raptures of Bonaventura, like the raptures of all
Mystics, tremble on the borders of Pantheism: he would
still keep up the distinction between the soul and God;
but the soul must aspire to absolute unity with God, in
whom all ideas are in reality one, though many according to human thought and speech. But the soul, by
contemplation, by beatic vision, is, as it were, to be lost
and merged in that Unity.[d]

Where the famous Duns Scotus was born, in Scot-

Duns Scotus.

land, in Ireland, in Northumberland; why
called the Scot, what was his parentage; all
is utter darkness, thick and impenetrable as his own
writings, from whence some derived his Greek name,
Scotos. He appeared a humble Franciscan at Oxford;

---

enim veros fideles nec per argumenta,
nec per tormenta, nec per blandimenta,
inclinari posse ut veritatem quam cre-
dunt, saltem ore tenus, negent. Stultus
etiam esset *geometra* qui pro quacunque
certâ conclusione geometriæ, auderet
subire mortem."—In Sentent. xxiii.
quæst. 11 a 14, quoted by Haurreau, p.
226. Strange prediction of Galileo!
" Verus fidelis etiam si sciret totam
physicam, mallet totam illam scientiam
perdere, quam unum solum articulum
perdere vel negare, adeo adhæreus veritati creditæ."—Ibid.

[d] " Et quoniam cognoscens est unum,
et cogita sunt multa, ideo omnes idea
in Deo sunt unum, secundum rem, sed
tamen plures secundum rationem intel-
ligendi sive dicendi."—In Intel. l. xav.
1-3, quoted by Ritter, p. 496. " Tu
autem, o amice, circa mysticas visiones
corroborato itinere et sensus desere et
intellectuales operationes, et sensibilia
et invisibilia, et omne non ens et ens,
et ad unitatem, ut possibile est, inscius
restituere ipsius, qui est super omnem
essentiam et scientiam." Itin. Ment. ad
Deum, 2, 5, 7.—Ibid. p. 498.

the subtle Doctor gathered around him 30,000 pupils.
At Paris he was not heard by less eager or countless
crowds. From Paris he went to Cologno, and there
died. The vast writings of Duns Scotus, which as lectures, thousands thronged to hear, spread out as the
dreary sandy wilderness of philosophy ; if its border be
now occasionally entered by some curious traveller, he
may return with all the satisfaction, but hardly the
reward, of a discoverer. The toil, if the story of his
early death be true, the rapidity, of this man's mental
productiveness, is perhaps the most wonderful fact in
the intellectual history of our race. He is said to have
died at the age of thirty-four, a period at which most
minds are hardly at their fullest strength, having written
thirteen closely-printed folio volumes, without an image,
perhaps without a superfluous word, except the eternal
logical formularies and amplifications.* These volumes
do not contain his Sermons and Commentaries, which
were of endless extent. The mind of Duns might seem
a wonderful reasoning machine; whatever was thrown
into it came out in syllogisms: of the coarsest texture,
yet in perfect flawless pattern. Logic was the idol of
Duns ; and this Logic-worship is the key to his whole
philosophy. Logic was asserted by him not to be an
art, but a science ; ratiocination was not an instrument,
a means for discovering truth : it was an ultimate end ;
its conclusions were truth. Even his language was

---

* Haureau adopts this account of the
age of Duns without hesitation ; it has
been controverted, however, rather from
the incredibility of the fact than from
reasons drawn from the very few known
circumstances or dates of his life. See
Schrockh, xxiv. 437. Trithemius, a
very inaccurate writer, makes him a
hearer of Alexander Hales in 1245; if
so, at his death in 1308, he must have
been above sixty. But no doubt the
authority, whoever he was, of Trithemius wrote Scholar (follower), not
Hearer.

Logic-worship. The older Schoolmen preserved something of the sound, the flow, the grammatical construction, we must not say of Cicero or Livy, but of the earlier Fathers, especially of St. Augustine. The Latinity of Duns is a barbarous jargon.[1] His subtle distinctions constantly demanded new words: he made them without scruple. It would require the most patient study, as well as a new Dictionary, to comprehend his terms. Logic being a science, not an art, the objects about which it is conversant are not representatives of things, but real things; the conceptions of human thought, things, according to the Thomist theory, of second intention, are here as things of first intention, actual as subsistent. Duns, indeed, condescended to draw a distinction between pure and applied Logic; the vulgar applied Logic might be only an instrument; the universals, the entities of pure logic, asserted their undeniable reality. Duns Scotus is an Aristotelian beyond Aristotle, a Platonist beyond Plato; at the same time the most sternly orthodox of Theologians.[g] On the eternity of matter he transcends his master: he accepts the hardy saying of Avicembron,[h] of the universality of

---

[1] Scotus has neither the philosophic dignity nor the calm wisdom of Thomas; he is rude, polemic. He does not want theologic hatred. "Sarmani—vilissimi porci—asini Manichei. Ille maledictus Averrhoes."—Ritter, p. 360.

[g] "Die Richtung, welche er seiner Wissenschaft gegeben hat, ist durchaus kirchlich."—Ritter, p. 336.

[h] "Je reviens, dit-il, à la thèse d'Avicembrou (ego autem ad positionem Avicembrouis redeo), et je soutiens d'abord que toute substance, creée, corporelle ou spirituelle, participe de la matière. Je prouve ensuite que cette matière est une en tous—quod sit unica materia."—Haureau, p. 328. "Sellst die Materie, obwohl sie die niedrigste von allem Seienden ist, muss doch also ein Seiendes gedacht werden und hat ihre Idee in Gott."—Ritter, p. 432. The modern Baconian philosophy may appear in one sense to have reached the same point as the metaphysical philosophy of Duns Scotus, to have subtilised matter into immateriality, to have reached the point where the distinction between the spiritual and material seems to be lost, and almost mocks definition. It is arrived at centres of

matter. He carries matter not only higher than the
intermediate world of Devils and Angels, but up into
the very Sanctuary, into the Godhead itself. And how
is this? by dematerialising matter, by stripping it of
everything which, to the ordinary apprehension, and not
less to philosophic thought, has distinguished matter;
by spiritualising it to the purest spirituality. Matter
only became material by being conjoined with form.
Before that it subsisted potentially only, abstract, unem-
bodied, immaterial; an entity conceivable alone, but as
being, conceivable, therefore real. For this end the
Subtle Doctor created, high above all vulgar common
matter, a primary primal, a secondary primal, a tertiary
primal matter; and yet this matter was One. The universal Primary primal matter is in all things; but as the
secondary primal matter has received tho double form
of the corruptible and incorruptible, it is shared between
these two. The tertiary primal matter distributes itself
among the infinite species which range under these ge-
nera.[1] It is strange to find Scholasticism, in both its
opposite paths, gliding into Pantheism. An universal
infinite Matter, matter refined to pure Spiritualism, com-
prehending the finite, sounds like the most extreme
Spinosism. But Scotus, bewildered by his own skilful
word-juggling, perceives not this, and repudiates the
consequence with indignation. God is still with him

---

force, powers impalpable, imponder-
able, infinite. But it is one thing to
refine away all the qualities of matter
by experiment, and to do it by stripping
words of their conventional meaning.
Mr. Faraday's discoveries and his fame
will not meet the fate of Duns Scotus.

[1] "Dicitur materia secunda prima
quæ est subjectum generationis et cor-

ruptionis, quam mutant et transmutant
agentia creata, seu angeli seu agentia
corruptibilia; quæ ut dixi, addit ad
materiam primo primam, quia esse
subjectum generationis non potest sine
aliquâ formâ substantiali aut sine quan-
titate, quæ sunt extra rationem materiæ
primo primæ."—Haurēau.

the high, remote Monad, above all things, though
throughout all things.ᵏ In him, and not without him,
according to what is asserted to be Platonic doctrine,
are the forms and ideas of things. With equal zeal, and
with equal ingenuity with the Thomists, he attempts to
maintain the free will of God, whom he seems to have
bound in the chain of inexorable necessity.ᵐ He saves
it by a distinction which even his subtlety can hardly
define. Yet, behind and without this nebulous circle,
Duns Scotus, as a metaphysical and an ethical writer, is
remarkable for his bold speculative views on the nature
of our intelligence, on its communication with the outward world, by the senses, by its own innate powers, as
well as by the influence of the superior Intelligence.
He thinks with perfect freedom ; and if he spins his
spider-webs, it is impossible not to be struck at once
by their strength and coherence. Translate him, as
some have attempted to translate him, into intelligible language, he is always suggestive, sometimes
conclusive.

The war of Scotists and Thomists long divided the

ᵏ Hauréau, p. 359.

ᵐ " L'origine de toutes les erreurs
propagées au sujet de la Création vient,
dit-il, de ce que les philosophes ont
témérairement assimilé la volonté divine à la volonté humaine, aussi com-
bat-il de toutes ses forces cette assimilation, sans réussir, toutefois, à démêler
d'une manière satisfaisante ce que c'est
la détermination temporelle d'une acte
éternelle." — Hauréau, p. 363. The
reader who may be curious to learn
how Duns Scotus solves other important physical and metaphysical questions, the principle of motion, the personality and immortality of the soul,

will do well to read the chapters of M.
Hauréau, compared, if he will, with
the heavier synopsis of Brucker, the
neater of Tenneman, the more full and
elaborate examination of Ritter. Ritter
dwells more on the theological and
ethical part of the system of Duns
Scotus, whom he ranks not only as
the most acute and subtlest, but, as
should seem, the highest of the Schoolmen. The pages in which he traces
the theory of Scotus respecting the
means by which our knowledge is acquired are most able, and full of interest for the metaphysical reader.

Schools, not the less fierce from the utter darkness in
which it was enveloped. It is not easy to define in
what consisted their implacable, unforgiven points of
difference. If each combatant had been compelled
rigidly to define every word or term which he employed,
concord might not perhaps have been impossible; but
words were their warfare, and the war of words their
business, their occupation, their glory. The Conceptualism or Eclecticism of St. Thomas (he cannot be
called a Nominalist) admitted so much Realism, under
other forms of speech; the Realism of Duns Scotus was
so absolutely a Realism of words, reality was with him
something so thin and unsubstantial; the Augustinianism
of St. Thomas was so guarded and tempered by his high
ethical tone, by his assertion of the loftiest Christian
morality; the Pelagianism charged against Scotus is so
purely metaphysical, so balanced by his constant, for
him vehement, vindication of Divine grace," only with
notions peculiar to his philosophy, of its mode of operation, and with almost untraceable distinctions as to its
mode of influence, that nothing less than the inveterate
pugnacity of Scholastic Teaching, and the rivalry of the
two Orders, could have perpetuated the strife.° That

* Ritter, p. 358. He is not only
orthodox on this point; he is hierarchical to the utmost. He adopts the
phrase ascribed to St. Augustine, that
he would not believe the Gospel but
on the witness of the Church. The
power of the keys he extends not only
to temporal, but to eternal punishments
—"doch mit dem Zusatze, dass hier-
bei, so wie in andern Dingen der Priester
nur als Werkzeug Gottes handle, wel-
cher selbst eines bösen Engels sich bedie-
nen könnte um einer gültige Taufe zu

vollziehn."—Scotus draws a distinction
(he saves everything by a distinction
which his subtlety never fails to furnish) between the absolute and secondary will of God.

° Ritter thinks their philosophy vi-
tally oppugnant (p. 364), but it is in
reconciling their philosophy with the
same orthodox theology that they again
approximate. One defines away necessity till it ceases to be necessity, the
other fetters free-will till it ceases to
be free.

strife was no doubt heightened and embittered by
their real differences, which touched the most sensitive
part of the Mediæval Creed, the worship of the Virgin.
This was coldly and irreverently limited by the refusal
of the Dominican to acknowledge her Immaculate Conception and birth; wrought to a height above all
former height by the passionate maintenance of that
tenet in every Franciscan cloister, by every Franciscan
Theologian.

But, after all, the mortal enemy of the Franciscan
scholasticism was in the Franciscan camp. The religious mysticism of Bonaventura, the high orthodox sub-
tilism of Duns Scotus, were encountered by a more
William of   dangerous antagonist. The schism of Francis-
Ockham.   canism was propagated into its philosophy; the
Fraticelli, the Spiritualists, must have their champion
in the Schools, and that champion in ability the equal
of those without and those within their Order, of Aquinas, Bonaventura, Duns Scotus. As deep in the very
depths of metaphysics, as powerful a wielder of the great
arm of the war, Logic; more fearless and peremptory,
as less under the awe of the Church, in his conclusions—
William of Ockham had already shaken the pillars of
the hierarchical polity by his audacious assertion of the
more than co-equal rights of the temporal Sovereign;
by his stern, rigid nominalism, he struck with scholastic
arguments, in the hardest scholastic method, at the
foundations of the Scholastic Philosophy. William was
of undistinguished birth, from the village of Ockham, in
Surrey; he entered into the Franciscan order, and was
sent to study theology under Duns Scotus at Paris. The
quarrel of Boniface VIII. and Philip the Fair was at its
height. How deeply the haughty and rapacious Pope
had injured the Franciscan order, especially the English

Franciscans, has been told.[p] How far William of Ockham was then possessed by the resentment of his Order,
how far he had inclined to the extreme Franciscanism,
and condemned his own Order, as well as the proud
Prelates of the Church, for their avarice of wealth, does
not clearly appear. He took up boldly, unreservedly, to
the utmost height, the rights of temporal Sovereigns.
In his Disputation on the ecclesiastical power[q] he refused to acknowledge in the Pope any authority whatever as to secular affairs. Jesus Christ himself, as far as
he was man, as far as he was a sojourner in this mortal
world, had received from his heavenly Father no commission to censure Kings; the partisans of the Papal
temporal omnipotence were to be driven as heretics
from the Church. In the strife of his Order with
John XXII., William of Ockham is, with Michael of
Cesena and Bonagratia, the fearless assertor of absolute
poverty.[r] These men confronted the Pope in his power,
in his pride, in his wealth. The Defence of Poverty by
William of Ockham was the most dauntless, the most
severely reasoned, the most sternly consequent, of the
addresses poured forth to astonished Christen-
dom by these daring Revolutionists.   Pope   A.D. 1323.
John commanded the Bishops of Ferrara and Bologna
to examine and condemn this abominable book.   Five
years after, William of Ockham, Michael de Cesena and
Bonagratia, were arraigned at Avignon, and in close
custody, for their audacious opinions.   William of Ockham might already, if he had any fear, shudder at the
stake and the fire in which had perished so many of his
brethren.   They fled, took ship at Aigues Mortes, found

---

[p] See vol. vii. p. 90.
[q] "Disputatio super potestate ecclesiastica prælatis atque principibus terrarum commissâ."—In Goldastus de
Monarchia. Compare Hauréau, p. 419
[r] Apud Brown, Fasciculus.

their way to the Court of Louis of Bavaria. They were
condemned by the Pope, cast off by their own Order.
The Order at the Synod of Perpignan renounced the
brotherhood of these men, who denounced their wealth
as well as that of the Pope, and would admit nothing
less than absolute, more than apostolic poverty. Their
sentence was that of heretics and schismatics, depriva-
tion of all privileges, perpetual imprisonment. But
William of Ockham, in the Court of Louis, at Munich,
laughed to scorn and defied their idle terrors. He
became the champion of the Imperial rights, of the
Franciscan Antipope, Peter of Corbara. He did not
live to put to shame by his firmer, and more resolute
resistance to the Pope, the timid, vacillating, yielding
Louis of Bavaria.

William of Ockham was in philosophy as intrepid and
as revolutionary as in his political writings. He is a
consummate schoolman in his mastery, as in his use of
logic; a man who wears the armour of his age, engages
in the spirit of his age, in the controversies of his age;
but his philosophy is that of centuries later.[1] The scholastic theologian can discuss with subtlety equal to the
subtlest, whether Angelic natures can be circumscribed
in a certain place; the Immaculate birth and conception
of the Virgin, on which he is faithfully Franciscan;
Transubstantiation, on which he enters into the most
refined distinctions, yet departs not from the dominant
doctrine. As a philosopher, Ockham reverently secludes
the Godhead[2] from his investigation. Logic, which deals

Quodlibeta. Compare Schrockh,
xxiv. 196-7.

[2] Quodlibet. ii. quæst. ii. Hauræau,
422.—In another part M. Hauræau
sums up Ockham's awful reserve on

the notion of God as boldly formed by
the older Schoolmen : " C'est précisé-
ment cette notion rationnelle de la
substance divine que Guillaume d'Ockham critique et réduit à un concept

with finite things, must not presume to discuss the Infinite First Cause. He at once, and remorselessly, destroys all the idols of the former schoolmen. Realism must surrender all her multifarious essences, her abstract virtues, her species, her ideas. Universals are but modes of thought; even the phantasms of Aquinas must disappear. Ideas are no longer things; they are the acts of the thinking being. Between the subject which knows and the object known there is nothing intermediate. The mind is one, with two modes or faculties,—sensibility and intelligence. Sensation is not sufficient to impart knowledge; there must be also an act of intelligence: the former is purely intuitive, the latter is, as it were, judicial. The difference between the sensitive and intelligent is thus partly by experience, partly by reason. By experience, the child sees through sensation, not through intelligence; by reason, because the soul, when separate, sees intellectually, but not through the senses. The sensitive vision is the potential cause of the intellectual vision, but not the potential cause of the intellectual assent. After intuition comes abstraction, sensation, or the intuitive notion, being always singular; abstraction may, as it were, insulate that which is singular, disengaging it from all its surrounding circumstances; it may introduce plurality, combine, compare, multiply. Thus ideas are simple perceptions, or

arbitrairement composé; composé de concepts qui expriment bien, sans doute, quelque chose de Dieu (*aliquod Dei*), mais ne désignent pas Dieu lui-même, la substance, l'essence de Dieu, *quod est Deus* . . . . cette notion abstraite de Dieu, cette notion qui, on le prouve bien, ne représente pas son objet, est la seule que possède la raison humaine, la seule qui lui permet de soupçonner, de deviner, de poser l'entité mystérieuse de la suprême cause. Faut-il désirer une connaissance plus parfaite de cette cause? Sans aucun doute; mais en attendant, il faut s'en tenir à ce qu'il sait."—p. 454. See also the preceding pages.

conceptions, and so not only fall away the Democritean
notions of actual images which have a local existence,
and pass from the object to the sense, but likewise even
the impressions, as of a seal, which is the doctrine of
Scotus, and the real phantasms of St. Thomas.[*] Of
course he denies not the images or similitude of things
in the organ of sight, but they are as the reflections in
a mirror: they do not precede and determine, though
they accompany the sensation. The universal is but a
conception of the mind; and as these conceptions are
formed or perpetuated by these processes, each is the
repetition, the reflection of the other, in intelligence,
speech, writing. Universals are words, whether conceived, spoken, or written words, which by common
consent express under one term many singular things.[*]
In this respect, then, is William of Ockham a Nominalist
in the strongest sense.

Thus may William of Ockham seem with fine and
prophetic discrimination to have assigned their proper,
indispensable, yet limited power and office to the senses;
to have vindicated to the understanding its higher,
separate, independent function; to have anticipated the
famous axiom of Leibnitz, that there is nothing in the
intellect but from the senses, except the intellect itself;
to have anticipated Hobbes; foreshadowed Locke, not
as Locke is vulgarly judged, according to his later
French disciples, but in himself;[y] to have taken his

---

[*] " Dès que les idées ne sont plus
considérées comme des choses mais
comme des actes du sujet pensant, que
de chimères s'évanouissent !"—p. 439,

[*] "Est . . . universale, vox vel
scriptum, aut quodcunque aliud signum ex meditatione vel voluntarie usu,
significans plura singularia universë."

—Quoted in Hauréau, p. 469.

[y] I must be allowed to refer to the
excellent article on Locke in Mr. Hallam's Literary History; and to a very
elaborate and able review of this groundwork of Locke's philosophy in the
' Edinburgh Review,' lately republished
among the Essays by Mr. Rogers.

stand on the same ground with Kant. What Abélard
was to the ancestors of the Schoolmen was Ockham to
the Schoolmen themselves. The Schoolmen could not
but eventuate in William of Ockham; the united stream
could not but endeavour to work itself clear; the incessant activity of thought could hardly fail to call forth a
thinker like Ockham.

Such was the character of the Scholastic Philosophy,
such the chief of the scholastic philosophers, such the
final assertion and vindication of the sole dominion of
Latin Christianity over the mind of man. Between the
close of this age, but before the birth of modern philosophy, was to come the Platonising, half Paganising
school of Marsilius Ficinus: the age to end in direct
rebellion, in the Italian philosophers, against Christianity itself. But it was an extraordinary fact, that in
such an age, when Latin Christianity might seem at the
height of its mediæval splendour and power, the age of
chivalry, of Cathedral and Monastic architecture, of
poetry in its romantic and religious forms, so many
powerful intellects should be so incessantly busy with
the metaphysics of religion; religion, not as taught by
authority, but religion under philosophic guidance, with
the aid, they might presume to say with the servile, the
compulsory aid, of the Pagan Aristotle and the Mohammedan Arabians, but still with Aristotle and the Arabians admitted to the honour of a hearing: not regarded
as odious, impious, and godless, but listened to with
respect, discussed with freedom, refuted with confessed
difficulty. With all its seeming outward submission to
authority, Scholasticism at last was a tacit universal
insurrection against authority; it was the swelling of
the ocean before the storm; it began to assign bounds
to that which had been the universal all-embracing

domain of Theology. It was a sign of the reawakening
life of the human mind that Theologians dared, that
they thought it their privilege, that it became a duty to
philosophise. There was vast waste of intellectual
labour; but still it was intellectual labour. Perhaps at
no time in the history of man have so many minds, and
those minds of great vigour and acuteness, been employed on subjects almost purely speculative. Truth
was the object of research; truth, it is true, fenced
about by the strong walls of authority and tradition,
but still the ultimate remote object. Though it was
but a trammelled reluctant liberty, liberty which locked
again its own broken fetters, still it could not but keep
alive and perpetuate the desire of more perfect, more
absolute emancipation. Philosophy once heard could
not be put to silence.

One man alone, Roger Bacon, even in his own day,
had stood aloof from this all-absorbing Theology, this
metaphysical or ontological philosophy, which, with all
the rest, was the dominant aim of all profound and
rigidly syllogistic investigation; the primary, if not
exclusive subject matter of all the vast volumes, in
which the same questions, argued in the same forms,
revolved in eternal round. Roger Bacon alone sought
other knowledge, and by other processes of thought and
reasoning. Not that physical, or mathematical, or even
experimental sciences were absolutely disdained or proscribed among the highest Theologians: they were pursued by Albert the Great with the ardour of his all-
grasping intellect. But with Roger Bacon they were
the predominant master-studies. Even he, on his side,
could not withdraw entirely from that which had been
so long, and was to be still, so exclusively the province
of all human thought, which must occupy it more or

less, Theology; but the others were manifestly the
engrossing pursuit, the passion, as far as such men are
capable of passion, of his mind. Yet Latin Christianity
can hardly lay claim to the glory, whatever that might
be, of Roger Bacon. The Church, which could boast
her Albert, Aquinas, Bonaventura, Duns Scotus, repudiated Roger Bacon with jealous suspicion. That which
is his fame in later days, heaped on him, in his own,
shame and persecution. For at least ten years he was
in prison; it is not quite clear that he ever emerged
from that prison. Yet, though he has no proper place,
though he is in no way the son or the scholar of Latin
Christianity, still, in justice to the rulers in Latin Christendom, as well as characterising their rule (the exceptional man often throws the strongest light on the
times), must be instituted a more close, yet of necessity
rapid investigation into the extent and causes of the
persecution of Roger Bacon.

At Oxford, his first place of study, Roger Bacon was
remarked for his zeal in mathematical and Born about
scientific studies.[1] But Paris was at that time 1214.
to Transalpine Christendom what Athens was to later
Rome. Without having attended lectures at Paris, no
one could aspire to learned, or philosophical, or theological eminence. At Paris his great talent and acquirements obtained him the name of the " Wonderful
Doctor." It was at Paris no doubt that he matured
those studies, which he afterwards developed in his
" Greater Work."[2] He could not but excite wonder;

---

[1] It is disputed whether at Merton
College or Brazenose Hall. As Bacon
was not a member of Merton College,
according to the fashion of the day he
may possibly at different times have

lodged both in one and in the other.
The halls were merely places of residence for Scholars.

[2] The Opus Majus.

doubtless he did excite more than wonder, for he dared
to throw off entirely the bondage of the Aristotelian
logic. When he judged Aristotle, it should seem, only
by those parts of his works, matured in the Dialectics
of the Schools, he would have been the Omar of Aristotle; he would willingly have burned all his books, as
wasting time, as causes of error, and a multiplication of
ignorance.[b] But Aristotle, as a philosopher, especially
as commented by Avicenna, after Aristotle the prince
of philosophers, is the object of his profound reverence.
The studies of Roger Bacon embraced every branch.
of physical science, Astronomy, Optics, Mechanics,
Chemistry. He seems even to have had some glimpses
of that which has first grown into a science in our own
day. He was an industrious student of all languages,
Hebrew, Greek, Arabic, the modern tongues. He had
a dim notion of their kindred and filiation. He had a
vision of a Universal Grammar, by which all languages
were to be learned in an incredibly short space of time.[c]
In Paris his fellow-student was the famous Robert Gros-

---

[b] "Si haberem potestatem super
libros Aristotelis, ego facerem omnes
cremari, quia non est nisi temporis
amissio studere in illis, et causa erroris,
et multiplicatii erroris." See on the
translators of Aristotle, Opus Majus,
quoted by Jebb in Præfat. I. c. viii.

[c] As his astronomy sometimes tam-
pered with astrology, his chemistry de-
generated into alchemy, so his knowledge of languages was not without
what, in modern times, might be
branded as charlatanism. He professed
that, according to his Universal Grammar, he could impart to an apt and
diligent scholar a knowledge of Hebrew
in three days, of Greek in as many

more. "Certum est mihi quod intrà
tres dies quæmcunque diligentem et
confidentem docerem Hebræum et simul
legere et intelligere quicquid sancti
dicunt et sapientes antiqui in exposi-
tione sacri textûs, et quicquid pertinet
ad illius textûs correctionem, et expo-
sitionem, si vellet se exercere secundum
doctrinam doctam; et per tres dies
sciret de Græco iterum, ut non solum
sciret legere et intelligere quicquid pertinet ad theologiam, sed ad philosophiam et
ad linguam Latinam."—Epist. de Laud.
S. Script. al P. Clement. IV. Here too
he is breaking up the way to Biblical
criticism.

tête: the intimate friendship of such a man could not
but commend him to the favour of some of the loftier
Churchmen. He returned to Oxford, and in an evil
hour took the fatal step (it is said by the advice of
Grostête, who was infatuated with the yet ardent zeal
of the Franciscans) of becoming a Franciscan Friar.
Thus he became not merely subject to the general discipline of the Church, but to the narrower, more rigid,
more suspicious rule of the Order.[d] It was difficult for
a man of great powers to escape being Dominican or
Franciscan. The Dominicans were severe and jealously
orthodox. The Inquisition was entrusted to them; but
they had a powerful and generous corporate spirit, and
great pride in men of their own Order who showed
transcendant abilities. The Franciscan Generals were,
with the exception perhaps of John of Parma, and of
St. Bonaventura, men of mean talent, of contracted and
jealous minds, with all the timidity of ignorance.[e] The
persecutor of Roger Bacon was Jerome of Ascoli, the
General of his own Order; first when as Cardinal he
was aspiring towards the steps of the Papal throne;
afterwards when he ascended that throne as Nicolas IV.[f]
Nor indeed were wanting at that time causes which
might seem to justify this ungenerous timidity in the
Franciscans. They were watched with the jealousy of
hatred by the Dominicans. Masters of the Inquisition,
the Dominicans would triumph in the detection of

---

[d] According to some he became a
Franciscan at Paris.

[e] "Les Franciscains, toujours gou-
vernés, si l'on excepte Saint Bonaventura, par des généraux d'un menu talent
et d'un médiocre savoir, ne se sentaient
qu' humiliés de la présence et de la
gloire des hommes de mérite, qui

s'étaient égarés parmi eux."—M. V.
de Clerc, Hist. Lit. de la France, xx.
p. 230.

[f] Jerome d'Ascoli was at Paris, the
probable date of Bacon's persecution,
in 1278. I cannot but doubt the date
usually assigned to his birth.

Franciscan heretics. There had been already the first
rending of their body by the fatal schism, under John
of Parma, hardly allayed by the gentle and commanding
rule of Bonaventura. The fierce democratic Ghibellinism was even now fermenting among them, hereafter to
break out in the Anti-Papal writings of William of Ockham. Roger Bacon himself might seem disposed to
tamper with perilous politics. On his return to Oxford,
he preached, it is said, before King Henry III., and
denounced, in no measured terms, the employment of
French and Gascon Nobles and Prelates in the great
offices of State; the prodigality of the King towards
these foreign favourites; his blind confidence in the
Bishop of Winchester; his placing foreign Poitevins
in possession of the chief forts and strongholds in the
realm. Even in his own Order, Roger Bacon is said
to have shown the natural contempt of a man of his
high acquirements for the ignorance and superstition
of his brethren; to have let fall alarming words about
Reform in the Franciscan Convents. Yet was he not
without powerful friends; Grostête, of Lincoln, and,
after Grostête's death, men at least of wealth and
liberality. He is reported to have received at Oxford
no less a sum than 2000 Paris livres for books and
instruments.

Even the Church as yet seemed more disposed to
admire and to honour, than to look with cold suspicion
A.D. 1266. on the wonderful man. Pope Clement IV.
accepted the dedication of the Work which
contained all the great principles of his philosophy; all
on which his awe-struck brethren looked as fearful
magic. He received the work itself with some instruments invented by Bacon to illustrate his experiments.
These Bacon, notwithstanding the direct prohibition of

the Rulers of his Order, who threatened him with the forfeiture of his book, and the penalty of con- Clement IV. finement on bread and water, if he dared to Pope.
1265-1268. communicate with any one what might be his unlawful discoveries,[a] despatched through John of Paris to Rome. Philosophy was thus as it were entering its appeal to the Pope. Clement IV. was a Frenchman; no doubt knew the fame of Bacon at Paris. He had written a letter to Bacon entreating the communication of his famous wonders. Bacon had not dared to answer this letter till Clement was on the Papal throne; and even the Pope himself dared not openly to receive this appeal of philosophy. He stipulated that the books and the instruments should be sent as secretly as possible.[b] For the ten years which followed the death of   A.D. 1268-
1278. Clement IV., Bacon lived an object of wonder, terror, suspicion, and of petty persecution by his envious or his superstitious brethren. He attempted to propitiate Honorius IV. by a treatise on 'The Mitigation of the Inconveniences of Old Age.'[i] At the close of these ten years, came to Paris, as Legate from Pope Nicolas III., Jerome of Ascoli, General of the Franciscan Order. Jerome was a true Franciscan; and before him the Franciscans found ready audience in the arraignment of that fearful magician, their Brother. It is singular that among the specific charges was that of undertaking to predict future events. Bacon's own words show that

---

[a] " Sub præcepto et pœnâ amissionis libri et jejunio in pane et aquâ pluribus diebus, prohibuerunt eum a communicando scriptum aliquod a se factum cum aliis quibuscunque." — Opus Majus, MS. Cott. fol. 3.

[b] " Hoc quanto secretius poteris, facias."—Wadling, Ann. 11, p. 294,

quoted in an extremely good article on Roger Bacon in Didot's new Biographie Universelle, which has avoided or corrected many errors in the old biographies.

[i] Honorius IV. not Nicolas IV. See Hist. Lit. de la France, p. 223.

the charge, however puerile, was true: "But for the stupidity of those employed, he would have framed astronomical tables, which, by marking the times when the heavenly bodies were in the same positions and conjunctions, would have enabled him to vaticinate their influence on human affairs."[k] That which to us was the rare folly of a wise man, to his own age was the crime of a wicked one. The general accusation was far more wide and indefinite, and from its indefiniteness more terrible. It was a compact with the Devil, from whom alone he had obtained his wonderful knowledge, and wrought his wonderful works. In vain Bacon sent out his contemptuous and defiant treatise on the nullity of magic: "Because things are above your shallow understandings, you immediately declare them works of the Devil!" In such words he arraigns not the vulgar alone: "Theologians and Canonists, in their ignorance, abhor these things, as works of magic, and unbecoming a Christian." And thus the philosopher spoke against his whole Order; and before a Cardinal Legate, a Master of that Order. Roger Bacon was consigned to a Monastic dungeon at least for ten years; and as it is not likely that Jerome of Ascoli, as Pope, would mitigate the rigour, no doubt conscientiously exercised, most probably for five years more, till the close of the Pontificate of Nicolas IV. If he emerged from the

---

[k] Throughout Bacon's astrological section (read from p. 247), the heavenly bodies act entirely through their physical properties, cold, heat, moisture, drought. The comet causes war (he attributes the wars then raging in Europe to a comet) not as a mere arbitrary sign, nor as by magic influence (all this he rejects as anile superstition), but as by its intense heat inflaming the blood and passions of men. It is an exaggeration (unphilosophical enough) of the influences of the planetary bodies, and the powers of human observation to trace their effects, but very different from what is ordinarily conceived of judicial astrology.

darkness of his prison, it was not more than a year
before his death.

The value and extent of Roger Bacon's scientific
discoveries, or prophecies of discoveries, how far his
own, or derived from Arabian sources, belongs rather
to the history of philosophy than of Latin Christianity.
His astronomy no doubt had enabled him to detect the
error in the Julian year: three centuries too soon he
proposed to Clement IV. to correct the Calendar by his
Papal authority: but I presume not to enter further
into this or kindred subjects. In Optics his admirers
assert that he had found out many remarkable laws, the
principle of the Telescope, the Refraction of Light, the
cause of the Rainbow. He framed burning glasses of
considerable magnitude. Mechanics were among his
favourite and most successful studies. In his Chemistry
he had reached, or nearly reached, the invention of
gunpowder: it is more certain that he sought the philosopher's stone, or at least a transmuting elixir with
unlimited powers. There are passages about mounting
in the air without wings, and self-moving carriages,
travelling at vast speed without horses, which sound
like vaticinations of still more wonderful things. He
had no doubt discovered the cause of the tides. It is
for others, too, to decide how far in the general principles of his philosophy he had anticipated his greater
namesake, or whether it was more than the sympathy
of two kindred minds working on the same subjects,
which led to some singular yet very possibly fortuitous
coincidences of thought and expression.[m] This, how-

* See Mr. Forster's 'Mohammedanism Unveiled,' and Mr. Hallam's judi-
cious remarks, Lit. Hist. Mr. Brewer
(in the Rolls publications) has made a

most valuable addition to the published
works of Roger Bacon. His volume
contains the Opus Tertium, the Opus
Minus, the Computus, &c. This pub-

ever, is certain, that although the second Bacon's great
work, as addressed to Europe, might condescend to
the Latin form, it was in its strong copious Teutonic
English that it wrought its revolution, that it became
the great fountain of English thought, of English sagacity, the prelude to and the rule of English scientific
discovery.

Roger Bacon has rather thrown us back in our chrono-
logy to the age of the older Scholasticism ; but Scholasticism ruled supreme almost to the close of exclusive
Latin Christianity ; it expired only by degrees ; its bonds
were loosened, but not cast off: if its forms had given
place to others more easy, natural, rhetorical, its modes
of thought, its processes of ratiocination, its logic, and
its definitions, still swathed the dead body of Christian
Theology.   Gerson was still in a great degree a schoolman, Wycliffe himself at Oxford was a schoolman.   But
Latin Christianity was not all scholastic theology, it
was religion also ; it did not altogether forget to be
piety, holiness, charity ; it was not content with its
laborious endeavours to enlighten the mind : it knew
still that the heart was its proper domain.   The religious
feelings, the religious affections, the religious emotions,
were not abandoned for the eternal syllogisms of the
schools, the interminable process of twentyfold assertion, twentyfold objection, twentyfold conclusion.   It
was not enough that the human intelligence should be
taught that it was an efflux, a part of the Divine intel-

---

lication (London, 1859) appears to have
been unknown to M. Charles, in whose
elaborate work, ' Roger Bacon, sa Vie,
ses Ouvrages, ses Doctrines' (Paris,
1861), these writings are quoted and
extracted from, as if still MSS.   M.

Charles, I observe, with all his admiration of Roger Bacon, reduces his
scientific attainments very consider-
ably, and seemingly on just grounds.—
Part iv, c. 3.

ligence. Nor was the higher office of training the soul of man to communion with Christ by faith, purity, and love, altogether left to what may be called Scholastic Mysticism. In one remarkable book was gathered and concentered all that was elevating, passionate, profoundly pious, in all the older mystics. Gerson, Rysbroek, Tauler, all who addressed the heart in later times, were summed up, and brought into one circle of light and heat, in the single small volume, the 'Imitation of Christ.' That this book supplies *Imitation of Christ.* some imperious want in the Christianity of mankind, that it supplied it with a fullness and felicity, which left nothing, at this period of Christianity, to be desired, its boundless popularity is the one unanswerable testimony. No book has been so often reprinted, no book has been so often translated, or into so many languages, as the 'Imitation of Christ.'[a] The mystery of its authorship, as in other cases, might have added to its fame and circulation; but that mystery was not wanted in regard to the 'Imitation.' Who was the author—Italian, German, French, Fleming?[o] With each of these races it is taken up as a question of national vanity. Was it the work of Priest, Canon, Monk? This, too, in former times, was debated with the eagerness of rival Orders.[p] The size of the book, the manner, the style, the arrange-

[a] According to M. Michelet (whose rhapsody, as usual, contains much which is striking truth, much of his peculiar sentimentalism) there are sixty translations into French; in some respects he thinks the French translation, the 'Consolation,' more pious and touching than the original.

[o] Italian, French, German idioms have been detected.

[p] Several recent writers, especially

M. Onésime Roy, 'Etudes sur les Mystères,' have thought that they have proved it to be by the famous Gerson. If any judgement is to be formed from Gerson's other writings, the internal evidence is conclusive against him. M. Michelet has some quotations from Thomas à Kempis, the author at least of a thick volume published under that name, which might seem equally to endanger his claim. But to me, though

ment, as well as its profound sympathy with all the
religious feelings, wants, and passions; its vivid and
natural expressions, to monastic Christianity what the
Hebrew Psalms are to our common religion, and to our
common Christianity; its contagious piety; all conspired to its universal dissemination, its universal use.
This one little volume contained in its few pages the
whole essence of the St. Victors, of Bonaventura without his Franciscan peculiarities, and of the later Mystic
school.   Yet it might be easily held in the hand,
carried about where no other book was borne,—in the
narrow cell or chamber, on the journey, into the solitude, among the crowd and throng of men, in the
prison.   Its manner; its short, quivering sentences,
which went at once to the heart, and laid hold of and
clung tenaciously to the memory with the compression
and completeness of proverbs; [1] its axioms, each of
which suggested endless thought; its imagery, scriptural and simple, were alike original, unique.   The
style is ecclesiastical Latin, but the perfection of ecclesiastical Latin,—brief, pregnant, picturesque; expressing
profound thoughts in the fewest words, and those words,
if compared with the scholastics, of purer Latin sound
or construction.   The facility with which it passed into
all other languages, those especially of Roman descent,
bears witness to its perspicuity, vivacity, and energy.
Its arrangement has something of the consecutive progress of an ancient initiation; it has its commencement,

inferior, the other devotional works there ascribed to Thomas à Kempis, the Soliloquium Animæ, the Hortulus Rosarum, and Vallis Liliorum, even the Sermons, if not quite so pure, are more than kindred, absolutely the same, in thought and language and style. See the Opera T. à Kempis: Antwerp, 1615.

[1] It is singular how it almost escapes or avoids that fatal vulgarism of most mystic works, metaphors taken from our lower senses, the taste, the touch.

its middle, and its close; discriminating yet leading up
the student in constant ascent; it is an epopee of the
internal history of the human soul.

The 'Imitation of Christ' both advanced and arrested
the development of Teutonic Christianity; it was prophetic of its approach, as showing what was demanded
of the human soul, and as endeavouring, in its own way,
to supply that imperative necessity; yet by its defi-
ciency, as a manual of universal religion, of eternal
Christianity, it showed as clearly that the human mind,
the human heart, could not rest in the Imitation. It
acknowledged, it endeavoured to fill up the void of
personal religion. The Imitation is the soul of man
working out its own salvation, with hardly any aid but
the confessed necessity of divine grace. It may be
because it is the work of an ecclesiastic, a priest, or
monk; but, with the exception of the exhortation to
frequent communion, there is nothing whatever of sacerdotal intervention: all is the act, the obedience, the
aspiration, the self-purification, self-exaltation of the
soul. It is the Confessional in which the soul confesses
to itself, absolves itself; it is the Direction by whose
sole guidance the soul directs itself. The Book absolutely and entirely supersedes and supplies the place of
the spiritual teacher, the spiritual guide, the spiritual
comforter: it is itself that teacher, guide, comforter.
No manual of Teutonic devotion is more absolutely
sufficient. According to its notion of Christian perfection, Christian perfection is attainable by its study, and
by the performance of its precepts: the soul needs no
other mediator, at least no earthly mediator, for its
union with the Lord.

But 'The Imitation of Christ,' the last effort of Latin
Christianity, is still monastic Christianity. It is abso-

M 2

lutely and entirely selfish in its aim, as in its acts. Its
sole, single, exclusive object, is the purification, the
elevation of the individual soul, of the man absolutely
isolated from his kind, of the man dwelling alone in the
solitude, in the hermitage of his own thoughts; with no
fears or hopes, no sympathies of our common nature :
he has absolutely withdrawn and secluded himself not
only from the cares, the sins, the trials, but from the
duties, the connexions, the moral and religious fate of
the world. Never was misnomer so glaring, if justly
considered, as the title of the book, the 'Imitation of
Christ.' That which distinguishes Christ, that which
distinguishes Christ's Apostles, that which distinguishes
Christ's religion—the Love of Man—is entirely and
absolutely left out. Had this been the whole of Christianity, our Lord himself (with reverence be it said) had
lived, like an Essene, working out or displaying his
own sinless perfection by the Dead Sea : neither on the
Mount, nor in the Temple, nor even on the Cross. The
Apostles had dwelt entirely on the internal emotions of
their own souls, each by himself, St. Peter still by the
Lake of Gennesaret, St. Paul in the desert of Arabia,
St. John in Patmos. Christianity had been without
any exquisite precept for the purity, the happiness of
social or domestic life; without self-sacrifice for the
good of others ; without the higher Christian patriotism,
devotion on evangelic principles to the public weal;
without even the devotion of the missionary for the
dissemination of Gospel truth; without the humbler
and gentler daily self-sacrifice for relatives, for the wife,
the parent, the child. Christianity had never soared to
be the civiliser of the world. " Let the world perish, so
the single soul can escape on its solitary plank from the
general wreck," such had been its final axiom. The

'Imitation of Christ' begins in self—terminates in self.
The simple exemplary sentence, "He went about doing
good," is wanting in the monastic gospel of this pious
zealot. Of feeding the hungry, of clothing the naked,
of visiting the prisoner, even of preaching, there is profound, total silence. The world is dead to the votary of
the Imitation, and he is dead to the world, dead in a
sense absolutely repudiated by the first vital principles
of the Christian faith. Christianity, to be herself again,
must not merely shake off indignantly the barbarism,
the vices, but even the virtues of the Mediæval, of
Monastic, of Latin, Christianity.

CHAPTER IV.

Christian Latin Poetry. History.

WHAT did Latin Christianity add to the treasures of
Latin poetry? Poetry, as in Greece, may have its distinct epochs in different forms, but it rarely, if ever,
renews its youth.* Hardly more than half a century
contains all that is of the highest order in Latin poetry—
Lucretius, Catullus, Virgil, Horace, the Elegiacs, Ovid.
Even that noble declamatory verse, which in the best
passages of Lucan, in Juvenal, and even in Claudian
(this, with the philosophic and didactic poetry, Lucretius, Virgil, and the exquisite poetry of common sense
and common life in Horace, the only indigenous poetry
of Rome), dies feebly out in the triumph of Christianity
over Heathenism, as celebrated by Prudentius in his
book against Symmachus.

The three earlier forms of Christian Latin poetry
were—I. Paraphrases of the Scripture, II. Legends of Saints, and III. Hymns—with a few
controversial poems, like that of S. Prosper on Pelagianism. I. In the Scriptural Poems the life and
energy of the biblical annalists or poets are beaten out
to pleonastic and wearisome length; the antithetic or

---

* It has done so besides in Greece,
in England alone, hardly in Italy, unless Alfieri be admitted to make a third
Epoch, with Dante and Petrarch, with
Ariosto and Tasso. Spain has had but
one, that of Lope, Cervantes, and Calderon; Germany but one, and that a
late one, of Schiller and Goethe. The
most striking parallel is in India, of
the vast Epics, the Mahabarata and
Ramayana, of the Drama of Calidasa,
of the Lyric Gita Govinda.

parallelistic form of the Hebrew poetry is entirely lost;
the uncongenial Orientalism of thought and imagery
will not submit to the hard involutions of the Latin: it
dislocates the harmony of the verse, if verse still retains
or strives after harmony, without giving its own rude
strength or emphatic force. The Vulgate alone, by
creating almost a new language, has naturalised the
biblical thoughts and figures, which obstinately refuse to
be bound in the fetters of the Latin Hexameter. The
infallible poetic sentiment of mankind will still refuse
the name of poetry to the prolix, though occasionally ·
vigorous, versifications of Fortunatus, Juvencus, Sedu-
lius, Arator, Avitus, and the rest. As to the old voy-
ager in the vast interminable ocean, if he beheld on
some dreary mass of rock a patch of brilliant green, a
tuft of graceful trees, a cool rush of water, it became
a paradise—a Tinian or a Juan Fernandez—and is
described as one of the Elysian islands: so the curious
reader, if, on traversing these endless poems, he dis-
covers some lines more musical, some images more
happily embodied in words, some finer or more tender
thoughts expressed not without nature, he bursts out
into rapture, and announces a deep mine of rich and
forgotten poetry. The high-wrought expectations of
the next visitants revenge their disappointment by
exaggerating perhaps the dreariness and the barren-
ness.[b] In these poems creative power there is and can be

---

[b] Even M. Guizot, in his Lectures
on Civilisation, cites passages from these
authors, with praise, as it seems to me,
far beyond their due. They are pre-
Miltonic, as he asserts, in some of their
thoughts, in some of their imagery,
that is, they are drawn from the same
sources; but what they want is, what

Milton has given them, Poetry. So
too M. Ampère in his valuable Lectures. The passage which I have
quoted from Dracontius the Spaniard,
in the History of Christianity (iii. p.
356), still appears to me the most
favourable example which has occurred
in the course of my reading; and I

none : invention had been a kind of sacrilege. The Hebrew poetry, in the coldest and most artificial translation, preserves something of its life and sententious vigour, its bold figures and imagery : in the many-folded shroud of the Latin poetic paraphrase it is a mummy.

The Epic Poetry of Latin Christianity (I feel the abuse of the words) had done its work of paraphrase, or had nearly exhausted itself in a few centuries; but if it sunk almost into silence from the fifth to the eighth, it rose again more ambitious, and seized the office of the historian, or that which had been the sole function of the humble orator under the later empire, that of the panegyrist. Hardly a great historic event took place, hardly a great man ascended a throne or achieved fame, but some monkish versifier aspired to immortalise him ·with an interminable length of harsh hexameter or of elegiac verse. Charlemagne indeed was mostly reserved for later romance, and happily had his historian, Eginhard. But Louis the Pious was celobrated by Ermoldus Nigellus in a long poem in elegiac verse; the siege of Paris by the Normans was sung in hexameters by Abbo ; the anonymous panegyrist endeavoured to raise the Italian Berengar into a hero; Hroswitha wrote of the deeds of the Emperor Otho; Gunther, the Ligurian, those of Barbarossa ; Donizo celebrated the Countess Matilda, from whom was inseparable the great name of Gregory VII. William the Apulian described the conquests of the Normans; William of Brittany, Philip Augustus ; and so in unexhausted succession to the Cardinal Poet of Cœlestine V. and Boniface VIII. But from all those historical poems, who has yet struck out

have tollsomely read much of that age. To me they are inferior as Christian Latin Poetry to Sanazzaro or Vida,   and to some of the Jesuits, who are at least correct, animated, harmonious.

for our admiration one passage of genuine poetry?
Perhaps their great merit is their want of poetry: they
can lie under no suspicion of invention, hardly of poetic
embellishment: they are simply verse chronicles, as
veracious as the works of the contemporary prose historians of the cloister.

Nor were these inexhaustible and indefatigable writers
in Latin verse content with the domain of his-   Later Latin
tory, or the reward of the panegyrical orator.   poems
They seized and petrified, either for their amusement,
or as a trial of skill, or for the solace and entertainment
of their brother Monks, the old traditional German
poetry, the fabulous histories, the initiatory romances,
which, in their rude vernacular form and language,
began to make themselves heard. What the Court or
the Castle Hall listened to in the Lay or the Tale of the
Wandering Minstrel, was heard in the Cloister in a
Latin version. The Monks converted to their own use,
perhaps supposed that they were saving from destruction, by transferring into imperishable Latin, the fleeting
or expiring songs, which became the Niebelungen and
the Heldenbuch. Such doubtless was the origin of the
remarkable poem called Waltharius, or the Expedition
of Attila, founded on the Legends of Dietrich, Siegfried,
and Etzel. But even in this very curious work it is
remarkable that, although the innate poetry of the subject has given more than usual animation to the monkish
versifier, yet the prosaic and historic element predominates. The cloister poet labours to make that history
which is pure mythic romance; the wild song is harden-
ing into a chronicle.[e] The epic of John of Exeter, on

[e] De Expeditione Attilæ, edited by
Fischer, Leipsic, 1780; and later by
Grimm and Schmeller, Göttingen,
1838. Compare Gervinus, Geschichte
der poetischen Nat. Lit. der Deutschen,
i. p. 99 et seqq.

the War of Troy (as no doubt his lost Antiocheis), is, in
verse, the romance history prevalent under the authority
of Dictys Cretensis and Dares Phrygius, during the
middle ages.[4] With other Poems of that class, it mingles in discordant confusion the wild adventures of the
romance writers, the long desultory tales and luxuriant
descriptions of the Trouvères, with the classical form of
verse. Throughout it is the Monk vainly labouring to
be the Bard; it is popular poetry cast in a form most
remote from popularity, not only in a language, but in
an artificial mould, which unfitted it for general acceptance. It was in truth the popular poetry of a small
class, the more learned of the clergy and of the Monks:
the unlearned of that class must still have sought, and
did seek, with the lay vulgar, their poetic enjoyment
from the vernacular minstrel or Trouvère. Latinised, it
was, as they no doubt thought, chastened and elevated
for their more pious and fastidious ears. Latin verse
condescended to this humbler office, little suspecting
that these popular songs contained elements of the true
poetic spirit, which would throw all the Latin epics of
the middle ages into irretrievable obscurity. Nothing
indeed could escape these all-appropriating indefatigable
versifiers of the cloister. Almost all the vernacular
poetry of the middle ages has its Latin counter-type,
poems of chivalry, poems of adventure, of course Saint-
Legends, even the long fables, which the Germans call
beast-poetry, and the amatory songs. The Latin version
of Reynard the Fox[5] has not been able, in the harsh

---

[4] Warton, in his History of English
Poetry, gives some spirited verses from
John of Exeter. The poem may be
read (it is hard reading) subjoined to
the edition of Dictys Cretensis and

Dares Phrygius. Amsterdam, 1702.

[5] Renardus Vulpes. Editio Princeps.
Edited by M. Mone. Stutgard et
Tubingæ, 1832.

and uncongenial form of Monkish elegiac verse, altogether to quench the drollery of the original. It was written by a man with a singular mastery over the barbarous but expressive Latin of his day, of extraordinary ingenuity in finding apt and fitting phrases for all the strange notions and combinations in this bestial allegory. But "Renardus Vulpes" is manifestly of a late period; it is a bitter satire on Monks and Monkery. The Wolf Isengrim is an Abbot: it contains passages violently and coarsely Anti-papal.[f] It belongs, the Latin version at least, rather perhaps to the class of satiric than of epic Latin poetry.

On the whole, this vast mass of Latin poetry offers no one exception to the eternal irrepealable law, that no great poet is inspired but in his native language. The Crusades were, perhaps happily, too late even to tempt the ambition of the Cloister poets. By that time, the art of Latin versification, if not lost, was not so common: the innate poetry of the subject breaks occasionally through the barbarous but spirited prose of William of Tyre and James de Vitry.

II. The poems on the Lives of the Saints, it might have been supposed, as treating on subjects in which the mythic and imaginative element of Christianity predominated, would at least display more freedom and originality. They were addressed to the higher emotions, which poetry delights to waken, wonder, sympathy, veneration, pity; they were legends in which noble men and beautiful women, Saints and Holy Vir-

Lives of the Saints.

---

[f] This alone would confute (if confutation were necessary) the theory of the editor M. Mone, who attributes the aim of the Satire to certain obscure personages in an obscure but early period in the history of Flemish Gaul. Note, p. 1 et seqq. The Flemish origin of the poem seems now proved, but the original was clearly Teutonic not Latin.

gins, were at issue with power, with cruelty, with fate.
The new poetic machinery of Angels and Devils was
at the command of the poet; the excited faith of the
hearers was ready to accept fiction for truth; to believe
the creation of the poet with unsuspecting belief. But
legend only reluctantly and ungraciously submitted to
the fetters of Latin verse; the artificial form seemed
to dull the inspiration. Even in the earliest period, the
Saint-Poems and the Martyrdoms (except perhaps some
pleasing descriptions in Paulinus of Nola) are, in my
judgement, far inferior, even in poetic merit, to the
prose legends. I know nothing equal to the "Martyrs of
Vienne," or the "Perpetua and Felicitas," even in the
best of Prudentius, who is in general insufferably long,
and suffocates all which is noble or touching (and there is
much of both) with his fatal copiousness. In later times
the lives of St. Boniface, St. Gall, and St. Anschar have
more of the imaginative tone of poetry than the hard
harsh verses of the period. I should almost say that the
Golden Legend awakens more of the emotion of poetry
than any of the poetic lives of the mediæval Saints.

III. Even in the Hymnology[s] of the Latin Church,
her lyric poetry, it is remarkable, that, with the exception of the Te Deum, those hymns, which have struck,
as it were, and cloven to the universal heart of Christendom, are mostly of a late period. The stanzas which
the Latin Church has handed down in her services from
Prudentius are but the flowers gathered from a wilderness of weeds.[b] The "Pange Lingua Gloriosi" is attri-

---

[s] Compare Thesaurus Hymnologi-
cus. H. A. Daniel. Halæ, 1841. A
copious and excellent collection.

[b] The two or three stanzas, 'Salvete
Flores Martyrum,' are from the middle

of a long, it must be confessed tiresome
Poem, Cathem. xii. v. 125. Praden-
tius, even in Germany, was the great
popular author of the Middle Ages; no
work but the Bible appears with so

buted to Venantius Fortunatus, or Mamertus Claudianus, in the fifth century; the "Stabat Mater" and the "Dies Iræ" are, the first probably by Jacopone da Todi, and the last by Thomas di Celano, in the fourteenth. These two, the one by its tenderness, the other by its rude grandeur, stand unrivalled; in melody, perhaps the hymn of St. Bonaventura to the Cross approaches nearest to their excellencies.[1] As a whole, the Hymnology of

many glosses (interpretations or notes) in high German, which show that it was a book of popular instruction. Rodolf Raumer, Einwirkung Christenthums auf die Altboch Deutsche Sprache, p. 222. — "Seine Hymnen und die des Ambrosius, bilden mit den übrigen Christlichen Lyrikern, das Gesangbuch des mittelalterlichen Kleros."—The hymns of Ambrose were translated into German in the ninth century.

[1] The two former are too well known to extract. Take two stanzas of the latter :—

"Recordare sanctæ crucis,
Qui perfectam viam ducis,
Delectare jugiter,
Sanctæ crucis recordare,
Et in ipsa meditare
Insatiabiliter.

"Quum quietus sui laboras,
Quando rhies, quando ploras,
Dolce sive gaudeas,
Quando vadis, quando venis,
In solatiis in pœnis
Crucem corde teneas."
—Apud Daniel, ii. p. 102.

Of the more general hymns I would select that for the Evening, the 'Deus Creator Omnium,' for its gentle cadence (p. 17); the Paschal Hymn of the Roman Breviary (usually the best), p. 83; In Exequiis Defunctorum (p. 137) :—

"Jam mœsta quiesce querela,
Lacrimas suspendite maires :

Nullus sua pignora plangat,
Mors hæc reparatio vitæ est.
Quidnam tibi saxa cavata,
Quid pulcra volunt monumenta
Res quod nisi creditur illis,
Non mortua, sed data somno."

Or, the two attributed to St. Bernard, p. 227 and 432, which show the height of his mysticism. Of what are called the Rhythms, by far the finest is that on Paradise, attributed, no doubt without ground, to St. Augustine, more likely by Damiani. It was never chanted in the church :—

"Ad perennis vitæ fontem mens sitivit arida,
Claustra carnis præsto frangi clausa quærit anima :
Gliscit, ambit, eluctatur exul frui frui patria?
Dum pressuris et ærumnis se gemit obnoxiam,
Quam amisit, dum deliquit, contemplatur gloriam,
Præsens malum auget boni perditi memoriam.

Nam quis promat summæ pacis quanta sit lætitia,
Ubi vivis margaritis surgunt ædificia,
Auro celsa micant tecta, radiant triclinia :
Solis gemmis pretiosis hæc structura nectitur,
Auro mundo, tanquam vitro, urbis via sternitur,
Abest limus, deest fimus, lues nulla cernitur.

Hiems horrens, æstas torrens illic numquam sæviunt,
Flos perpetuus rosarum ver agit perpetuum,
Candent lilia, rubescit crocus, sudat balsamum.

Virent prata, vernant sata, rivi mellis confluunt,

the Latin Church has a singularly solemn and majestic
tone. Much of it, no doubt, like the lyric verse of the
Greeks, was twin-born with the music; it is inseparably
wedded with the music; its cadence is musical rather
than metrical. It suggests, as it were, the grave full
tones of the chant, the sustained grandeur, the glorious
burst, the tender fall, the mysterious dying away of the
organ. It must be heard, not read. Decompose it into
its elements, coldly examine its thoughts, its images, its
words, its versification, and its magic is gone. Listen to
it, or even read it with the imagination or the memory
full of the accompanying chant, it has an unfelt and
indescribable sympathy with the religious emotions, even
of those of whose daily service it does not constitute a
part. Its profound religiousness has a charm to foreign
ears, wherever there is no stern or passionate resistance
to its power. In fact, all Hymnology, vernacular as
well as Latin, is poetry only to predisposed or habituated
ears. Of all the lyric verse on the noblest, it might be
supposed the most poetic subject, how few hymns take
their place in the poetry of any language.

But out of the Hymnology, out of the Ritual, of which
the hymns were a considerable part, arose that which
was the initiatory, if rude, form of religious tragedy.
The Christian Church made some bold advance to be
the theatre as well as the temple of the people. But it
had an intuitive perception of the danger; its success
appalled its religious sensitiveness. The hymn which,
like the Bacchic song of the Greeks, might seem

Pigmentorum spirat odor, liquor et aro-
matum,
Pendent poma floridorum nec lapsura ne-
morum.
Non alternat luna vices, sol vel cursus
siderum.

Agnus est felicis orbis lumen inocciduum,
Nox et tempus deerunt et, diem fert coun-
tinuum.
        —Daniel, I. p. 116; and in works of
        St. Augustine.
There are thirteen more stanzas.

developing into scenic action, and becoming a drama,
shrank back into its simpler and more lonely grandeur.
The Ritual was content to worship, to teach the facts of
the Scripture history only by the Biblical descriptions,
and its significant symbolic ceremonial.   Yet the Latin
Mysteries, no doubt because they were Latin, maintained
in general their grave and serious character.   It was
when, to increase its power and popularity, the Mystery
spoke in the vulgar tongue, that it became vulgar;[k]
then buffoonery, at first perhaps from rude simplicity,
afterwards from coarse and unrestrained fun, mingled with
the sacred subjects.   That which ought to have been the
highest, noblest tragedy, became tragi-comedy, and was
gradually driven out by indignant and insulted religion.

In its origin, no doubt the Mystery was purely and
essentially religious.   What more natural than to
attempt, especially as the Latin became more unfamiliar
to the common ear, the representation rather than the
description of the striking or the awful scenes of the
Gospel history, or those in the lives of the Saints; to
address the quick, awakened and enthralled eye, rather
than the dull and palled ear.[m]   There was already on
the walls, in the chapels, in the cloisters, the painting
representing the history, not in words, but in act; by
gesture, not by speech.   What a theatre!   Such religious uses could not desecrate buildings so profoundly
hallowed; the buildings would rather hallow the spectacle.   That theatre was the Church, soaring to its

---

[k] See in Walton (the passage is worth
reading) the dull buffoonery introduced
into the Mystery on the Murder of the
Innocents, performed by the English at
the Council of Constance.   This, however, must have been in Latin, but

probably from an English original.—
vol. ii. p. 75.

[m] "Segnius irritant animos demissa per
aurem
Quam quæ sunt oculis subjecta fi-
delibus."—A. P. l. 180.

majestic height, receding to its interminable length,
broken by its stately divisions, with its countless chapels,
and its long cloister, with its succession of concentric
arches. What space for endless variety, if not for
change of scene! How effective the light and shade,
even by daylight; how much more so heightened by the
command of an infinity of lamps, torches, tapers, now
pouring their full effulgence on one majestic object,
now showing rather than enlightening the deep gloom!
How grand the music, either pervading the whole space
with its rolling volumes of sound, or accompanying some
solemn or tender monologue! If it may be said without
offence, the Company was already enrolled, to a certain
degree practised, in the dramatic art; they were used to
enforce their words by significant gesture, by movement, by dress. That which was considered the great
leap in the Greek drama, the introduction of the second
actor, was already done: different parts of the service
were assigned to priest, or humbler deacon. The anti-
phonal chant was the choir breaking into two responsive
parts, into dialogue. There were those who recited the
principal parts; and, besides them the choir of men or
of boys, in the convent of females and young girls;
acolyths, mutes without number. Take, as an illustration of the effect of these dramas in their simple form,
the Massacre of the Innocents.[a] It opens with a procession of Innocents, doubtless children in white robes,
who march in long lines, rejoicing, through the long
cloister of the Monastery, and chanting, " How glorious

---

[a] Published by Mr. Wright—Early
Mysteries, London, 1838. Several
Latin Mysteries have been published in
Paris, but only a small number of copies
by Bibliographical Societies, and so not
of general access. But in truth the
Poem, the Mystery itself, forms a very
subordinate part of these representations.

is Thy Kingdom! Send down, O God, Thy Lamb."
The Lamb immediately appears; a man, with a banner,
bearing the Lamb, takes his place at their head, leading
them up and down, in long gleaming procession. Herod
(doubtless clad in all the splendour of barbaric and
Oriental attire) is seated on his throne. A squire
appears, hands him his sceptre, chanting, "On the
throne of David." In the mean time, an Angel alights
upon the manger, singing, "Joseph, Joseph, Joseph,
thou son of David;" and reciting the verse of the Gospel
commanding the flight into Egypt, "Weep not, O
Egypt." His armour-bearer informs Herod of the departure of the Wise Men: he bursts out into wrath.
While he is raging, the children are still following the
steps of the Lamb, and sweetly chanting.° Herod
delivers the fatal sword to his armour-bearer. The
Lamb is silently withdrawn; the children remain, in
their fearless innocence, singing, "Hail, Lamb of God!
O hail!" The mothers entreat mercy. An Angel
descends while the slain children are dying, while they
lie dead: "Ye who dwell in the dust, awake and cry
aloud!" The Innocents answer: "Why, O God, dost
thou not defend us from bloodshed?" The Angel
chants: "Wait but a little time till your number is
full." Then enters Rachel, with two women comforting
her: their musical dialogue is simple, wild, pathetic.ᵖ

° "Agno qui sancto pro nobis mortificato, ｜
splendorem patris, splendorem virgini-
tatis.
Offerimus Christo, sub signo rumbnis
isto."

ᵖ After her first lament they reply:—
"Noli, Virgo Rachel, noli dulcissima mater,
Pro nece parvorum fletus redinere do-
lorem,
Si quæ i- lataris exulta quæ lacrimaris,
Namque tui nati vivunt super astra
beati."

RACHEL dolens.
"Heu! hen! heu!
Quomodo gaudebo, dum mortua membra
videbo!
Dum sic communia furem per viscera tota;
Me faciunt verè pueri sine fine dolere!
O dolor, o patrum militisque gaudia ma-
trum!
Ad lugubres luctus lacrimarum favilte
fluctus,
Judicæ florem patriæ lacrimando dolorem"
After some more verses the consolations

VOL. IX.   N

As they lead off the sad mother, an Angel, hovering above, sings the antiphone, "Suffer little children to come unto me." At the voice of the Angel all the children enter the choir, and take up their triumphant song. Herod disappears; Archelaus is on his throne. The Angel summons Joseph and the Virgin from Egypt. Joseph breaks out into a hymn to the Virgin. The cantor of the Church intones the Te Deum; the whole Church rings with the august harmony.

I have chosen this brief and simple episode, as it were, in the Gospel, to show in what spirit, with what aim, and doubtless with what wonderful effect, these sacred representations were introduced in the Middle Ages.⁴ But there was no event, however solemn and

---

end:—

"Numquid Herodem est iste
Qui regnum possidet coeleste!
Quisque preces frequente
Miseris fratribus
Apud Deum auxiliator."

Was Rachel represented by a male or a female? A Nun deploring the loss of her children had been somewhat incongruous: Did the Monks and Nuns ever join their companies? In one stage direction it appears the women were personated by men. "Primum prorodunt tres fratres præparati et vestiti in similitudinem trium Mariarum."— Mysterium Resurrectionis, quoted by M. Onésime de Roy, Mystères, p. 4.

"Gaude, gaude, gaude—
Maria Virgo, cunctas hæreses," &c.

⁴ A recent publication of the great Thuringian Mystery of the Wise and Foolish Virgins (Halle, 1855), deserves especial notice. Not only is this Mystery (performed at Eisenach, A.D. 1322, not in a Church, but in an open space adjoining), remarkable for its poetic beauty, for the mixture, as it seems, of Latin Responsives and Sequences, with the chief passages in the dialect of Thuringia; but as having caused the death of Frederick the Joyous (Friederich der Freudige), Landgrave of Thuringia. The characters are the Saviour, the Virgin Mary, a Choir of Angels, the Wise and Foolish Virgins. There seems to have been a representation, at least, of the opening of hell, into which Lucifer and Beelzebub drag down the miserable Foolish Virgins, shrieking "Woe, woe!" as in a Greek tragedy. But the most remarkable part of this remarkable Poem is, that Frederick the Joyous is not struck to death by his compassion for the Foolish Virgins, or by his horror at their fate: but for his wrath and indignation, that the intercessory prayers of the Blessed Virgin in their favour are ineffectual, and do not at once prevail with her inexorable Son. This wrath and indignation in a few days brought on an apoplectic seizure, under which Frederick lingered, and died in two or three years.

appalling, up to the Passion, the Resurrection, the
Ascension, which was not in like manner wrought into
action, and preached in this impressive way to awe-struck
crowds.   Legend, like the Gospels, lent itself to the
same purpose: instead of being read, it was thrown into
a stirring representation, and so offered to spectators as
well as to hearers. When all were believers (for those
who had not the belief of faith and love, had that of
awe and fear), these spectacles no doubt tended most
powerfully to kindle and keep alive the religious interest; to stamp upon the hearts and souls of men the
sublime truths, as well as the pious fictions of religion.
What remains, the dry skeleton of these Latin mysteries, can give no notion of what they were when alive;
when alive, with all their august, impressive, enthralling
accessories, and their simple, unreasoning, but pro-
foundly-agitated hearers.   The higher truths, as well as
the more hallowed events of our religion, have in our
days retired into the reverential depths of men's hearts
and souls: they are to be awfully spoken, not, what
would now be thought too familiarly, brought before
our eyes. Christian tragedy, therefore, could only exist
in this early initiatory form.   The older Sacred history
might endure to be poeticised in a dramatic form, as in
the 'Samson Agonistes;' it might even, under certain
circumstances, submit to public representation, as in the
Esther and Athalie of Racine, and the Saul of Alfieri.
A martyrdom like that of Polyeucte might furnish
noble situations. But the history of the Redeemer, the
events on which are founded the solemn mysteries of
our religion, must be realised only, as it were, behind
the veil; they will endure no alteration, no amplification, not the slightest change of form or word: with

N 2

them as with the future world, all is an object of " faith,
not of sight." [r]

---

[r] Since the publication of this work I have had the great good fortune to be present at the performance of the last of the ancient mysteries, which still lingers in Europe, the Passion Spiel, by the peasants of the Ammergau. No one who has not actually seen such a representation can fully and justly imagine the character and influence of these Mediæval plays. During my early life I have seen the drama in all its forms, as exhibited in the most splendid theatres of Europe. I have never witnessed a performance more striking from its scenic effect: the richness and harmony of the decorations and dresses, brilliant and blended in their colours as in an old Italian picture (by Gentile da Fabriano); the music, though this was of a modern cast (much was chanted by a chorus or semichorus alternating, as on the Greek stage); and the general sustained interest and impressiveness of the whole. There was nothing, I think, which could offend the most sensitive religiousness. All was serious, solemn, I may say devout; actors and audience were equally in earnest. The Saviour himself was represented with a quiet gentle dignity, admirably contrasting with the wild life and tumult, the stern haughty demeanour of the Pharisees and rulers in their secret plottings and solemn council (the Sanhedrin,) and the frantic agitation of the Jewish people. Even in the most perilous passages — the washing the feet of the disciples — there was no departure from the commanding repose of the Master. The one or two comic touches (no doubt the coarser jests and rude peasantries have been refined away by the greater fastidiousness of modern manners),— the greedy grasping of Judas after the pieces of silver; the eager quarrelling of the Roman soldiers, throwing dice for the seamless coat, did not disturb the general grave impressiveness, but rather gave a certain reality to the scene. Legend, too, had entirely dropped away; it was the evangelic history cast, with no mean skill, into a dramatic form. I never passed a day (it lasted from 7 in the morning till 3 in the afternoon,) in more absorbed and unwearied attention. The theatre was not roofed over by human hands, but with the bright blue sky above, at the bottom of a green valley, flanked by picturesque mountains, which closed in the remoter distance. And to crown the whole, on that occasion, the day, which had been bright, gradually darkened; the clouds in their thick heavy masses rolled slowly down the mountain sides, looming blacker and blacker, till just at the moment of the Crucifixion, the storm — the thunderstorm — burst, in awful grandeur. It disturbed, but did not close the drama; there was some confusion, especially among the audience, who were most exposed (we were under partial shelter). But the end, if hurried, was still grave, serious, and conscientiously carried on to the close, the Resurrection, and the appearance of the Lord to the Disciples.

I was assured that the moral and religious effect on the peasants them-

The Abbess of a German convent made a more extraordinary attempt to compel the dramatic art into the
service of Latin Christianity. The motive of Hroswitha,
declared by herself, is not less strange than her design.[*]
It was to wean the age (as far as we can judge, the
age included the female sex—it included nuns, even
the nuns of her own rigid order) from the fatal admiration of the licentious comedy of Rome.[1] "There are
persons," writes the saintly recluse, "who prefer the
vanity of heathen books to the Sacred Scriptures, and
beguiled by the charms of the language, are constantly
reading the dangerous fictions of Terence, and defile
their souls with the knowledge of wicked actions."
There is a simplicity almost incredible, but, from its
incredibility, showing its perfect simplicity, in Hroswitha's description not only of her motives but of her
difficulties. The holy poetess blushes to think that she
too must dwell on the detestable madness of unlawful
love, and the fatally tender conversations of lovers. If
however she had listened to the voice of modesty, she
could not have shown the triumph of divine Grace, as
of course Grace in every case obtains its signal triumph.
Each of the comedies, instead of its usual close, a marriage, ends with the virgin or the penitent taking the
vow of holy celibacy. But in the slender plots the
future saints are exposed to trials which it must have
been difficult to represent, even to describe, with
common decency. Two relate to adventures in which

gives was excellent. Of the audience I
could judge : and it was an audience
gathered from all quarters, many more
than could obtain accommodation. No
one (the preparations last for a year or
two) is permitted to appear, even in
the chorus, unless of unimpeachable
character.

[*] These plays have been recently
edited and translated into French with
great care by M. Magnin.—Théâtre de
Hroswitha. Paris, 1845.

[1] Hroswitha wrote also a long poem
in hexameters, Panegyris Oddonum.

holy hermits set forth in the disguise of amorous youths,
to reclaim fallen damsels, literally from the life of a
brothel, and bear them off in triumph, but not without
resistance, from their sinful calling. Of course the
penitents become the holiest of nuns. And the curious
part of the whole seems to be that these plays on such
much more than dubious subjects should not only have
been written by a pious abbess, but were acted in the
convent, possibly in the chapel of the convent. This is
manifest from the stage directions, the reference to stage
machinery, the appearance and disappearance of the
actors. And nuns, perhaps young nuns, had to per-
sonate females whose lives and experiences were certainly most remote from convent discipline.* The plays
are written in prose, probably because in those days the
verse of Terence was thought to be prose: they are
slight, but not without elegance of style derived, it
should seem, from the study of that perilously popular
author, whom they were intended to supersede. There
are some strange patches of scholastic pedantry, a long
scene on the theory of music, another on the mystery
of numbers, with some touches of buffoonery, strange
enough, if acted by nuns before nuns, more strange if
acted by others, or before a less select audience, in a
convent. A wicked heathen, who is rushing to commit
violence on some Christian virgins, is, like Ajax, judicially blinded, sets to kissing the pots and pans, and
comes out with his face begrimed with black, no doubt
to the infinite merriment of all present. The theatre of
Hroswitha is indeed a most curious monument of the
times.

---

* See note of M. Magnin (p. 457), in answer to Price, the editor of Warton, ii. 28. M. Magnin has studied with great industry the origin of the
Theatre in Europe.

No wonder that the severer Churchmen took alarm,
and that Popes and Councils denounced these theatric
performances, which, if they began in reverent sanctity,
soon got beyond the bounds not merely of reverence,
but of decency. But, like other abuses, the reiteration
of the prohibition shows the inveterate obstinacy and
the perpetual renewal of the forbidden practice.[x] The
rapid and general growth of the vernacular Mysteries,
rather than the inhibition of Pope and Council, drove
out the graver and more serious Latin Mysterics, not
merely in Teutonic countries—in England and Germany—but in France, perhaps in Italy.[y]

Latin, still to a certain extent the vernacular language
of the Church and of the cloister, did not confine itself
to the grave epic, the hymn, or the Mystery which
sprang out of the hymn. The cloisters had their
poetry, disguised in Latin to the common ear, and often
needing that disguise. Among the most curious,
original, and lively of the monkish Latin poems, are
those least in harmony with their cold ascetic discipline.
Anacreontics and satires sound strangely, though inter-
mingled with moral poems of the same cast, among the

---

[x] The prohibitions show that the
ancient use of masks was continued :—
" Interdum ludi fiunt in ecclesia theatrales, et non solum ad ludibriorum
spectacula introducuntur in eis mon-
stra larvarum, verùm etiam in aliqui-
bus festivitatibus diaconi, presbyteri ac
subdiaconi insaniæ suæ ludibria exercere præsumunt, mandamus, quatenus
ne per hujusmodi turpitudinem eccle-
siæ inquinetur honestas, prælibatum
ludibriorum consuetudinem, vel potius
corruptelam curetis a vestris ecclesiis
extirpare."—Decret. Greg. Borhmer,
Corpus Juris Canon. t. II. fol. 418.—

" Item, non permittant sacerdotes, ludos theatrales fieri in ecclesia et alios
ludos inhonestos."—Conc. Trev. A.D.
1227. Hartzheim, III. p. 529. Compare Synod Diœc. Worm. A.D. 1316.
Ibid. iv. p. 258.

[y] Mary Magdalene was a favourite
character in these dramas. Her earlier
life was by no means disguised or softened. See the curious extract from a
play partly Latin, partly German, published by Dr. Hoffman, Fundgruben
für Geschichte Deutschen Sprache,
quoted by Mr. Wright. Preface to
'Early Mysteries.' London, 1838.

disciples of S. Benedict, S. Bernard, and S. Francis. If
the cloister had its chronicle and its hymn-books, it
often had its more profane song-book, and the songs
which caught the ear seem to have been propagated
from convent to convent.[a] The well-known convivial
song, attributed to Walter de Mapes, was no doubt
written in England; it is read in the collection of a
Bavarian convent.[a] These, and still more, the same
satires, are found in every part of Latin Christendom;
they rise up in the most unexpected quarters, usually in
a kind of ballad metre, to which Latin lends itself with
a grotesque incongruity, sometimes with Leonine,
sometimes with more accurate rhyme. The Anacreontic
Winebibber's song, too well known to be quoted at
length, by no means stands alone: the more joyous
monks had other Bacchanalian ditties, not without fancy
and gay harmony.[b]

---

[a] Among the collections which I have
read or consulted on this prolific subject are the old one, of Flaccius Illyricus.—Early Mysteries and other Latin
Poems, by Thomas Wright, London,
1838.—Lateinische Gedichte des X.
und XI. J. H., von Grimm und Axel.
Schmeller. Göttingen, 1838.—Poëvias
Populaires Latines du Moyen Age. Edelstan du Meril. Paris, 1847.—Populær
Songs.—Poems of Walter de Mapes.
Camden Society by Thomas Wright.

[a] This Collection, the ' Carmina Benedicto-Burana ' (one of the most curious publications of the Stuttgard
Union), the Latin Book of Ballads, it
may be called, of the Convent of Benedict Buren, contains many love-verses,
certainly of no ascetic tendency; and
this, among many other of the coarser
monkish satires.

[b] " Mihi est propositum in tabernâ mori,
Vinum sit appositum morientis ori,
Ut dicant cum venerint Angelorum
chori,
Deus sit propitius huic potatori."

" Ave i color vini clari,
Dulcis potus non amari,
Tua nos inebriari
Digneris potentiâ.
O quam felis creatura,
Quam produxit vitis pura,
Omnis mensa sit secura
In tuâ præsentiâ.

O i quam pincens in colore !
O i quam fragrans in odore !
O i quam sapidum in ore !
Indoe linguæ vinculum !
Felix venter quem inicabis !
Felix guttur quod rigabis !
Felix os quod tu lavabis !
Et beata labia !

Ergo vinum collaudemus !
Potatores exaltemus !
Non potantes confundamus
In æterna supplicia ! "
—Wright, p. 120.

The Anacreons of the cloister did not sing only of
wine : they were not silent on that subject, least appro-
priate, but seemingly not least congenial, to men under
the duty, if not under the vow, of perpetual chastity.
From the variety and number of these poems, which
appear scattered about as freely and carelessly as the
moral poems and satires, it might seem that there was
a constant interchange between the troubadour or the
minnesinger and the ecclesiastic or the monk. Many
of the amatory Latin poems are apparently versions,
many the originals of those sung by the popular poets
in the vulgar tongue ; and there can be no doubt about
the authorship of most of the Latin poems. They were
the growth as they were the amusement of the cloister.
They were written for the monks and clergy, to whom
alone they were intelligible. It may suffice in a grave
history (which, however, as endeavouring to reveal the
whole character of past times, cannot altogether decline
such topics) to select one of the most curious, certainly
the most graceful of the poems of this class, in its
language at least, if not altogether in its moral, inoffen-
sive. It is a kind of Eclogue, in which two fair damsels,
Phyllis and Flora, one enamoured of a Knight, the
other of a Clerk, contend for the superior merit of their
respective lovers, and submit their cause to the decision
of the old heathen god, Cupid. The time of this Idyl
is a beautiful noon in spring, its scene a flowery meadow,
under the cool shade of a pine by a murmuring stream.[c]

---

[c] It is in the Carmina Benedicto-
burana, p. 155:—

6.

" Susurrabat modicum
Ventus temperativus,
locus erat viridi
gramine festivus,

et in ipso gramine
defluebat rivus,
brevis atque garrulo
Murmure lascivus.

7.

Ut puellis nocent
Calor nolis minus
fuit juxta rivulum
Spatiosa pinus

The fair champion of the knight taunts the indolence,
the luxuriousness, the black dress and shaven crown of
the clerk. She dwells on the valour, noble person,
bravery, and glory of the knight: the champion of the
clerk, on his wealth, superior dignity, even his learning.
His tonsure is his crown of dominion over mankind; he
is the sovereign of men: the knight is his vassal.[d]
After some dispute, they mount, one a fine mule, the
other a stately palfrey, and set off, both splendidly
accoutred, to the Court of the God of Love. The
Paradise of Cupid is described rapidly, but luxuriantly,
with much elegance, and a profusion of classical lore.

venustata foliis,
late pandens sinus,
nec intrare poterat
calor peregrinus.

2.

Comedere virginm,
Herba eadem dedit,
Phillis prope rivulum,
Flora longe sedet,
Et dum sedet utrisque
ac in aeve redit,
amor corda vulnerat
et utrumque ladit.

3.

Amor uni interius
latens et occultus,
et corde certissimos
elicit singultus,
pallor genas inficit,
alternatur vultus,
sed in verecundia
furor est sepultus."

[d] I omit other objections of Phyllis
to a clerical lover. This is the worst
she can say:—

37.

"Orbem cum laetificat
hora lucis festae,
tunc apparet clericus
satis inhoneste,
in tonsura capitis
et in atra veste
portans testimonium
voluntatis maestae."

To this Flora rejoins :—

37.

" Non dicas opprobrium
si cognoscas mores,
vestem nigram clerici
carnem breviorem ;
habet ista clericus
ad communem bonorum,
ut esse similis et
omnibus majorem.

38.

Universa clerico
Constat esse prona,
et signum imperii
portat in corona,
imperat militibus,
et largitur dona,
famulante major est
imperans persona.

39.

otiosum clericum
semper esse juras,
vitae spernit operas
fateor et duras,
sed cum ejus solimus
Evolat ad curas,
coeli vias dividit
et rerum naturas.

40.

Mens est in purpura
tuus in lorica ;
tuus est in praelio
meus in lectica,
ubi facta principum
recolit antiqua,
scribit, querit, cogitat—
totum de amica. "

Silenus is not forgotten. The award is in favour of the
clerk; an award which designates him as fitter for love:
and this award is to be valid to all future times.* Few
will question whence came this poem: that any layman
should be so studious, even in irony, of clerical interests,
can scarcely be suspected. If the ballad poetry of a
people, or of a time, be the best illustration of their
history, this poem, without doubt, is significant enough.

It were unjust not to add that there is a great mass
of this rhyme, not less widely dispersed, of much more
grave and religious import—poems which embody the
truths and precepts of the faith, earnest admonitions on
the duties of the clergy, serious expostulations on the
sufferings and oppressions of the poor, moral reflections
on the times. The monkish poets more especially
dwelt on the Crusades. Though there was no great
poem on the subject, there were songs of triumph at
every success—at every disaster a wild poetic wail.†
The Crusade was perpetually preached in verse, half
hymn, half war-song.‡

Yet, after all, the strength of these Monk-Poets was

---

* The close is delightfully naïve. I
must only subjoin the award:—

78.

" Fient et justitiæ,
ventilant vigorem
ventilant et retrahunt
Curiæ rigorem
secundum actentiam
et secundum morem.

79.

ad amorem clericum
dicant optiorem.
Comprobavit curia,
distinxere juris.
et teneri voluit
etiam futuris."

This poem is also in Mr. Wright's
English collection, who has subjoined
a translation of the time of Queen

Elizabeth, with very many of the
beauties, some of the faults of that
age.

† Carmina Benedicto-Burana, xxii.
to xxviii.:—

" Agedum Christicola,
surge vide
Ne de fide
reputeris frivola,
suda martyr in agone,
ape mercedis et corone,
derelicta Babylone
pugna,
pro cœlesti regione
et ad vitam te compone
Pugna."

‡ See xxvi. on the conquests of Sa-
ladin; and in Edelstan du Méril's Collection—" Lætare Hierusalem."

in satire. They have more of Juvenal, if not of his
majestic march and censorial severity, of his pitilessness,
of his bitterness, it may be said of his truculency, than
of Catullus, Terence, or Horace. The invectives against
Rome, against her pride, avarice, venality—against
Popes and Cardinals—against the Hierarchy, its pomp,
its luxury—against the warlike habits of the Prelates,
the neglect of their holy duties—even against the
Monks—put to the test their rude nerve and vigour;
and these poems in the same or in similar strain turn
up out of the convent libraries in many parts of Germany,
in France, in England, in every country beyond the
Alps (Italy mostly expressed her Antipapal passions in
other ways). They are of all ages; they have the merit
that they are the outpourings of overburthened hearts,
and are not the frigid and artificial works of mechanics
in Latin verse; they are genial even in their ribaldry;
they are written by men in earnest, bitterly deploring
or mercilessly scourging the abuses of the Church.
Whether from righteous indignation or malignity, from
moral earnestness or jealousy and hatred of authority,
whether its inspiration was holy and generous or sordid
and coarse, or, as in most human things, from mingling
and contradictory passions, the monkish Latin satire
maintained its unretracted protest against the Church.
The Satirists impersonated a kind of bold reckless antagonist against Rome and the hierarchy,[h] confounding

[h] Mr. Wright has abundantly proved
this in his preface to the poems of
Walter de Mapes. (Introd. p. ix.,
&c.) He is equally successful, according to my judgement, in depriving
of the glory, or relieving from the reproach, of these compositions the celebrated Walter de Mapes. De Mapes
had a feud with the Cistercians or
White Monks, and did not spare his
enemies; but he was not Golias. Under that name ranked bards of a considerable period, and in my opinion of
more than one country. Mr. Wright
is not so satisfactory in claiming them
all for England; one poem seems to

together in their Golias, as Rabelais in later days, solemnity and buffoonery, pedantic learning and vulgar humour, a profound respect for sacred things and freedom of invective against sacred persons. The Goliards became a kind of monkish rhapsodists, the companions and rivals of the Jongleurs (the reciters of the merry and licentious fabliaux); Goliardery was a recognised kind of mediæval poetry. Golias has his Metamorphoses, his Apocalypse, his terrible Preachment, his Confession,[i] his Complaint to the Pope, his Address to the Roman Court, to the impious Prelates, to the Priests of Christ, to the Prelates of France; and, finally, a Satire on women, that is, against taking a wife, instinct with true monastic rigour and coarseness. Towards the Pope himself—though Golias scruples not to arraign his avarice, to treat his Bulls with scorn—there is yet some awe.[k] I doubt if

---

show itself written in Pavia. Compare the copy of the Confession in Wright (p. 71), and the Carmina Benedicto-Burana (p. 57).

[i] The Confession contains the famous drinking song. The close is entirely different, and shows the sort of common property in the poems. Both poems mention Pavia. Yet the English copy names the Bishop of Coventry, the German "the Elect of Cologne," as Diocesan.

[k] I have already quoted the lines in one of those songs in which he derives the word Papa, by apocope, from pagare, "pay, pay." In his complaint to the Pope, Golias is a poor clerical scholar poet:—

"Tange tibi, pastor bone,
Si divina lectione
Spretâ flam laicus,
Vel absolve clericatu,
Vel fac ut in ci-ri statu,
Prævertem clericus,
Dulcis erit mihi status,
Si prebenda muneratus

Reddita vel alio,
Vivam licet non laboande,
Saltem mihi detur unde,
Studeam de proprio."

From a very different author in a different tone is the following:—

1.

"Die XII veritas,
Dic cara raritas,
Dic rara charitas,
Ubi nunc habitas?
Aut in valle Visionis,
Aut in throno Pharaonis,
Aut in alto cum Nerone,
Aut in antro cum Timone,
Vel in viscella scirpea
Cum Moyse plorante,
Vel in domo Romulea
Cum bulla fulminante.

2.

Bulla fulminante
Sub judice tonante,
Reo appellante,
Sententia gravante,
Veritas opprimitur,
Distrahitur et renditur,
Justitia prostante,
Itur et recurritur
Ad curiam, nec ante
Quis quid consequitur
Inæ exuitur
Ultimo quadrante.

the Roman Pontiff was yet to the fiercest of these poets, as to the Albigensians and to the Spiritual Franciscans, Antichrist. The Cardinals meet with less respect; that excessive and proverbial venality, which we have heard denounced century after century, is confirmed, if it needed confirmation, by these unsparing satirists.[m]

The Bishops are still arraigned for their martial habits,[n] their neglect of their sacred functions, their pride, their venality, their tyranny. Some were married: this and universal concubinage is the burthen of the complaint against the Clergy.[o] The Satirists are stern monks to others, however their amatory poetry may tell against

---

[3.]

[m] " Respondit Caritas
Homo quid dubitas,
Quid me sollicitas ?
Non sum quod putas,
Nec in rure, nec in amaro,
Nec in foro, nec in claustro,
Nec in byrso, nec in cuculla,
Nec in brilo, nec in bulla
De Jericho sum veniens
Ploro cum sauciato,
Quem duplex levi transiens
Non sublili grabato."
Carmina Benedicto-Burana, p. 61.

One of these stanzas is contained in a long poem made up very uncritically from a number of small poems (in Flaccius Illyricus, p. 29, &c.) on Papal absolution and Indulgences :—

" Nos peccata relaxamus
Absolutos collocamus
Sedibus ethereis,
Nec habemus nostras leges,
Alligantes omnes reges
In manicis aureis."
Carm., B. B., p. 11.

[n] See the Poem de Ruina Romæ.
Wright, p. 217. Carmina B. B. 16 :—

3.

" Vidi vidi caput mundi
instar maris et profundi
Vorax guttur Scylli ;
ibi mundi bithalassus,
ibi sorbet aurum Crassus
et argentum sæculi.
* * *

---

ibi pugna galearum
et concursus piratarum
id est cardinalium.
* * *

23.

Cardinales ut prædixi,
Novo jure Crucifixi
Vendunt patrimonium,
Petrus foris, intus Nero,
intus lupa, foris vero
sicut agni ovium."

This is but a sample of these Poems.

[n] " Episcopi cornuti
Conticuere muti,
ad prædam sunt parati
et indecenter coronati
pro virga ferunt lanceam,
pro infula galeam,
clipeum pro stola,
(hæc mortis erit mola)
loricam pro alba,
hæc occasio calva,
pellem pro humerali,
pro ritu seculari
Silent fortes inveniunt,
et a Deo discordant," &c.

Carm. B. Burana, p. 15. Compare Wright, Sermo Golia ad Prælatos, p. 48.

[o] " Nec in participes
Conjugiæ vitæ vitio
Namque multos invenio
qui sunt hujus participes,
ecclesiarum principes."

themselves.[p] The Archdeacons' Court is a grievance which seems to have risen to a great height in England. Henry II. we have heard bitterly complaining against its abuses: it levied enormous sums on the vices of the people, which it did not restrain.[q] All are bitterly reproached with the sale of the services of the Church, even of the Sacraments.[r] The monks do not escape; but it seems rather a quarrel of different Orders than a general denunciation of all.

The terrible preachment of Golias on the Last Judgement ought not to be passed by. The rude doggrel rises almost to sublimity as it summons all alike before the Judge, clerk as well as layman; and sternly cuts off all reply, all legal quibble, all appeal to the throne of St. Peter. The rich will find no favour before Him who is the Judge, the Author of the sentence, the Witness. God the Judge will judge Judges, he will judge Kings; be

---

[p] " O sacerdos haec responde,
qui frequenter et jocunde
cum uxore dormis, unde
Mane surgens, missam dicis,
corpus Christi benedicis,
post amplexus meretricis,
minus quam tu peccatricis.

*   *   *   *

Miror ego, miror plane
quod sub lito latet pane
Corpus Christi, quod prophana
Tractat manus illa mane,
Miror, nisi te mireris,
quod a terrā non aufferis,
cumque saepe prohiberis
Iterare non vereris."
— Wright, pp. 49, 50.

[q] Compare in Wright the three curious poems, De Concubinis Sacerdotum, Consultatio Sacerdotum, Convocatio Sacerdotum, pp. 171, 174, 180.

[r] " Ecce capitinium legi de moribus
Archidiaconi, qui sola vicibus
quicquid a praesulis evadit manibus
Capit et lacerat rostris et ungulbus.

Hic plenus orulis sedet ad synodum,
Lynx ad timidias, Janus ad commodum,

Argus ad anima welus omnimodum,
in Polyphemus est ad artis metodum.

Doctorum statuit decreta mililum,
Quorum est pondus supra jus jorium,
Unum qui solverit, reus est omnium,
Nisi resolverit prius marsuplum.

*   *   *   *   *

Ecclesiastica jura venalia,
facti propatulo, sed venialia
cum venium dederit, vocal a veniā
quam non invenions venit Ecclesia."
—Wright, p. 9.

[s] " Jacet ordo clericalis
in respectu laicalis,
spina Christi fit mercalis
generosa generalia
Vepunat altaria,
venit eucharistia,
cum sit mgatoria
gratis venalis."
— Carmin, B. Burana, p. 41.

This and the following poems dwell on simony of all kinds. See the Poem De Grisis Monachis, Wright, p. 54. De Claravallensibus et Clunisacensibus, ib. p. 237. De Malis Monachorum, 157.

he Bishop or Cardinal, the sinner will be plunged into the stench of hell. There will be no fee for Bull or Notary, no bribe to Chamberlain or Porter. Prelates will be delivered up to the most savage tormentors; their life will be eternal death.[*]

History throughout these centuries bore on its face that it was the work not of the statesman or the warrior, unless of the Crusader or of the warrior Bishop, it was that of the Monk. It is universally Latin during the earlier period: at first indeed in Italy, in Latin which may seem breaking down into an initiatory Romance or Italian. Erchempert and the Salernitan Chronicle, and some others of that period, are barbarous beyond later barbarism. When history became almost the exclusive property of the Monks, it was written in their Latin, which at least was a kind of Latin. Most of the earlier Chronicles were intended each to be a universal history for the instruction of the brotherhood. Hence monkish historians rarely begin lower than the Creation or the Deluge. According to the erudition of the writer, the historian is more or less diffuse on the pre-Christian History, and that of the Cæsars. As the writers approach their own age, the brief Chronicle expands and registers at first all that relates to the institution and interests of the monastery, its

Latin history.

---

[*] " Quid dicturi miseri sumus ante thronum,
Ante tantum judicem, ante summum
bonum;
Tunc non erit aliquis locus hic pec-
corum,
Cum nostrorum præmia rediet ac-
tionum.
Cum perventum fuerit examen veri,
Ante thronam stabimus judicis severi,
Nec erit distinctio laici vel cleri.
Nulla nos exceptio poterit meri.
Hic non erit licitum qulequam alle-
gare,
Neque jus replicare, neque replicare,
Nec ad Apostolicam sedem appellare,

Reus tunc damnabitur, nec dicetur
quare.
Contitate divites qui vel quales estis.
Quod in hac judicio facere potestis;
Tunc non erit aliquis locus hic Digestis,
Idem erit Deus hic judex, autor, testis.
Judicabit judices judex generalis,
Nihil ibi proderit dignitas regalis;
Sed factorem mittet parvae gehennalis,
Sive ait Episcopus, sive Cardinalis,
Nihil ibi dabitur bullæ vel scriptori.
Nihil camerario, nihil janitori;
Nec dabuntur præmia pessimo tortori,
Quibus erit vivere sine fine mori."
—Wright, p. 52.

founders and benefactors, their lives and miracles, and
condescends to admit the affairs of the times in due subordination. But there is still something of the legend.
Gradually, however, the actual world widens before the
eyes of the monkish historian; present events in which
he, his monastery, at all events the Church, are mingled,
assume their proper magnitude. The universal-history
preface is sometimes actually discarded, or shrinks into a
narrower compass. He is still a chronicler; he still,
as it were, surveys everything from within his convent-
walls; but the world has entered within his convent. The
Monk has become a Churchman, or the Churchman,
retired into the monastery, become almost an historian.
The high name of Historian, indeed, cannot be claimed
for any mediæval Latin writer; but as chroniclers of
their own times (their value is entirely confined to their
own times; on the past they are merely servile copyists
of the same traditions) they are invaluable.[1] Their very
faults are their merits. They are full of, and therefore
represent the passions, the opinions, the prejudices, the
partialities, the animosities of their days. Every kingdom, every city in Italy, in Germany every province,
has its chronicler.[2] In England, though the residence
of the chronicler, the order to which he belongs, and the
office which he occupies, are usually manifest, it is more
often the affairs of the realm which occupy the annals.
France, or rather the Franco-Teutonic Empire, began
with better promise; Eginhard has received his due
praise; the Biographers of Louis the Pious, Thegan, and
the Astronomer, may be read with pleasure as with instruction: Nithard falls off. In England Matthew Paris,

[1] E.g. in the Saxon Chronicle.
[2] To characterise the Chronicles, even those of the different nations, would
be an endless labour.

or rather perhaps Roger of Wendover, takes a wider range: he travels beyond the limits of England; he almost aspires to be a chronicler of Christendom. The histories of the Crusades are lively, picturesque, according as they come directly from the Crusaders themselves. Perhaps the most elaborate, William of Tyre, being a compilation, is least valuable and least effective. Lambert of Hertzfield (vulgarly of Aschaffenburg) in my judgement occupies, if not the first, nearly the first place, in mediæval history. He has risen at least towards the grandeur of his subject. Our own chroniclers, Westminster, Knighton, and Walsingham, may vie with the best of other countries. As to their Latinity, Saxo Grammaticus, the Sicilian Ugo Falcandus, command a nobler and purer style.

Yet after all the Chronicle must, to attain its perfection, speak in the fresh picturesqueness, the freedom, and the energy of the new vernacular languages. The Latin, though in such universal use, is a foreign, a conventional tongue even among Churchmen and in the monastery. Statesmen, men of business, men of war, must begin to relate the affairs of States, the adventures and events of war. For the perfect Chronicle we must await Villehardouin, Joinville, Froissart. Villani is more than a chronicler; he is approaching to the historian.

CHAPTER V.

Christian Letters in the New Languages of Europe.

CHRISTIANITY, indeed, must await, and not in history alone, the creation, growth, perfection of new languages, before she can become the parent of genuine Christian letters and arts—of letters and arts which will maintain permanent influence and ascendancy over the mind of man. But the abrogation of the Latin as the exclusive language of Christian letters and arts must be inevitably and eventually the doom of Latin Christianity. Latin must recede more and more into a learned language understood by the few. It may linger in the religious service of all who adhere to the Church of Rome, not absolutely unintelligible to those whose language is of Latin descent, and among them with a kind of mysterious and venerable indistinctness not unfavourable to religious awe. The Latin is a congenial part of that imposing ritual system which speaks by symbolic gestures and genuflexions, by dress, by music, by skilful interchange of light and darkness, by all which elevates, soothes, rules the mind through the outward senses. A too familiar Liturgy and Hymnology might disturb this vague, unreasoning reverence. With the coarsest and most vulgar Priesthood these services cannot become altogether vulgar; and except to the strongest or most practical minds, the clear and the definite are often fatal to the faith. Yet for popular instruction either from the Pulpit or through the Printing Press, Christianity

o 2

must descend, as it does descend, to the popular language. In this respect Latin has long discharged its mission—it is antiquated and obsolete.

But while the modern languages of Europe survive; and we can hardly doubt the vitality of French, Italian, Spanish, German, and our own English (now the vernacular tongue of North America and Australia, that too of government and of commerce in vast regions of Africa and Asia), the great Christian writers, Dante, Ariosto, Tasso, Calderon; Pascal, Bossuet, and the pulpit orators of France, with Corneille and Racine; the German Bible of Luther, the English Bible, Shakspeare, Milton, Schiller, some of our great divines, Hooker, Jeremy Taylor, will only die with the languages in which they wrote. Descartes, Bacon, Locke, Reid, Kant, will not share the fate of the scholastic philosophers, till the French, English, and German are to new races of men what mediæval Latin is to us. And religion must speak to mankind in the dominant languages of mankind.

It might seem indeed that in the earliest Latin as distinguished from the Teutonic languages, the Romance in its various forms, Sicilian, Italian, Catalan, Provençal, poetry, the primal form of vernacular literature was disposed to break loose from Latin Christianity, from hierarchical unity, even from religion. The Clergy in general remained secluded or shrunk back into the learned Latin; the popular poetry, even the popular prose, became profane, unreligious, at length in some part irreligious. The Clergy, as has been seen, for their own use and amusement, transmuted much of the popular poetry into Latin, but it ceased thereby to be popular except among themselves. They shut themselves up from the awakening and stirring world in their sanctity, their authority, their learning, their wealth. The

Jongleurs, the Trouvères, the Troubadours, became in a certain sense the popular teachers; the Bards and the sacerdotal order became separate, hostile to each other. The Clergy might seem almost content with the intellect of man; they left the imagination, except so far as it was kept enthralled by the religious ceremonial, to others. Perhaps the Mysteries, even the early Latin Mysteries, chiefly arose out of the consciousness of this loss of influence; it was a strong effort to recover that which was gliding from their grasp. Some priests were Troubadours, not much to the elevation of their priestly character; Troubadours became priests, but it was by the renunciation of their poetic fame; and by setting themselves as far asunder as possible from their former brethren. Fulk of Marseilles [a] became the furious persecutor of those who had listened with rapture to his poetry. Later one of the most famous of the schoolmen was said to have been a Troubadour.[b]

Chivalry alone, so far as chivalry was Christian, held poetry to the service of Christianity, and even of the Church; but this was chiefly among the Trouvères of Northern France or the Langue d'Oil. The Provençal poetry of the South, the cradle of modern song, contains some noble bursts of the Crusading religious sentiment; it is Christian, if chivalry be Christian, in tone and thought. But, in general, in the castle courts of the

---

[a] For the history of Fulk of Marseilles, whose poetic fame endured to the days of Dante, see back, vol. v. p. 412.

[b] No less a person than William Durand, the great general of the Pope, the great Ecclesiastical Legist, almost the last great Schoolman, the author of the Speculum and the Rationale, is traditionally reported to have been a Troubadour. A tale is told of him very similar to that of Romeo and Juliet. Conceive Romeo growing up into a High Churchman and a Schoolman!—Ritter, Christliche Philosophie, vii. p. 19. The question is examined with fairness and sagacity in the xxth vol. of the Hist. Lit. de la France, p. 435.

Provençal Princes and Nobles poetry not only set itself above Christian religion, but above Christian morals. The highest Idealism was amatory Platonism, which while it professed religious adoration of woman, degraded her by that adoration. It may be doubted whether it could ever have broken forth from that effeminacy to which it had condemned itself. Grace, perhaps tenderness, was its highest aim; and Poetry soars not above its aim. But this subject has already found its place in our history. In its lower and popular form Provençal poetry, not less immoral, was even more directly anti-hierarchical. It was not heretical, for it had not religion enough to be heretical: religion was left to the heretic. The Fabliau, the Satire, the Tale, or the Song, were the broad and reckless expression of that aversion and contempt into which the Clergy of Southern France had fallen, and tended immeasurably to deepen that aversion and contempt. But it has been sadly shown how the Albigensian war crushed the insurrection of Provençal poetry against Latin letters, together with the insurrection against the Latin hierarchy. The earliest vernacular poetry perished almost without heirs to its fame; its language, which once divided France, sunk into a provincial dialect.[c]

Christendom owes to Dante the creation of Italian Poetry, through Italian, of Christian Poetry. It required all the courage, firmness, and prophetic sagacity of Dante to throw aside the inflexible bondage of the established hierarchical Latin of Europe. He had almost yielded and had actually commenced the Divine Comedy in the ancient, it seemed, the universal and eternal language.[d]

---

[c] Even in our days Provence has undergone much change. poet, and that of no undeserved fame, Jasmine: of course, the language has

[d] Compare among other authorities the valuable essay of Perticari, the

But the Poet had profoundly meditated, and deliberately resolved on his appeal to the Italian mind and heart. Yet even then he had to choose, to a certain extent to form, the pure, vigorous, picturesque, harmonious Italian which was to be intelligible, which was to become native and popular to the universal ear of Italy. He had to create; out of a chaos he had to summon light.[e] Every kingdom, every province, every district, almost every city, had its dialect, peculiar, separate, distinct, rude in construction, harsh, in different degrees, in utterance. Dante in his book on Vulgar Eloquence ranges over the whole land,[f] rapidly discusses the Sicilian and Apulian,

son-in-law of Monti (in Monti, Pro-
posta di Alcune Correzioni, &c. al
Vocab. della Crusca, v. ll. pte. ii.).
Perticari quotes the very curious letter
of the Monk Ilario to Uguccione della
Fagginola. To this Monk the wandering Dante showed part of his great
work. The Monk was astounded to
see that it was written in the vulgar
tongue. "Io mi stupiva ch' egli avesse
cantato in quella lingua, perchè paren
cosa difficile, anzi da non credere, chè
quegli altissimi intendimenti si potess-
ero significare per parole di vulgo; ne
mi parea convenire chè una tanta e sì
degna scienza fosse vestita a quel modo
così plebeo." Dante replied, that so he
himself had originally thought. He
had once begun his poem in Latin, and
these were the lines—

"Ultima regna canam, fluido contermina
　mundo,
Spiritibus quæ lata patent, quæ præmia
　solvunt
Pro meritis cuicunque suis."

But he had thrown aside that lyre, "ed
un altra ne temperal conveniente all'
orecchio de' moderni." The Monk
concludes "molte altre cose con sublimi

affetti soggionse" (p. 328). Perticari
quotes another remonstrance addressed
to the poet by Giovanni di Virgilio da
Cesena, closing with these words : "Se
ti giova la fama, non sii contento a sì
brevi confini, nè all' esser fatto glorioso
dal vil giudicio del volgo" (p. 330).
Conceive the Divine Comedy strangled,
with Petrarch's Africa, high on the
barren and unapproachable shore of
ecclesiastical Latin.

[e] "Poscia nel libro ch' ei nomina
della Vulgare Eloquenza, cominciò ad
illustrare l' idioma poetico ch' egli
creava." See the excellent observations
on writing in a dead language, in Foscolo,
Discorso sul Testo di Dante, p. 250.

[f] I can have no doubt whatever of
the authenticity of the De Vulgari
Eloquentia; contested because Dante
threw aside the vulgar Tuscan or Florentine as disdainfully as the rest, and
even preferred the Bolognese. To a
stranger it is extraordinary that such
an Essay as that of Perticari should be
necessary to vindicate Dante from the
charge of ingratitude and want of patriotism, even of hatred of Florence

the Roman and Spoletan, the Tuscan and Genoese, the
Romagnole and the Lombard, the Trevisan and Venetian, the Istrian and Friulian; all are coarse, harsh,
mutilated, defective. The least bad is the vulgar
Bolognese. But high above all this discord he seems to
discern, and to receive into his prophetic ears, a noble
and pure language, common to all, peculiar to none, a
language which he describes as Illustrious, Cardinal,
Courtly, if we may use our phrase, Parliamentary, that
is, of the palace, the courts of justice, and of public
affairs.[r] No doubt it sprung, though its affiliation is by
no means clear, out of the universal degenerate Latin,
the rustic tongue, common not in Italy alone, but in all
the provinces of the Roman Empire.[b] Its first domicile was the splendid Sicilian and Apulian Court of
Frederick II., and of his accomplished son. It has been
boldly said, that it was part of Frederick's magnificent
design of universal empire: he would make Italy one

(Florence which had exiled him), because Florentine vanity was wounded
by what they conceived injustice to
pure Tuscan. See also the Preface to
the De Vulgari Eloquio in the excellent
edition of the Opere Minori, by Fraticelli. Florence, 1833.

[r] " Itaque adepti quod quærebamus,
dicimus, Illustre, Cardinale, Aulicum
et Curiale Vulgare in Latio, quod omnis Latiæ civitatis est et nullius esse
videtur, et quo municipia Vulgaria
omnia Latinorum mensurantur, ponde-
rantur et comparantur."—Lib. i. cxvi.

[b] Perticari has some ingenious observations on the German conquests,
and the formation of Italian from the
Latin. The German war-terms were
alone admitted into the language. But
his theory of the origin of the Romance

out of the ecclesiastical Latin, and still
more his notion that the ecclesiastical
Latin was the old lingua rustica, rests on
two bold and unproved assumptions,
though doubtless there is some truth
in both: " La fina Industria degli Ecclesiastici, che in Romano spiegando la
dottrina Evangelica, ed in Romano
scrivendo i fatti della chiesa cattolica,
facevano del Romano il linguaggio
pontifical e Cattolica cioè universale.
Ma quella non era più il Latino Illustre;
non l' usato da Lucrezio e da Tullio,
non l' udito nel Senato e nella Corte
di Cesare; era quel rustico che parlava
l'intero volgo dell' Europa Latina" (p.
92). Still I know no treatise on the
origin of the Italian language more full,
more suggestive, or more valuable than
Perticari's.

realm, under one king, and speaking one language.[1]
Dante does homage to the noble character of Frederick II.[2] Sicily was the birthplace of Italian Poetry.
The Sicilian Poems live to bear witness to the truth of
Dante's assertion, which might rest on his irrefragable
authority alone. The Poems, one even earlier than the
Court of Frederick,[3] those of Frederick himself, of Pietro
della Vigna,[4] of King Enzio, of King Manfred, with
some peculiarities in the formation, orthography, use

[1] " Federigo II. sperava a riunire
l' Italia sotto un solo principe, una
sola forma di governo, e una sola lingua."—Foscolo sulla lingua Italiana,
p. 159. This essay, printed (1850)
in the fourth volume of my poor
friend's Works, has only just reached
me.

[2] " Quicquid poetantur Itali Sicilianum vocatur .... Sed hæc fama
Trinacriæ terræ, si recte signum ad
quod tendit inspiciamus, videtur tantum in opprobrium Italorum Principum remansisse qui non heroico more,
sed plebeo sequuntur superbiam. Siquidem illustres heroes Fredericus Cæsar,
et hæc genitus ejus Manfredus, nobilitatem ac rectitudinem suæ formæ
pandentes, donec fortuna permansit,
humana secuti sunt, brutalia dedignantes, propter quod corde nobiles
atque gratiarum dotati inhærere tantorum principum majestati conati sunt:
ita quod eorum tempore quicquid excellentes Latinorum nitebantur, primitus in tantorum Coronatorum aulâ
prodibat. Et quia regale solium erat
Sicilia, factum est quicquid nostri prædecessores vulgariter protulerunt, Sicilianum vocatur. Quod quidem retinemus et nos, nec posteri nostri permutare valebunt, Racha! Racha! Quid

nunc personat tuba novissimi Frederici? quid tintinnabulum II. Caroli?
quid corona Johannis et Azzonis Marchionum potentum? quid aliorum
Magnatum tibiæ? nisi Venite carnifices! Venite altriplices! Venite avaritiæ sectatores. Sed præstat ad propositum repedare quam frustra loqui."
—De Vulgar. Eloquio, i. xii. p. 46.
There is a splendid translation of this
passage in Dantesque Italian by Foscolo, Discorso, p. 255.

[3] See the Rosa fresca olentissima,
Foscolo, della Lingua, p. 150.

[4] " Cosi ne' versi seguenti non v' e
un unico grammaticamento de sintassi, nè un modo d' esprimersi inelegante, nè un solo vocabolo che possa
parere troppo antico.

" Non dico ch' alla vostra gran bellezza
Orguglio non convegna e stiavi bene,
Che a bella donna orguglio ben convene,
Che la mantiene in pregio ed in grandezza;
Troppo altereza e quella che scun vene.
Il grande orguglio mai ben non avvene."
Fatti del 1mo See. I. p. 196.
See Foscolo, p. 166.

Peter della Vigna (Peter de Vinea) did
not write Sicilian from want of command
of Latin; his letters, including many
of the State Papers of his master Frederick II., are of much higher Latinity
than most of his time.

and sounds of words, are intelligible from one end of
the Peninsula to the other.[o] The language was echoed
and perpetuated, or rather resounded spontaneously,
among poets in other districts. This courtly, aristocratical, universal Italian, Dante heard as the conventional dialect in the Courts of the Cæsars,[p] in
the republics, in the principalities throughout Italy.[q]
Perhaps Dante, the Italian, the Ghibelline, the assertor
of the universal temporal monarchy, dwelt not less
fondly in his imagination on this universal and noble
Italian language, because it would supersede the Papal
and hierarchical Latin; the Latin with the Pope himself, would withdraw into the sanctuary, into the service
of the Church, into affairs purely spiritual.

However this might be, to this vehicle of his noble
thoughts Dante fearlessly entrusted his poetic immortality, which no poet anticipated with more confident
security. While the scholar Petrarch condescended to
the vulgar tongue in his amatory poems, which he had
still a lurking fear might be but ephemeral, in his

---

o See the passages from Frederick II.
and King Enzio, Foscolo, p. 165.

p See, among other instances, the
pure Italian quoted from Angelati by
Perticari, written at Milan the year
before the birth of Dante. Perticari's
graceful essay, as far as the earlier
Italian poetry may be compared with
that of Foscolo, sulla Lingua; the
other poets Cino da Pistoia, the Guidos
(Foscolo ranks Guido Cavalcanti,
Dante's best friend, very high) may
be read in a collection printed at Florence, referred to in a former volume.
Nor must the prose be forgotten; the
history of Matteo Spinelli is good universal Italian. The maritime code of

Amalfi has been recently discovered,
in Italian perfectly intelligible in the
present day. I owe this information
to my accomplished friend Sign'. La-
mita.

q "La lingua ch' ei nomina corte-
giana, e della quale ei disputa tuttavia,
la sua fantasia vedevala nascere ed am-
pliarsi per la perpetua residenza de'
Cesari in Roma, e fra le republiche e
le tirannikli, tutte confuse in un solo
reame. Di questo ei ti pare certissimo
come di legge preordinata dalla Provi-
denza e connessa al sistema del' Uni-
verso."—Compare quotations, Foscolo,
Discorso, p. 254.

Africa and in his Latin verses he laid up, as he
fondly thought, an imperishable treasure of fame.'
Even Boccaccio, happily for his own glory, followed
the example of Dante, in, as he probably supposed,
his least enduring work, his gay Decamerone. Yet
Boccaccio doubted, towards the close of his life,
whether the Divine Comedy had not been more sublime, and therefore destined to a more secure eternity
in Latin.'

Thus in Italy, with the Italian language, of which, if
he was not absolutely the creator, he was the first who
gave it permanent and vital being, arose one of the
great poets of the world. There is a vast chasm between the close of Roman and the dawn of Italian
letters, between the period at which appeared the last
creative work written by transcendent human genius
in the Roman language, while yet in its consummate
strength and perfection, and the first, in which Italian
Poetry and the Italian tongue came forth in their
majesty; between the history of Tacitus and the Divina
Comedia. No one can appreciate more highly than
myself (if I may venture to speak of myself), the great
works of ecclesiastical Latin, the Vulgate, parts of the
Ritual, St. Augustine: yet who can deny that there is

' Compare Petrarch's letter (Epist.
Fam. xi. 12), in which he haughtily
vindicates himself from all jealousy of
Dante. How should he, who is the
companion of Virgil and Homer, be
jealous of one who enjoys the hoarse
applause of taverns and markets. I
may add that Mr. Bruce Whyte, in his
curious volumes, Histoire des Langues
Romanes, has given a careful analysis
of Petrarch's " Africa," which he has
actually read, and discovered in it,

some passages of real merit (vol. iii.
ch. xl.).

' " Non dico però che se in versi
Latini fosse (non mutato il peso delle
parole vulgari) ch' egli non fosse molto
più artificioso e più sublime; percio-
chè molto più arte e nel parlare latino
chè nel moderno."—Boerne. Comm.
Div. Com. f. f. As if sublimity in
poetry consisted in skilful triumph over
difficulty. But on the old age of Boccaccio, see Foscolo, p. 213.

barbarism, a yet unreconciled confusion of uncongenial
elements, of Orientalism and Occidentalism, in the language? From the time of Trajan, except Claudian,
Latin letters are almost exclusively Christian; and
Christian letters are Latin, as it were, in a secondary
and degenerate form. The new era opens with
Daute.

To my mind there is a singular kindred and similitude
between the last great Latin, and the first great
Italian writer, though one is a poet, the other
a historian. Tacitus and Dante have the same penetrative truth of observation as to man and the external
world of man; the same power of expressing that truth.
They have the common gift of flashing a whole train of
thought, a vast range of images on the mind by a few
brief and pregnant words; the same faculty of giving
life to human emotions by natural images, of imparting
to natural images, as it were, human life and human
sympathies: each has the intuitive judgement of saying
just enough; the stern self-restraint which will not say
more than enough; the rare talent of compressing a
mass of profound thought into an apophthegm; each
paints with words, with the fewest possible words, yet
the picture lives and speaks. Each has that relentless
moral indignation, that awful power of satire which in
the historian condemns to an immortality of earthly
infamy, in the Christian Poet aggravates that gloomy
immortality of this world by ratifying it in the next.
Each might seem to embody remorse.[1] Patrician, high,
imperial, princely, Papal criminals are compelled to
acknowledge the justice of their doom. Each, too,

Margin note: Tacitus and Dante.

---

[1] It is a saying attributed to Talleyrand of Tacitus, "Quand on lit cet homme-là on est au Confessional."

writing, one of times just past, of which the influences
were strongly felt in the social state and fortunes of
Rome: the other of his own, in which he had been
actively concerned, throws a personal passion (Dante of
course the most) into his judgements and his language,
which, whatever may be its effect on their justice, adds
wonderfully to their force and reality. Each, too, has a
lofty sympathy with good, only that the highest ideal of
Tacitus is a death-defying Stoic, or an all-accomplished
Roman Proconsul, an Helvidius Thrasea, or an Agricola;
that of Dante a suffering, and so purified and beatified
Christian saint, or martyr; in Tacitus it is a majestic
and virtuous Roman matron, an Agrippina, in Dante an
unreal mysterious Beatrice.

Dante is not merely the religious Poet of Latin or
mediæval Christianity; in him that mediæval Christianity is summed up as it were, and embodied for perpetuity. The Divine Comedy contains in its sublimest
form the whole mythology, and at the same time the
quintessence, the living substance, the ultimate conclusions of the Scholastic Theology. The whole course of
Legend, the Dæmonology, Angelology, the extra-mun-
dane world, which in the popular belief was vague, frag-
mentary, incoherent, in Dante, as we have seen, becomes
an actual, visible, harmonious system. In Dante heathen
images, heathen mythology are blended in the same
living reality with those of Latin Christianity, but they
are real in the sense of the early Christian Fathers.
They are acknowledged as part of the vast hostile Demon
world, just as the Angelic Orders, which from Jewish
or Oriental tradition obtained their first organisation in
the hierarchy of the Areopagite. So, too, the schools of
Theology meet in the Poet. Aquinas, it has been said,
has nothing more subtle and metaphysical than the

Paradise, only that in Dante single lines, or pregnant
stanzas, have the full meaning of pages or chapters of
divinity. But though his doctrine is that of Aquinas,
Dante has all the fervour and passion of the Mystics; he
is Bonaventura as well as St. Thomas.

Dante was in all respects but one, his Ghibellinism,
Dante's Ghibellinism. the religious poet of his age, and to many minds
not less religious for that exception. He was
anti-Papal, but with the fullest reverence for the spiritual
supremacy of the successor of St. Peter. To him, as to
most religious Imperialists or Ghibellines, to some of
the spiritual Franciscans, to a vast host of believers
throughout Christendom, the Pope was two distinct personages. One, the temporal, they scrupled not to condemn with the fiercest reprobation, to hate with the
bitterest cordiality: Dante damns Pontiffs without fear
or remorse. But the other, the Spiritual Pope, was
worthy of all awe or reverence; his sacred person must
be inviolate; his words, if not infallible, must be heard
with the profoundest respect; he is the Vicar of Christ,
the representative of God upon earth. With his Ghibelline brethren Dante closed his eyes against the incongruity, the inevitable incongruity, of these two discordant
personages meeting in one: the same Boniface is in hell,
yet was of such acknowledged sanctity on earth that it
was spiritual treason to touch his awful person. The
Saints of Dante are the Saints of the Church; on the
highest height of wisdom is St. Thomas, on the highest
height of holiness, St. Benedict, St. Dominic, St. Francis.
To the religious adversaries of the Church he has all
the stern remorselessness of an inquisitor. The noble
Frederick II., whom we have just heard described as
the parent of Italian poetry, the model of a mighty
Emperor, the Cæsar of Cæsars, is in hell as an arch-

heretic, as an atheist." In hell, in the same dreary
circle, up to his waist in fire, is the noblest of the Ghibellines, Farinata degli Uberti. In hell for the same sin is
the father of his dearest friend and brother poet Guido
Cavalcanti. Whatever latent sympathy seems to transpire for Fra Dolcino, he is unrelentingly thrust down
to the companionship of Mohammed. The Catholic
may not reverse the sentence of the Church.

Petrarch, as an Italian poet, excepting in his Ode to the
Virgin, stands almost aloof from the mediæval
religion ; it is only as a Latin poet, and in his
familiar Letters, that he inveighs against the vices, the
irreligion of the Court of Avignon.

Boccaccio, the third of this acknowledged Triumvirate,
was, on the other hand, in his one great work,
unquestionably as regards the dominant religion of his times, its monkhood and hierarchism, the
most irreligious, on account of his gross immoralities,
to all ages an irreligious writer. The Decamerone
centres in itself all the wit, all the indecency, all the
cleverest mockery of the French and Provençal Fabliaux, and this it has clothed in that exquisite, all-ad-
mired Florentine which has secured its undying fame.
The awful description of the Plague in Florence has
been compared, but by no means with justice, to that of
Thucydides and that of Lucretius. This grave opening
of the Decamerone might be expected to usher in a
book of the profoundest devotion, the most severe,
ascetic penitential. After this, another Dante might
summon the smitten city to behold its retributive doom

Petrarch.

Boccaccio.

---

* Inferno, i. 119. Pietro della Vigna calls him—
  " Al mio Signor, che fu d' onor sì degno."—*Inferno,* xiii. 74.

in the Infernal Regions; a premature Savonarola might
thunder his denunciations, and call on Florence, thus
manifestly under divine visitation, to cast all her pomps
and vanities, her ornaments, her instruments of luxury,
upon the funeral pyre; to sit and lament in dust and
ashes. This terrific opening leads, but not in bitter
irony, to that other common consequence of such dark
visitations, the most reckless licence. Tale follows tale,
gradually sinking from indecency into obscenity, from
mockery to utter profaneness. The popular religion,
the popular teachers, are exposed with the coarsest,
most reckless pleasantry. Erasmus, two centuries later,
does not scoff with more playful freedom at pilgrimages,
reliques, miracles: Voltaire himself, still two centuries
after Erasmus, hardly strips their sanctity from monks,
nuns and friars, with more unsparing wit. Nothing,
however sung or told in satiric verse or prose against
the Court of Rome, can equal the exquisite malice of
the story of the Jew converted to Christianity by a visit
to Rome, because no religion less than divine could
have triumphed over the enormous wickedness of its
chief teachers, the Cardinals, and the Pope. Strange
age of which the grave Dante and the gay Boccaccio
are the representatives! in which the author of the
Decamerone is the biographer of Dante, the commen-
tator on the Divine Comedy, expounding, pointing, echo-
ing, as it were, in the streets of Florence the solemn
denunciations of the poet. More strange, if possible,
the history of the Decamerone. Boccaccio himself
bitterly repented of his own work: he solemnly warned
the youth of Florence against his own loose and profane
novels; the scoffer at fictitious reliques became the
laborious collector of reliques not less doubtful; the

scourge of the friars died in the arms of friars, bequeath-
ing to them his manuscripts, hoping only for salvation
through their prayers.[x] Yet the disowned and proscribed
Decamerone became the text-book of pure Italian. Florence, the capital of letters, insisted on the indefeasible
prerogative of the Florentine dialect, and the Decamerone was ruled to be the one example of Florentine.
The Church was embarrassed; in vain the Decamerone
was corrected, mutilated, interpolated, and indecencies,
profanenesses annulled, erased: all was without effect;
the Decamerone must not be degraded from its high
and exemplary authority. The purity of morals might
suffer, the purity of the language must remain unat-
tainted; till at length an edition was published in
which the abbesses and nuns, who were enamoured
of their gardeners, became profane matrons and damsels; friars, who wrought false miracles, necromancers;
adulterous priests, soldiers. But this last bold effort
of jesuitical ingenuity was without effect: the Decamerone was too strong for the censure in all its forms;
it shook off its fetters, obstinately refused to be altered,
as before it had refused to be chastened; and remains
to this day at once the cleverest and bitterest satire,

---

[x] See in the works of Petrarch the very curious letter to Boccaccio, de Vaticinio Morientium, Opera, p. 740. Boccaccio had written in a paroxysm of superstitious terror to Petrarch concerning the prophecies of a certain holy man, Peter of Sienna, on the death of the two poets. Petrarch evidently does not believe a word of what had frightened poor Boccaccio. He alleges many causes of suspicion. "Non estenuo vaticinii pondus, quicquid a Christo dicitur verum est. Fieri nequit ut veritas mentiatur. At id quæritur Christiane rei hujus autor sit, an alter quispiam ad commenti fidem, quod sæpe vidimus, Christi nomen assumpserit." The poet urges Boccaccio, at great length, not to abandon letters, but only the lighter letters of his youth.

and the most curious illustration of the religion of the age.[7]

---

[7] "Se non che un Domiuicano Italiano e di natura più facile (chiamavasi Eustachio Locatelli, e morì vescovo in Reggio) vi s' interpose; e per essere stato confessore de Pio V., impetrò da Gregorio XIII. che il Decamerone non fosse mutato, se non in quanto bisognava al buono nome degli Ecclesiastici."—I'. 43. The account of the whole transaction at length may be read in the Discorso prefixed to Foscolo's edition of the Decamerone, London, 1825. Compare the fifth and sixth discourse of Foscolo; the most just criticism with which I am acquainted on Boccaccio, his merits, his influence, his style, and his language. I quote Boccaccio's will on Foscolo's authority. There is nothing new under the sun, nothing obsolete. I possess a translation of Eugene Sue's Wandering Jew, printed on the coarsest paper, the rudest type, and cheapest form, obviously intended for the lower Roman Catholics, in which the Jesuit becomes a Russian spy; all that is religious is transformed into political satire.

CHAPTER VI.

Language of France.

·NOTHING is more remarkable in the civil or in the religious history of the West, nothing led to more momentous or enduring results, than the accession, as it were, of the great kingdom of France from the Teutonic, and its adhesion to the Latin division of Christendom ; the fidelity of its language to its Roman descent, and its repudiation of the German conqueror. For about four centuries, loosely speaking, Gaul, from the days of Julius Cæsar, was a province of the Roman Empire. During that period it became Romanised in manners, institutions, language. The Celtic dialect was driven up into the North-Western corner of the land. If it subsisted, as seems to have been the case in the time of Irenæus, still later in that of Jerome, or in the fifth century,[a] as the dialect of some of the peasantry ; if it left its vestiges in the names of plains, of forests and mountains ; if even some sounds and words found their way into the supervening Latin, and became a feeble

France.

---

[a] According to Ulpian in the second century wills might be drawn in Latin or in the language of Gaul, the Celtic therefore had a legal existence. St. Jerome in the fourth century compares the language of the Asiatic Galatians with that which he had heard spoken in the neighbourhood of Treves. In the fifth, Sulpicius Severus desires one of the interlocutors in a dialogue to speak in Gallic or Celtic (Dialog. i. sub fine). Sidonius Apollinarius says that the nobles of his province (Auvergne) had only just cast off all the scales of their Celtic speech; this may have been the pronunciation. The father of Ausonius, a physician at Bazas in Aquitaine, spoke Latin imperfectly. Compare Ampère, Hist. Lit. de la France, pp. 36 and 136.

constituent of French; yet there can be no doubt that
the great mass of the French language, both the Langue
d'Oil of the North, and the Langue d'Oc of the South,
is of Latin origin.[b]

For about four centuries, Teutonic tribes, Goths,
Burgundians, Alemannians, Franks, ruled in Gaul, from
the first inroad and settlement of the Visigoths in the
South, down to the third generation after Charlemagne.
Clovis and his race, Charlemagne and his immediate de-
scendants, were Teutons; the language at the Court of
Soissons, in the capitals of Neustria and Austrasia, as
afterwards in that of Charlemagne at Aix-la-Chapelle, was
German. Nor was it only so in the Court; there were
Germans throughout the Frankish realm of Charlemagne.
The Council of Tours enacts that every Bishop should
have homilies in both languages; he should be able to
expound them in the rustic Roman and in the Teutonic,
so as to be intelligible to the whole people.[c]

But the grandsons of Charlemagne behold Latin and
Teutonic nationality, the Latin and Teutonic
language, dividing the Western Empire. The
German is withdrawing, if not beyond the Rhine, to the
provinces bordering on the Rhine; Latin is resuming
its full dominion over France and the French language.
At Strasburg, only thirty years after the Council of
Tours, France has become French, Germany German.

Separation. A.D. 842.

---

[b] M. Fauriel (Histoire de la Poésie
Provençale, L p. 195) observes of the
Provençal that there are more words
not of Latin origin than is commonly
supposed. He had collected 3000. The
whole Provençal literature might perhaps furnish him as many. A great
part he could trace to no known language. Some few are Arabic, many

Greek, some Celtic, some Basque; not
above fifteen Teutonic. The whole investigation is worthy of study.

[c] A.D. 812. Labbe, Concil. vii.
1263. This injunction was renewed
at Rheims and at Mentz A.D. 847.
There are fragments of old German
sermons.—Raumer, p. 66.

The two Kings of the same race, equally near in blood
to Charlemagne, take their oaths in languages not only
dialectically different, but distinct in root and origin.
Germany still recedes, leaving but few traces of its long
dominion ; the Celtic element probably contributes more
to the French language than the German. In truth
the Germans after all were but an armed oligarchy in
France, like the Turks in their European provinces, but
by no means so inaccessibly shut up in their Oriental
habits, in their manners, in their religion. Even in the
Visigothic South, no sooner had the conquest passed
over, than the native language, or rather the naturalised
Latin, reasserted its independence, its jealous and
exclusive superiority : and this, although the Goths
were routed and driven out by another Teutonic race,
the Franks of the North. France returned entirely to
its Latinity ; and from its rustic Roman gradually formed
that language which was to have such wide influence on
later civilisation.

In this conservation of France to Latin and Latin
Christianity, no doubt Latin Christianity, and the hierarchy so long, even under the German sway, of Latin
descent, powerfully contributed. The unity of religion in
some degree broke down the barrier between the Teuton
and the Roman Gaul ; they worshipped the same God in
the same Church ; looked for absolution from their sins,
trembled before, or sought humbly the counsel of the same
Priest. But the Clergy, as has been seen, remained long
almost exclusively Roman. The Teutons, who aspired to
the high places of the Church (for the services remained
obstinately Roman), were compelled to possess one qualification, the power of ministering in that Latin service.
The most rude, most ignorant, most worldly Bishop or
Priest must learn something, and that lesson must be the

recitation at least, or pronunciation of Latin. Charlemagne's schools, wherever the Teutonic element was the
feeblest, would teach in the Rustic Roman, or the Roman
more or less rapidly tending to its new form. At least in
the Church and in the Cloister the Latin ruled without
rival ; among the people the Latin element was far the
stronger : the stronger is ever aggressive ; and the Teutonic was by degrees renounced, and driven towards the
Rhine, or over the Rhine. The German Teuton, mind-
ful of his descent, might still call himself a Frank, but
the Gallic Frank had ceased to be a German.[d]

It is not the least singular fact in the history of the
French language, that another German, or kindred Scandinavian race, wrests a large province
from France. Normandy takes its name from its Norman
conquerors : the land, according to Teutonic usage, is par-
titioned among those adventurers ; they are the lords of the
soil. In an exceedingly short time the Normans cease to be
Teutons ; they are French or Latin in language. About
a century and a half after the establishment
of the Normans in France, the descendants of
Rollo conquer England, and the Conqueror introduces
not a kindred dialect, but the hostile and oppugnant
Norman-French, into Anglo-Saxon England. The im-
position of this foreign tongue, now the exclusive language of the Normans, is the last and incontestable sign
of their complete victory over the native inhabitants.
This is not the less extraordinary when the Italian Normans also are found for some time obstinately refusing

The Nor-
mans.

A.D. 912.
1066.

---

[d] In the epitaph on Gregory V.
(997), he is said to have spoken three
languages; Frankish (German), the Vulgar (Romance or Italian), and Latin :—
"Usus Francisca, vulgari, et voce Latina
Instituit populos eloquio triplici."

Gregory (Bruno, cousin of the Emperor Otho) was a German.—Murator.
Diss. li. 91. At this time in Italy
traces of Italian begin to appear in
wills and deeds.—Ibid. p. 93.

to become Italians. They endeavour to compel the
Italians to adopt their French manners and language;
histories of the Norman conquest are written at Naples
or within the kingdom, in Norman-French.[*] The dialect
has adopted some Italian words, but it is still French.[f]
Thus within France Teutonism absolutely and entirely
surrenders its native tongue, and becomes in the North
and in the South of Europe a powerful propagator of a
language of Latin descent.

It is not the office of this history to trace the obscure
growth of the French language out of the pre-existing
elements—the primal Celtic and the Latin. It must
not be forgotten that higher up the Celtic and the Latin
branch off from the same family—the Indo-Teutonic;[g]
so that the actual roots of French words may be reason-
ably deduced from either. The Christian language, all
the titles, terms, and words which related to the religion,
were doubtless pure Latin, and survived, but slightly
modified, in the French. Pronunciation is among the
most powerful agents in the change and formation of
language, in the silent abrogation of the old, the silent
crystallisation of the new. Certain races, nations, tribes,
families, have a predilection, a predisposition, a facility
for the utterance of certain sounds. They prefer labial

[*] "Moribus et lingua, quascunque venire
videbant,
Informenti propria, gens efficiatur ut
unum."—Gul. Appul. Lib. i.; Muratori, v. 258.

[f] Compare on this subject M. Cham-
pollion Figeac's preface to the French
Chronicle of the Italian Normans,
'Les Normans' (publication of the
Société Historique), p. xliv., &c., with
the references to Falconet, Lebœuf,
Le Grand d'Aussy, and Tiraboschi.

[g] This fact in the history of language, first established by our coun-
tryman, Dr. Prichard, in his Essay on
the Eastern Origin of the Celtic Nations, is now admitted by all writers
of authority. See also the excellent
treatise of M. Pictet, 'L'Affinité des
Langues Celtiques avec le Sanscrit.'
Mr. Bruce Whyte was unfortunately
not master of this branch of Philology,
which supersedes at once or modifies
his whole system.

or guttural, hard or soft letters; they almost invariably substitute the mute, the surd, or the aspirate letter for its equivalent; there is an uniformity, if not a rule of change, either from organism or habit. The Italian delights in the termination of words with a soft vowel, the Langue d'Oc with a consonant, the French with a mute

Effect of Church service. vowel. The Latin of the Ritual being a written language, in its structure as well as in its words would inflexibly refuse all change; it would not take the auxiliary verb in place of its conjugations, the article or the preposition to designate its cases; it would adhere to its own declensions, conjugations, inflexions, and thus far would stand aloof from the gradual change going on around it; it would become in so far unintelligible to the vulgar ear. But not only, the roots remaining the same, would the great mass of the words retain their significance; there would also be some approximation in the tone and accent. The Clergy, being chiefly of the country, and in their ordinary conversation using the language of the country, would pronounce their Latin with a propensity to the same sounds which were forming the French. Latin as pronounced by an Italian, a Frenchman, or a Spaniard, during the formation, and after the formation, of the new tongue, would have a tinge of Italian, French, or Spanish in its utterance. The music being common throughout the Church might perhaps prevent any wide deviation, but whatever deviation there might be would tend to make the meaning of the words more generally and easily comprehensible. So there would be no precise time when the Latin Ritual would become at once and perceptibly a foreign tongue; the common rustic Roman, or the Romance, if not the offspring was probably akin to the ecclesiastical Latin, at all events all Church words or terms would

form part of it. And so on the one hand Latin Christianity would have a powerful influence in the creation
of the new language, and at the same time never be an
unintelligible stranger; hers would be rather a sacred
and ancient form of the same language among her lineal
and undoubted descendants.

The early poetry of the Langue d'Oil was either the
Legend or the Poem of Chivalry. The Trouvère of the
North was far more creative than the Troubadour of the
South. In his lighter Fabliaux the Trouvère makes no
less free with the Christian Clergy and with Christian
morals than his brother of the South, but his is the freedom of gaiety or of licentiousness, not of bitter hatred, or
pitiless, and contemptuous satire. There is nothing of
the savage seriousness of the Provençal.[b]

But the higher Epopee of the Northern Trouvère was
almost contemporaneous in its rise with the Crusades;
its flourishing period was that of the Crusades, and as
far as that was a real and actual state of society, of
Chivalry. It is the heroic poetry of mediæval Christianity. The Franks were the warriors, the Franks the
poets of the Cross. In both the great Cycles, of Charlemagne and his Peers, of Arthur and the Knights of the
Round Table, in the subordinate cycles, as of Rinaldo,
or the four Sons of Aymon, the hero was ever a Christian
knight, the enemy, whether knight, giant, or even dragon, was anti-Christian, Saracen, misbeliever, or devil.
Charlemagne's war is of the West against the East, of
Latin Christianity against Islam; the Gascons and the
Basques at Roncesvalles become the splendid Saracens

---

[b] It must not be forgotten that
Brunetto Latini, the master of Dante
(so little prescient was he of the glory
of his pupil), wrote his Tesoretto not
in Italian but in French, as of all the
vernacular tongues the most likely to
be enduring.

of Spain; the whole misbelieving East is gathered
around Christian Paris. The Church avouched the
wonders of Archbishop Turpin, adopted the noble fictions
about Charlemagne and his Peers. These became part
of authorised Christian Legend, when Legend and History were one; when it would have been equal impiety
to assert the mythic character of the former as that of
the authentic Gospel.[1] So, too, whether Arthur and his
Knights sprung, as is most probable, from Breton or
from British lays, the Saxondom of his foes recedes, the
Paganism, even the Saracenism takes its place. It is
not the ancient British King and his British warriors
warring with Saxons and Anglians on the borders of
Wales, Cumberland, or Cornwall for the dominion of
Britain; it is the Christian King and the Christian
Knight waging a general war of adventure against unbelievers. It is not the independence of Britain, it is
the mystic Sangreal, the cup with the blood of the Redeemer, which is the holy object, the ideal reward of
their valour; it is to be the triumph of the most chaste
and virtuous as well as of the bravest knight. The sons
of Aymon are Southern knights keeping the Spanish
borders (Spain reserved her Cid for her own noble old
poem), but the Sons of Aymon are adopted Northerns;
the Troubadour Poetry knows little or nothing of their
chivalry. Toulouse owns only her own unidealised, un-
romanticised Counts: the few Provençal poems of chivalry are of doubtful origin: their Epic is the dull verse
chronicle of the Albigensian War.

But, after all, in this inexhaustible fecundity of her
Romance, whether from the rudeness and imperfection
of the language at this period of her prolific creativeness,

---

[1] Tiraboschi, l. v.

or from some internal inaptitude in French for this high
class of poetry, from want of vigour, metrical harmony,
and variety, or even from its excellence, its analytical
clearness and precision, the Mediæval Poetry of Northern France, with all its noble, chivalrous, and crusading
impulses, called forth no poet of enduring fame. The
Homer of this race of cyclic poets was to be an Italian.
It was not till these poems had sunk into popular tales;
till, from the poem recited in the castle or the court of
the King or the Baron, they had become disseminated
among the people;[k] not till they had spread into
Italy, and as the 'Reali di Francia' had been over
and over again recited by the professional story-tellers,
and been rudely versified by humbler poets, that they
were seized first by the bold and accomplished Boiardo,
afterwards by the inimitable Ariosto, and in their full
ancient spirit, yet with some fine modern irony, bequeathed to mankind in the most exquisite and harmonious Italian. Even the Crusades were left to the
gentle and romantic Tasso, when the religious fire of the
Crusades and of Chivalry was all but extinct in its cold
faint embers.

But if the Crusades, and by the Crusades Latin Christianity, did not create enduring French poetry, they
created the form of history in which France has excelled

---

[k] "Tutte le meraviglie ch' oggi leg-
giamo ne' romanzi o poemi, che hanno
per suggetto i Paladini, erano allora
raccontate al popolo dai novellatori; e
quest' uso rimane in alcune città, e
specialmente in Venezia e in Napoli
sino a quest' ultimi anni. Chiunque
non sapeva leggere, si raccoglieva quasi
ogni sera d' estate intorno il novellatore
su la riva del mare," &c. &c.—Foscolo,
Discorso, v. p. 229. This accounts at
once for the adoption of such subjects
by Pulci, Boiardo, and Ariosto, when
the high tide of classical letters had not
passed away; as well as for the unbounded popularity of their poems,
and of countless other epics, once
common as the stones in the streets,
now the rarities of the choicest libraries.

all Europe. Perhaps of vernacular history, properly so
called, the Florentine Villani is the parent; of political
history, Dino Compagni; but that history, which delights from its reality and truth, as springing from the
personal observation, instinct with the personal character, alive with all the personal feelings of the historian,
the model and type of the delightful Memoir, is to be
found first in Villehardouin and Joinville, to rise to
still higher perfection in Froissart and in De Comines.
No cold later epic on St. Louis will rival the poetry of
Joinville.

CHAPTER VII.

Teutonic Languages.

In all the Romance languages, as it has appeared, in all languages of Latin descent, Italian, French both in its northern and southern form, Spanish in all its dialects, the religious vocabulary, every word which expressed Christian notions, or described Christian persons, was Latin, only lengthened out or shortened, deflected, or moulded, according to the genius of each tongue; they were the same words with some difference of pronunciation or form, but throughout retaining their primal sense: the words, even if indistinctly understood, had at least an associated significance, they conveyed, if not fully, partially to all, their proper meaning.

In the Teutonic languages it was exactly the reverse. For all the primal and essential Christian notions the German found its own words; it was only what may be called the Church terms, the ecclesiastical functions and titles, which it condescended or was compelled to borrow from the Latin.[a] The highest of all, "God," with all

---

[a] M. Regnier, in a Mémoire in the last year's Transactions of the Academy (p. 324), has summed up in a few clear French sentences, the substance of a learned work by Rudolf Raumer, 'Die Einwirkung des Christenthums auf die althochdeutsche Sprache.' Berlin, 1851. "Un fait remarquable, et qui prouve bien avec quel soin jaloux la langue se conservait pure de toute mélange étrangère, c'est qu'au moment même de l'introduction du Christianisme, qui apportait tant d'idées nouvelles, elle n'eut pas besoin d'emprunter au Grec et au Latin les mots qui les rendaient, que ses propres ressources lui suffirent en grande partie, surtout

its derivatives, the "Godhead, godly, godlike," was in
sound entirely remote from "Deus, the deity, the
divinity, the divine." As to the attributes of God, the
German had his own word for allmightiness, for the
titles the all-merciful or all-gracious.[b] For the Trinity,
indeed, as in all Indo-Teutonic languages, the numerals
are so nearly akin, that there would be at least a close
assonance, if not identity, in the words; and the primitive word for "father" is so nearly an universal, that
the Latin "Pater" might be dimly discerned under the
broader Teutonic pronunciation, "Fader." But the
"Son and the Holy Ghost"[c] were pure, unapproaching
Teuton. The names of the Saviour, "Jesus," and "the
Christ," passed of course into the creed and ritual; but
the "Lord," and the German "Herr," were Teuton, as
were the "healer, health," for the "Saviour and salvation," the "atonement" for the "propitiation."[d] In
the older versions the now ignoble words "hanging and
the gallows" were used instead of the Crucifixion and
the Cross: the "Resurrection" takes the German form.[e]
The "Angels and the Devils" underwent but little
change; but all the special terms of the Gospel, "the
soul, sin, holiness, faith, prayer, repentance, penance,
confession, conversion, heaven and hell, Doomsday, even
Baptism and the Lord's Supper," were new and peculiar.[f]

---

pour l'expression des sentiments qui
appartenaient à la foi Chrétienne, et
que ce ne fut guère que pour l'organisation extérieure de l'Eglise, qu'elle
reçut en partie du dehors les mots
avec les faits."—In a note M. Regular
illustrates these assertions by examples,
many of them the same as those cited
in my text.

[b] Compounds from Macht—Barm-
herzigkeit—Gnade.

[c] Der Sohn, der Heilige Geist.

[d] Der Herr, Heiland, Heil.

[e] Notker and Otfried use "hrogan
und galgen."—Auferstehung. Rudolf
Raumer. b. iii.

[f] Seele, Sünde, Schuld, Heiligkeit,
Glaube, Gebete, Reue, Busse, Beichte,
Bekehrung, Himmel, Hölle, Taufe,
Heiliger Abendmahl.

The Book;[f] the Seer not the Prophet;[h] above all, the great Festivals of Christmas and Easter,[i] were original, without relation in sound or in letters to the Latin. Of the terms which discriminated the Christian from the Unbeliever one was different; the Christian, of course, was of all languages, the Gentile or the Pagan became a "heathen." So too "the world" took another name. To the German instructed through these religious words, the analogous vocabulary of the Latin service was utterly dead and without meaning; the Latin Gospel was a sealed book, the Latin service a succession of unintelligible sounds. The offices and titles of the Clergy alone, at least of the Bishop and the Deacon, as well as the Monk, the Abbot, the Prior, the Cloister, were transferred and received as honoured strangers in the land, in which the office was as new as the name.[k] "The Martyr" was unknown but to Christianity, therefore the name lived. "The Church" the Teuton derived, perhaps through the Gothic of Ulphilas, from the Greek;[m] but besides this single word there is no sign of Greek more than of Latin in the general Teutonic Christian language.[n] The Bible of Ulphilas was that of an ancient race, which

[f] Rudolf Raumer, b. iii.

Ulphilas used the word praufetus. See Zahn's glossary to his edition of Ulphilas, p. 70. The German word is Seher, or Wahrsager.

[i] Weihnacht. "Ostarn" (in Anglo-Saxon, Easter) "paraît avoir désigné dans des temps plus anciens une fête Germanique dont la fête se célébrait vers la même époque que notre Fête de Pâques, et qui avait donné son nom au mois d'Avril."— Grimm, Mythologie, p. 267, 8vo., 2e edit., &c. &c. M. Regnier might have added to his authorities that of

Bede, who in his de Comp. Temporum gives this derivation. . . . Pfingsten is Pentecost.

[h] Pfaffe, the more common word for Clericus, is from Papa.—Raumer, p. 295. It is curious that in the oldest translations the High Priests, Annas and Caiaphas, are Bishops.— Ibid. 297.

[m] Walafrid Strabo gives this derivation from the Greek through the Gothic. The word is, I believe, not found in the extant part of Ulphilas.

[n] Even the word "Catholic" is superseded by "Allgemeine."

passed away with that race; it does not appear to have
been known to the Germans east of the Rhine, or to the
great body of the Teutons, who were converted to Christianity some centuries later, from the seventh to the
eleventh. The Germans who crossed the Rhine or the
Alps came within the magic circle of the Latin; they
submitted to a Latin Priesthood; they yielded up their
primitive Teuton, content with forcing many of their
own words, which were of absolute necessity, perhaps
some of their inflexions, into the language which they
ungraciously adopted. The descendants of the Ostro-
goths, the Visigoths, the Burgundians, the Lombards,
by degrees spoke languages of which the Latin was
the groundwork; they became in every sense Latin
Christians.

Our Anglo-Saxon ancestors were the first Teutonic

Anglo-
Saxon.   race which remained Teuton. It is a curious
problem how the Roman Missionaries from the
South, and the Celtic Missionaries from the North, ·
wrought the conversion of Anglo-Saxondom.[*] Probably
the early conversions in most parts of the island were
hardly more than ceremonial; the substitution of one
rite for another; the deposing one God and accepting
another, of which they knew not much more than the
name; and the subjection to one Priesthood, who seemed
to have more powerful influence in heaven, instead of
another who had ceased to command success in war, or
other blessings which they expected at his hands. This
appears from the ease and carelessness with which the
religion was for some period accepted and thrown off
again. As in the island, or in each separate kingdom,

---

[*] Augustine addressed Ethelbert through an interpreter. The Queen
and her retinue were French, and used to intercourse with a Latin priesthood.

the Christian or the Heathen King, the Christian or the
Heathen party was the stronger, so Christianity rose
and fell. It was not till the rise of a Priesthood of
Anglo-Saxon birth under Wilfrid, or during his time,
that England received true Christian instruction ; it was
not till it had, if not an Anglo-Saxon ritual, Anglo-
Saxon hymns, legends, poetry, sermons, that it can be
properly called Christian ; and all those in their religious
vocabulary are Teutonic, not Latin. It was in truth
notorious that, even among the Priesthood, Latin had
nearly died out, at least if not the traditional skill of
repeating its words, the knowledge of its meaning.

Our Anglo-Saxon Fathers were the first successful
missionaries in Trans-Rhenane Germany. The Celt
Columban and St. Gall were hermits and cœnobites, not
missionaries ; and in their Celtic may have communicated, if they encountered them, with the aboriginal
Gauls, but they must chiefly have made their way
through Latin. They settled within the pale of Roman
Gaul, built their monasteries on the sites of old Roman
cities ; their proselytes (for they made monks at least, if
not numerous converts to the faith) were Gallo-Romans.[p]
But no doubt the Anglo-Saxon of Winfrid (Boniface)
and his brother apostles of Germany was the means of

---

[p] Columban has left a few lines of
Latin poetry. While his Celticism
appears from his obstinate adherence
to the ancient British usage about
Easter, it is strange that he should
be mixed up with the controversy
about the "three Chapters." M.
Ampère has pointed out the singular
contrast between the adulation of Columban's letter to Pope Boniface on
this subject, "pulcherrimo omnium
totius Europæ ecclesiarum capiti . . .

Papæ prædicto, præcelso, præsenti
(præstanti ?) pastorum pastori . . .
humillimus celsissimo, agrestis ur-
bano," and the bold and definite language of the letter itself : " Tamdiu
enim potestas apud vos erit, quamdiu
recta ratio permanserit. Dolere æ de
infamiâ quæ cathedræ S. Petri inuri-
tur."—Annal. Benedict. l. 274. Compare Ampère, Hist. Lit. de la France,
iii. p. 9. The Celt is a Latin in language rather than in thought.

intercourse; the kindred language enabled them to communicate freely and successfully with the un-Romanised races: Teutons were the apostles of Teutons. It was through the persuasive accents of a tongue, in its sounds as in its words closely resembling their own, not in the commanding tones of foreign Latin, that the religion found its way to their hearts and minds. Charlemagne's conversions in the further north were at first through an instrument in barbarous ages universally understood, the sword. Charlemagne was a Teuton warring on Teutons: he would need no interpreter for the brief message of his evangelic creed to the Saxons—" Baptism or death." Their conversion was but the sign of submission, shaken off constantly during the long wars, and renewed on every successful inroad of the conqueror. But no doubt in the bishoprics and the monasteries, the religious colonies with which Charlemagne really achieved the Christianisation of a large part of Germany, though the services might be in Latin, the schools might instruct in Latin, and the cloister language be Latin, German youths educated as Clergy or as Monks could not forget or entirely abandon their mother tongue.[a] Latin and German became insensibly mingled, and interpenetrated

<hr>

[a] " Dem Kloster S. Gallen wird im 10ten Jahrhundert nachgerühmt, dass nur die Kleinsten Knaben seiner Schule sich der Deutschen Sprache bedienten; alle übrigen aber mussten ihre Conversation Lateinisch führen. In den meisten Fällen aber lief natürlich der Gebrauch der Deutschen Muttersprache neben dem der Lateinischen her. Daher enstand jene Mischung Lateinischer mit Deutsche Worte, die wir in so vielen Glossen handschriften der Althochdeutschen Zeit finden. Man erklärte bei der Auslegung Lateinischer Texte die schwiergeren Wörter entweder durch geläufigere Lateinische oder auch durch entsprechende Deutsche. Dadurch musste eine fortdauernde Wechselwirkung zwischen dem Lateinischen und Deutschen in den Klöstern entstehen."— Raumer, p. 201. Otfried, the German sacred poet, owed his education to the scholar and theologian, H. Rhabanus Maurus.

each other. As to the general language of the country,
there was an absolute necessity that the strangers should
yield to the dominant Teutonism, rather than, like
Rome of old in her conquered provinces, impose their
language on the subject people. The Empire of Charlemagne till his death maintained its unity. The great
division began to prevail during the reign of Louis the
Pious, between the German and the Frank portions of
the Empire. By that time the Franks (though German
was still spoken in the north-east, between the Rhine
and the Meuse) had become blended and assimilated
with those who at least had begun to speak the Langue
d'Oïl and the Langue d'Oc.[7] But before the oath at
Strasburg had as it were pronounced the divorce between
the two realms, Teutonic preachers had addressed German homilies to the people, parts of the Scripture had
found their way into Germany, German vernacular
poets had begun to familiarise the Gospel history to the
German ear, the Monks aspired to be vernacular poets.[8]
As in Anglo-Saxon England, so in the dominions of
Louis the Pious, and of Lothaire, the Heliand, and the
Harmony of the Gospels by Otfried, had opened the
Bible, at least the New Testament, to the popular ear.
The Heliand was written in the dialect of Lower Saxony.
Otfried, a Monk of Weissenberg in Alsace, wrote in
High German. The Heliand is alliterative verse,
Otfried in rhyme. Otfried wrote his holy poem to wean
the minds of men from their worldly songs; the history
of the Redeemer was to supplant the songs of the old
German heroes. How far Otfried succeeded in his pious

[7] See above, from the canons of the Councils of Tours, Rheims, and Mentz.
[8] See on the Vienna fragments of the old German translation of St. Matthew, and the version of the Gospel Harmony of Ammianus, Notker's Psalms, the Lord's Prayer and Creed.—Raumer, pp. 35 et seqq.

design is not known, but even in the ninth century, other Christian poetry, a poem on St. Peter, a legend of St. Gall, a poem on the miracles of the Holy Land, introduced Christian thoughts and Christian imagery into the hearts of the people.[t]

Thus Christianity began to speak to mankind in Greek; it had spoken for centuries in the commanding Latin; henceforth it was to address a large part of the world in Teutonic. France and Spain were Romanised as well as Christianised. Germany was Christianised, but never Romanised. England, Germanised by the Anglo-Saxon conquest, was partially Romanised again by the Normans, who, in their province of France, had entirely yielded to the Gallo-Roman element. Westward of the Rhine and south of the Danube, the German conquerors were but a few, an armed aristocracy; in Germany they were the mass of the people. However, therefore, Roman religion, to a certain extent Roman law, ruled eastward of the Rhine, each was a domiciled

---

[t] On the Heliand and on Otfried see the powerful criticism of Gervinus, Geschichte der Poetischen National Literatur der Deutschen, L. p. 84, et seqq. Neither are translators; they are rather paraphrasts of the Gospel. The Saxon has more of the popular poet, Otfried more of the religious teacher; in Otfried the poet appears, in the Saxon he is lost in his poetry. Where the Saxon leaves the text of the Gospel, it is in places where the popular poetry offers him matter and expression for epic amplification or adornment, as in the Murder of the Innocents; and where in the description of the Last Judgment he reminds us of the Scandinavian imagery of the destruction of the world; in this not altogether unlike the fragment of the Muspell edited by Schmeller. Instead of this, Otfried cites passages of the Prophets Joel and Zephaniah. On the whole, the Saxon has an epic, Otfried a lyric and didactic character. Gervinus thinks but meanly of Otfried as a poet. The whole passage is striking and instructive. The Heliand has been edited by Schmeller; and Otfried best by Graff, Königsberg. 1831. Compare Lachmann's article in Ersch und Gruber's Encyclopädie. The Poem on St. Gall exists only in a fragment of a Latin translation in Pertz, ii. p. 33. The first is in Hoffman, Geschichte des Deutschen Kirchenliedes; the last in Vit. Altman. in Prz. Script. Rer. Austriac. i. p. 117.

stranger. The Teuton in character, in habits, in language, remained a Teuton. As their tribes of old united for conquest; the conquest achieved, severed again to erect independent kingdoms; as the Roman Empire in Germany was at last but a half-naturalised fiction, controlled, limited, fettered by the independent Kings, Princes, and Prelates: so, as our History has shown, there was a constant struggle in the German Churchman between the Churchman and the Teuton—a gravitating tendency towards Roman unity in the Churchman, a repulsion towards independence in the Teuton. But for the Imperial claims on Italy and on Rome, which came in aid of the ecclesiastical centralisation under the Papacy, Teutonism might perhaps have much earlier burst free from the Latin unity.

The Norman conquest brought England back into the Roman pale; it warred as sternly against the independence of the Anglo-Saxon Bishop as against that of the Anglo-Saxon thane; it introduced the Latin religions phraseology. Hence in England we in many cases retain and use almost indifferently both the Latin and the Teutonic terms; in some instances only we inflexibly adhere to our vernacular religions language, and show a loyal predilection for the Saxon tongue. "God" and "the Lord" retain their uninvaded majesty. "The Son" admits no rival, but we admit the Holy *Spirit* as well as the Holy *Ghost*, but the Holy Ghost "sanctifies." The attributes of God, except his Almightiness and his wisdom, are more often used in theological discussion than in popular speech. Therefore his "omnipresence," his "omniscience" (he is also "all-knowing"), his "ubiquity," his "infinity," his "incomprehensibility," are Latin. In the titles of Christ, "the Saviour," the "Redeemer," the "Intercessor," except in the "Atonement," instead of the "Propitiation or Reconciliation," Latin has obtained the mastery. "Sin" is Saxon; "righteousness" a kind of common property; "mercy and love" may contend for pre-eminence; "goodness" is genuine German; "faith and charity" are Latin; "love," German. We await "Doomsday, or the Day of Judgement;" but "Heaven and Hell" are pure Teutonisms.* "Baptism" is Latinised Greek. The "Lord's Supper" contests with the "Eucharist;" the "Holy Communion" mingles the two. "Easter" is our Paschal Feast. We speak of Gentiles and Pagans, as well as "Heathens." Our inherited Greek, "Church," retains its place; as does "Priest," from the Greek presbyter. In common with all Teutons, our ecclesiastical titles, with this exception, are borrowed.

During this period of suspended Teutonic life in England, Germany had not yet receded into her rigid Teutonism. The Crusades united Christendom, Latin and German, in unresisting and spontaneous confederacy. The Franks, as has been seen, were in the van; Germany followed sluggishly, reluctantly, at intervals, made at least two great paroxysmal efforts under the Emperors, who themselves headed the armaments, but then collapsed into something bordering on apathy. From that time only single Princes and Prelates girt themselves with the Cross. The long feud, the open war of the Emperors and the Popes, was no strife between the races; the Emperor warred not for German interests, but for his own; it was as King of the Romans, with undefined rights over the Lombard and Tuscan cities, later as King of Naples as well as Emperor of

---

* The German Heiden is clearly analogous in its meaning to Pagan; the word is not the Greek Ethnic.

Germany, that he maintained the internecine strife. If
Frederick II. had been a German, not a Sicilian; if his
capital had been Cologne or Mentz or Augsburg, not
Palermo or Naples; if his courtly language, the language of his statesmen and poets, had been a noble
German, rising above the clashing and confused dialects
of High and Low, Franconian, Swabian, Bavarian; if
he had possessed the power and the will to legislate for
Germany as he legislated for Apulia, different might
have been the issue of the conflict.

Throughout all this period, the true mediæval period,
Germany was as mediæval as the rest of Christendom.
Her poets were as fertile in chivalrous romances;
whether translated or founded on those of the Trouvères,
there is not a poem on any of the great cycles, the
classical or that from ancient history, those of Charlemagne or of Arthur, not a tale of adventure, which has
not its antitype in German verse, in one or other of the
predominant dialects. The legends of the Saints of
all classes and countries (the romances of religious
adventure) are drawn out with the same inexhaustible
fecundity, to the same interminable length.[x] The somewhat later Minnesingers echo the amatory songs of the
Troubadours; and everywhere, as in France and England,
the vernacular first mingles in grotesque incongruity
with the Latin Mystery; scenes of less dignity, sometimes broadly comic in the vulgar tongue, are interpolated into the more solemn and stately Latin
spectacle.

When the Norman dynasty, and with the Norman

---

[x] Many of these poems, sacred and
profane, of enormous length, Titurel,
the Kaiser Chronik, Kutrun, as well
as the great " Passional " and the

" Marienleben," are in course of publication at Quedlinburg, in the Bib-
liothek der Deutschen National Literatur.

dynasty the dominance of the Norman language came
to an end, nearly at the same period the English constitution and the English language began to develope
themselves in their mingled character, but with Teutonism resuming its superiority. As in the constitution
the Anglo-Saxon common law, so in the structure and
vocabulary of the language the Anglo-Saxon was the
broad groundwork.   Poetry rose with the language;
and it is singular to observe that the earliest English
poems of original force and fancy (we had before only
the dry dull histories of Wace, and Robert of Gloucester,
Norman rather than English[7]), the Vision and the Creed
of Piers Ploughman, while they borrow their allegorical
images from the school of the Romance of the Rose,
adopt the alliterative verse of the old Anglo-Saxon.
The Romance of the Rose, by its extraordinary popularity had introduced the Impersonated Virtues and
Vices, which had almost driven out the knights and the
saints of the Romance and the Legend; instead of the
wild tale of chivalrous adventure, or the holy martyrdom, poetry became a long and weary allegory: even
the Mystery before long gave place to the Morality. In
some degree this may have been the Morals of Christianity reasserting coequal dignity and importance
against ritual observances and blind sacerdotal authority: it is constantly rebuking with grave solemnity,
or keen satire, the vices of the Clergy, the Monks, and
the Friars.

Before Chaucer, even before Wycliffe, appeared with

[7] The Ormulum, excellently edited
by Dr. Meadows White, Oxford, 1852,
is a paraphrase of the Gospels (it is
curious to compare it with the older
Teutonic Heliand and Otfried) in verse
and language, of a kind of transition
period, by some called semi-Saxon. See
on the Ormulum, Introduction to Bos-
worth's Anglo-Saxon Dictionary.

his rude satire, his uncouth alliterative verse, his homely
sense, and independence of thought, the author of Piers
Ploughman's Vision.* This extraordinary manifestation
of the religion, of the language, of the social and political
notions, of the English character, of the condition, of the
passions and feelings of rural and provincial England,
commences, and with Chaucer and Wycliffe completes
the revolution of this transition period, the reign of
Edward III. Throughout its institutions, language,
religious sentiment, Teutonism is now holding its first
initiatory struggle with Latin Christianity. In Chaucer
is heard a voice from the court, from the castle, from
the city, from universal England. All orders of society
live in his verse, with the truth and originality of individual being, yet each a type of every rank, class, every
religious and social condition and pursuit. And there
can be no doubt that he is a voice of freedom, of more
or less covert hostility to the hierarchical system, though
more playful and with a poet's genial appreciation of all
which was true, healthful, and beautiful in the old faith.
In Wycliffe is heard a voice from the University, from
the seat of theology and scholastic philosophy, from the
centre and stronghold of the hierarchy; a voice of revolt
and defiance, taken up and echoed in the pulpit
throughout the land against the sacerdotal domination.
In the Vision of Piers Ploughman is heard a voice from
the wild Malvern Hills, the voice it should seem of an
humble parson, or secular priest. He has passed some
years in London, but his home, his heart is among the
poor rural population of central Mercian England. Tra-

---

* The Vision bears its date about
1305. Chaucer's great work is about
twenty years later. Wycliffe was
hardly known, but by his tract on the
Last Days, before 1370. Whittaker,
p. xxxvi. and last note to Introduction.
Also Wright's Preface.

dition, uncertain tradition, has assigned a name to the
Poet, Robert Langland, born at Cleobury Mortimer, in
Shropshire, and of Oriel College, Oxford. Whoever he
was, he wrote in his provincial idiom, in a rhythm
perhaps from the Anglo-Saxon times familiar to the
popular ear; if it strengthened and deepened that
feeling, no doubt the poem was the expression of a strong
and wide-spread feeling. It is popular in a broader and
lower sense than the mass of vernacular poetry in
Germany and England. We must rapidly survey the
religion, the politics, the poetry of the Ploughman.

The Visionary is no disciple, no precursor of Wycliffe
in his broader religious views: the Loller of Piers
Ploughman is no Lollard; he applies the name as a
term of reproach for a lazy indolent vagrant.[a] The
Poet is no dreamy speculative theologian; he acquiesces
seemingly with unquestioning faith in the creed and
in the usages of the Church. He is not profane but
reverent as to the Virgin and the Saints. Pilgrimages,
penances, oblations on the altar, absolution, he does not
reject, though they are all nought in comparison with
holiness and charity; on Transubstantiation and the
Real Presence and the Sacraments he is almost silent,
but his silence is that of submission not of doubt.[b] It is
in his intense absorbing moral feeling that he is beyond

---

[a] Passus Sextus, p. 75 and elsewhere, Loller's life is begging at but-
tery hatches, and loitering on Fridays
or Feast Days at Church, p. 76.

[b] There is a very curious passage as
to the questions even then agitated :—
"I have Heard High men,—eating at the
table,
Carp as though they Clerks were,—of
Christ and his might,
And laid Faults on the Father—that
Formed us all . . . .

Why would our Saviour Suffer,—Such a
worm in his bliss
That beguiled the woman,—and the man
after."—Wright, 119.

The religious poet puts down these
questions with holy indignation.

I quote mostly from Dr. Whittaker's
edition, sometimes from Wright's,
taking the liberty of modernising only
the spelling, which shows how near
most of it is to our vernacular English.

his age : with him outward observances are but hollow
shows, mockeries, hypocrisies, without the inward power
of religion. It is not so much in his keen cutting satire
on all matters of the Church as in his solemn installation of Reason and Conscience as the guides of the self-
directed soul, that he is breaking the yoke of sacerdotal
domination : in his constant appeal to the plainest, sim-
plest Scriptural truths, as in themselves the whole of
religion, he is a stern reformer. The sad serious
Satirist, in his contemplation of the world around him,
the wealth of the world and the woe," sees no hope, no
consolation but in a new order of things, in which if the
hierarchy shall subsist, it shall subsist in a form, with
powers, in a spirit totally opposite to that which now
rules mankind. The mysterious Piers the Ploughman
seems to designate from what quarter that reformer is
to arise. Piers the Ploughman, who at one time was a
sort of impersonation of the industrious and at the same
time profoundly religious man, becomes at the close
Piers Pardon Ploughman, the great publisher of the
pardon of mankind through Christ. In him is the
teaching, absolving power of the Church ; he is the great
assertor and conservator of Unity.

With Wycliffe, with the spiritual Franciscans, Langland ascribes all the evils, social and religious, of the
dreary world to the wealth of the Clergy, of the Monks,
and the still more incongruous wealth of the Mendicants.
With them he asserts the right, the duty, the obligation
of the temporal Sovereign to despoil the hierarchy of
their corrupting and fatal riches.[d] As he has nothing of

---

c " And Marvellously me Met—as I May
      you tell,
   All the Wealth of the World—and the
      Woe both."—p. 2.

d " For if Possession be Poison—and im-
      Perfect these make

The Heads of Holy Church,
It were Charity to disCharge them for
   Holy Church sake,
And Purge them of the old Poison."
                                   —p. 236.

   See the whole passage.

the scholastic subtlety, of the Predestinarianism, or speculative freedom of Wycliffe, so he has nothing of the
wild spiritualist belief in the prophecies of ages to come.
With the Fraticelli, to him the fatal gift of Constantine
was the doom of true religion; with them he almost
adores poverty, but it is industrious down-trodden rustic
poverty; not that of the impostor beggar,[e] common in
his days, and denounced as sternly as by the political
economy of our own, still less of the religious mendicant.
Both these are fiercely excluded from his all-embracing
charity.[f]

Langland is Antipapal, yet he can admire an ideal
Pope, a general pacificator, reconciling the Sovereigns
of the world to universal amity.[g] It is the actual Pope,
the Pope of Avignon or of Rome, levying the wealth of
the world to slay mankind, who is the object of his bitter invective.[h] The Cardinals he denounces with the
same indignant scorn; but chiefly the Cardinal Legate,
whom he has seen in England riding in his pride and
pomp, with lewdness, rapacity, merciless extortion, inso-
lence in his train.[i] Above all, his hatred (it might seem

[e] See Passus iv. where Waster refuses to Work, and Piers summons
Want to seize him by the paunch, and
wring him well. The whole contrast
of the industrious and idle poor is remarkable. Also the Impostors and
Jolly Beggars, as of our own days, and
the favourable view of "God's Min-
strels,"—Whitaker, p. 154. This
passage was not in Mr. Wright's
copy.

[f] Pass. vi. p. 76.

[g] "Sithen Prayed to the Pope,—have Pity
    of Holy Church,
And no Grace to Grant—till Good love
    were,
Among all Kind of Kings—over Christ-
    ian people,

Command all Confessors that any King
    shrive
Enjoin him Peace for his Penance—and
    Perpetual forgiveness."—p. 63.

[h] Simony and Civil go to Rome to
put themselves under the Pope's protection.—P. iii. p. 36.

"And God amend the Pope—that Pilleth
    Holy Church,
And Claimeth by force to be King—to be
    Keeper over Christendom,
And Counteth not how Christian Men be
    Killed and robbed,
And Findeth Folk to Fight,—and Christian
    blood to spill."—Do best, p. 1, p. 389.

Compare p. 207.

[i] "The Country is the Crusader,—that
    Cardinals Come in,
And where they Lie and Linger,—
    Lechery there reigneth."
            —Wright, p. 120.

that on this all honest English indignation was agreed)
is against the Mendicant orders. Of the older monks
there is almost total silence. For St. Benedict, for St.
Dominic, for St. Francis he has the profoundest reverence.[k] But it is against their degenerate sons that he
arrays his allegorical Host; the Friars furnish every
impersonated vice, are foes to every virtue; his bitterest
satire, his keenest irony (and these weapons he wields
with wonderful poetic force) are against their dissoluteness, their idleness, their pride, their rapacity, their arts,
their lies, their hypocrisy, their intrusion into the functions of the Clergy, their delicate attire, their dainty
feasts, their magnificent buildings,[m] even their proud
learning; above all their hardness, their pitilessness to
the poor, their utter want of charity, which with Langland is the virtue of virtues.

Against the Clergy he is hardly less severe;[n] he
sternly condemns their dastardly desertion of their
flocks, when during the great plague they crowded to
London to live an idle life: that idle life he describes
with singular spirit and zest. Yet he seems to recognise the Priesthood as of Divine institution. Against
the whole host of officials, pardoners, summoners, Archdeacons, and their functionaries; against lawyers, civil
as well as ecclesiastical, he is everywhere fiercely and
contemptuously criminatory.

---

[k] Pass. v. p. 70.

[m] He scoffs at those who wish their names to appear in the rich painted windows of the Franciscan churches. The Friar absolves Mede (Bribery):—

> And sithen he seyde,
> We have a window in werkynge,
> Woldest thou glaze that gable,
> And grave there thy name,
> Sigher should thy soul be
> Heaven to have."—Wright, p. 44.

There is a full account in " the Creed " of a spacious and splendid Dominican Convent, very curious. " The Creed " is of a later date, by another author, an avowed Lollard.

[n] He declares that the Clergy shall fall as the Templars had fallen.—Do Bet., i. p. 297. But compare Wright, i. p. 233.

His political views are remarkable.[o] He has a notion of a king ruling in the affections of the people, with Reason for his chancellor, Conscience for his justiciary. On such a King the commonalty would cheerfully and amply bestow sufficient revenue for all the dignity of his office, and the exigencies of the state, even for his conquests. No doubt that Commonalty would first have absorbed the wealth of the hierarchy.[p] He is not absolutely superior to that hatred of the French, nor even to the ambition for the conquest of France engendered by Edward's wars and by his victories. And yet his shrewd common sense cannot but see the injustice and cruelty of those aggressive and sanguinary wars.[q]

As a Poet Langland has many high qualities. He is creating his own language, and that in a rude and remote province: its groundwork is Saxon-English, exclusively so in most of its words and in its idiom. It admits occasionally French words, but they appear like strangers; his Latinisms, and words of Latin descent, might seem drawn directly from the Vulgate Scriptures and the Church services. These he constantly cites in

---

[o] There is a strange cross of aristocratical feeling in Langland's levelling notions. That slaves and bastards should be advanced to be clergymen is a crying grievance. They should be sons of franklins and freemen, if not of Lords :—

"And such Bondamens Bairns have been made Bishops,
And Barons Bastards have been Archdeacons,
And Soapers (soap-boilers) and their sons for Silver have been Knights,
And Lords sons their Labourers."

The Barons mortgaged their estates to go to the wars. They were bought, this is curious, by traders.

[p] What the Commons require of the

King is Law, Love, and Truth, and himself for their Lord antecedent (p. 57) :—

"And I dare Lay my Life that Love would Lend that silver
To Wage (to pay the wages of) them, and help Win that thou Wittest after,
More than all the Merchants, or than the Mitred Bishops,
Or Lombards of Lacca, that Live by Love as Jews."—p. 14.

[q] Had Mede been Seneschal in France, K. Edward would have conquered the length and breadth of the land.—Pass. iv. p. 51. In another passage, he had won France by gentleness.—Do Wel, p. 250.

the original Latin. With his Anglo-Saxon alliteration
there is a cadence or rhythm in his verse; while Chaucer
is writing in rhyme Langland seems utterly ignorant of
that poetic artifice. The whole poem is an allegory, by
no means without plan, but that plan obscure, broken,
and confused; I am inclined to think wanting its close.
The Allegory is all his own. The universal outburst of
Allegory at this time in Paris, in Germany, in England
is remarkable. It had full vogue in Paris, in Rutebeuf,
and in the Romance of the Rose, which Chaucer translated into English. As the chivalrous romance and the
fabliaux had yielded to the allegorical poem, so also the
drama. It might seem, as we have said, as if the
awakening moral sense of men, weary of the saints, and
angels, and devils, delighted in those impersonations of
the unchristian vices and Christian virtues. That which
to us is languid, wearisome, unreal, seized most powerfully on the imagination of all orders. Nor had allegory
fulfilled its office in the imaginative realm of letters till
it had called forth Spenser and Bunyan. Langland, I
am disposed to think, approaches much nearer to Bunyan
than the Romance of the Rose to the Faëry Queen.
But Langland, with all his boldness, and clearness, and
originality, had too much which was temporary, much
which could not but become obsolete. Bunyan's vision
was more simple, had more, if it may be so said, of the
moral, or of the scheme, of perpetual, universal Christianity. But Spenser himself has hardly surpassed some
few touches by which Langland has designated his personages: and there is at times a keen quiet irony too
fine for Bunyan.

The Poem is manifestly in two parts: the poet, asleep
on the Malvern Hills, beholds the whole world; eastward
a magnificent tower, the dwelling of Truth; opposite a

deep dale, the abode of unblessed spirits; between them
a wide plain, in which mankind are following all their
avocations. He dwells rapidly on the evils and abuses
of all Orders. A stately lady, in white raiment (Holy
Church) offers herself as guide to the Castle of Truth,
in which is seated the Blessed Trinity. The first five
passages of the first part are on the redress of civil
wrongs, the last on the correction of religious abuses.
Mede (Bribery) with all her crew are on one side; Conscience, who refuses to be wedded to Mede,' with Reason
on the other. It closes with the King's appointment of
Conscience as his Justiciary, of Reason as his Chancellor. In the Sixth Passage the Dreamer awakes; he
encounters Reason. As Reason with Conscience is the
great antagonist of social and political evil, so again,
Reason, vested as a Pope, with Conscience as his Cross
Bearer, is alone to subdue religious evil. For that evil
God is visiting the earth with awful pestilences and
storms. To avert God's wrath the domestic duties must
be observed with fervent affection; the Pope must have
pity on the Church, the religious Orders keep to their
rule, those who go on pilgrimages to the Saints seek

' Conscience objects to Mede that
she is false and faithless, misleading
men by her treasure, leading wives
and widows to wantonness. Falsehood
and she undid the King's Father (Edward II.), poisoned Popes, impaired
holy Church; she is a trumpet to the
basest Simony of the common law;
summoners of the civil law prize her
highly; sheriffs of counties would be
undone without her, for she causes men
to forfeit lands and lives; she bribes
gaolers to let out prisoners, imprisons
true men, hangs the innocent. She
cares not for being excommunicated in
the Consistory Court; she buys absolution by a cope to the Commissary.
She can do almost as much work as the
King's Privy Seal in 120 days. She is
intimate with the Pope, as provisors
show. She and Simony seal his
Bulls. She consecrates Bishops without learning. She presents Rectors
to prebends, maintains priests in keeping concubines and begetting bastards
contrary to the Canon, &c. &c.—P. iii.
p. 46.

rather Truth. Truth is the one eternal object of man. After Repentance has brought all the seven deadly sins to confession [1] (a strange powerful passage), Hope blows a trumpet, whose blast is to compel mankind to seek Grace from Christ to find out Truth. But no pilgrim who has wandered over the world can show the way to Truth. Now suddenly arises Piers Ploughman; he has long known Truth; he has been her faithful follower. Meekness and the Ten Commandments are the way to, Grace is the Portress of, the noble Castle of Truth. After some time Truth reveals herself. She commands Piers to stay at home, to tend his plough; of the young peasantry industry in their calling is their highest duty; to the laborious poor is offered plenary pardon, and to those who protect them, Kings who rule in righteousness, holy Bishops who justly maintain Church discipline. Less plenary pardon is bestowed on less perfect men, merchants, lawyers who plead for hire. What is this pardon? it is read by a Priest; it contains but these words: "They that have done good shall go into life eternal, they that have done evil into everlasting fire." [2]

Thus with Piers Ploughman, a holy Christian life, a

---

[1] The confession of Covetousness is admirable :—

"Didst thou ever make restitution ? Yes, I once Robbed some Chapmen, and Rifled their trunks."

Covetousness would go hang herself— but even for her Repentance has comfort :—

"Have Mercy in thy Mind—and with thy Mouth beseech it, For Goddes Mercy is More—than all his other works, And all the Wickedness of the World— that man might Work or think Is no More to the Mercy of God—than in the Sea a glede (a spark of fire)."
Wright, p. 84.

[2] It is added—

"For wise men ben holden To Purchase you Pardon and the Popes bulles, At the Dreadful Doom when the Dead shall arise, And Come all before Christ, accounts to yield How thou leddest thy Life here, and his Laws kept. A Pouch full of Pardons there, nor Provincials Letters, Though ye be Found in the Fraternity of all the Four Orders, And have Indulgences Double fold, If he Wol you help, I set your Patents and your Pardons at one Pies worth."—Wright, L p. 156.

life of love, of charity, of charity especially to the poor,
is all in all; on the attainment of that life dwells the
second Vision, the latter part of the poem. There are
three personages by the plain names of Do Well, Do
Bet (do better), and Do Best. The whole of this ascent
through the different degrees of the Christian life is
described with wonderful felicity; every power, attribute, faculty of man, every virtue, every vice is impersonated with the utmost life and truth. The result of
the whole is that the essence of the Christian life, the
final end of Do Well, is charity. Do Bet appears to
have a higher office, to teach other men; and this part
closes with a splendid description of the Redeemer's life
and passion, and that which displays the poetic power of
Robert Langland higher perhaps than any other passage,
that mysterious part of the Saviour's function between
his passion and resurrection commonly called the " har-
rowing of hell," the deliverance of the spirits in prison.[a]

---

[a] It is odd that Mahamet (Mahomet)
defends the realm of Lucifer against
the Lord with guns and mangonels
—a whimsical anticipation of Milton.
" There had been a loud cry, Lift up
your heads, ye gates, and be ye lift up,
ye everlasting doors." At length,

" What Lord art thou? quoth Lucifer. A
　　voice aLoud said.
The Lord of Might and of Heaven, that
　　Made all things,
Dame of this Dim place. Anon unDo the
　　gates
That Christ may comen in, the King's son
　　of heaven.
And with that Break Hell Brake, with
　　all Belial's Bars,
Nor any Wight or Ward Wide opened the
　　gates,
Patriarchs and Prophets, Populus in tene-
　　bris,
Sang out with Saint John, Ecce Agnus
　　Dei."

I am tempted to give the close of this
canto—so characteristic of the poem.

He had said in Latin, Mercy and
Charity have met together; Right-
ousness and Peace have kissed each
other:—

" Truth Trumpeted them, and sung 'To
　　Deum laudamus.'
And then saLuted Love, in a Loud note.
Ecce quam bonum et quam jocundum est
　　habitare fratres in unum.
Till the Day Dawned, there Damsels
　　Daunsed,
That men Rang to the Revurrection. And
　　with that I awaked,
And called Kitty my wife, and Kalotte
　　my daughter,
A Rise and go Reverence Gods Resur-
　　rection,
And Creep on knees to the Cross, and Kiss
　　it for a jewel,
And Rightfullest of Reliques, none Richer
　　on earth.
For Gods Blessed Body it Bare for our
　　Bote (good).
And it a Feareth the Fiend; for such is
　　the might,
May no Grisly Ghost Glide where I
　　shadoweth."

In Do Best Piers Ploughman appears as a kind of impersonation of the Saviour, or of his faith; the Holy Ghost
descends upon him in lightning; Grace arrays him with
wonderful power to sustain the war with coming Antichrist; Piety has bestowed upon him four stout oxen
(the Evangelists) to till the earth; four bullocks to harrow the land (the four Latin Fathers), who harrow into
it the Old and New Testaments; the grain which Piers
sows is the cardinal virtues. The poem concludes with
the resurrection and war of Antichrist, in which Piers,
if victor, is hardly victor—"a cold and comfortless conclusion," says the learned editor, Dr. Whittaker. I am
persuaded that it is not the actual or the designed conclusion. The last Passage of Do Best can hardly have
been intended to be so much shorter than the others.
The poet may have broken off indeed in sad despondency,
and left his design unfinished; he may have been prevented from its completion; or, what is far less impro-
bable, considering the way in which the Poem has
survived, the end may have been lost.

The Poet who could address such opinions, though
wrapt up in prudent allegory, to the popular ear, to the
ear of the peasantry of England; the people who could
listen with delight to such strains, were far advanced
towards a revolt from Latin Christianity. Truth, true
religion, was not to be found with, it was not known by,
Pope, Cardinals, Bishops, Clergy, Monks, Friars. It
was to be sought by man himself, by the individual man,
by the poorest man, under the sole guidance of Reason,
Conscience, and of the Grace of God, vouchsafed directly,
not through any intermediate human being, or even
Sacrament, to the self-directing soul. If it yet respected
all existing doctrines, it respected them not as resting on
traditional or sacerdotal authority. There is a manifest

appeal throughout, an unconscious installation of Scripture alone,[*] as the ultimate judge; the test of everything is a moral and purely religious one, its agreement with holiness and charity.

English prose in Wycliffe's Bible, the higher English poetry in its true father, Chaucer, maintained this prevailing and dominant Teutonism. Wycliffe's Bible, as translated from the Vulgate, had not so entirely shaken off the trammels of Latinity as our later versions; but this first bold assertion of Teutonic independence immeasurably strengthened, even in its language, that independence. It tasked the language, as it were, to its utmost vigour, copiousness, and flexibility: and by thus putting it to the trial, forced out all those latent and undeveloped qualities. It was constantly striving to be English, and by striving became so more and more. Compare the freedom and versatility of Wycliffe's Bible with Wycliffe's Tracts. Wycliffe has not only advanced in the knowledge of purer and more free religion, he is becoming a master of purer and more free English.

Geoffrey Chaucer, among the most remarkable of poets, was in nothing more remarkable than in being most emphatically an English poet. Chaucer lived in courts and castles: he was in the service of the King, he was a retainer of the great Duke of Lancaster. In the court and in the castle, no doubt, if anywhere, with the Norman chivalrous magnificence lingered whatever

[*] "And is Han to Religion, and hath Rendered the Bible, And Preacheth to the People St. Paul's words."—Wright, p. 164. He quotes, "Ye suffer fools gladly" (1 Cor.) Is this Wycliffe? Clergy (Theology) weds a wife; her name is Scripture.—Wright, p. 182. I take the opportunity of observing that the famous prophecy, ascribed to Langland, about the King who should suppress the monasteries, is merely a vague and general prediction; though the naming the Abbot of Abingdon is a lucky coincidence.—See Wright, p. 192.

remained of Norman manners and language. Chaucer
had served in the armies of King Edward III.; he had
seen almost all the more flourishing countries, many of
the great cities, of the Continent, of Flanders, France,
Italy. It may be but a romantic tradition, that at the
wedding of Violante to the great Duke of Milan he had
seen Petrarch, perhaps Boccaccio, and that Froissart too
was present at that splendid festival. It may be but a
groundless inference from a misinterpreted passage in
his poems, that he had conversed with Petrarch (Novem-
ber, 1372); but there is unquestionable evidence that
Chaucer was at Genoa under a commission from the
Crown. He visited brilliant Florence, perhaps others of
the noble cities of Italy. Five years later he was in
Flanders and at Paris. In 1378 he went with the Embassy to demand the hand of a French Princess for the
young Richard of Bordeaux. Still later he was at the
gorgeous court of the Visconti at Milan.[7] Chaucer was
master of the whole range of vernacular poetry, which
was bursting forth in such young and prodigal vigour, in
the languages born from the Romance Latin. He had
read Dante, he had read Petrarch; to Boccaccio he
owed the groundwork of two of his best poems—the
Knight's Tale of Palamon and Arcite, and Griselidis. I
cannot but think that he was familiar with the Troubadour poetry of the Langue d'Oc; of the Langue d'Oïl,
he knew well the knightly tales of the Trouvères and
the Fabliaux, as well as the later allegorical school,
which was then in the height of its fashion in Paris. He
translated the Romance of the Rose.

It is indeed extraordinary to see the whole of the
mediæval, or post-mediæval poetry (with the great ex-

---

[7] Compare the lives of Chaucer, especially the latest by Sir Harris Nicolas.

ception of the Dantesque vision of the other world)
summed up, and as it were represented by Chaucer in
one or more perfect examples, and so offered to the
English people. There is the legend of martyrdom in
Constance of Surrie; the miracle legend, not without its
harsh alloy of hatred to the unbeliever, in Hugh of
Lincoln; the wild, strange, stirring adventures told in
the free prolix Epopee of the Trouvère, in its romanticised classic form, in Troilus and Cressida; in the wilder
Oriental strain of magic and glamour in the half-told
tale of Cambuscan; the chivalrous in Palamon and
Arcite; to which perhaps may be added the noble
Franklin's Tale. There is the Fabliau in its best, in its
tender and graceful form, in Griselidis; in its gayer and
more licentious, in January and May; in its coarser,
more broadly humorous, and, to our finer manners, repulsive, Miller's Tale; and in that of the Reve. The
unfinished Sir Thopas might seem as if the spirit of
Ariosto or Cervantes, or of lighter or later poets, was
struggling for precocious being. There is the genial
apologue of the Cock and the Fox, which might seem
an episode from the universal brute Epic, the Latin, or
Flemish, or German or French Reynard. The more
cumbrous and sustained French allegory appears in the
translation of the Romaunt of the Rose; the more rich
and simple in the Temple of Fame. There are a few
slighter pieces which may call to mind the Lais and
Serventes of the South.

Yet all the while Chaucer in thought, in character, in
language, is English—resolutely, determinately, almost
boastfully English.[1] The creation of native poetry was

<hr>

[1] There is a curious passage in the
Prologue to the Testament of Love on
the soveran wits in Latin and in French.

"Let then Clerkes enditen in Latin,
for they have the propertie of science,
and the knowledge in that faculte:

his deliberate aim; and already that broad, practical, humorous yet serious view of life, of life in its infinite variety, that which reaches its height in Shakspeare, has begun to reveal itself in Chaucer. The Canterbury Tales, even in the Preface, represent, as in a moving comedy, the whole social state of the times; they display human character in action as in speech; and that character is the man himself, the whole man, with all his mingling, shifting, crossing, contradictory passions, motives, peculiarities, his greatnesses and weaknesses, his virtues and his vanities; every one is perfectly human, yet every one the individual man, with the very dress, gesture, look, speech, tone of the individual. There is an example of every order and class of society, high, low, secular, religious. As yet each is distinct in his class, as his class from others. Contrast Chaucer's pilgrims with the youths and damsels of Boccaccio. Exquisitely as these are drawn, and in some respects finely touched, they are all of one gay light class; almost any one might tell any tale with equal propriety; they differ in name, in nothing else.

In his religious characters, if not in his religious tales (religion is still man's dominant motive), Chaucer is by no means the least happy. In that which is purely religious the poet himself is profoundly religious; in his Prayer to the Virgin, written for the Duchess Blanche of Lancaster, for whom also he poured forth his sad elegy; in his Gentle Martyrs S. Constantia and S. Cecilia: he is not without his touch of bigotry, as has been said, in Hugh of Lincoln. But the strong Teutonic good sense of Chaucer had looked more deeply into the

and let Frenchmen in their French also enditen their quaint termes, for it is kindely to their mouthes; and let us | shew our fantasies in such wordes as wee learneden of our dames tongue."— Fol. 271.

whole monastic and sacerdotal system. His wisdom betrays itself in his most mirthful, as in his coarsest humour. He who drew the Monk, the Pardoner, the Friar Limitour, the Summoner, had seen far more than the outer form, the worldliness of the Churchman, the abuse of indulgences, the extortions of the friars, the licentiousness of the Ecclesiastical Courts, of the Ecclesiastics themselves: he had penetrated into the inner depths of the religion. Yet his wisdom, even in his most biting passages, is tempered with charity. Though every order, the Abbot, the Prioress, the Friar, the Pardoner, the Summoner, are impersonated to the life, with all their weaknesses, follies, affectations, even vices and falsehoods, in unsparing freedom, in fearless truth, yet none, or hardly one, is absolutely odious; the jolly hunting Abbot, with his dainty horses, their bridles jingling in the wind, his greyhounds, his bald shining head, his portly person, his hood fastened with a rich pin in a love-knot: the tender and delicate Prioress, with what we should now call her sentimentality, virtuous no doubt, but with her broad and somewhat suspicious motto about all-conquering love: the Friar, who so sweetly heard confession, and gave such pleasant absolution, urging men, instead of weeping and prayers, to give silver to the friars; with his lisping voice and twinkling eyes, yet the best beggar in his house, to whom the poorest widow could not deny a farthing: the Pardoner with his wallet in his lap, brimful of pardons from Rome, with his reliques or pillowbere covered with part of our Lady's veil and the glass vessel with pig's bones; yet in Church the Pardoner was a noble Ecclesiast, read well, chanted with such moving tones, that no one could resist him and not throw silver into the offertory. The Summoner, whose office and the

Archdeacon's Court in which he officiated seem to have
been most unpopular, is drawn in the darkest colours,
with his fire-red cherubim's face, lecherous, venal, licentious.   Above all, the Parish Priest of Chaucer has
thrown off Roman mediæval Sacerdotalism; he feels his
proper place; he arrays himself only in the virtues
which are the essence of his holy function.   This unrivalled picture is the most powerful because the most
quiet, uninsulting, unexasperating satire.   Chaucer's
Parish Priest might have been drawn from Wycliffe,
from Wycliffe at Lutterworth, not at Oxford, from
Wycliffe, not the fierce controversialist, but the affec-
tionate and beloved teacher of his humble flock.   The
Priest's Tale is a sermon, prolix indeed, but, except in
urging confession and holding up the confessorial office
of the Priesthood, purely and altogether moral in its
scope and language.[a]   The translation of the Romaunt
of the Rose, with all its unmitigated bitterness against
the Friars, is a further illustration of the religious mind
of Chaucer.   If we could interpret with any certainty
the allegory and the mystic and poetic prose in the
Testament of Love, we might hope for more light on
the religion and on the later period of Chaucer's life.[b]
It is evident that at that time, towards the close of his
life, he was in disgrace and in prison.   Other documents
show that his pensions or allowances from the Crown
were, for a time at least, withdrawn.   There is no doubt
that his imprisonment arose out of some turbulent and

[a] I have little doubt that in the Retractation ascribed to Chaucer at the close of this Sermon, Tyrwhitt is right in that part which he marks for interpolation. Read the passage without it, all is clear.

[b] Speght in his argument to the Testament of Love, if it be Speght's. "Chaucer did compile this booke as a comfort to himselfe after great greefes conceived for some rash attempts of the Commons, with which hee had joyned, and thereby was in feare to lose the favour of his best friends."—Fol. 272.

popular movements in the City of London. There is
every probability that these movements were connected
with the struggle to reinvest the Wycliffite (and so long
as the Lancastrian party was Wycliffite) Lancastrian
Mayor,[*] John of Northampton, in the civic dignity. The
Londoners were Lollards, and if on the people's side,
Chaucer was on the Lollards' side. Chaucer, in his imprisonment, would, like Boethius of old, from whom the
Testament of Love was imitated, seek consolation, but
his consolation is in religion, not philosophy. His aspiration is after the beautiful and all-excelling Margarita,
the pearl of great price, who, like the Beatrice of Dante,
seems at once an ideal or idealised mistress, and the
impersonation of pure religion. Love alone can bestow
on him this precious boon; and divine love, as usual,
borrowing some of its imagery and language from human
love, purifies and exalts the soul of the poet for this
great blessing by imparting the knowledge of God in
the works of his power, and the works of his grace and
glory. More than this the obstinate obscurity of the
allegory refuses to reveal.

We must turn again to Germany, which we left in its
intermediate state of slowly dawning Teutonism. Germany, it has been seen, rejected the first free movement
of her kindred Teutons in England, because it was taken
up with such passionate zeal by the hostile Sclavonians.
The reformation in Bohemia, followed by its wild and
cruel wars, civil and foreign, threw back the German

* See the whole very curious but
obscure passage. fol. 277: "Then,
Lady, I thought that every man that
by auye way of right, rightfully done,
may helpe any commune (helpe) to
been saved." Chaucer was in the
secrets of his party, which he was urged
to betray. He goes on to speak of the
"citie of London, which is to me so deare
and sweet, in which I was forth growen;
and more kindly love have I to that
place than to anye other in yearth."

mind in aversion and terror upon Latin Christianity.
Yet Teutonism only slumbered, it was not extinguished;
it was too deeply rooted; it had been slowly growing up
from its undying root for centuries. The strife of ages
between the Emperor and the Pope could not but leave
a profound jealousy, and even antipathy, in a great mass
of the nation. Throughout there had been a strong
Imperialist, a German faction. The haughty aggression
of John XXII. (a Pontiff not on the Papal throne at
Rome) was felt as a more wanton and unprovoked insult.
It was not now the Pope asserting against the Emperor
the independence of Italy or of Rome; not defending
Rome and Italy from the aggression of Transalpine
barbarians by carrying the war against the Emperor
into Germany.   Louis of Bavaria would never have
descended into Italy if the Pope had left him in peace
on his own side of the Alps.   The shame of Germany
at the pusillanimity of Louis of Bavaria wrought more
strongly on German pride: the Pope was more profoundly hated for the self-sought humiliation of the
Emperor.   At the same time the rise of the great and
wealthy commercial cities had created a new class with
higher aspirations for freedom than their turbulent
princes and nobles, who were constantly in league with
the Pope against the Emperor, of whom they were more
jealous than of the Pope: or than the Prince Bishops,
who would set up a hierarchical instead of a papal
supremacy. The burghers, often hostile to their Bishops
and even to the cathedral Chapters, with whom they
were at strife for power and jurisdiction in their towns,
seized perpetually the excuse of their papalising to eject
their Prelates, and to erect their lower Clergy into a
kind of spiritual Republic.   The Schism had prostrated
the Pope before the temporal power; the Emperor of

Germany had compelled the Pope to summon a Council; at that Council he had taken the acknowledged lead, had almost himself deposed a Pope. It is true that at the close he had been out-manœuvred by the subtle and pertinacious Churchman. Martin V. had regained the lost ground; a barren, ambiguous, delusive Concordat had baffled the peremptory demand of Germany for a reformation of the Church in its head and in its members.[d] Yet even at the height of the Bohemian war, dark, deepening murmurs were heard of German cities, German Princes, joining the Antipapal movement. During the Council of Basle, when Latin Christianity was severed into two oppugnant parties, that of the Pope Eugenius IV. and that of the Transalpine reforming hierarchy, Germany had stood aloof in cold, proud neutrality: but for the subtle policy of one man, Æneas Sylvius, and the weak and yielding flexibility of another, the Emperor Frederick III., there might have been a German spiritual nationality, a German independent Church. The Pope was compelled to the humiliation of restoring the Prelate Electors whom he had dared to degrade, to degrade their successors whom he had appointed. Gregory of Heimberg, the representative of the German mind, had defied the Roman Court in Rome itself, had denounced Papal haughtiness to the face of the Pope.[e] But for one event, all the policy of Æneas Sylvius, and all the sub-

<hr />

[d] Ranke has written thus (I should not quote in English, if the English were not Mrs. Austin's): " Had this course been persevered in with union and constancy, the German Catholic Church, established in so many great principalities, and splendidly provided with the most munificent endowments, would have acquired a perfectly independent position, in which she might have resisted the subsequent political storms with as much firmness as England."—Reformation in Germany, vol. i. p. 48.

[e] Ranke, p. 49. Compare these passages above.

serviency of Frederick III. to him who he supposed
was his counsellor, but who was his ruler, had been un-
availing. As the aggressive crusade to Palestine gave
the dominion of Latin Christendom to the older Popes,
so the defensive crusade against the terrible progress of
the Turk, which threatened both Teutonic and Latin
Christendom, placed the Pope again at the head, not in
arms, but in awe and influence, of the whole West. Germany and the Pope were in common peril, they were
compelled to close alliance. In justice to Æneas Sylvius,
when Pius II., it may be acknowledged that it was his
providential sagacity, his not ungrounded apprehension
of the greatness of the danger, which made him devote
his whole soul to the league against the Ottoman; if
it was also wise policy, as distracting the German mind
from dangerous meditations of independence, this even
with Pius II. was but a secondary and subordinate consideration. The Turk was the cause of the truce of
more than half a century between the Papacy and the
Empire.

But throughout all that time the silent growth of the
German languages, the independent Teutonic thought
expressed in poetry, even in preaching, was widening
the alienation. During the century and a half in which
English Teutonism was resolutely bracing itself to
practical and political religious independence, and the
English language ripening to its masculine force, with
the Anglo-Saxon successfully wrestling for the mastery
against the Southern Latin; in Germany a silent rebellious mysticism was growing up even in her cloisters,
and working into the depths of men's hearts and minds.
The movement was more profound, more secret, and
unconscious even among those most powerfully under its
influence. There was not only the open insurrection of

Marsilio of Padua and William of Ockham against the
Papal or hierarchical authority, and the wild revolt of
the Fraticelli; there was likewise at once an acknow-
ledgement of and an attempt to satisfy that yearning of
the religious soul for what the Church, the Latin
Church, had ceased to supply, which was no longer to
be found in the common cloister-life, which the new
Orders had ceased to administer to the wants of the
people. During this time, too, while Germany luxu-
riated in the Romance Legend as well as in the
Chivalrous Romance, and the Hymn still in some
degree vied with the Lay of the Minnesinger, German
prose had grown up and was still growing up out
of vernacular preaching. From the earliest
period some scanty instruction, catechetical or
oral, from the glosses or from fragments of the Scripture, had been communicated in German to the people:
some German homilies, translated from the Latin, had
been in use. But the great impulse was given by the
new Orders. The Dominican, Conrad of Marburg, had
been forced at times to leave the overcrowded church
for the open air, on account of the multitudes which
gathered round the fierce Inquisitor, to hear his sermons, to witness the conclusion of his sermons, the
burning of a holocaust of heretics. Far different was
the tone of the Franciscan Bertholdt of Win-
terthur,[f] who from 1247 to 1272 preached
with amazing success throughout Bavaria, Austria,
Moravia, Thuringia. His sermons, taken down by the

German preaching.

Bertholdt.

[f] Compare Leyser, Einleitung, Deutsche Predigten des viii. und xiv. Jahrhundert, Quedlinburg, 1838, p. xvi.,
for the life of Bartholdt. Gervinus
(Deutsche Poesie) writes, " Die Vortreff-
lichkeit der Berthold'schen Predigten,
die weit die Schriften Taulers über-
trifft."—Vol. ii. p. 142. Schmidt,
Joannes Tauler, p. 82.

zeal of his hearers, were popular in the best sense; he
had the instinct of eloquence; he is even now by the
best judges set above Tauler himself. In earnestness, in
energy, in his living imagery from external nature,
Bertholdt was the popular preacher in the open field,
on the hill-side, Tauler the contemplative monk in the
pulpit of the cloister-chapel.[f] Nor did Bertholdt stand
alone in these vivid popular addresses. That which,
notwithstanding these examples, was at least inefficiently
bestowed by the Church, stirring and awakening vernacular instruction, was prodigally poured forth from
other quarters. The dissidents under their various
names, and the Beghards, were everywhere. At the
beginning of the fourteenth century Alsace was almost
in possession of the Brethren and Sisters of the Free
Spirit; they were driven out and scattered, but expulsion and dispersion, if it does not multiply the numbers,
usually increases the force and power of such communities.[h] Mysticism within the Church strove to fill the
void caused by their expulsion. Of these Mystics the
most famous names are Rysbroeck of Cologne, Master
Eckhart, John Tauler, Nicolas of Suso. The life of
Tauler will show us the times and the personal influence of these men, and that of their opinions. It occupies all the early part of the fourteenth century.

John Tauler[i] was born in Strasburg in 1290. At
the age of eighteen the religious youth entered the
Dominican cloister. He went to study at Paris; but at
Paris the Doctors were ever turning over the leaves of
huge books, they cared not for the one book of life.[k]

[f] Leyser, Deutsche Predigten.
[h] Schmidt, Tauler, p. 7. In 1317,
there was a violent persecution by John
of Ochsenstein, Bishop of Strasburg.

[i] Joannes Tauler von Strasburg, von
D. Carl Schmidt. Hamburg, 1841.
[k] Tauler, p. 3. Quotation from
Tauler's Sermon in note.

Probably on his return to Strasburg he came under the influence of Master Eckhart. This remarkable man preached in German; countless hearers thronged even to Eckhart's vernacular sermons. But Eckhart was a Schoolman in the incongruous office of a popular preacher; he was more than a Schoolman, he aspired to be a philosopher. His was not a passionate, simple, fervent theology, but the mystic divinity of Dionysius the Areopagite; it approached the Arabic Aristotelian philosophy. He held, indeed, the Creation out of nothing, and in theory repudiated the Eternity of Matter; but Creation seemed a necessity of the divine nature. The Universal could not but be particular; so God was all things, and all things were God. The soul came forth from God, it was an emanation; it had part of the light of God, in itself inextinguishable, but that light required kindling and quickening by divine grace.[m] Thus man stands between the spiritual and the corporeal, between time and eternity. God will reveal himself fully, pour himself wholly into the reasonable soul of man. It is not by love but by intelligence that the mystic reunion takes place with God; by knowledge we are one with God; that which knows and that which is known are one. Master Eckhart is the parent of German metaphysical theology. But if Tauler was caught with the glowing language in which Eckhart clothed these colder opinions, he stood aloof from the kindred teaching of the Beghards, with their more pas-

---

[m] See the Chapter on Eckhart, Ritter, Christliche Philosophie, iv. p. 408, &c. "Eckhart ist mit den Theologen seiner Zeit von der Ueberzeugung durchdrungen, dass die vernünftige Seele des Menschen dazu bestimmt sei in der innigsten Verbindung mit Gott, des höchsten Gutes, ganz und ohne alle Schmälerung, theilhaftig zu werden . . . Gott soll sich ganz offenbaren, wir ihn ganz erkennen: er soll ganz unser werden."—P. 502.

sionate, more religious Pantheism—the same in thought
with Eckhart, more bold and fearless in expression.

But if of itself the soul of Tauler sought a deeper and
more fervent faith, the dark and turbulent times would
isolate or make such a soul seek its sympathy within a
narrower circle. It was the height of the war between
John XXII. and Louis of Bavaria, and nowhere did that
war rage more violently than in Strasburg. The Bishop
John of Ochsenstein was for the Pope, the Magistrates
and the people, for the Emperor, or rather for insulted
Germany. The Bishop laid his interdict on the city; the
Magistrates, the Town Council, declared that the Clergy
who would not perform their functions must be driven
from the city.[a] The Clergy, the Monks, the Friars,
were divided: here the bells were silent, the churches
closed; there they tolled for prayers, and the contumacious Clergy performed forbidden services. No
wonder that religious men sought that religion in themselves which they found not in the church or in the
cloister; they took refuge in the sanctuary of their own
thoughts, from the religion which was contesting the
world. In all the great cities rose a secret unorganised
brotherhood, bound together only by silent infelt sympathies, the Friends of God. This appellation was a
secession, a tacit revolt, an assumption of superiority.
God was not to be worshipped in the church alone, with
the Clergy alone, with the Monks alone, in the Ritual,
even in the Sacraments; he was within, in the heart, in
the life. This and kindred brotherhoods embraced all
orders, Priests, Monks, Friars, Nobles, Burghers, Peasants; they had their Prophets and Prophetesses, above

a " Do solltent su such fürbas singen,
      Oder aber us der stall springen."
                —Konigshofen Chronicle, 128 -9. Schmidt, p. 14.
             See Book xii. c. 7.

all, their Preachers.* Some convents were entirely in
their power. In one thing alone they sided with the

---

* On the "Friends of God," see
Schmidt, Anhang. M. Carl Schmidt
has now discovered and printed some
very curious documents, which throw
more full but yet dubious light on the
"Friends of God," and their great
leader, Nicolas of Basle. They were
Mystics to the height of Mysticism;
each believer was in direct union with
God, with the Trinity, not the Holy
Ghost alone. They were not Walden-
sians. They were faithful to the whole
mediæval imaginative creed, Transubstantiation, worship of the Virgin and
Saints, Purgatory. Their union with
the Deity was not that of Pantheism,
or of passionate love; it was rather
through the phantasy. They had wonders, visions, special revelations, prophecies. Their peculiar heresy was the
denial of all special prerogative to the
Clergy, except the celebration of the
Sacraments; the layman had equal
sanctity, equal communion with the
Deity, saw visions, uttered prophecies.
Their only sympathy with the Walden-
sians was Anti-Sacerdotalism. Neither
were they Biblical Christians; they
honoured, loved the Bible; but sought
and obtained revelation beyond it. They
rejected one clause of the Lord's Prayer.
Temptations were marks of God's favour not to be deprecated. But though
suffering was a sign of the Divine Love,
it was not self-inflicted suffering. They
disclaimed asceticism, self-maceration,
self-torture. All things to the beloved
were of God; all therefore indifferent,
seclusion, poverty. In 1367 Nicolas
of Basle, with his twelve friends or
disciples (so commanded by a dream),

set forth from the Oberland under the
guidance of a dog to find a domicile.
After a wild journey over moss and
moor, the dog barked and scratched up
the earth. They determined to build
(with the permission of the Duke of
Austria to whom the land belonged) a
chapel, with a pleasant chamber for
each; here they dwelt, recluses, not
monks, under no vows, withdrawn
from the world, but well informed of
what passed in the world. Eight of
them afterwards went into foreign
lands, to Hungary, to Italy.

They had other places of retreat,
and it should seem multitudes of followers attached to them with more or
less intimacy. Nicolas of Basle, as
specially inspired, held boundless influence and authority over all, whether
"Friends of God," or not, over Tauler,
Rulman Merswin, and others.

As the days of the Church grew
darker under the later Popes at Avignon, and during the Schism, visions,
dreams multiplied and darkened around
them. Nicolas visited Gregory XI. at
Rome; he reproved the Pope's inert-
ness, his sins. Gregory, at first indignant, was overawed by the commanding holiness of Nicolas. In 1276
Nicolas with his followers prayed together from the 17th to the 25th of
March to God, to dispel the dark weather which overhung the Church. They
were directed to "wait." The time
of "waiting" lasted to March 25th,
1383. In the mean time they scrupled
not to speak with the utmost freedom
of the Pope and the Clergy. They
disclaimed both Popes. Many awful

Town Councils—in denouncing the unlawfulness, the
wickedness of closing the churches against the poor;
they rejected the monstrous doctrine that the Pope and
the Bishops might withhold the blessings of religion
from the many for the sins, or what they chose to call
the sins, of the few.   Christian love was something
higher, holier than Bishop or than Pope.   John Tauler
was an earnest disciple, a powerful apostle of this lofty
mysticism; he preached with wonderful success in Strasburg, in some of the neighbouring convents, in towns
and villages, in the cities.   He journeyed even to
Cologne, the seat of this high mysticism; there the
famous Rysbroeck taught with the utmost power and
popularity.   Tauler was often at Basle, where Henry of
Nordlingen, who had respected the Papal interdict at
Constance, resumed his forbidden functions.   Tauler
threw aside all scholastic subtleties; he strove to be
plain, simple, comprehensible to the humblest understanding; he preached in German, but still with deferential citations in Latin.   Tauler sought no Papal
licence; it was his mission, it was his imperative duty as
a Priest, to preach the Gospel.

But Tauler was to undergo a sterner trial, to be
trained in another school.   In Basle he had been marked
by men of a different cast, the gauge of his mind had
been taken, the depth of his heart sounded, his religion
weighed and found wanting.   In Strasburg appeared a
stranger who five times sat at the feet of Tauler, and
listened to his preaching with serious, searching earnest-

visions were seen by many believers;
many terrible prophecies were sent
abroad.

At length Nicolas and some of his
chief followers set out as preachers of
repentance.   In 1393 Martin of Maintz

was burned in Cologne; others in Heidelberg; Nicolas with two of his chief
and constant disciples at Vienne in
Dauphiny.—See Die Gottesfreunde in
xiv Jahrhundert von Carl Schmidt
Jena, 1855.

ness. He was a layman, he sought an interview with Tauler, confessed to him, received the Sacrament at his hands. He then expressed his wish that Tauler would preach how man could attain perfection, that perfection to which he might aspire on earth. Tauler preached his loftiest mysticism. The stern man now spoke with authority, the authority of a more determinate will, and more firm convictions. "Thou art yet in slavery to the letter; thou knowest not the life-giving spirit; thou art but a Pharisee; thou trustest in thine own power, in thine own learning; thou thinkest that thou seekest God's honour, and seekest thine own." Tauler shuddered. "Never man before reproved me for my sins." He felt the spell of a master. "Twelve years," said the layman (who was rebuking the self-righteousness of Tauler!), "I have been toiling to the height of spiritual perfection, which I have now attained, by the study of German writings, by self-mortification and chastisements which have now ceased to be necessary." He gave Tauler certain simple moral rules, counselled him to preach no more, to hear no more confession, to deny himself, and to meditate on the life and death of Christ till he had attained humility and regeneration.[9] The stronger, the more positive and peremptory mind subdued the gentler. Tauler, for above two years, despite the wonder of his friends, the taunts of his enemies, was silent. The first time, at the end of that period, when he attempted, under permission (for the inflexible layman watched him unceasingly), he broke down in floods of tears. This stranger was the

A.D. 1340.

---

[9] Dr. Carl Schmidt has taken the whole of this from an old narrative "of a Teacher of Holy Scripture and a Layman," of which he does not doubt the authenticity. It is well translated in Miss Winkworth's Life and Times of Tauler. London, 1857.

famous Nicolas of Basle. The secret influence of these
teachers, unsuppressed by years of persecution, may
appear from the work thus wrought on the mind of
Tauler, and from the fact that it was not till towards
the close of the century, long after Tauler's death, that
Nicolas of Basle, venturing into France, was seized and
burned as a heretic at Vienne in Dauphiny.   .

Tauler adhered to the Church; many of the Wal-
denses and others did so to escape persecution,⁴ and to
infuse their own zeal; Tauler, it seems, in honesty and
simplicity. But from that time the German preaching
of Tauler—now unmingled with Latin, in churches, in
private assemblies, in the houses of Beguines, in nun-
neries—was more plain, earnest, and, as usual, flowed
from his own heart to the hearts of others. He taught
estrangement from the world, self-denial, poverty of
spirit, not merely passive surrender of the soul to God,
but, with this, love also to the brethren and the discharge of the duties of life. Men were to seek peace,
during these turbulent times, within their own souls.
He not only preached in German, he published in
German, "the following the lowly life of Christ."ʳ The
black plague fell on the city of Strasburg, on _{A.D. 1348-9.}
Strasburg still under the ban of the Pope. In
Strasburg died 16,000, in Basle 14,000 victims. Amid
these terrible times of wild visions, wild processions of
self-scourged penitents, of crowded cloisters, massacred
Jews, the calm voice of Tauler, and of some who spoke
and wrote in the spirit of Tauler, rose against the un-

---

⁴ " Auf diese Weise die Waldenser
in die Kirche selber Eingang fanden und
auf die berühmtesten Doctoren und
nämlich auf Dominikaner, deren Beruf
es war die Ketzer zu bekämpfen, so

mächtig wirkten."—Schmidt, p. 37.
But M. Schmidt's new authorities show
that Nicolas was not a Waldensian.
   ʳ Die Nachfolgung des armen Lebens
Christi.

pitying Church. A remonstrance was addressed to the
Clergy, that the poor, innocent, blameless people were
left to die untended, unabsolved, under the interdict,
and boldly condemning the Priests who refused them
the last consolations of the Gospel.* "Christ died for
all men; the Pope cannot, by his interdict, close heaven
against those who die innocent." In another writing
the abuse of the spiritual sword was clearly denounced,
the rights of the Electors asserted. The broad maxim
was laid down, that "he who confesses the true faith of
Christ, and sins only against the person of the Pope, is
no heretic." It is said that the people took comfort,
and died in peace, though under the Papal interdict.
It was for these unforgiven opinions that Tauler and
his friends, Thomas of Strasburg, an Augustinian, and
Ludolph of Saxony, first a Dominican then a Carthu-
sian, fell under the suspicion of the new Bishop Bertholdt and the Clergy. He had been called to render
an account of his faith before Charles IV.,
"the Priests' Emperor," when at Strasburg.
The Mystics were commanded to recant, and to withdraw from their writings these obnoxious tenets.

A.D. 1348.

Tauler disappeared from Strasburg; he was now heard
in Cologne; there he taught his own simpler doctrines,
and protested against the Pantheistic tenets of the
Beghards, and even of those dreamy fanatics who would
yield up their passive souls to the working of Divine
grace. He returned to Strasburg only to die. His last
hours were passed in the garden of the convent in which his only sister had long dwelt, a
holy and blameless nun. He sought her gentle aid and
consolation. One hard Mystic reproached his weakness

A.D. 1361.

---

* Schmidt, Tauler, p. 52.

in yielding to this last earthly affection. He was buried in the cloisters, amid the respectful sorrow of the whole city.

Tauler had been dead nearly a century before the close of our History, but his Sermons lived in the memory of men; they were transcribed with pious solicitude, and disseminated among all who sought something beyond what was taught in the Church, or taught by the Clergy; that which the Ritual, performed perhaps by a careless, proud, or profligate Priest, did not suggest; which was not heard in the cold and formal Confessional; which man might learn for himself, teach to himself, which brought the soul in direct relation with God, trained it to perfection, to communion, to assimilation, to unity with God. Herder, perhaps the wisest of German critics, condemns the Sermons of Tauler for their monotony:[1] "He who has read two of Tauler's Sermons has read all."[a] But perhaps in that monotony lay much of their strength. Religious men seek not variety but emotion; it is the key-note which vibrates to the heart. Tauler had Mysticism enough to awaken and keep alive all the most passionate sentiments of religion, yet with a seeming clearness and distinctness as if addressed to the reason; his preaching appeared at least to be intelligible; it addressed the whole man, his imagination, his reason, his affection.

But Tauler's Mysticism was far beyond the sublime selfishness of the Imitation of Christ: it embraced fully, explicitly the love of others; it resembled the Imitation of à Kempis, in that it was absolutely and entirely per-

---

[1] The two latter parts of Dr. Schmidt's Tauler are on the writings and doctrines of Tauler, illustrated with abundant extracts. Miss Wink-worth has well chosen, and rendered well some of his best Sermons. 1857.

[a] Theologische Briefe 41, quoted by Schmidt, p. 84.

sonal religion, self-wrought out, self-disciplined, self-matured, with nothing necessarily intermediate between the grace of God and the soul of man. The man might be perfect in spirit and in truth within himself, spiritualised only by the Holy Ghost. Tauler's perfect man was a social being, not a hermit; his goodness spread on earth, it was not all drawn up to heaven. Though the perfect man might not rise above duties, he might rise above observances; though never free from the law of love to his fellow-creatures, he claimed a dangerous freedom as regarded the law and usage of the Church, and dependence on the ministers of the Church. Those who were content with ritual observances, however obedient, were still imperfect; outward rites, fastings, were good as means, but the soul must liberate itself from all these outward means. The soul, having discharged all this, must still await in patience something higher, something to which all this is but secondary, inferior; having attained perfection, it may cast all these things away as unnecessary. Tauler's disciple respects the laws of the Church because they are the laws of the Church; he does not willingly break them, but he is often accused of breaking them when intent on higher objects. But the whole vital real work in man is within. Penance is nought without contrition: "Mortify not the poor flesh, but mortify sin." Man must confess to God; unless man forsakes sin, the absolution of Pope and Cardinals is of no effect; the Confessor has no power over sin. Tauler's religion is still more inflexibly personal: "His own works make not a man holy, how can those of others? Will God regard the rich man who buys for a pitiful sum the prayers of the poor? Not the intercession of the Virgin, nor of all the Saints, can profit the unrepentant sinner."

All this, if not rebellion, was sowing the seeds of rebellion against the sacerdotal domination; if it was not the proclamation, it was the secret murmur preparatory for the assertion of Teutonic independence.

Tauler lived not only in his writings; the cherished treasure of Mysticism was handed down by minds of kindred spirit for nearly two centuries. When they were appealed to by Luther as the harbingers of his own more profound and powerful religiousness, the Friends of God subsisted, if not organised, yet maintaining visibly if not publicly their succession of Apostolic holiness.

Ten years after the death of Tauler, Nicolas of Basle, not yet having ventured on his fatal mission into France, is addressing a long and pious monition to the Brethren of St. John in Strasburg.[a]

Near the close of the century, Martin, a Monk, was arraigned at Cologne as an infatuated disciple of Nicolas of Basle.[b] From this process it appears that many Friends of God had been recently burned at Heidelberg.[c] The heresies with which Martin is charged are obviously misconceptions, if not misrepresentations, of the doctrine of perfection taught by Tauler and by most of the German Mystics.

---

[a] Schmidt, Anhang 5, p. 233, dated 1377.

[b] "Quod quidam Laicus nomine Nicolaus de Basilea, cui te funditus submisisti, clarius et perfectius evangelium quam aliqui Apostoli, et beatus Paulus hoc intellexerit . . . . . quod prædicto Nicolao ex perfectione submissionis sibi facta contra præcepta cujuscunque Prælati etiam Papæ licite et sine peccato obedire."—He was accused of having said, That he was restored to his state of primitive innocence, emancipated from obedience of the Church, with full liberty to preach and administer the Sacraments without licence of the Church. Of course the charge was darkened into the grossest Antinomianism.

[c] 1393. "Quod judicialiter convicti et per ecclesiam condemnati ac impœnitentes heretici aliquando in Heidelbergâ concremati fuerunt et sunt amici Dei."—Anhang 6, p. 238.

Tauler was thus only one of the voices, if the most
powerful and influential, which as it were appealed
directly to God from the Pope and the Hierarchy;
which asserted a higher religion than that of the
Church; which made salvation dependent on personal
belief and holiness, not on obedience to the Priest;
which endeavoured to renew the long-dissolved wedlock
between Christian faith and Christian morality; and
tacitly at least, if not inferentially, admitted the great
Wycliffite doctrine, that the bad Pope, the bad Bishop,
the bad Priest, was neither Pope, Bishop, nor Priest.
It was an appeal to God, and also to the moral sense of
man; and throughout this period of nearly two centuries
which elapsed before the appearance of Luther, this
inextinguishable torch passed from hand to hand, from
generation to generation. Its influence was seen in the
earnest demand for Reformation by the Councils; the
sullen estrangement, notwithstanding the reunion to
the sacerdotal yoke, during the Hussite wars; the dis-
dainful neutrality when reformation by the Councils
seemed hopeless; it is seen in the remarkable book, the
" German Theology," attributed by Luther to Tauler
himself, but doubtless of a later period.* Ruder and
coarser works, in all the jarring and various dialects,
betrayed the German impatience, the honest but homely
popular alienation from ecclesiastical dominion, and
darkly foreshowed that when the irresistible Revolution
should come, it would be more popular, more violent,
more irreconcileable.

---

* Two translations have recently
appeared in England of this book, of
which the real character and importance cannot be appreciated without a
full knowledge of the time at which it
originally appeared. It was not so
much what it taught as " German
Theology," but what it threw aside as
no part of genuine Christian Faith.

CHAPTER VIII.

Christian Architecture.

LITERATURE was thus bursting loose from Latin Christianity; it had left the cloister to converse with men of the world; it had ceased to be the prerogative of the Hierarchy, and had begun to expatiate in new regions. In Italy erelong, as in its classical studies, so in the new Platonism of Marsilius Ficinus and the Florentine school, it almost threatened to undermine Christianity, or left a Christianity which might almost have won the assent of the Emperor Julian. In all the Teutonic races it had begun to assert its freedom from sacerdotal authority; its poets, even its preachers, were all but in revolt.

But Art was more faithful to her munificent patron, her bold and prolific creator, her devout wor- Architecture shipper. Of all the arts Architecture was that _{faithful to} the Church. which owed the most glorious triumphs to Christianity. Architecture must still be the slave of wealth and power, for majestic, durable, and costly buildings can arise only at their command; and wealth and power were still to a great extent in the hands of the Hierarchy. The first sign and prophetic omen of the coming revolution was when in the rich commercial cities the town halls began to vie in splendour with the Churches and Monasteries. Yet nobler gratitude, if such incentive were possible, might attach Architecture to the cause of the Church. Under the Church she had perfected old forms, invented new; she had risen to an unrivalled

majesty of design and skill in construction. In her
stateliness, solemnity, richness, boldness, variety, vastness, solidity, she might compete with the whole elder
world, and might almost defy future ages.

Latin Christianity, during a period of from ten to
twelve centuries, had covered the whole of
Western Europe with its still multiplying
Churches and religious buildings. From the Southern
shores of Sicily to the Hebrides and the Scandinavian
kingdoms, from the doubtful borders of Christian Spain
to Hungary, Poland, Prussia, not a city was without its
Cathedral, surrounded by its succursal churches, its
monasteries, and convents, each with its separate church
or chapel. There was not a town but above the lowly
houses, almost entirely of wood, rose the churches, of
stone or some other solid material, in their superior
dignity, strength, dimensions, and height; not a village
was without its sacred edifice: no way-side without its
humbler chapel or oratory. Not a river but in its course
reflected the towers and pinnacles of many abbeys; not
a forest but above its lofty oaks or pines appeared the
long-ridged roof, or the countless turrets of the con-
ventual church and buildings. Even now, after periods
in some countries of rude religious fanaticism, in one,
France (next to Italy, or equally with Italy prodigal in
splendid ecclesiastical edifices), after a decade of wild
irreligious iconoclasm; after the total suppression or
great reduction, by the common consent of Christendom, of monastic institutions, the secularisation of their
wealth, and the abandonment of their buildings to decay
and ruin; our awe and wonder are still commanded, and
seem as if they would be commanded for centuries, by
the unshaken solidity, spaciousness, height, majesty,
and noble harmony of the cathedrals and churches

throughout Western Europe. We are amazed at the
imagination displayed in every design, at the enormous
human power employed in their creation; at the wealth
which commanded, the consummate science which
guided that power; at the profound religious zeal which
devoted that power, wealth, and science to these high
purposes.

The progress and development of this Christian Architecture, Roman, Byzantine, Romanesque or Lombard,
Norman, Gothic in its successive forms, could not be
compressed into a few pages: the value of such survey
must depend on its accuracy and truth, its accuracy and
truth on the multiplicity and fulness of its details and
on the fine subtlety of its distinctions, and might seem
to demand illustrations from other arts. It is hardly
less difficult to express in a narrow compass the religious, hierarchical, and other convergent causes which
led to the architectural Christianisation of the West in
its two great characteristic forms. These forms may
perhaps be best described as Cisalpine (Italian) and
Transalpine (Gothic), though neither of them respected
the boundary of the other, and the Teutonic Gothic in
the North arose out of the Southern Romanesque.

Our former history has surveyed Christian Architecture in its origin; it has traced the primitive form of
the churches in the East;[a] so far as they differed in
their distribution from the Western, resembling the
Pagan rather than the Jewish temple, yet of necessity
assuming their own peculiar and distinct character. It
has seen in the West the Basilica, the great hall of
imperial justice, offering its more commodious plan and
arrangements, and becoming with far less alteration a

---

[a] History of Christianity, vol. ii. p. 239. Church of Tyre, described by Eusebius.

Christian edifice for public worship and instruction.[b]
This first epoch of Christian Architecture extended,
even after the conversion of Constantine and the building of Constantinople, to the reign of Justinian, under
whom Byzantine Architecture, properly so distinguished,
drew what may be called the architectural division
between the East and the West. Even in Architecture
the Greek and Latin Churches were to be oppugnant;
though the Byzantine, as will appear, made a strong
effort, and not without partial success, to subjugate the
West.

To Rome, not to Greece, Christian Architecture owed
Roman its great elementary principle, the key-stone,
architecture. as it were, to all its greatness; and this principle was carried out with infinitely greater boldness and
fulness in the West than in the East. And surely it is
no fanciful analogy that, as the Roman character contributed so powerfully to the great hierarchical system
of the West, so the Roman form of building influenced
most extensively Christian Architecture, temporarily
and imperfectly that of the East, in perpetuity that
of the Latin world. After a few centuries the more
dominant hierarchism of the West is manifest in the
oppugnancy between Greek and Latin Church Architecture. The East, having once wrought out its
architectural type and model, settled down in unpro-
gressive, uncreative acquiescence, and went on copying
that type with servile and almost undeviating uniformity. In the West, within certain limits, with certain principles, and with a fixed aim, there was freedom,
progression, invention. There was a stately unity,
unity which seemed to imply immemorial antiquity, and

[b] Vol. II. pp. 340, 343, and vol. III. p. 373.

to aspire to be an unalterable irrepealable law for perpetuity, in the form and distribution, in the proportions
and harmony of the sacred buildings; but in the details,
in the height, the dimensions, the character, the ornaments, the mechanical means of support, infinite inexhaustible variety; it ranged from the most bare and
naked Romanesque up to the most gorgeous Gothic.[c]

Latin Christianity by its centralisation, its organisation arising out of Roman respect for law and usage, its
rigid subordination, its assertion of and its submission to
authority, with a certain secondary freedom of action,
had constituted its vast ecclesiastical polity; so one
great architectural principle carried out in infinite
variety and boundless extent, yet in mutual support and
mutual dependence, that of the Arch (if not absolutely
unknown, of rare and exceptional application among the
Greeks), had given solidity and stability to the gigantic
structures of Rome, which spread out and soared above
each other in ambitious unending rivalry. Hence the
power of multiplying harmonious parts, of inclosing
space to almost infinite dimensions, of supporting almost
in the air the most ponderous roofs, of making a vast

---

[c] Compare Hope on Architecture, p. 59. All that has been discovered of the knowledge and use of the Arch in Egypt and in other countries, tends to the same result as that to which Mr. Hope arrived: "The Arch which the Greeks knew not, or if they knew, did not employ." So with other nations. It was first among the Romans an elementary and universal principle of construction. It is impossible not to refer with respect to the first modern philosophical and comprehensive work on Architecture, that by the author of Anastasius. Some corrections, manifold details, much scientific knowledge, have been added by the countless writers on Christian Architecture, of which England has furnished her full share,—Whewell, Willis, Petit, the Author of the Glossary of Architecture, the late Mr. Gally Knight. But who of all these will not own his obligations to Mr. Hope? The recollection of much friendly kindness in my youth enhances the pleasure with which I pay this tribute to a man of real and original genius.

complicated whole, one in design, one in structure, one
in effect. The Greek temples and the Roman temples
on the Greek model, limited in size and extent by the
necessity of finding support for horizontal pressure, were
usually isolated edifices, each in its exquisite harmony
and perfection, complete, independent, simple. If they
were sometimes crowded together, as in the Acropolis
of Athens, or the Forum at Rome, yet each stood by
itself in its narrow precincts; it was a separate republic,
as it were the domain and dwelling of its own God, the
hall of its own priesthood.

But through that single principle of the Arch the
Roman had attained a grandeur and vastness of construction as yet unknown. It was not like the colossal
fanes of Egypt, either rocks hewn into temples, or rocks
transported and piled up into temples; or the fabrics
supported on the immense monolithic pillars in the
Eastern cities (which the Romans themselves in the
time of the Antonines and their successors rivalled at
Baalbec and Palmyra); nor yet the huge terraced
masses of brickwork in the further East. The transcendant and peculiar Architecture of the Romans was
seen in their still more vast theatres and amphitheatres,
which could contain thousands and thousands of spectators; in their Cæsarean palaces, which were almost
cities; in their baths, in which the population of considerable towns, or whole quarters of Rome, found space
not for bathing only, but for every kind of recreation
and amusement; in their bridges, which spanned the
broadest and most turbulent rivers; and their aqueducts, stretching out miles after miles, and conveying
plentiful water to the central city. It remained only to
apply this simple, universal principle. By resting not
the horizontal entablature, but the succession of arches

on the capitals of the pillars, the length might be
infinitely drawn out; the roof, instead of being limited
in its extent by the length of the rafters, might be vaulted
over and so increased enormously in width; and finally,
suspended as it were in the air, soar to any height.

Christian Architecture, when the world under Constantine became Christian, would of course Constantine the Great.
begin to display itself more boldly, more ostentatiously. It would aspire to vie with the old religion in
the majesty of its temples. Not but that long before it
had its public sacred edifices in the East and the West.
Still it would be some time before it would confront
Paganism, the Paganism of centuries. It must still in
vastness and outward grandeur submit to the supremacy
of the ancestral temples of the city. The Basilica,
too, in its ordinary form, though in its length, height,
and proportions there might be a severe and serious
grandeur, was plain. A high unadorned wall formed its
sides, its front was unbroken but by the portals: it had
not its splendid rows of external columns, with their
interchanging light and shade; nor the rich and sculp-
tured pediment over its entrance. Constantine, before
his departure to the East, erected more than one church,
no doubt worthy of an imperial proselyte, for the new
religion of the empire. But earthquakes, conflagra-
tions, wars, tumults, the prodigal reverence of some
Popes, the vast ambition of others, have left not a ves-
tige of the Constantinian buildings in Rome. The
Church of the Lateran, thrown down by an earthquake,
was rebuilt by Sergius III. That built in honour of
St. Peter[4] (it was asserted and believed over the place

---

[4] On the old St. Peter's see the curious work of Bonanni, Historia Templi
Vaticani (Roma, 1708), and the elaborate chapter in Bunsen and Platner,
Köln's Beschreibung.

of his martyrdom), with its splendid forecourt and its
five aisles, which to the time of Charlemagne, though
the prodigal piety of some Popes had no doubt violated
its original, it should seem, almost cruciform, outline,
and sheathed its walls in gold and precious marbles,
yet maintained the plan and distribution of the old
church. It stood, notwithstanding the ravages of the
Saracens, the sieges of the Emperors, the seditions of
the people, on its primitive Constantinian site for many
hundred years after, and was only swept away by the
irreverent haughtiness of Julius II., to make way for
what was expected to, and which does, command the
universal wonder of mankind, the St. Peter's of Bra-
mante and Michael Angelo. The noble church of St.
Paul, without the walls, built by Theodosius the Great,
stood as it were the one majestic representative of the
Imperial Christian Basilica till our own days.[*]   The
ground plan of the Basilica must be sought in the hum-   •
bler Church of S. Clemente,[f] which alone retains it in
its integrity: S. Maria Maggiore, S. Lorenzo, and one
or two others, have been so overlaid with alterations as
only to reveal to the most patient study distinct signs of
their original structure.

Constantinople rose a Christian city, but a Christian
city probably in most parts built by Roman hands, or
by Greeks with full command of Roman skill and
science, and studiously aspired to be an eastern Rome.
As her Senators, her Patricians, so probably many of
her architects and artists came from Rome ; or if

---

[*] The author saw this stately and
venerable building in the summer of
1822; it was burned down in July,
1823.

[f] See the S. Clemente in Mr. Gally

Knight's splendid and munificent work ;
which has the rare excellence, that the
beauty of the engravings does not
interfere with their scrupulous accuracy.

Greeks, were instructed and willing to conform to
Roman habits and usage. The courtiers of Constantinople, who migrated from the old to the new Rome,
were surprised, it is said, to find palaces so closely
resembling their own, that they hardly believed themselves to have been transported from the banks of the
Tiber to the shores of the Bosphorus. Constantine himself was a Western by birth and education; Rome therefore, rather than the East, would furnish the first model
for the Christian Churches. In old Byzantium there
were probably few temples of such magnificence as to
tempt the Christians to usurp them for their own uses,
or allure them to the imitation of their forms. Nor did
such temples, dilapidated and deserted, as in later times
in Rome and Italy, furnish inexhaustible quarries from
which triumphant Christianity might seize and carry off
her legitimate spoils. There were not at hand rows of
noble pillars, already hewn, fluted or polished, with their
bases and capitals, which, accustomed to form the porch,
or to flank the heathen temple, now took their stand
along the nave of the church, or before the majestic
vestibule. Though Constantine largely plundered other
works of art, statues of bronze or marble (somewhat
incongruous heathen ornaments of a Christian city), yet
he can have had no great quantity of materials from
old temples, unless at much cost of freight from more
remote cities, to work up in his churches.[f] On the
other hand neither were there many, if there was a
single Basilica, such as were found in most Italian cities,
ready to undergo the slight necessary transmutation.
Yet there can be no doubt that the first churches in
Constantinople were in the Basilican form; that S.

<hr>

[f] See Hist. of Christianity, ii. p. 338.

Sophia was of an oblong shape there is satisfactory authority; it was not till the reign of Constantius that the area was enlarged to a square.[b]

This, then, which may be called the Roman or Basilican, may be considered as the first Age of Christian Architecture.

II. Of true Byzantine Architecture Justinian was the parent. Time, earthquakes, seditions nowhere so furious and destructive as in Constantinople, especially the famous one in the reign of Justinian; more ambitious or more prodigal Emperors, or more devout and wealthy Christians, denied duration to the primitive Churches of Constantinople. The edifices of Constantine, in all likelihood hastily run up, and, if splendid, wanting in strength and solidity, gave place to more stately and enduring churches. The S. Sophia of Constantine was razed to the ground in a fierce tumult; but on its site arose the new S. Sophia, in the East the pride, in the West the wonder, of the world.[i] The sublime unity and harmony of the design, above all the lightness and vastness of the cupola, were too marvellous for mere human science. Even the skill of the famous architects Anthi-

---

[b] It was of great length, δρόμικος, the form of a Dromos, or Circus for races. See Ducange, Descriptio S. Sophiæ; and also on the enlargement by Constantius. The Church in the Blachernæ, built so late as Justin, had straight rows of pillars and a timber roof. The Church of S. John Studius, still existing, is of the Basilican form of that period.—Schnaase, Geschichte der Bildenden Kunst, iii. p. 123, note. On the other hand the Church of Antioch, described by Eusebius and by Theophilus, was an octagon, as was

that of Nazianzum.—Schnaase, p. 124. The round form, not unknown in the East, nor in the West, as that of S. Constanza near Rome, was more used for Baptisteries, and for monumental chapels, as the tomb of Galla Placidia at Ravenna.

[i] To the poem of Paulus Silentiarius, on the building and dedication of S. Sophia (Edition Bonn), are appended the laborious dissertation of Ducange, and the perspicuous illustrative essay of Banduri. They contain everything relating to the structure.

mus of Tralles and Isidore of Miletus were unequal to
the conception. An angel revealed to the Emperor
(Justinian hinself must share in the glory) many of the
forms of the building; the great principle of the construction of the cupola, sought in vain by the science of
the architects, flashed across the mind of the Emperor
himself in a dream. The cupola did not seem, according
to the historian Procopius, to rest on its supports, but to
be let down by a golden chain from heaven.[k] Santa
Sophia was proclaimed in the West as the most consummate work of Christian Architecture.[m]

But Justinian was not content to be the founder and
lawgiver of Christian art; as in empire, so he aspired in
all things, to bring the whole Roman world under his
dominion. To conquered Italy he brought back the
vast code of the Civil Law, which he had organised and
adapted to Christian use; to Italy came also his architecture, an immense amplification of the Roman arch,
which was to be, if not the law, the perfect form of the
Christian Church. San Vitale arose in Ravenna, the
Constantinople of the West. In dimensions only and
in the gorgeousness of some of its materials, San Vitale
must bow before its Byzantine type Santa Sophia, but

---

[k] τούτου δὲ τοῦ κυκλοτεροῦς ταμι-
μεγέθης ἐπαναστηκυῖά τις σφαιροει-
δὴς θόλος ποιεῖται, αὐτὸ διαφερόντως
εὐπρόσωπον δοκεῖ δὲ οὐκ ἐπὶ στερρᾶς
τῆς οἰκοδομίας διὰ τὸ παρειμένον τῆς
οἰκοδομίας ἑστάναι ἀλλὰ τῇ σειρᾷ τῇ
χρύσῃ ἀπὸ τοῦ οὐρανοῦ ἐξημμένη κα-
λύπτειν τὸν χῶρον.—Procop. de Ædif.
i. p. 177, Edit. Bonn.

[m] " Cujus opus adeo cuncta ædificia
excellit ut in totis terrarum spatiis
huic simile non possit inveniri."—Paul
Warnefrid. S. Sophia and some other

Constantinopolitan churches have become better known during the last
year (1854) from the splendid work
published by M. Salzenberg, at the
expense of the King of Prussia. An
Italian architect, M. Fossato, having
been intrusted with the repairs, the whole
structure has been surveyed, measured,
and drawn. Many mosaics covered up
since the transmutation into a mosque
have for a time revealed again in all
their brilliancy some very remarkable
specimens of Byzantine mosaic art.

it closely resembled it in plan and arrangement. The
Mosaics of the Emperor and of the Empress Theodora
in the choir might seem as though they would commend San Vitale as the perfect design for a Christian
Church to subject Italy and to the West. Rome indeed
might seem, even in Ravenna, to offer a more gallant
resistance to the arts than to the arms of Justinian.
To San Vitale she would oppose the noble S. Apollinaris, in her own Basilican form. Of the ancient
Basilicas, since the destruction of St. Paul without the
walls at Rome, S. Apollinaris at Ravenna, with its
twenty-four columns of rich Greek marble from Constantinople, and its superb mosaics, is undoubtedly the
most impressive and august in the world."

Thus, then, there were two forms which contested
for the supremacy in Italy. One was the old Roman
Basilica, with its stately length, which by slow and
imperceptible degrees became cruciform by the extension into transepts of the space between the end of the
nave (where rose a great arch, called the Arch of
Triumph, as opening upon the holy mysteries of the
faith), and the conch or apse, before which stood the
high altar. The other was square or octagon, which in
the same manner and by the same slow process broke
into the short equal-limbed Greek cross.° This latter
form, with the cupola, was the vital distinction of the
Byzantine style.ᴾ Rome remained faithful to her

ⁿ See this church in Gally Knight.

° It is not known when the form of
the Cross began. Mr. Gally Knight
observes that the form of the Cross was
for many centuries the exception rather
than the rule.

ᴾ Procopius states of S. Sophia, εὖρος
δὲ αὐτῆς καὶ μῆκος οὕτως ἐν ἐπιτη-
δείῳ ἐπιτετόρνευεται, ὥστε καὶ περι-
μήκης, καὶ ὅλως εὐρεῖα οὐκ ἀπὸ
τρόπου εἰρήσεται, p. 174.—So too
that of S. Mary and S. Michael, c. iii.
p. 174. S. Anthimus, c. vi. p. 194.
That of the Apostles was a Greek Cross,
c. iii. p. 188.

ancient basilican form; but in many of the cities of
Northern Italy the more equal proportion of the length
and width, with the central cupola, sometimes multiplied on the extended limbs of the transept; these, the
only creations of Byzantine architecture, found favour.
Venice early took her eastern character; the old church
of S. Fosca in Torcello, in later times St. Mark's maintained the Byzantine form.[e] St. Mark's, with her Greek
plan, her domes, her mosaics, might seem as if she had
prophetically prepared a fit and congenial place for
the reception of the spoils of the Constantinopolitan
Churches after the Latin conquest.   But many other of
the Lombard Churches, in Pavia, Parma, the old cathedral at Brescia, were square, octagon, or in the form of
the Greek cross.   As late as the tenth century Ancona,
still a Greek city, raised the Church of S. Cyriac, with
much of what is called Lombard, more properly Romanesque ornament, but in form a strictly Byzantine Church.[f]

   Yet on the whole the architectural, as the civil conquests of Justinian, were but partial and un-
enduring.   The Latin Architecture, with these
exceptions, even in Italy, adhered to the Basilican form
or to the longer Latin cross: beyond the Alps the
square form was even more rare.   But it is singular to
observe in both the development of the hierarchical
principle according to the character and circumstances
of the Eastern and the Western Church.   As the worship throughout Christendom became more local, more

Marginal note: Difference of Greek and Latin services.

---

[e] The round churches, which were few, gave place to Baptisteries, for which or for sepulchral chapels they were mostly originally designed.

[f] It is curious that Charlemagne's cathedral at Aix-la-Chapelle is the one true Byzantine church or type of a Byzantine church beyond the Alps—in form, construction, even in mosaics. Charlemagne had perhaps Greek architects, he had seen Ravenna, he drew ornaments and materials from Ravenna. Compare Schnaase, vol. xiv. 486 et seqq.

material, the altar was now the Holy of Holies, the
actual abode of the Real Presence of Christ. The
Clergy withdrew more entirely into their unapproachable sanctity; they would shroud themselves from all
profane approximation by solemn mystery, the mystery
which arises from remoteness, from obscurity or dim-
ness, or even from secrecy. For this end, to heighten
the awe which he would throw around the tremendous
sacrifice, and around himself the hallowed minister of
that sacrifice, the Greek, in himself less awful, had
recourse to artificial means. The Latin trusted to his
own inherent dignity, aided only by more profound distance, by the splendour which environed him, splendour
more effective as heightened by surrounding darkness.
The shorter Greek cross did not repel the adoring worshipper far enough off; the Greek therefore drew a veil.
At length he raised a kind of wall between himself and
the worshippers, and behind, in that enclosed sanctuary,
he performed the mystery of consecration, and came
forth and showed himself in turn at each of the side
doors of the Holy of Holies, rarely at the central or
royal gate, with the precious paten and chalice in his
hands. When the service was over, he withdrew again
with his awful treasure into its secret sanctuary.[*] In
the longer Latin cross the hierarchy might recede to a
commanding distance from the great mass of worshippers, yet all might remain open; the light rails of the
chancel were sufficient, with their own inherent majesty,
to keep the profane on their lower level, and in their
humble posture of far-off adoration. In the West the
crypt under the altar, to contain the bones of the saint
or martyr, was more general; the altar therefore was

---

* Smith's account of the Greek Church, p. 64. This, called the Iconostasis, is
general in the Russian churches. There is a curious example at Pesth in Hungary.

more usually approached by a flight of steps, and thus
elevation was added to distance: and to distance and
elevation were added by degrees the more dazzling
splendour of the altar-furniture, the crosses, the candlesticks, the plate, the censers, and all the other gorgeous
vessels, their own dresses, the violet, green, scarlet, cloth
of gold, the blaze of lamps and tapers, the clouds of
incense. At one time the altar and the officiating
clergy were wrapped in the mystery of sublime gloom,
at the next the whole altar, and all under the stately
Baldachin, burst out into a concentred brilliancy of
light. The greater length of the building, with its succursal aisles and ambulatories and chapels, as so admirably adapted for processional services, would greatly
promote their introduction and use. The Clergy would
no longer be content with dim and distant awe and
veneration ; this was now inherent in their persons : and
so, environed with their sacred symbols, bearing their
banners emblazoned with the image of the crucified
Redeemer, of the Virgin, of the Saints, and the crosses,
the emblems of their own authority and power, and in
their snow-white or gorgeous dresses, they would pass
through the rows of wondering and kneeling worshippers, with their grave and solemn chant, or amid the
peals of the thundering organ, bringing home, as it
were, to the hearts of all, the most serious religious
impressions, as well as those of their own peculiar
inalienable sanctity.

But the oppugnancy was not only in the internal
form and arrangements of the sacred buildings or the
more effective display of ecclesiastic magnificence. In
splendour of dress, in the richness of their church fur-
niture and vessels, in the mysterious symbolism of their
services, the East boasted itself even superior to the

West. But the more vigorously developed hierarchical
spirit among the Latins displayed itself in nothing more
than in its creativeness, in its progressive advancement
in Christian Architecture. The Emperors were in general the founders and builders of the great Eastern
Churches, in the West to a vast extent the Church
herself. Though kings and nobles were by no means
wanting in these signs of prodigal piety—the Catholic
Lombard kings, the priest-ruled Merovingians, Charlemagne and his descendants, the sovereigns in England
—there were also, besides these royal and noble devotees,
the magnificent Prelates, the splendid Abbots, the opulent Chapters. In the East it was the State acting it
might be under the influence, in obedience to, or at the
suggestion of the Priesthood; in the West, with the
Monarch and the Baron, it was the whole ecclesiastical
Wealth of Order out of its own enormous wealth, its own
the clergy. vast possessions, and still accumulating property. From the seventh at least to the close of the
fourteenth century this wealth was steadily on the
increase, at times pouring in like a flood; if draining
off, draining but in narrow and secret channels. It was
in the nature of things that a large portion of this
wealth should be consecrated, above all others, to this
special use. It had long been admitted that a fifth, a
fourth, a third of the ecclesiastical endowments belonged
to the sustentation, to the embellishment of the religious
fabrics. But it needed no law to enforce on a wide scale
this expenditure demanded at once by every holy and
generous principle, by every ambitious, among the more
far-sighted and politic, as well as by every more sordid,
motive. Throughout Christendom there was the high
and pure, as well as the timid and superstitious religion,
which invited, encouraged, commanded, exacted, pro-

mised to reward in this world and in the next, these
noble works of piety. Without as within the Church
these motives were in perpetual, unslumbering activity.
Church-building was, as it were, the visible personal
sacrifice to God, a sacrifice which could never be fully
accomplished; it was the grateful or expiatory oblation
to the Redeemer and to the Saints. The dying king,
the dying noble, the dying rich man, or the king, noble,
or rich man, under strong remorse during his lifetime,
might with more lofty and disinterested urgency be
pressed by the priest or the confessor to make the bequest or the gift to a holy work in which the clergy
had no direct advantage, and which was in some sort a
splendid public benefaction. The Church was built for
the poor, for the people, for posterity. What the splendour of the old Asiatic monarchs had done for the per-
petuation of their own luxury and glory, the Egyptians
for their burying-places, as well as in honour of their
gods; what the narrower patriotism of the Greeks for
the embellishment of their own cities, for the comfort
and enjoyment of the citizens; what the stern pride of
the older, the enormous wealth and ostentation of the
later republicans at Rome; what the Pagan Emperors
had done, the elder Cæsars, to command the wonder,
gratitude, adulation of the mistress of the world; Trajan,
Hadrian, the Antonines, from policy, vanity, beneficence,
on a wider and more cosmopolitan scale throughout the
Empire; what had been thus done in many various ways,
was now done by most kings and most rich men in one
way alone.[1] Besides temples the heathen Cæsars had

---

[1] Let it be remembered that in Paris,
in the time of Philip the Fair, the
house of the Templars was stronger if
not more magnificent than the King's
palace in the Louvre. What in comparison were the more sumptuous religious buildings?

raised palaces, theatres, amphitheatres, circuses, baths, roads, bridges, aqueducts, senate-houses, porticoes, libraries, cemeteries. Now the only public buildings, unless here and there a bridge (until the burghers in the commercial cities began to raise their guildhalls), were the church and the castle. The castle was built more for strength than for splendour. Architecture had the Church alone and her adjacent buildings on which to lavish all her skill, and to expend the inexhaustible treasures poured at her feet. To build the Church was admitted at once as the most admirable virtue, as the most uncontested sign of piety, as the fullest atonement for sin, as the amplest restitation for robbery or wrong, as the bounden tribute of the loyal subject of God, as the most unquestioned recognition of the sovereignty and mercy of God.

If these incentives were for ever working without the
Incentives for Church buildings.
Church, besides these, what powerful concurrent and subsidiary motives were in action within the Church! Every Prelate, even each member of a Chapter (if he had any noble or less sordid feeling than personal indulgence in pomp and luxury, or the least ecclesiastical public spirit), would feel emulation of his spiritual ancestors: he would delight to put to shame the less prodigal, the more parsimonious, generosity of his predecessor, would endeavour to transcend him in the richness of his oblation to God or to the Patron Saint. He would throw down that predecessor's meaner work, and replace it by something more splendid and enduring. Posthumous glory would assume a sacred character: the Prelate would not be inflexibly and humbly content with obscure goodness, or with the unwitnessed virtues, which would rest entirely on the reward in the world to come. The best and wisest

might think that if their names lived on earth with
their imperishable Cathedrals, it was a pardonable, if
not a pious and laudable ambition.   Their own desire of
glory would so mingle with what they esteemed the
glory of God, as to baffle their discrimination.   So too
national, municipal, corporate, local pride and interest
would disguise themselves as the love of God and man.
The fane of some tutelary saint, or some shrine of peculiar holiness or of wonder-working power, which attracted
more numerous and more devout pilgrims, as it enriched
the Church, the city, the town, the village, so it would
demand even from gratitude a larger share of the votive
offerings.   The Saint must be rewarded for his favours,
for his benefits; his church, his chapel, and his shrine
must be more splendid, as more splendid would be more
attractive; and thus splendour would beget wealth, wealth
gladly devote itself to augment the splendour.

Throughout, indeed, there was this latent, and unconscious it might be, but undeniable influence The Church.
operating through the whole sacerdotal Order, The Priests.
through the whole Monkhood, and not less among the
more humble Friars.   Every church was not merely
the house of God, it was also the palace where the religious Sovereign, the Ecclesiastic, from the Pope to the
lowliest Parish Priest, held his state; it was the unassailable fortress of his power; it was, I use the word
with reluctance, the Exchange where, by the display of
his wealth, he immeasurably increased that wealth.   To
the Ecclesiastic belonged the chancel, not to be entered
by unsanctified feet; to him in his solitary or in his corporate dignity, only attended by a retinue of his own
Order; his were the costly dresses, the clouds of incense.
The more magnificent the church, and the more sumptuous the services, the broader the line which divided

him from the vulgar, the rest of mankind. If he vouchsafed some distinction, some approach towards his unapproachable majesty, as when the Emperor took his seat
at the entrance or within the chancel, read the Gospel,
and was graciously permitted to perform some of the
functions of a Deacon, this but threw back the rest of
mankind to more humble distance. Those passages
which the haughtiest Popes alleged in plain words, as
"Ye are Gods," which was generally read, "Ye are
Christs (the anointed of God)," almost revoked, or neu-
tralised in the minds of the Priesthood, the specious
reservation that it was God in them, and not themselves,
which received these honours. Popular awe and reverence know no nice theological discrimination; at least
a large share of the veneration to the Saint or the Redeemer, to God, rested, as it passed, on the Hierarchy.
They were recognised as those without whose mediation
no prayer passed onward to the throne of grace; they
stood on a step, often a wide step, higher in the ascent
to heaven. Everywhere, through the whole framework
of society, was this contrast, and the contrast was to the
advantage of the Hierarchy. The highest and richest
Bishop in his episcopal palace might see the castle of
the Baron not only in its strength, but in its height, its
domains, its feudal splendour, its castellated richness,
frowning contemptuously down upon him; he might
seem to be lurking, as it were, a humble retainer under
its shadow and under its protection. But enter the
church! the Baron stood afar off, or knelt in submissive,
acknowledged, infelt inferiority; and it was seldom that
in the city the cathedral did not outsoar and outspread
with its dependent buildings—its baptistery, chapter-
house, belfry, cloisters—the rival castle with all its out-
buildings. That which in the cathedral city long held

the Ecclesiastics in their separate peculiar majesty, went
down in due proportion through the town to the village,
to the meanest hamlet. In the feudal castle itself the
chapel was almost always the most richly decorated.
During war, in the siege, in the boisterous banquet, the
chaplain might be self-levelled, or levelled by a lawless
chief and lawless soldiery, to a humble retainer; in the
chapel he resumed his proper dignity. It was his fault,
his want of influence, if the chapel was not maintained
in greater decency and splendour than the rude hall or
ruder chamber; and reverence to the chapel reacted on
the reverence to himself.

Add to all this the churches or chapels of the religious
houses, and there was hardly a religious house without
its church or chapel, many of them equal or surpassing
in grandeur, in embellishment, those of the town or of
the city. In a religious foundation the Church could
not, for very shame, be less than the most stately and
the most splendid edifice. Year after year, century after
century, if any part of the monastery was secure from
dilapidation, if any part was maintained, rebuilt, re-
decorated, it would be the church. The vow of humility,
the vow of poverty was first tacitly violated, first disdainfully thrown aside, by the severest Order, in honour
of God. The sackcloth-clad, bare-foot Friar would watch
and worship on the cold stone or the hard board; but
within walls enriched with the noblest paintings, tapes-
tried with the most superb hangings, before an altar
flashing with the gold pix, with the jewelled vessels,
with the rich branching candlesticks. Assisi, not
many years after the death of St. Francis, had begun
to be the most splendid and highly adorned church in
Italy.

Thus then architecture was the minister at once and

servant of the Church, and a vast proportion of the wealth
The Church of the world was devoted to the works of
the people's. architecture. Nor was it in a secular point of
view a wasteful pomp and prodigality. If the church
was the one building of the priest, so was it of the
people. It was the single safe and quiet place where
the lowest of the low found security, peace, rest, recreation, even diversion. If the chancel was the Priest's,
the precincts, the porch, the nave were open to all; the
Church was all which the amphitheatre, the bath, the
portico, the public place, had been to the poor in the
heathen cities. It was more than the house of prayer
and worship, where the peasant or the beggar knelt side
by side with the burgher or the Baron; it was the
asylum, not of the criminal only, but of the oppressed,
the sad, the toil-worn, the infirm, the aged. It was not
only dedicated to God; it was consecrated to the consolation, the peace, even the enjoyment of man. Thus
was it that architecture was raising all its wondrous
structures in the West, if for the advancement of the
Hierarchy, so too at the perpetual unsleeping instigation,
at the cost, and it should seem under the special direction, of the Hierarchy: for no doubt within the precincts
of the cathedral, within the cloister, much of the science
of architecture was preserved, perpetuated, enlarged; if
the architects were not themselves Ecclesiastics, they
were under the protection, patronage, direction, instruction of Ecclesiastics. But it was also of the most indu-
bitable benefit to mankind. Independent of the elevating,
solemnising, expanding effects of this most material and
therefore most universally impressive of the Fine Arts,
what was it to all mankind, especially to the prostrate
and down-trodden part of mankind, that though these
buildings were God's, they were, in a certain sense, his

own; he who had no property, not even in his own
person, the serf, the villain, had a kind of right of pro-
prietorship in his parish church, the meanest artisan in
his cathedral. It is impossible to follow out to their
utmost extent, or to appreciate too highly the ennobling,
liberalising, humanising, Christianising effects of church
architecture during the Middle Ages.

III. The third period of Christian architecture (reckoning as the first the Roman Basilica, as the second the
proper Byzantine, with its distinctive Greek cross and
cupolas) lasted, with the Norman, till the introduction of
the Pointed or so-called Gothic in the twelfth century.
This style has been called Lombard, as having first
flourished in the cities of Northern Italy, which under
the later Kings attained unwonted peace and prosperity,
and in which the cities rose to industry, commerce,
wealth and freedom. Assuredly it was no in-   Third style.
vention of the rude Lombards, who brought   Lombard.
over the Alps only their conquering arms and   Byzantine, or Romanesque.
their hated Arianism. It has been called also Byzan-
tine, improperly, for though it admitted indiscriminately
Byzantine and Roman forms and arrangements, its characteristics seem either its own or the traditions of
Roman principles, the appropriation and conversion to
its use of Roman examples. Its chief characteristic is
delight in the multiplication of the arch, not only for
the support, but for the ornamentation of the building.
Within and without there is the same prodigality of
this form. But these rows or tiers of arches, without
supporting or seeming to support the roof, or simply
decorative, appear to be no more than the degenerate
Roman, as seen in the Palace of Diocletian at Spalatro,
and usefully as well as ornamentally employed in the
Coliseum and in other amphitheatres. Gradually the

west front of the Church, or the front opposite to the
altar, grew into dignity and importance. The central
portal, sometimes the three portals, or even five portals,
lost their square-headed form, became receding arches,
arches within arches, decorated with graceful or fantastic mouldings. Above, tier over tier, were formed
rows of arches (unless where a rich wheel or rose window
was introduced) up to the broad bold gable, which was
sometimes fringed as it were just below with small
arches following out its line. Sometimes these arches
ran along the side walls; almost always either standing
out more or less, or in open arcades, they ran round the
semicircular eastern apse. Besides these, slender com-
pound piers or small buttresses are carried up the whole
height to the eaves. They arrive at length at the
severer model of this form, San Zeno at Verona, or the
richer, the San Michele at Lucca. Within the church
the pillars, as the models of those in the ancient buildings disappeared (the Roman Corinthian long survived),
or rather as the ruins of ancient buildings ceased to be
the quarries for churches, gradually lost their capitals.
From those sprung the round arches in a bolder or more
timid sweep, according to the distance or solidity of the
pillars. Above the nave a second row of arches formed
the clerestory windows. The roof, in general of timber,
was first flat, then curved, at length vaulted. Over the
centre of the cross rose the cupola, round, octagon, or
of more fanciful forms. In the seventh century the
introduction of bells, to summon to the service, drew on
the invention of the architect. The dome or cupola was
not a convenient form for a belfry. Beside the building
it had not been unusual to erect a baptistery, circular or
polygonal, such as are still seen in the richest form, and
almost rivalling the churches, in Florence and in Parma.

Throughout Lombardy, in most parts of Italy, rose the
detached campanile, sometimes round, in general square,
terminating at times with a broad flat roof, more rarely
towering into a spire. In Italy this third epoch of
architecture culminated in the Cathedral of Pisa. It
was the oblation of the richest and most powerful city
in Italy, at the height of her prosperity, her industry,
her commerce, her fame; it was made in the pride of
her wealth, in a passion of gratitude for a victory and
for rich plunder taken from the Mohammedans in the
harbour of Palermo. Pisa found an architect worthy of
her profuse magnificence; the name of Boscheto lives
in this his unrivalled edifice. It is not only that the
cathedral makes one of those four buildings—the Dome,
the Baptistery, the Leaning Tower, the Campo Santo—
which in their sad grandeur in the deserted city surpass
all other groups of buildings in Europe: the cathedral
standing alone would command the highest admiration.
On the exterior the west front displays that profusion of
tiers of arches above arches, arranged with finer proportion, richness, and upward decreasing order, than elsewhere. But its sublimity is within. Its plan, the Latin
cross in the most perfect proportion, gives its impressive
unity to its central nave, with its double aisles, its aisled
transepts, its receding apse. Its loftiness is far more
commanding than any building of its class in Italy had
as yet aspired to reach. The Corinthian pillars along
the nave are of admirable height and proportion;[*]
those of the aisles lower, but of the same style. The
arches spring boldly from the capitals of the pillars;
the triforium above, running down the long nave, is

---

[*] The pointed arch from the nave to the transepts is of later date; incongruous but not without effect.

singularly picturesque. While the long, bold, horizontal architrave gives the sedate regularity of the Basilica; the crossings of the transepts, the sweep of the curved apse, even without the effective mosaic of Cimabue, close the view with lines of the most felicitous and noble form.

Nothing can contrast more strongly, in the same architecture, than the Transalpine Romanesque with Pisa.[x] It is seen in all the old cities on the Rhine (the earliest form in St. Castor at Coblentz), later at Spires, Worms, Mentz, Bonn, the older churches at Cologne; east of the Rhine in the older cities or monasteries, as in Corvey. It is more rude but more bold; these churches might seem the works of the great feudal Prelates; with a severe grandeur, not without richness of decoration, but disdaining grace or luxuriance. They are of vast size, as may beseem Prelate Princes, but of the coarse red or grey stone of the country, no fine-wrought freestone, no glittering marble. The pillars are usually without capitals, or with capitals fantastic and roughly hewn; they would impress by strength and solidity rather than by harmony or regularity. In the south of France this style is traced not only in cathedral cities, but in many very curious parochial churches.[y] With few exceptions, it is there more picturesque and fanciful than grand or solemn. In the north of France and in England this architecture received such a powerful impulse from the Normans as almost to form a new epoch in the art.

IV. That wonderful people the Normans, though without creative power, seemed as it were to throw

---

[x] See for the Saxon Romanesque Schnaase.

[y] Mr. Petit has published engravings of many of these buildings.

their whole strength and vigour into architecture, as into
everything else.   They had their kingdoms   The Nor-
on the Mediterranean, and on either side of   mans.
the British Channel.   In the South they had become
Southerns; even in architecture they anticipated from
the Mohammedans some approximation to the Gothic,
the pointed arch.   In the North, on the other hand, as
by adopting and domiciling men of Roman or Italian
cultivation, they had braced the intellect of the degenerate Church to young energy, and had trained learned
Churchmen and theologians, Lanfrancs and Anselms;
so taking the form, the structure, the architectural
science of universal Latin Christendom, they gave it a
grandeur, solidity, massiveness, even height, which might
seem intended to confront a ruder element, more wild
and tempestuous weather.   The Norman cathedrals
might almost seem built for warlike or defensive purposes; as though their Heathen ancestors, having in
their fierce incursions destroyed church and monastery,
as well as castle and town, they would be prepared for
any inroad of yet un-Christianised Northmen.   That
great characteristic of the Norman churches, the huge
square central tower, was battlemented like a castle.
The whole impression is that of vast power in the architect, unshaken duration in the edifice; it is the building
of a Hierarchy which has unfailing confidence in its own
strength, in its perpetuity.   On the exterior, in the
general design there is plainness, almost austerity; the
walls, visibly of enormous thickness, are pierced with
round arched windows of no great size, but of great
depth; the portals are profound recesses, arch within
arch resting on short stubborn pillars; the capitals are
rude, but boldly projecting; the rich ornaments cut with
a vigorous and decisive hand : the zigzag or other

mouldings with severity in their most prodigal richness.
In the interior all again is simple to the disdain, in its
greater parts, of ornament. The low, thick, usually
round pillars, with capitals sometimes indulging in wild
shapes, support, with their somewhat low arches, the
ponderous wall, in its turn pressed down as it were by
the ponderous roof. Such are the works of our Norman
Kings, the two abbeys at Caen, Jumieges in its ruins,
St. George de Boscherville; such in our island, Durham,
parts of Peterborough and Ely, and Gloucester, the two
square towers of Exeter. If later and more splendid
cathedrals inspire a higher devotion, none breathe more
awe and solemnity than the old Norman.[*]

V. On a sudden, in a singularly short period, the
Gothic archi-
tecture. latter half of the twelfth century (though discerning eyes[*] may trace, and acute minds
have traced with remarkable success and felicity, this
transition), Christian architecture beyond the Alps, in
Germany, in France, in England, becomes creative.
Nothing but the distribution and arrangement of the
parts of the church remains the same; and even in that
respect the church, instead of standing alone or nearly
alone, with the other edifices in humble subordination,
is crowded around by a multitude of splendid vassals,
partaking in all her decorative richness, the Lady
chapel and other chapels, the chapter-house, the monastery, the episcopal palace, the cloisters, sometimes the
belfry.

In the church not only are there new forms, not only
is there a new principle of harmony, not only a constant

---

* See Mr. Gally Knight's Norman   own excellent judgement by the well-
Tour, and 'Normans in Sicily.' Mr.   remunerated labours of accomplished
Knight dedicated part of a noble for-   artists.
tune to these studies, illustrating his   * Dr. Whewell, Mr. Willis, Mr. Petit.

substitution of vertical for horizontal lines, new and
most exquisite proportions, an absolutely original character, but new principles of construction seem to have
revealed themselves. Architecture is not only a new
art, awakening different emotions of wonder, awe, and
admiration, but a new science. It has discovered the
secret of achieving things which might appear impossible, but which once achieved, seem perfectly simple,
secure, justificatory of their boldness, from the perfect
balance and equable pressure of every part, pressure
disguised as it were, as distributed on a multitude of
supports, and locked down by superincumbent weights.
Such is the unity, however multifarious, of the whole,
that the lightest, though loftiest and most vast Gothic
cathedral has a look of strength and duration as manifest, as unquestioned, as the most ponderous and massive
Romanesque or Norman.

The rapid, simultaneous, and universal growth of this
so-called Gothic, its predominance, like its ⟨Rapid rise
predecessor the Romanesque, through the ⟨and exten-
⟨sion.
whole realm of Latin Christendom, is not the least
extraordinary fact in the revolution. It has had marked
stages of development (now defined with careful discrimination by the able and prolific writers on the art)
during several centuries and in all countries, in Germany, France, England, the Netherlands, Spain, even
Italy ; but its first principles might almost seem to have
broken at once on the wondering world. Everywhere
the whole building has an upward, it might seem
heaven-aspiring tendency ; everywhere the arches become more and more pointed, till at length they arrive
at the perfect lancet ; everywhere the thick and massy
walls expand into large mullioned windows ; everywhere
the diminished solidity of the walls is supported from

without by flying buttresses, now concealed, now become
lighter and more graceful, and revealing themselves,
not as mere supports, but as integral parts of the building, and resting on outward buttresses; everywhere
pinnacles arise, singly or in clusters, not for ornament
alone, but for effect and perceptible use; everywhere
the roof becomes a ridge more or less precipitate;
everywhere the west front becomes more rich and
elaborate, with its receding portals covered with niches,
which are crowded with statues; everywhere the central
tower assumes a more graceful form, or tapers into a
spire; often two subordinate towers, or two principal
towers, flank the west front; everywhere, in the exube-
rant prodigality of ornament, knosps, shrine-work, cor-
bels, gurgoyles, there is a significance and a purport.
Within the church the pillars along the nave break into
graceful clusters around the central shaft; the vaulted
roof is formed of the most simple yet intricate ribs;
everywhere there are the noblest avenues of straight
lines of pillars, the most picturesque crossings and inter-
minglings of arches; everywhere harmony of the same
converging lines; everywhere the aim appears to be
height, unity of impression, with infinite variety of
parts; a kind of heavenward aspiration, with the most
prodigal display of human labour and wealth, as an
oblation to the temple of God.

The rise of Gothic Architecture, loosely speaking, was
contemporaneous with the Crusades.[b] It was natural to

---

[b] The theory of Warburton deriving
the Gothic Cathedrals from an imitation of the overarching forests of the
ancient Germans (he is disposed to go
back to the Druids) is curious as illustrating the strange and total neglect of
Mediæval Church History in this
country. Here is a divine of almost
unrivalled erudition (Jortin excepted)
in his day, who seems to suppose that
the Germans immediately, that they
emerged from their forests, set to work
to build Gothic cathedrals. He must
either have supposed Gothic architec-

suppose that the eyes of the pilgrims were caught by
the slender, graceful, and richly decorated forms of the
Saracenic mosques, with their minarets and
turrets. Pointed windows were discovered in
mosques, and held to be the models of the Gothic cathedrals. Even earlier, when the Normans were piling up
their massy round arches in the North, they had some
pointed arches in Sicily, apparently adopted from the
Mohammedans of that island.[c] But the pointed arch is
only one characteristic of Gothic Architecture, it is a
vast step from the imitation of a pointed arch or window
(if there were such imitation, which is extremely doubtful), to the creation of a Gothic cathedral.[d] The connexion of the Crusades was of another kind, and far
more powerful; it was the devotion aroused in all orders
by that universal movement, which set into activity all
the faculties of man; and the riches poured into the
lap of the Clergy, which enabled them to achieve such
wonders in so short a period. Religion awoke creative
genius, genius worked freely with boundless command
of wealth.

This apparently simultaneous outburst, and the universal promulgation of the principles, rules, Theory of
and practice of the Gothic Architecture, has Freemasons.
been accounted for by the existence of a vast secret
guild of Freemasons, or of architects.[e] Of this guild,
either connected with or latent in the monasteries and
among the Clergy, some of whom were men of profound
architectural science, and held in their pay and in their
subservience all who were not ecclesiastics, it is said,

ture of the fourth or fifth century, or
quietly annihilated the intervening centuries to the twelfth.

[c] Gally Knight, 'Normans in Sicily.'

[d] Compare Whewell, 'Architectural
Notes,' p. 35.

[e] Hope on Architecture.

the centre, the quickening, and governing power was in
Rome. Certainly of all developments of the Papal
influence and wisdom none could be more extraordinary
than this summoning into being, this conception, this
completion of these marvellous buildings in every part
of Latin Christendom. But it is fatal to this theory
that Rome is the city in which Gothic Architecture,
which some have strangely called the one absolute and
exclusive Christian Architecture, has never found its
place ; even in Italy it has at no time been more than a
half-naturalised stranger. It must be supposed that
while the Papacy was thus planting the world with
Gothic cathedrals, this was but a sort of lofty concession
to Transalpine barbarism, while itself adhered to the
ancient, venerable, more true and majestic style of
ancient Rome. This guild too was so secret as to elude
all discovery. History, documentary evidence maintain
rigid, inexplicable silence. The accounts, which in some
places have been found, name persons employed. The
names of one or two architects, as Erwin of Strasburg,
have survived, but of this guild not one word.[f] The
theory is not less unnecessary than without support.
Undoubtedly there was the great universal guild, the
Clergy and the monastic bodies, who perhaps pro-
State of
Europe. duced, certainly retained, employed, guided,
directed the builders. During this period Latin
Christendom was in a state of perpetual movement,

---

[f] All the documentary evidence adduced by Mr. Hope amounts to a Papal
privilege to certain builders or masons,
or a guild of builders, at Como, published by Muratori (Como was long
celebrated for its skill and devotion to
the art), and a charter to certain painters
by our Henry VI. Schnaase (Geschichte der Bildenden Kunst, iv. c. 5)
examines and rejects the theory. He
cites some few instances more of guilds,
but local and municipal. The first
guild of masons, which comprehended
all Germany, was of the middle of the
15th century.

intercommunication betweeu all parts was frequent,
easy, uninterrupted. There were not only now pilgrimages to Rome, but a regular tide setting to and from the
East, a concourse to the schools and universities, to
Paris, Cologne, Montpellier, Bologna, Salerno: rather
later spread the Mendicants. The monasteries were the
great caravansaries; every class of society was stirred to
its depths; in some cases even tho villains broke the
bonds which attached them to the soil; to all the abbey
or the church opened its hospitable gates. Men skilled
and practised in the science of architecturo would not
rest unemployed, or but poorly employed, at home.
Splendid prizes would draw forth competition, emulation. Sacerdotal prodigality, magnificence, zeal, rivalry
would abroad be famous, attractive at home; they would
be above local or national prepossessions. The prelate
or the abbot, who had determined in his holy ambition
that his cathedral or his abbey should surpass others,
and who had unlimited wealth at his disposal, would
welcome the celebrated, encourage tho promising,
builder from whatever quarter of Christendom he came.
Thus, within certain limits, great architects would be
the architects of the world, or what was then tho
Western world, Latin Christendom: and so there would
be perpetual progress, communication, sympathy in
actual design and execution, as well as in the principles
and in the science of construction. Accordingly, foreign
architects are frequently heard of. Germans crossed
the Alps to teach Italy the secret of tho new architecture.[e] Each nation indeed seems to have worked

[e] " All countries, in adopting a
neighbouring style, seem however to
have worked it with some peculiarities
of their own, so that a person conversant with examples can tell, upon in-
specting a building, not only to what
period it belongs, but to what nation.
Much depends on material, much on

out its own Gothic with certain general peculiarities,
Germany, France, the Netherlands, England, and later
Spain. All seem to aim at certain effects, all recognised
certain broad principles, but the application of these
principles varies infinitely. Sometimes a single building, sometimes the buildings within a certain district,
have their peculiarities. Under a guild, if there had
been full freedom for invention, originality, boldness of
design, there had been more rigid uniformity, more close
adherence to rule in the scientifical and technical parts.

The name of Gothic has ascended from its primal
meaning, that of utter contempt, to the highest honour;
it is become conventional for the architecture of the
Middle Ages, and commands a kind of traditionary
reverence. Perhaps Teutonic, or at least Transalpine,
might be a more fit appellation. It was born, and
reached its maturity and perfection north of the Alps.
Gothic, properly so called, is a stranger and an alien in
Italy. Rome absolutely repudiated it. It was brought
across the Alps by German architects; it has ever borne
in Italy the somewhat contemptuous name German-
Gothic.[b] Among its earliest Italian efforts is one remarkable for its history, as built by a French architect
with English gold, and endowed with benefices in England. The Cardinal Gualo, the legate who placed the
young Henry III. on the throne of England, as he came
back laden with the grateful or extorted tribute of the
island, 12,000 marks of silver, encountered an architect
of fame at Paris: he carried the Northern with him
to his native Vercelli, where the Church of S. Andrea

---

the style of sculpture," &c.—Willis on
Architecture, p. 11. Mr. Hickman's
book is most instructive on the three
styles predominant successively in England.—Compare Whewell.

[b] Gotico Tedesco, Compare Hope,
c. xxxix.

astonished Italy with its pointed arches, as well as
the Italian clergy with the charges fixed for Italian-Gothic. A.D. 1916.
their maintenance on Preferments in remote
England.[i] Assisi, for its age the wonder of the world,
was built by a German architect. What is called the
Lombard or Italian-Gothic, though inharmonious as
attempting to reconcile vertical and horizontal lines,
has no doubt its own admirable excellencies, in some
respects may vie with the Transalpine. Its costly
marbles, inlaid into the building, where they do not
become alternate layers of black and white (to my
judgement an utter defiance of every sound principle
of architectural effect), its gorgeousness at Florence,
Sienna, its fantastic grace at Orvieto, cannot but awaken
those emotions which are the world's recognition of
noble architecture.[k] Milan to me, with all its match-
less splendour, and without considering the architectural
heresy of its modern west front, is wanting in religiousness. It aspires to magnificence, and nothing beyond
magnificence. It is a cathedral which might have been
erected in the pride of their wealth by the godless
Visconti. Nothing can be more wonderful, nothing
more graceful, each seen singly, than the numbers
numberless, in Milton's words, of the turrets, pinnacles,

---

[i] Compare on Cardinal Gualo, vol.
vi. p. 61.

[k] Professor Willis lays down "that
there is in fact no genuine Gothic
building in Italy."—On Italian Architecture, p. 4. He is inclined to make
exceptions for some churches built in
or near Naples by the Angevine dynasty.
"The curious result is a style in which
the horizontal and vertical lines equally
predominate; and which, while it wants
alike the lateral extension and repose

of the Grecian and the lofty upward
tendency and pyramidal majesty of the
Gothic, is yet replete with many an
interesting and valuable architectural
lesson. It exhibits pointed arches,
pinnacles, buttresses, tracery and clus-
tered columns, rib-vaultings, and lofty
towers; all these characteristics, in
short, the bare enunciation of which is
considered by many writers to be a
sufficient definition of Gothic."—Ibid.

statues, above, below, before, behind, on every side.
But the effect is confusion, a dazzling the eyes and
mind, distraction, bewilderment. The statues are a host
of visible images basking in the sunshine, not glorified
saints calmly ascending to heaven. In the interior the
vast height is concealed and diminished by the shrine-
work which a great way up arrests the eye and prevents
it from following the columns to the roof, and makes
a second stage between the pavement and the vault; a
decoration without meaning or purport.

There can be no doubt that the birthplace of true
Gothic Architecture was north of the Alps; it should
seem on the Rhine, or in those provinces of France
which then were German, Burgundy, Lorraine, Alsace,
bordering on the Rhine. It was a splendid gift of Teutonism before Germany rose in insurrection and set
itself apart from Latin Christendom. North of the Alps
it attained its full perfection; there alone the Cathedral
became in its significant symbolism the impersonation
of mediæval Christianity.

The Northern climate may have had some connexion
with its rise and development. In Italy and
the South the Sun is a tyrant; breadth of
shadow must mitigate his force; the wide eaves, the
bold projecting cornice must afford protection from his
burning and direct rays; there would be a reluctance
altogether to abandon those horizontal lines, which cast
a continuous and unbroken shadow; or to ascend as it
were with the vertical up into the unslaked depths of
the noonday blaze. The violent rains would be cast off
more freely by a more flat and level roof at a plane of
slight inclination. In the North the precipitate ridge
would cast off the heavy snow, which might have lodged
and injured the edifice. So, too, within the church the

Italian had to cool and diminish, the Northern would admit and welcome the flooding light. So much indeed did the Gothic Architecture enlarge and multiply the apertures for light, that in order to restore the solemnity it was obliged to subdue and sheathe as it were the glare, at times overpowering, by painted glass. And thus the magic of the richest colouring was added to the infinitely diversified forms of the architecture.

The Gothic cathedral was the consummation, the completion of mediæval, of hierarchical Christianity. Of that mediævalism, of that hierarchism (though Italy was the domain, and Rome the capital of the Pope), the seat was beyond the Alps. The mediæval hierarchical services did not rise to their full majesty and impressiveness, till celebrated under a Gothic cathedral. The church might seem to expand, and lay itself out in long and narrow avenues, with the most gracefully converging perspective, in order that the worshipper might contemplate with deeper awe the more remote central ceremonial. The enormous height more than compensated for the contracted breadth. Nothing could be more finely arranged for the processional services; and the processional services became more frequent, more imposing. The music, instead of being beaten down by low broad arches, or lost within the heavier aisles, soared freely to the lofty roof, pervaded the whole building, was infinitely multiplied as it died and rose again to the fretted roof. Even the incense curling more freely up to the immeasurable height, might give the notion of clouds of adoration finding their way to heaven.

The Gothic cathedral remains an imperishable and majestic monument of hierarchical wealth, Symbolism of Gothic architecture. power, devotion; it can hardly be absolutely called self-sacrifice, for if built for the honour of God

and of the Redeemer, it was honour, it was almost worship, shared in by the high ecclesiastic. That however
has almost passed away; God, as it were, now vindicates
to himself his own. The cathedral has been described
as a vast book in stone, a book which taught by symbolic language, partly plain and obvious to the simpler
man, partly shrouded in not less attractive mystery. It
was at once strikingly significant and inexhaustible;
bewildering, feeding at once and stimulating profound
meditation. Even its height, its vastness might appear
to suggest the Inconceivable, the Incomprehensible in
the Godhead, to symbolise the Infinity, the incalculable
grandeur and majesty of the divine works; the mind felt
humble under its shadow as before an awful presence.
Its form and distribution was a confession of faith; it
typified the creed. Everywhere was the mystic number;
the Trinity was proclaimed by the nave and the aisles
(multiplied sometimes as at Bourges and elsewhere to
the other sacred number, seven), the three richly orna-
mented recesses of the portal, the three towers. The
Rose over the west was the Unity; the whole building
was a Cross. The altar with its decorations announced
the Real Perpetual Presence. The solemn Crypt below
represented the under world, the soul of man in darkness and the shadow of death, the body awaiting the
resurrection. This was the more obvious universal
language. By those who sought more abstruse and
recondite mysteries, they might be found in all the
multifarious details, provoking the zealous curiosity, or
dimly suggestive of holy meaning. Sculpture was called
in to aid. All the great objective truths of religion had
their fitting place. Even the Father, either in familiar
symbol or in actual form, began to appear, and to assert
his property in the sacred building. Already in the

Romanesque edifices the Son, either as the babe in the
lap of his Virgin Mother, on the cross, or ascending into
heaven, had taken his place over the central entrance,
as it were to receive and welcome the worshipper.
Before long he appeared not there alone, though there
in more imposing form; he was seen throughout all his
wondrous history, with all his acts and miracles, down
to the Resurrection, the Ascension, the return to Judgement. Everywhere was that hallowed form, in infancy,
in power, on the cross, on the right hand of the Father,
coming down amid the hosts of angels. The most
stupendous, the most multifarious scenes were represented in reliefs more or less bold, prominent, and
vigorous, or rude and harsh. The carving now aspired
to more than human beauty, or it delighted in the most
hideous ugliness; majestic gentle Angels, grinning hateful sometimes half-comic Devils. But it was not only
the New and the Old Testament, it was the Golden
Legend also which might be read in the unexhausted
language of the cathedral. Our Lady had her own
chapels for her own special votaries, and toward the
East, behind the altar, the place of honour. Not only
were there the twelve Apostles, the four Evangelists,
the Martyrs, the four great Doctors of the Latin Church,
each in his recognised form, and with his peculiar symbol,—the whole edifice swarmed with Saints within and
without, on the walls, on the painted windows, over the
side altars. For now the mystery was so awful that it
might be administered more near to the common eye,
upon the altar in every succursal chapel which lined the
building: it was secure in its own sanctity. There were
the Saints local, national, or those especially to whom
the building was dedicated; and the celestial hierarchy
of the Areopagite, with its ascending orders, and con-

ventional forms, the winged seraph, the cherubic face.
The whole in its vastness and intricacy was to the outward sense and to the imagination what Scholasticism
was to the intellect, an enormous effort, a waste and
prodigality of power, which confounded and bewildered
rather than enlightened; at the utmost awoke vague
and indistinct emotion.

But even therein was the secret of the imperishable
power of the Gothic cathedrals. Their hieroglyphic
language, in its more abstruse terms, became obsolete
and unintelligible; it was a purely hierarchical dialect;
its meaning, confined to the hierarchy, gradually lost its
signification even to them. But the cathedrals themselves retired as it were into more simple and more
commanding majesty, into the solemn grandeur of their
general effect. They rested only on the wonderful boldness and unity of their design, the richness of their
detail. Content now to appeal to the indelible, inextinguishable kindred and affinity of the human heart to
grandeur, grace, and beauty, the countless statues from
objects of adoration became architectural ornaments.
So the mediæval churches survive in their influence on
the mind and the soul of man. Their venerable antiquity comes in some sort in aid of their innate religiousness. It is that about them which was temporary and
accessory, their hierarchical character, which has chiefly
dropped from them and become obsolete. They are
now more absolutely and exclusively churches for the
worship of God. As the mediæval pageantry has passed
away, or shrunk into less imposing forms, the one object
of worship, Christ, or God in Christ, has taken more
full and absolute possession of the edifice. Where the
service is more simple, as in our York, Durham, or
Westminster, or even where the old faith prevails, in

Cologne, in Antwerp, in Strasburg, in Rheims, in
Bourges, in Rouen, it has become more popular, less
ecclesiastical : everywhere the priest is now, according
to the common sentiment, more the Minister, less the
half-divinised Mediator. And thus all that is the higher
attribute and essence of Christian architecture retains
its nobler, and in the fullest sense, its religious power.
The Gothic cathedral can hardly be contemplated without awe, or entered without devotion.

CHAPTER IX.

Christian Sculpture.

During almost all this period Christian Sculpture was accessory, or rather subsidiary to architecture The use of Statues was to ornament and enrich the building. In her Western conquests under Justinian, Constantinople sent back no sculptors; only architects with her domes, and her Greek cross, and her splendid workers in mosaic. The prodigality with which Constantine, as Rome of old, despoiled the world to adorn his new city with ancient works of sculpture, put to shame, it should seem, rather than awoke the emulation of Christian Art. We have seen Constantine usurp the form, the attributes, even the statue, of Apollo.[a] We have heard even Theodosius do homage to art, and spare statues of heathen deities for their exquisite workmanship. Christian historians, Christian poets, lavish all their eloquence, and all their glowing verse on the treasures of ancient art. They describe with the utmost admiration the gods, the mythological personages, those especially that crowded the baths of Zeuxippus;[b] which perished with the old Church of St. Sophia in the fatal conflagration in the fifth year of Justinian. In the Lausus stood the unrivalled Cnidian

---

[a] History of Christianity, vol. II. p. 337; III. 378. The whole passage.
[b] Cedrenus, v. I. p. 648, Ed. Bonn. The Ecphrasis of Christodorus, is a

Poem, for its age, of much spirit and beauty. See especially the descriptions of Hecuba and of Homer.—Jacobs, Anthologia.

Venus of Praxiteles; the Samian Juno of Lysippus; [c]
the ivory Jove of Phidias.   The whole city was thronged
with statues of the Emperors and their Queens, of Constantine, Theodosius, Valentinian, Arcadius, and Honorius, Justinian, Leo, Theodora, Pulcheria, Eudocia.[d]   It
is even said that there were marble statues of Arius,
Macedonius, Sabellius, and Eunomius, which were exposed to filthy indignities by the orthodox Theodosius.[e]
It appears not how far Sculpture had dared to embody
in brass or in marble the hallowed and awful objects of
Christian worship.   It should seem indeed that the
Iconoclastic Emperors found statues, and those statues
objects of adoration, to war upon.   Though in the word
Iconoclast, the image-breaker, the word for image is
ambiguous; still the breaking seems to imply something more destructive than the effacing pictures, or
picking out mosaics; it is the dashing to pieces something hard and solid.   This controversy in the second
Nicene Council comprehends images of brass or stone;
one of the perpetual precedents is the statue of the
Redeemer said to have been raised at Paneas in Syria.[f]
The carved symbolic images of the Jewish ark are constantly alleged.[g]   Those are accursed who compare the
images of the Lord and of the Saints to the statues of
Satanic Idols.[h]   If we worship stones as Gods, how do

[c] So at least says Cedrenus, p. 564.
[d] All these will be found in the description of Constantinople by Petrus
Gyllius. The work was translated by
John Ball, London, 1729.
[e] Gyllius, b. II. c. xxlii.
[f] Act. Concil. Nicen. iL A.D. 737,
ἀνδριάντι τῷ Χριστῷ.   It was said to
have been raised by the woman cured
of an issue of blood, p. 14; ἔστησαν

δὲ καὶ εἰκόνα—of a certain Saint in an
oratory, p. 23.
[g] The Sculptilia in the Old Testament, p. 45.
[h] These are anathematised — τὴν
εἰκόνα τοῦ κυρίου καὶ τῶν ἁγίων
αὐτοῦ ὁμοίως τοῖς Ἑσανοας τῶν Σατα-
νικῶν εἰδώλων ὀνομάσαντες σεκτὰς
καὶ ἁγίας εἰκόνας τὰς ἐκ χρωμάτων
καὶ ψηφίδος καὶ ἑτέρας ὕλης ἐπιτη-

we worship the Martyrs and Apostles who broke down
and destroyed idols of stone?[1] The homage paid to
the statues of the Emperors was constantly urged to
repel the accusation of idolatry. Yet probably statues
which represented objects of Christian worship were
extremely rare; and when Image-worship was restored,
what may be called its song of victory, is silent as to
Sculptures:[k] the Lord, the Virgin, the Angels, Saints,
Martyrs, Priesthood, take their place over the portal
entrance; but shining in colours to blind the eyes of
the heretics. To the keener perception of the Greeks
there may have arisen a feeling that in its more rigid
and solid form the Image was more near to the Idol.
At the same time, the art of Sculpture and casting in
bronze was probably more degenerate and out of use;
at all events it was too slow and laborious to supply the

θείως ἐχουσῆς ἐν ταῖς ἁγίαις τοῦ
Θεοῦ ἐκκλησίαις, ἐν ἱεροῖς σκεύεσι
καὶ ἐσθῆσι τοίχοις τε καὶ σανίσιν,
οἴκοις τε καὶ ὁδοῖς, p. 375. In this
minute enumeration the first must be
statues. The letter of Tarasius is less
clear: it mentions only painting, mosaics, waxen tablets, and σανίδες; and
in the Treatise of the Patriarch Ger-
manus, published by Mai, Spicilegium,
Romanum, vii. p. 62, σανίδες (qu.,
reliefs) are mentioned and contrasted
with γραφίδες, paintings.

[l] Εἰ τοὺς λίθους ὡς θεοὺς δοξάζω
(if I give really divine worship to
these stones, as I am accused) was τιμῶ
καὶ προσκυνῶ τοὺς μάρτυρας καὶ
ἀποστόλους συντρίψαντας καὶ ἀπο-
λέσαντας τὰ λίθινα ξόδια. — The
address of Leontius, p. 48.

[k] See the Poem in the Anthologia
(Χριστιάνικα Ἐπιγράμματα), Jacobs,
i. 28.

Λάμψον ἀντὶς τῆς ἀληθείας πόλιν
καὶ τὰς κόρας ἤμβλυνε τῶν ψευδηγόρων
γύμνου συστολία. νόστιμος πλάνη·
καὶ πίστιν ἀντεῖ, καὶ πλανῶνται χέρι.
Ἰδοῦ γὰρ αὖθις Χριστὸν εἰσοιτομένος
λάμπει· πρὶν ὕφοι τῆς καθέδρας τοῦ ἐρατοῦ,
καὶ τὰς συστιχίδα αἱμόνεις ἀνατρέψει.
Τὴν εἴσοδου δ' ὕπερθεν, ὡς θεία πύλη,
στηλογραφεῖται, καὶ φυλακῆ, ἢ παμῆνει,
ἀναξ δὲ καὶ πρόεδρος, ὡς ἐλαστήριον
σὺν τοῖς συνέργοις ἱστορούντες Ἀμφίον·
σύλλας δὲ παντὸς αἷα ἐρεμμοὶ τοῦ δόμου,
ποὺς (Angeli) μαθηταί, μάρτυρες, θεράπνεις.
ὅθεν καλοῦμεν Χριστοτυπίάλαων οἶκον,
τὸν πρὶν λαχόντα καθέσμαι χρυσαντόραον,
ὡς τὸν θρόνον ἔχοντα Χριστοῦ κυρίου.
Χριστοῦ δὲ μιγάδι, Χριστοτυπώμεν τύπους,
καὶ τοῦ σοφουργοῦ Μιχαὴλ τὴν εἰκόνα.

This was Michael the Drunkard, son of
Theodora (Jacobs' Note). Compare
vol. ii. p. 411. Was the Painting of
Michael the Archangel, celebrated in
two other Epigrams, erected on this
occasion?—(Pp. 12, 13.)

[k] Λάμπων ἀγγελίαρχος, ἀσώματον εἰδεῖ
μορφῆς·
ἤ μέγα τολμήεις κηροῖς ἀνεπλάσσατο·
οἶδα δὲ τέχνη
χρώμασι πορθμεῦσαι τὴν φρενὸς ἱκεσίην.

demand of triumphant zeal in the restoration of the persecuted Images. There was therefore a tacit compromise; nothing appeared but painting, mosaics, engraving on cups and chalices, embroidery on vestments. The renunciation of Sculpture grew into a rigid passionate aversion. The Greek at length learned to contemplate that kind of more definite and full representation of the Deity or the Saints with the aversion of a Jew or a Mohammedan.[m] Yet some admiration for ancient Sculpture of heathen objects lingered behind in the Grecian mind. In his vehement and bitter lamentation over the destruction of all the beautiful works of bronze by the Crusaders in the Latin Conquest of Constantinople, Nicetas is not content with branding the avarice which cast all these wonderful statues into the melting-pot to turn them into money; he denounces the barbarians as dead to every sense of beauty,[n] who remorselessly destroyed the colossal Juno, the equestrian Bellerophon, the Hercules; as regardless of the proud reminiscences of old Rome, they melted the swine and the wolf which suckled Romulus and Remus, and the ass with its driver set up by Augustus after the battle of Actium; they feared not to seize the magic eagle of Apollonius of Tyana. Even the exquisite Helen, who set the world in arms, notwithstanding her unrivalled beauty and her fame, touched not, and did not soften those iron-hearted,

Christian Sculpture proscribed in the East.

---

[m] Nicephorus Critopulus, a late writer, φησι, τούτων οὐκ εἰκόνας ἢ ἱακλησία ἱνοίει οὐ γλυπτὰς εὔθι Λαξευτὰς ἀλλὰ γραπτὰς μόνον, quoted in Suicer, who speaks justly of "Imagines sculptas et excisas, ipsiusque Dei repræsentationes apud Græcos etiamnum ignotas." The exquisite small carvings in ivory were permitted seemingly in all ages of Byzantine art.

[n] Nicetas Choniata de Signis, οἱ τοῦ καλοῦ ἀνέραστοι οὗτοι βάρβαροι. Some called the equestrian Bellerophon Joshua the Son of Nun. This is remarkable.

those unlettered savages, who could not read, who had never heard of Homer.°

The West might seem to assert its more bold and
Sculpture in the West. free image-worship by its unrestrained and prodigal display of religious sculpture; still it was mostly sculpture decorative, or forming an integral part of Architecture. It was not the ordinary occupation of Sculpture to furnish the beautiful single statue of marble or of bronze. Rome had no succession of Emperors, whose attribute and privilege it was to a late period in Constantinople to have their image set up for the homage of the people, and so to keep alive the art of carving marble or casting bronze. But gradually in the Romanesque, as in the later Gothic Architecture, the west front of the Churches might seem, as it were, the chosen place for sacred Images. Not merely did the Saviour and the Virgin appear as the Guardian Deities over the portal, gradually the Host of Heaven, Angels, Apostles, Martyrs, Evangelists, Saints spread over the whole façade. They stood on pedestals or in niches; reliefs more or less high found their panels in the walls; the heads of the portal arches were carved in rich designs; the semicircle more or less round or pointed, above the level line of the door, was crowded with sacred scenes, or figures. But in all these, as in other statues if such there were, within the Churches, Christian modesty required that human or divinised figures must be fully clad. Sculpture, whose essence is form, found the naked human figure almost under proscription. There remained nothing for the sculptor's

---

° Of Helen he says—ἄρ᾽ ἐμείλιξε | καὶ τέλεον ἀναλφάβητοι ἀναγνόσις τοὺς δισμειλίπτους; ἄρ᾽ ἐμάθεξε καὶ γνῶσις τῶν ἐπὶ σοὶ ῥαψῳβηθέντων τοὺς εὐηρόφορους; . . . . . ἄλλως ἐκείνων ἐτῶν.—Edit. Bonn., p. 863. τὰ τοῦ παρὰ ἀγραμμάτοις βαρβάροις

art but the attitude, the countenance, and the more or
less graceful fall of the drapery; all this too, in strict
subordination to the architectural effect; with this he
must bo content, and not aspire to centre on himself
and his work the admiring and long dwelling eye.[p] The
Sculptor, in general, instead of the votary and master
of a high and independent art, became the workman of
the architect; a step or two higher than the carver of
the capital, or the moulding, the knosp or the finial.[q] In
some respects the progress of Gothic, though it multiplied images to infinity, was unfavourable; as the niches
became loftier and narrower, the Saints rose to disproportionate stature, shrunk to meagre gracility, they
became ghosts in long shrouds. Sometimes set on high
upon pinnacles, or crowded in hosts as at Milan, they
lost all distinctness, and were absolutely nothing more
than architectural ornaments.

All, no doubt, even as regards sculptural excellence,
is not equally rude, barbarous, or barren. So many
artists could not be employed, even under conventional
restrictions, on subjects so suggestive of high and solemn
emotion, men themselves under deep devotional feelings,
without communicating to the hard stone some of their
own conceptions of majesty, awfulness, serenity, grace,
beauty. The sagacious judgement among the crowds of
figures in front of our Cathedrals may discern some of
the nobler attributes of Sculpture, dignity, expression,
skilful and flowing disposition of drapery, even while that
judgement is not prompted and kindled by reverential

---

[p] Even of the Crucifix Schnaase has
justly said, " Gleichzeitig änderte sich
auch die Tracht des Gekreuzigten; die
lange Tunica, welche früher den Kör-
per ganz verhüllte, wird schon in 12

Jahr. kurzer, im 13 und noch allge-
meiner in 14 vertritt ein Schurz um
die Hüfte ihre Stelle."—iv. p. 390.

[q] It is to be observed that the Statues
were only intended to be seen in front.

religiousness, as is often the case, to imagine that in the
statue which is in the man's own mind. In the reliefs,
if there be more often confusion, grotesqueness, there
is not seldom vigour and distinctness, skilful grouping,
an artistic representation of an impressive scene. The
animals are almost invariably hard, conventional emblems
not drawn from nature; but the human figure, if without anatomical precision, mostly unnecessary when so
amply swathed in drapery, in its outline and proportions
is at times nobly developed. Yet, on the whole, the
indulgence usually claimed and readily conceded for
the state of art at the period, is in itself the unanswerable testimony to its imperfection and barbarism. Christian Sculpture must produce, as it did afterwards produce, something greater, with John of Bologna and
Michael Angelo, or it must be content to leave to
heathen Greece the uncontested supremacy in this wonderful art. Sculpture, in truth, must learn from ancient
art those elementary lessons which Christianity could
not teach, which it dared not, or would not venture to
teach; it must go back to Greece for that revelation of
the inexhaustible beauties of the human form which had
long been shrouded from the eyes of men. The anthropomorphism of the Greeks grew out of, and at the same
time fully developed the physical perfection of the
human body. That perfection was the model, the ideal
of the Sculptor. The gods in stature, force, majesty,
proportion, beauty, were but superhuman men. To the
Christian there was still some disdain of the sensual
perishable body; with monasticism, that disdain grew
into contempt; it must be abased, macerated, subdued.
The utmost beauty which it could be allowed was
patience, meekness, gentleness, lowliness. To the fully
developed athlete succeeded the emaciated saint. The

man of sorrows, the form "of the servant," still lingered
in the Divine Redeemer; the Saint must be glorified in
meekness; the Martyr must still bear the sign and
expression of his humiliation. The whole age might
seem determined to disguise and conceal, even if not to
debase, the human form, the Sculptor's proper domain
and study, in its free vigorous movement or stately
tranquillity. The majestic Prelate was enveloped in
his gorgeous and cumbrous habiliments, which dazzled
with their splendour; the strong, tall, noble Knight
was sheathed in steel; even the Monk or Friar was
swathed in his coarse ungainly dress, and cowl. Even
for its draperies reviving Sculpture must go back to the
antique.

There was one branch, however, of the art—Monumental Sculpture—which assumed a peculiar Monumental
character and importance under Christianity, Sculpture.
and aspired to originality and creativeness. Even
Monumental Sculpture, in the Middle Ages, was in
some degree architectural. The tomb upon which, the
canopy under which, lay the King, the Bishop, or the
Knight, or the Lady, was as carefully and as elaborately
wrought as the slumbering image. In the repose, in
the expression of serene sleep, in the lingering majesty,
gentleness, or holiness of countenance of these effigies
there is often singular beauty.[1] Repose is that in which
Sculpture delights; the repose, or the collapsing into
rest, of a superhuman being, after vigorous exertion;
nothing, therefore, could be more exquisitely suited to

---

[1] Among the noblest tombs in Italy
are that of Benedict XI. at Perugia,
by John, son of Nicolo Pisano; of
Gregory X., by Margaritone, at Arezzo;
of John XXIII., at Florence, by Donatello.   Our own Cathedrals have noble
specimens of somewhat ruder work—
the Edward III., Queen Philippa, and
Richard II. in Westminster Abbey.

the art than the peace of the Christian sleeping after a
weary life, sleeping in conscious immortality, sleeping
to awake to a calm and joyful resurrection. Even the
drapery, for Sculpture must here, above all, submit to
conceal the form in drapery, is at rest. But Monumental Sculpture did not confine itself to the single
recumbent figure. The first great Christian Sculptor,
Nicolo Pisano, in the former part of the 14th century,
showed his earliest skill and excellence in the reliefs
round the tomb of St. Dominic at Bologna.[1] It is remarkable that the first great Christian Sculptor was a
distinguished architect. Nicolo Pisano had manifestly
studied at Rome and elsewhere the remains of ancient
art; they guide and animate, but only guide and animate his bold and vigorous chisel. Christian in form
and sentiment, some of his figures have all the grace
and ease of Grecian Art. Nicolo Pisano stood, indeed,
alone almost as much in advance of his successors, as of
those who had gone before.[1] Nor did Nicolo Pisano
confine himself to Monumental Sculpture. The spacious
pulpits began to offer panels which might be well filled
up with awful admonitory reliefs. In those of Pisa and
Sienna the master, in others his disciples and scholars,
displayed their vigour and power. There was one scene
which permitted them to reveal the naked form—the
Last Judgement. Men, women, rose unclad from their

---

[1] See on Nicolo Pisano, Cicognara, Storia de Scultura, v. 111, with the illustrative Prints. In Count Cicognara's engravings the transition from the earliest masters to Nicolo Pisano, is to be transported to another age, to overleap centuries.

[1] Count Cicognara writes thus: all that I have seen, and all the Count's illustrations, confirm his judgement:—"Tutto ciò che lo avera preceduto era molto al di sotto de lui, e per elevarsi ad un tratto fu forza d'un genio straordinario," p. 223. "E le opere degli scolari di Niccolo ci sembrerano talvolta della mano de suoi predecessori," p. 234. Guilds of sculpture now arose at Sienna and elsewhere.

tombs. And it is singular to remark how Nicolo Pisano seized all that was truly noble and sculptural. The human form appears in infinite variety of bold yet natural attitude, without the grotesque distortions, without the wild extravagances, the writhing, the shrinking from the twisting serpents, the torturing fiends, the monsters preying upon the vitals. Nicolo wrought before Dante, and maintained the sobriety of his art. Later Sculpture and Painting must aspire to represent all that Poetry had represented, and but imperfectly represented in words : it must illustrate Dante.

But in the first half of the fifteenth century, during the Popedom of Eugenius and Nicolas V., Sculpture broke loose from its architectural servitude, and with Donatello, and with Brunelleschi (if Brunelleschi had not turned aside and devoted himself exclusively to architectural art), even with Ghiberti, asserted its dignity and independence as a creative art.* The Evangelist or the Saint began to stand alone trusting to his own majesty, not depending on his position as part of an harmonious architectural design. The St. Mark and the St. George of Donatello are noble statues, fit to take their place in the public squares of Florence. In his fine David, after the death of Goliath, above all in his Judith and Holofernes, Donatello took a bolder flight. In that masterly work (writes Vasari) the simplicity of the dress and countenance of Judith manifest her lofty spirit and the aid of God ; as in Holofernes wine, sleep,

---

* Donatello born 1383, died 1466 ; Brunelleschi 1398 ; Ghiberti 1378, died 1455. I ought perhaps to have added Jacobo della Quercia, who worked rather earlier at Bologna and Sienna. Read in Vasari the curious contest be- | tween Donatello and Brunelleschi, in which Donatello owned that while himself made an unrivalled Contadino, Brunelleschi made a Christ. See Vasari on the works of Donatello.

and death are expressed in his limbs; which, having lost their animating spirit, are cold and failing. Donatello succeeded so well in portrait statuary, that to his favourite female statue he said—Speak! speak! His fame at Padua was unrivalled. Of him it was nobly said, either Donatello was a prophetic anticipation of Buonarotti, or Donatello lived again in Buonarotti.

Ghiberti's great work was the gates of the Baptistery at Florence, deserving, in Michael Angelo's praise, to be called the Gates of Heaven; and it was from their copiousness, felicity, and unrivalled sculptural designs, that these gates demanded and obtained their fame.

CHAPTER X.

Christian Painting.

PAINTING, which, with architecture and music, attained its perfect and consummate excellence under the influence of Latin Christianity, had yet to await the century which followed the pontificate of Nicolas V. before it culminated, through Francia and Perugino, in Michael Angelo, Leonardo, Raffaelle, Correggio, and Titian. It received only its first impulse from mediæval Christianity; its perfection was simultaneous with the revival of classical letters and ancient art. Religion had in a great degree to contest the homage, even of its greatest masters, with a dangerous rival. Some few only of its noblest professors were at that time entirely faithful to Christian art. But all these, as well as the second Teutonic school, Albert Durer and his followers, are beyond our bounds.[a]

Of the great Epochs of Painting, therefore, two only, preparatory to the Perfect Age, belong to our present history: I. That which is called (I cannot but think too

---

[a] It were unwise and presumptuous (since our survey here also must be brief and rapid) to enter into the artistic and antiquarian questions which have been agitated and discussed with so much knowledge and industry by modern writers, especially (though I would not pass over Lanzi, still less the new Annotated Edition of Vasari) by the Baron Rumohr (Italienische Forschungen), my friend M. Rio (Art Chrétien), by Kugler and his all-accomplished Translators, and by Lord Lindsay (Christian Art). In my summary I shall endeavour to indicate the sources from which it can be amplified, justified, or filled up.

exclusively) the Byzantine period ; II. That initiatory branch of Italian art which I will venture to name, from the subjects it chose, the buildings which it chiefly adorned, and the profession of many of the best masters who practised it, the Cloistral epoch. The second period reached its height in Frà Angelico da Fiesole.[b]

It is impossible to doubt that Painting, along with the conservation of some of its technical processes, and with some traditionary forms, and the conventional representation of certain scenes in the Scriptural History or in Legends, preserved certain likenesses, as they were thought to be, of the Saviour and his Apostles and Martyrs, designated by fixed and determinate lineaments, as well as by their symbolical attributes. The paintings in the Catacombs at Rome show such forms and countenances in almost unbroken descent till nearly two centuries after the conversion of Constantine.[c] The history of Iconoclasm has recorded how such pictures were in the East religiously defended, religiously destroyed, religiously restored ; how the West, in defiance, as it were, and contempt of the impious persecutor, seemed to take a new impulse, and the Popes of the Iconoclastic

---

[b] Born 1397—became a Dominican 1407.

[c] Much has been done during the last few years in the Catacombs. The great French Publication, by M. Louis Perret, is beautiful ; if it be as true as beautiful, by some inexplicable means, some of the paintings have become infinitely more distinct and brilliant, since I saw them some thirty years ago. It is unfortunate that the passion for early art, and polemic passion, are so busy in discovering what they are determined to find, that sober, histori-

cal, and artistic criticism is fairly bewildered. There are two important questions yet to be settled : When did the Catacombs cease to be places of burial ? (what is the date of the later cemeteries of Rome ?). When did the Catacomb Chapels cease to be places not of public worship, but of fervent private devotion ? To the end of that period, whenever it was, they would continue to be embellished by art, and therefore the difficulty of allying dates to works of art is increased.

age lavished large sums on decorations of their churches
by paintings, if not by sculpture. No doubt, also, many
monk-artists fled from the sacrilegious East to practise
their holy art in the safe and quiet West. Even a century or more before this, it is manifest that Justinian's
conquest of Italy, as it brought the Byzantine form of
architecture, so it brought the Byzantine skill, the modes
and usages of the subsidiary art. The Byzantine painting of that age lives in the mosaics (the more durable
process of that, in all its other forms, too perishable art)
on the walls of the Church of San Vitale, and in S. Apollinaris in Ravenna, and in other Italian cities under
Greek influence. These mosaics maintain the indefeasible character[d] of Greek Christianity. The vast,
majestic image of the Saviour broods indeed over the
place of honour, above the high altar ; but on the chan-
cel-walls, within the Sanctuary, are on one side the
Emperor, Theodora on the other, not Saints or Martyrs,
not Bishops or Popes. It cannot be argued, from the
survival of these more lasting works, that mosaic predominated over other modes of painting, either in Constantinople or in the Byzantinised parts of the West.
But as it was more congenial to the times, being a work
more technical and mechanical, so no doubt it tended
to the hard, stiff, conventional forms which in general
characterise Byzantine art, as well as to their perpetuity.
The traditions of painting lived on. The descriptions of
the paintings on the walls of the Romans[e] by the poets

---

[d] On the Mosaics of Leo III., Anastasius in vit. compare Schnaase, Bildende Kunst, iii. p. 505.

[e] In the Castle Villa of Pontius
Leontius on the Garonne, in the verses
of Sidonius Apollinaris, Carm. xxii.,

were painted on one part scenes from
the Mithridatic war waged by Lucul-
lus; on the other the opening Chapters
of the Old Testament. "Recutitorum
primordia Judæorum." Sidonius seems
to have been surprised at the splendour

of the fourth or fifth centuries bear striking resemblance
to those of the poets of Charlemagne and Louis the
Pious, of the works which adorned Aix-la-Chapelle and
the Palace of Ingelheim. How far, during all this
period, it was old Roman art, or Roman art modified by
Byzantine influences, may seem a question unimportant
to general history, and probably incapable of a full
solution. We must confine ourselves to that which is
specially and exclusively Christian art.

Of all Christian painting during this long period, from
the extinction of Paganism to the rise of Italian art
(its first dawn at the beginning of the twelfth century,
brightening gradually to the time of Nicolas V.), the
one characteristic is that its object was worship, not art.
It was a mute preaching, which addressed not the
refined and intelligent, but the vulgar of all ranks.[f] Its
utmost aim was to awaken religious emotion, to suggest
religious thought. It was therefore—more, no doubt,
in the East than in the West—rigidly traditional, conventional, hierarchical. Each form had its special type,
from which it was dangerous, at length forbidden, to
depart. Each scene, with its grouping and arrangement, was consecrated by long reverence; the artist
worked in the trammels of usage; he had faithfully to
transmit to others that which he had received, and
no more. Invention was proscribed; novelty might

---

and duration of the colours :
" Perpetuum pictura nical, nec tempora
longo
Depreciata suas turpant pigmenta figuras."
—C. 212.
Fortunatus mentions wood-carving as
rivalling painting,
   " Quæ pictura solet, ligna dedere jocos."
See Ermondus Nigellus, for the paint-
ings at Ingelheim.

[f] See the Greek Epigram on the
painting of Michael the Archangel.
'Ὡς θρασὺ μορφῶσαι τὸν ἀσώματον ἀλλὰ
καὶ εἰκὼν
ἡ μορφὴν ἀνάγει μᾶλλον ἐπουρανίαν.
                                          Jacobs, p. 14.
This whole series of Epigrams was in-
scribed, no doubt, either under paintings, or under illuminations in MSS.

incur the suspicion almost of heresy—at all events it would be an unintelligible language. Symbolism without a key; it would either jar on sacred associations, or perplex, or offend.[f]

From the earliest period there had been two traditional conceptions of that which was the central figure of Christian art, the Lord himself. One represented the Saviour as a beautiful youth, beardless—a purely ideal image, typical perhaps of the rejuvenescence of mankind in Christ.[b] Such was the prevailing, if not the exclusive conception of the Redeemer in the West. In the East, the Christ is of mature age, of tall stature, meeting eyebrows, beautiful eyes, fine-formed nose, curling hair, figure slightly bowed, of delicate complexion, dark beard (it is sometimes called wine-coloured beard), his face, like his mother's, of the colour of wheat, long fingers, sonorous voice, and sweet eloquence (how was this painted?),[i] most gentle, quiet, long-suffering, patient, with all kindred graces, blending the manhood with the attributes of God. In the fabulous letter ascribed to

---

[f] Kugler has the quotation from the Acts of the Council of Nice, which show that the Byzantine painters worked according to a law θέσμος. But M. Didron's work, Manuel d'Iconographie Chrétienne, at once proved the existence, and in fact published this law, according to which, in his vivid words —" L'artiste Grec est asservi aux traditions comme l'animal à son instinct, Il fait une figure comme l'hirondelle son nid ou l'abeille sa ruche," p. iv. The Greek Painter's Guide, which fills the greater part of M. Didron's book, gives all the rules of technical procedure and design.

[b] Didron, Hist. de Dieu, and a trans-

lation published by Bohn, p. 249. But compare the two heads from the Catacombs, engraved in the Translation of Kugler. These, if both indeed represent the Redeemer, and are of the period supposed, approximate more nearly to the Eastern type.

[i] Didron, p. 248, from John of Damascus. M. Didron has fully investigated the subject, but with an utter and total want of historical criticism. He accepts this controversial tract of John of Damascus (he does not seem to read Greek) as an authority for all the old Legends of Abgarus of Edessa, and the likenesses of Christ painted or carved by order of Constantine.

Y 2

Lentulus, descriptive of the person of the Redeemer, this conception is amplified into still higher beauty.[k] The truth seems to be that this youthful Western type was absolutely and confessedly ideal; it was symbolic of the calm, gentle, young, world-renewing religion. In one place the Christ seems standing on the mystic mountain from whence issue the four rivers of Paradise, the Gospels of everlasting life.[m] The tradition of the actual likeness was Eastern (it was unknown to Augustine), and this tradition in all its forms, at the second Council of Nicæa, and in the writings of John of Damascus, became historical fact. Though at that time there was not much respect for Scripture or probability, yet the youthful, almost boyish type of the Western Church, if it still survived, was so directly at issue with the recorded age of Jesus, that even in the West the description in John of Damascus, embellished into the bolder fiction of Lentulus, the offspring, and not the parent of the controversy, found general acceptance in the West as in the East.[n]

---

[k] Compare Hist. of Christianity, iii. p. 390, for the translation of Lentulus. I am astounded at finding in a book like Kugler's (the English translation especially having undergone such supervision) the assertion that this letter of Lentulus may "possibly be assigned to the third century," p. 12. What evidence is there of its existence before the ninth or even the eleventh century? It is a strange argument, the only one that I can find, that the description resembles some of the earliest so-called Portraits of the Saviour, even one in the Catacombs. It is clear that it was unknown to the early Fathers, especially to St. Augustine. If known, it must have been adduced at the Council of Nicæa, and by John of Damascus. But even the fable had not been heard of at that time. I have not the least doubt that it was a fiction growing out of the controversy.

[m] Didron, p. 251.

[n] Hence too the Veronica, the vera eixav, a singular blending of Greek and Latin fiction and language. William Grimm, however, in his "Die Sage von Ursprung der Christus Bilder," treats this as a fancy of Mabillon and Papebroch. He derives it from the traditional name, Berenice, of the woman whose issue of blood was stanched, who traditionally also was the S. Veronica. —Berlin. Transact., 1843.

But the triumph of Iconoclasm had been a monastic triumph—a triumph for which the monks had suffered, and admired each other's martyr sufferings. Gradually misery and pain became the noblest, dearest images; the joyous and elevating, if still lowly, emotions of the older faith, gave place altogether to gloom, to dreary depression. Among one class of painters, the monks of St. Basil, there was a reaction to absolute black- *Monks of St. Basil. Black School.* ness and ugliness. The Saviour became a dismal, macerated, self-tortured monk. Light vanished from his brow; gentleness from his features; calm, serene majesty from his attitude.

Another change, about the tenth century, came over the image of the Lord. It was no longer the *Change in the tenth century.* mild Redeemer, but the terrible Judge, which painting strove to represent. As the prayers, the hymns, gradually declined from the calm, if not jubilant tone of the earliest Church, the song of deliverance from hopeless unawakening death, the triumph in the assurance of eternal life,—so the youthful symbol of the new religion, the form which the Godhead, by its in-dwelling, beautified and glorified, the still meek, if commanding look of the Redeemer, altogether disappeared, or ceased to be the most ordinary and dominant character: he became the King of tremendous majesty, before whom stood shuddering, guilty, and resuscitated mankind.[c] The Cross, too, by degrees, became the Crucifix.[p] The image of the Lord on the Cross was at first *The Crucifix.* meek, though suffering; pain was represented, but pain overcome by patience; it was still a clothed

---

[c] See the observations of Schnaase above, p. 599, note.

[p] Schnaase says that the first By-santine representation of the Cruci- fixion is in a Codex of the time of Basil the Macedonian (867-886), iii. p. 216.

form, with long drapery. By degrees it was stripped to ghastly nakedness; agony became the prevailing, absorbing tone. The intensity of the suffering strove at least to subdue the sublime resignation of the sufferer; the object of the artist was to wring the spectator's heart with fear and anguish, rather than to chasten with quiet sorrow or elevate with faith and hope; to aggravate the sin of man, rather than display the mercy of God. Painting vied with the rude sculpture which arose in many quarters (sculpture more often in wood than in stone), and by the red streaming blood, and the more vivid expression of pain in the convulsed limbs, deepened the effect; till, at last, that most hideous and repulsive object, the painted Crucifix, was offered to the groaning worship of mankind.[q]

But this was only one usage, though the dominant one—one school of Byzantine art. Painting, both at Constantinople and in Italy, was more true to its own dignity, and to Christianity. It still strove to maintain nobler conceptions of the God-Man, and to embody the Divinity glorifying the flesh in which it dwelt. In this respect, no doubt, the more durable form of the art would be highly conservative; it prevented deeper degeneration. If other painting might dare to abrogate the

[q] The curious and just observations of M. Didron should be borne in mind in the History of Christian Painting. "Nous dirons à cette occasion, qu'il n'y aurait rien de plus intéressant qu'à signaler dans l'ordre chronologique les sujets de la Bible, du Martyrologe, et de la Légende, que les différentes époques ont surtout affectionnés. Dans les catacombes il n'y a pas une scène de martyre, mais une foule de sujets relatifs à la résurrection. Les Martyrs et les jugements derniers, avec les représentations des supplices de l'enfer, abondent pendant le moyen âge. A partir de la renaissance à nos jours c'est la douceur, et, disons le mot, la sentimentalité, qui dominent; alors on adopte la bénédiction des petits enfants, et les dévotions qui ont le cœur pour l'objet. Il faut chercher la raison de tous ces faits."—Didron, Manuel d'Iconographie, p. 182, note. The reason is clear enough.

tradition or the law, Mosaic would be more unable, or
more unwilling, to venture upon dangerous originality.
It would be a perpetual protest against the encroachments of ugliness and deformity: its attribute, its excellence being brilliancy, strongly contrasted diversity
and harmony of rich colouring, it would not consent to
darken itself to a dismal monotony. Yet Mosaic can
hardly become high art; it is too artificial, too mechanical. It may have, if wrought from good models, an
imposing effect; but the finely-evanescent outline, the
true magic of colouring, the depth, the light and shade,
the half-tints, the blending and melting into each other
of hues in their finest gradations, are beyond its powers.
The interlaying of small pieces cannot altogether avoid
a broken, stippled, spotty effect: it cannot be alive.
As it is strong and hard, we can tread it under foot on
a pavement, and it is still bright as ever: but in the
church, the hall, or the chamber, it is an enamelled
wall—but it is a wall;[1] splendid decoration, but aspiring
to none of the loftier excellences of art. But throughout
this period faithful conservation was in truth the most
valuable service. Mosaic fell in with the tendency to
conventionalism, and aided in strengthening conventionalism into irresistible law.[2]

Thus Byzantine art, and Roman art in the West, so

[1] Kugler (p. 20) is almost inclined
to suspect that historic painting on
walls in Mosaic arose under Christian
influences in the fourth century. It
was before on pavements.

[2] The account of the earlier Mosaics,
and the description of those at Rome
and at Ravenna, in Kugler's Handbook,
is full and complete. Kugler, it is to
be observed, ascribed those in San Vitale, and other works of Justinian and
his age in the West, to Roman, not
Byzantine Art. This, perhaps, can
hardly be determined. The later, at
S. Apollinaris in Ravenna, at S. Pras-
sede, and other Churches in Rome, are
Byzantine in character; on those of
Venice Kugler is fuller. The Art
was lost in Italy at the close of the
ninth century, to revive again more
free and Italian in the eleventh and
twelfth.

far as independent of Byzantine art, went on with its
perpetual supply of images, relieved by a blazing golden
ground, and with the most glowing colours, but in general stiff, rigid, shapeless, expressionless. Worship still
more passionate multiplied its objects; and those objects
it was content to receive according to the established
pattern. The more rich and gaudy, the more welcome
the offering to the Saint or to the Deity, the more
devout the veneration of the worshipper. This character—splendid colouring, the projection of the beautiful
but too regular face, or the hard, but not entirely un-
pliant form, by the rich background—prevails in all the
subordinate works of art in East and West—enamels,
miniatures, illuminations in manuscripts. In these, not
so much images for popular worship, as the slow work
of artists dwelling with unbounded delight on their own
creations, seem gradually to dawn glimpses of more
refined beauty, faces, forms, more instinct with life:
even the boundless luxuriance of ornament, flowers,
foliage, animals, fantastic forms, would nurse the sense
of beauty, and familiarise the hand with more flowing
lines, and the mind with a stronger feeling for the graceful for the sake of its grace. It was altogether impossible that, during so many ages, Byzantine art, or the
same kind of art in the West, where it was bound by
less rigid tradition, and where the guild of painters did
not pass down in such regular succession, should not
struggle for freedom.[1] The religious emotions which

---

[1] I must decline the controversy
how far Western Art was Byzantine.
It may be possible for the fine sagacity
of modern judgement to discriminate
between the influences of Byzantine
and old Roman Art, as regards the
forms and designs of Painting. Yet
considering that the Byzantine Artists
of Justinian, and the Exarchs of Ravenna, to a far greater extent those
who, flying from the Iconoclastic persecution, brought with them the secrets

the painter strove to excite in others would kindle in
himself, and yearn after something more than the cold
immemorial language. By degrees the hard, flat lineaments of the countenance would begin to quicken themselves; its long ungraceful outline would be rounded into
fulness and less rigid expression; the tall, straight,
meagre form would swell out into something like movement, the stiff, fettered extremities separate into the
attitude of life; the drapery would become less like the
folds which swathe a mummy; the mummy would begin
to stir with life. It was impossible but that the Saviour
should relax his harsh, stern lineaments; that the child
should not become more child-like; the Virgin-Mother
waken into maternal tenderness.[*] This effort after
emancipation would first take place in those smaller

---

and rules of their art, were received
and domiciliated in the Western Monasteries, and that in those Monasteries
were chiefly preserved the traditions
of the older Italian Art; that at no
time was the commercial or political
connexion of Constantinople and the
West quite broken off, and under the
Othos the two Courts were cemented
by marriage; that all the examples of
the period are to be sought in the rigid
Mosaic, in miniatures, ivories, illuminations—there must have been so much
intermingling of the two streams, that
such discrimination must at least be
conjectural.—Compare Rio, on what he
calls Romano-Christian, independent of
Byzantine Art, pp. 32 *et seqq.* Rumohr, Italienische Forschungen, and
Kugler. Lord Lindsay is a strong
Byzantine; and see in Kugler, p. 77;
but Kugler will hardly allow Byzantine
Art credit for the original conception
or execution of the better designs.

[*] Durandus, in his Rationale, l. c. 3,
would confine the representation of the
Saviour in Churches to three attitudes,
either on his throne of glory, on the
cross of shame, or in the lap of his
Mother. He adds another, as teacher
of the world, with the Book in his
hand.—See Schnaase, iv. 387, for the
various postures (il. p. 136) of the
Child in his Mother's arms. Schnaase,
Geschichte der Bildende Kunst, says
that about the middle of the fifth century the paintings of the Virgin Mary
became more common (one has been
discovered, which *is asserted to be of
an earlier period*, but we have only
the authority of enthusiastic admiration
and polemic zeal for its age) in the
Catacombs. The great Mosaic in S.
Apollinare Nuovo is of the first quarter
of the sixth century. Her image, as
has been said, floated over the fleet of
the Emperor Heraclius I.

works, the miniatures, the illuminations of manuscripts.[*] On these the artist could not but work, as has been said, more at his ease; on the whole, in them he would address less numerous perhaps, but more intelligent spectators; he would be less in dread of disturbing popular superstition: and so Taste, the parent and the child of art, would struggle into being. Thus imperceptibly, thus in various quarters, these better qualities cease to be the secret indulgences, the life-long labours of the emblazoner of manuscripts, the illuminator of missals. In the higher branches of the art, the names of artists gradually begin to transpire, to obtain respect and fame; the sure sign that art is beginning, that mere technical traditionary working at images for popular worship is drawing to its close. Already the names of Guido of Sienna, Giunto of Pisa, and of Cimabue, resound through Christendom. Poetry hails the birth and the youth of her sister art.

Such, according to the best authorities, appears to have been the state of painting from the iconoclastic controversy throughout the darker ages. Faintly and hesitatingly at the commencement of the twelfth century,[†] more boldly and vigorously towards its close, and

[*] The exquisite grace of the ivory carvings from Constantinople, which show so high and pure a conception for art, as contrasted with the harsh glaring paintings, is perfectly compatible with these views. The ivories were the works of more refined artists for a more refined class. The paintings were the idols of the vulgar—a hard, cruel, sensual vulgar; the ivories, as it were, talismans of the hardly less superstitious, but more opulent, and polished; of those who kept up, some the love of letters, some more cultivated tastes. Even the illuminations were the quiet works of the gentler and better and more civilised Monks: their love and their study of the Holy Books was the testimony and the means of their superior refinement.

[†] "Mir selbst aber ist es während vieljähriger Nachforschung durchaus nicht gelungen, irgend ein Beispiel des Wiederaufstrebens und Fortschreitens der Italienischen Kunstübung auszufinden, dessen Alter den Anbeginn des

during the thirteenth and half the fourteenth, Italian
painting rose by degrees, threw off with Giotto the last
trammels of Byzantinism which had still clung around
Cimabue; and at least strove after that exquisite harmony of nature and of art, which had still great progress
to make before it reached its consummation. Turn from
the vast, no doubt majestic Redeemer of Cimabue, which
broods, with its attendant figures of the Virgin and St.
John, over the high altar at Pisa, to the free creations
of Giotto at Florence or Padua. Giotto was Giotto,
the great deliverer. Invention is no sooner $\begin{smallmatrix}\text{born 1276,}\\\text{died 1334.}\end{smallmatrix}$
free than it expatiates in unbounded variety. Nothing
more moves our wonder than the indefatigable activity,
the unexhausted fertility of Giotto: he is adorning Italy
from the Alps to the Bay of Naples; even crossing the
Alps to Avignon. His works either exist or have existed
at Avignon, Milan, Verona, Padua, Ferrara, Urbino,
Ravenna, Rimini, Lucca, Florence, Assisi, Rome, Gaeta,
Naples.[1] Bishops, religious orders, republics, princes
and potentates, kings, popes, demand his services, and
do him honour. He raises at once the most beautiful
tower in architecture—that of Florence—and paints the
Chapel of the Arena at Padua, and the Church at Assisi.
Giotto was no monk, but, in its better sense, a man of
the world. Profoundly religious in expression, in character, in aim; yet religious not merely as embodying
all the imagery of the mediæval faith, but as prophetic,
at least, if not presentient of a wider Catholicism.[2] Be-

zwölften Jahrhunderts übersteige."—
Rumohr, Italienische Forschungen, i. p.
250.

For the works of the twelfth century, Kugler, p. 94 et seqq. Never-
theless full eighty years elapsed before
this development made any further

progress, p. 98. Sculpture in relief
was earlier than Painting.

[1] Rio says, perhaps too strongly,
that all his works at Avignon, Milan,
Verona, Ferrara, Modena, Ravenna,
Lucca, Gaeta, have perished, p. 65.

[2] There is great truth and beauty

sides the Scriptural subjects, in which he did not entirely
depart from the Byzantine or earlier arrangement, and
all the more famous Legends, he opened a new world of
real and of allegorical beings. The poetry of St. Francis
had impersonated everything; not merely, therefore,
did the life of St. Francis offer new and picturesque
subjects, but the impersonations, Chastity, Obedience,
Poverty, as in the hymns of St. Francis they had taken
being, assumed form from Giotto.   Religious led to
civil allegory.   Giotto painted the commonwealth of
Florence.   Allegory in itself is far too unobjective for
art : it needs perpetual interpretation, which art cannot
give; but it was a sign of the new world opening, or
rather boldly thrown open, to painting by Giotto.   The
whole Scripture, the whole of Legend (not the old permitted forms and scenes alone), the life of the Virgin, of
the Saints, of the founders of Orders, even the invisible
worlds which Dante had revealed in poetry, now expanded in art.   Dante, perhaps, must await Orcagna,
not indeed actually to embody, but to illustrate his
transmundane worlds.   Italy herself hailed, with all her
more powerful voices—her poets, novelists, historians—
the new epoch of art in Giotto.   Dante declares that he
has dethroned Cimabue.   "The vulgar," writes Petrarch,
"cannot understand the surpassing beauty of Giotto's
Virgin, before which the masters stand in astonishment."
"Giotto," says Boccaccio, "imitates nature to perfect.

---

in the character of Giotto as drawn by   Chapel at Padua.   III. Assisi,   IV.
Lord Lindsay (ii. p. 268).   The three   Longer residence in Florence, North of
first paragraphs appear to me most   Italy, Avignon, Naples, p. 165.—See
striking and just.   Lord Lindsay divides   also Mr. Ruskin's Memoir.   For Giotto's
his life into four periods.   I. His youth   remarkable poem against voluntary
in Florence and Rome.   II. About   poverty, see Rumohr, i. c. 9.
A.D. 1306 in Lombardy, the Arena

illusion;" Villani describes him as transcending all former artists in the truth of nature.[b]

During the latter half of the thirteenth, and throughout the fourteenth century, the whole of Italy, the churches, the monasteries, the cloisters, many of the civil buildings, were covered with paintings aspiring after, and approximating to the highest art. Sienna, then in the height of her glory and prosperity, took the lead; Pisa beheld her Campo Santo peopled with the wonderful creations of Orcagna. Painting aspired to her Inferno, Purgatorio, Paradiso: Painting will strive to have her Dante.

This outburst was simultaneous with, it might seem to originate in, the wide dissemination, the ubiquitous activity, and the strong religious passion felt, Mendicant propagated, kept alive in its utmost intensity Orders. by the Mendicant Orders. Strange it might appear that the Arts, the highest luxuries, if we may so speak, of religion, should be fostered, cultivated, cherished, distributed throughout Italy, and even beyond the Alps, by those who professed to reduce Christianity to more than its primitive simplicity, its nakedness of all adornment, its poverty; whose mission it was to consort with the most rude and vulgar; beggars who aspired to rank below the coarsest mendicancy; according to whose rule there could be no property, hardly a fixed residence. Strange! that these should become the most munificent patrons of art, the most consummate artists; that their cloistered palaces should be the most sumptuous in architecture, and the most richly decorated by sculpture

b   "Credette Cimabue nella pittura
Tener lo campo, ed or' ha Giotto il grido."
                                    Purg. xi. 94.

" Mitte tabulam meam beatæ Virginis, operis Jotti pictoris egregii in

cujus pulcritudinem nec intelligunt, magistri autem artis stupent."—Quoted by Vasari. Decameron. Giorn. vi. Nov. 5. Villani, 11. 12.

and painting; at once the workshops and the abodes
of those who executed most admirably, and might seem
to adore with the most intense devotion, these splen-
dours and extravagances of religious wealth. Assisi—
the birthplace of St. Francis, the poor, self-denying
wanderer over the face of the earth, who hardly owned
the cord which girt him, who possessed not a breviary
of his own, who worshipped in the barren mountain, at
best in the rock-hewn cell, whose companions were the
lepers, the outcasts of human society—Assisi becomes
the capital, the young, gorgeous capital of Christian
Art. Perhaps in no single city of that period was such
lavish expenditure made in all which was purely decorative. The church, finished by a German architect
but five years after the death of St. Francis, put to
shame in its architecture, as somewhat later in the
paintings of Cimabue, Simon Memmi, Giunto, Giotto,
probably the noblest edifices in Rome, those in the
Lombard Republics, in Pisa, Sienna, Florence, and as
yet those of the capitals and cathedral cities of Transalpine Christendom. The Dominicans were not far
behind in their steady cultivation, and their profuse
encouragement of art.[e]

Yet this fact is easy of explanation, if it has not
already found its explanation in our history. There is
always a vast mass of dormant religiousness in the
world; it wants only to be seized, stimulated, directed,
appropriated. These Orders swept into their ranks and
within their walls all who yearned for more intense
religion. Devout men threw themselves into the movement, which promised most boldly and succeeded most
fully in satisfying the cravings of the heart. There

---

[e] Simon Memmi of Sienna painted the legend of St. Dominic in the Chapel of
the Spaniards in Santa Maria Novella at Florence.—Vasari and Rio, p. 55.

would be many whose vocation was not that of the
active preacher, or the restless missionary, or the argute
schoolman. There were the calm, the gentle, the contemplative. Men who had the irresistible calling to be
artists became Franciscans or Dominicans, not because
mendicancy was favourable to art, but because it awoke,
and cherished, and strengthened those emotions which
were to express themselves in art. Religion drove
them into the cloister; the cloister and the church
offered them its walls; they drew from all quarters the
traditions, the technicalities of art. Being rich enough
(the communities, not the individuals) to reward the
best teachers or the more celebrated artists, they soon
became masters of the skill, the manipulation, the rules
of design, the practice of colouring. How could the
wealth, so lavishly poured at their feet, be better employed than in the reward of the stranger-artist, who
not only adorned their walls with the most perfect
models, but whose study in the church or in the cloister
was a school of instruction to the Monks themselves who
aspired to be their pupils or their rivals?

The Monkish painters were masters of that invaluable
treasure, time, to work their study up to perfection;
there was nothing that urged to careless haste. Without labour they had their scanty but sufficient sustenance; they had no further wants. Art alternated with
salutary rest, or with the stimulant of art, the religious
service. Neither of these permitted the other to languish
into dull apathy, or to rest in inexpressive forms or hues.
No cares, no anxieties, probably not even the jealousies
of art, intruded on these secluded Monks; theirs was
the more blameless rivalry of piety, not of success.
With some, perhaps, there was a latent unconscious
pride, not so much in themselves as in the fame and

influence which accrued to the Order, or to the convent, which their works crowded more and more with wondering worshippers. But in most it was to disburthen, as it were, their own hearts, to express in form and colour their own irrepressible feelings. They would have worked as passionately and laboriously if the picture had been enshrined, unvisited, in their narrow cell. They worshipped their own works, not because they were their own, but because they spoke the language of their souls. They worshipped while they worked, worked that they might worship; and works so conceived and so executed (directly the fetters of conventionalism were burst and cast aside, and the technical skill acquired) could not fail to inspire the adoration of all kindred and congenial minds. Their pictures, in truth, were their religious offerings, made in single-minded zeal, with untiring toil, with patience never wearied or satisfied. If these offerings had their meed of fame, if they raised the glory or enlarged the influence and so the wealth of the Order, the simple artists were probably the last who would detect within themselves that less generous and less disinterested motive.

If the Dominicans were not inferior to the Franciscans in the generous encouragement of the art of painting, in its cultivation among their own brethren they attained higher fame. If Assisi took the lead, and almost all the best masters kindled its walls to life, the Dominican convent in Florence might boast the works of their own brother Frà Angelico. To judge from extant paintings, Angelico was the unsurpassed, if not unrivalled, model of what I presume to call the cloistral school of painting. The perfect example of his inspiration as of his art was Frà Giovanni Angelico da Fiesole. Frà Angelico became a monk that he

Frà Angelico.

might worship without disturbance, and paint without
reward. He left all human passions behind him; his
one passion was serene devotion, not without tenderness,
but the tenderness of a saint rather than of a man.
Before he began to paint, he knelt in prayer; as he
painted the sufferings of the Redeemer, he would break
off in tears. No doubt, when he attained that expression of calm, unearthly holiness which distinguishes his
Angels or Saints, he stood partaking in their mystic
ecstacy. He had nothing of the moroseness, the self-
torture of the monk; he does not seem, like later
monastic painters in Italy and Spain, to have delighted
in the agony of the martyrdom; it is the glorified, not
the suffering, Saint which is his ideal. Of the world,
it was human nature alone from which he had wrenched
away his sympathies. He delights in brilliant colours;
the brightest green or the gayest hues in his trees and
flowers; the richest reds and blues in his draperies,
with a profusion of gold. Frà Angelico is the Mystic
of painting, the contemplative Mystic, living in another
world, having transmuted all that he remembers of this
world into a purer, holier being. But that which was
his excellence was likewise his defect. It was spiritualism, exquisite and exalting spiritualism, but it was
too spiritual. Painting, which represents humanity,
even in its highest, holiest form, must still be human.
With the passions, the sympathies and affections of
Giovanni's mind had almost died away. His child is
not a child, he is a cherub. The Virgin and the Mother
are not blended in perfect harmony and proportion; the
colder Virgin prevails; adoration has extinguished
motherly love. Above all, the Redeemer fails in all
Angelico's pictures. Instead of the orthodox perfect
God and perfect Man, by a singular heresy the humanity

is so effaced that, as the pure Divinity is unimaginable,
and, unincarnate, cannot be represented, both the form
and the countenance are stiffened to a cold, unmeaning
abstraction. It is neither the human nature with the
infused majesty and mercy of the Godhead; nor the
Godhead subdued into the gentleness and patience of
humanity.   The God-Man is neither God nor Man.
Even in the celestial or beatified beings, angels or
saints, exquisite, unrivalled as is their grace and beauty,
the grace is not that of beings accustomed to the free
use of their limbs; the beauty is not that of our atmosphere. Not merely do they want the breath of life,
the motion of life, the warmth of life, they want the
truth of life, and without truth there is no consummate
art.   They have never really lived, never assumed the
functions nor dwelt within the precincts of life.   Painting having acquired in the cloister all this unworldliness,
this profound devotion, this refined spirituality, must
emerge again into the world to blend and balance both,
first in Francia and Perugino, up to the perfect Leonardo
and Raffaelle. Even the cloister in Frà Bartolomeo
must take a wider flight; it must paint man, it must
humanise itself that it may represent man and demand
the genuine admiration of man. It is without the walls
of the cloister that painting finds its unrivalled votaries,
achieves its most imperishable triumphs.

Transalpine Painting is no less the faithful conservator of the ancient traditions. In the German
missals and books of devotion there is, throughout the earlier period, the faithful maintenance of the
older forms, rich grounds, splendid colours. The walls
of the older churches reveal paintings in which there is
at least aspiration after higher things, some variety of
design, some incipient grace and nobleness of form.

Transalpine, German and Flemish art.

The great hierarchical cities on the Rhine seem to take the lead. William of Cologne and Master Stephen seem as if they would raise up rivals in Teutonic to Italian art. Above all, at the close of this period, about contemporary with Angelico da Fiesole, the Flemish Van Eycks, if not by the invention, by the perfection of oil-painting, gave an impulse of which it is difficult to calculate the importance. Those painters of the rich commercial cities of the Low Countries might seem as deeply devout in their conceptions as the cloistral school of Italy, yet more human as living among men, nobler in their grouping, nobler in their dresses and draperies; and already in their backgrounds anticipating that truth and reality of landscape which was hereafter to distinguish their country. In this the later Flemish painters rise as much above the Van Eycks as Leonardo and Raffaelle above their predecessors. But at first Teutonic might seem as if it would vie for the palm of Christian painting.[4]

The works of Nicolas V. in letters and in arts have ended our survey of these two great departments of Christian influence, and summed up the account of Latin Christendom. The papacy of Nicolas V. closed the age of mediæval letters; it terminated, at least in Italy, if Brunelleschi had not already closed it, the reign of mediæval architecture.[5] In painting, by his muni-

---

[4] Hubert Van Eyck, born about 1366, died 1426. John Van Eyck, born about 1400, died 1445.—See for German Painting the Translation of Kugler, by Sir Edmund Head. On the Van Eycks, Waagen's Dissertation.

[5] Two sentences of Vasari show the revolution arrived at and taught by that great Architect, who boasted to have raised the majestic cupola of Florence. "Solo l'intento suo era l' architettura che gia era spenta, dico gli ordini antichi *buoni*, e non la *Tedesca e barbara* la quale molto si usava nel suo tempo. * * * E aveva in se due concetti grandissimi ; l' uno era il tornare a luce la buona architettura, credendo egli, ritrovandola non lasciare

ficent patronage of that which was then the highest art,
but which was only the harbinger of nobler things to
come, the pontificate of Nicolas marked the transition
period from the ancient to the modern world.

But Nicolas V. was only a restorer, and a restorer
not in the hierarchical character, of the mediæval architecture. That architecture had achieved its great works,
Strasburg, all that was to rise, till the present day, of
Cologne, Antwerp, Rheims, Bourges, Amiens, Chartres,
St. Ouen at Rouen, Notre Dame at Paris, our own
Westminster, York, Salisbury, Lincoln. This great art
survived in its creative power, only as it were, at the
extremities of Latin Christendom. It had even passed
its gorgeous epoch, called in France the Flamboyant;
it was degenerating into luxury and wantonness; it had
begun to adorn for the sake of adornment. But Rome
was still faithful to Rome; her architecture would not
condescend to Teutonic influence. That which is by
some called Christian architecture, as has been said,
was to the end almost a stranger in the city still acknowledged as the capital of Christendom.ᶠ Rome at least,
if not Italy, was still holding aloof from that which was
the strength of Rome and of Latin Christendom—
Mediævalism; Nicolas V., as it were, accomplished the
divorce. In him Rome repudiated the whole of what
are called the Dark Ages. Rome began the revival
which was to be in the end the ruin of her supremacy.

Nicolas V., as Pope, as sovereign of Rome, as patron
of letters and arts, stood, consciously perhaps, but with

---

manco memoria di se, che fatto si
aveva Cimabue e Giotto; l' altro di
tiovar modo, se e al potesse, a voltare
la cupola di S. Maria del Fiore di
Firenze," p. 207, edit. Milan. Compare

p. 265.

ᶠ It was in Rome that Brunelleschi
" ritrovò le cornici antiche, e l' ordine
Toscano, Corinthio, Dorico, e Ionico
alle primarie forme restituiti. '—Vasari.

a dim perception of the change, at the head of a new
era. It was an epoch in Christian civilisation. To him
the Pope might seem as destined for long ages to rule
the subject and tributary world ; the great monarchies,
the Empire, France, Spain, England, were yet to rise,
each obedient or hostile to the Pope as might suit their
policy. He could not foresee that the Pope, from the
high autocrat over all, would become only one of the
powers of Christendom. To be a sovereign Italian
prince might appear necessary to his dignity, his
security. It was but in accordance with the course of
things in Italy. Everywhere, except in stern oligar-
chical Venice, in Milan, in Verona, in Ferrara, in
Florence, princes had risen, or were arising, on the ruins
of the Republics, Viscontis, Sforzas, della Scalas, Estes,
Medicis. Thomas of Sarzana (he took this name, he
had no other, from his native town), so obscure that his
family was unknown, had no ancestry to glorify, no
descendants whom he might be tempted to enrich or
to ennoble. He had no prophetic fears that, as sovereign princes, his successors would yield to the inevitable
temptation of founding princely families at the expense
of the interests, of the estates and dominions of the
Church. Not only was the successor of St. Peter to be
merged in the more ambitious politics of the world, but
trammelled in the more mean and intricate politics of
Italy. Almost from this time the names of the successive Popes may be traced in the annals of the cities
and petty principalities of Italy, in the rolls of the
estates of the Church, of which they have become lords,
in their magnificent palaces in Rome. Among those
palaces there is but one, the Colonna, which boasts an
ancient name ; but few which bear not the name of a
papal house. Too often among the Popes of the next

century the character (and dark indeed was that character) of the Italian sovereign prince prevailed over
that of the Pope. If his house was not perpetuated, it
was solely from the indignant hostility and execration
of mankind.[*]

As to Nicolas V. Italy, or rather Latin Christianity,
mainly owes her age of learning, as well as its fatal consequences to Rome and to Latin Christianity, so those
consequences, in his honest ardour, he would be the last
to prognosticate or to foresee. It was the splendid vision
of Nicolas V. that Christianity was to array herself in
the spoils of the ancient world, and so maintain with
more universal veneration her supremacy over the
human mind. This, however, the revival of
learning, was but one of the four great principles in slow, silent, irresistible operation in Western
Christendom, mutually co-operative, blending with and
strengthening each other, ominous of and preparing the
great revolution of the next century. But to all these,
signs at once and harbingers of the coming change,
Nicolas could not but be blind; for of these signs some
were those which a Pope, himself so pious and so prosperous, might refuse to see; or, if not dazzled by his
prosperity, too entirely absorbed in dangers of far other
kind, the fall of Constantinople, the advance of the Turks
on Western Christendom, might be unable to see. This
one danger, as it (so he might hope) would work reformation in the startled Church, would bring the alienated world into close and obedient confederacy with
her head. The Pope, like Urban of old, would take his
place at the head of the defensive crusade.

Revival of Letters.

---

[*] Pius II. alienated Radicofani, not to his family, but to his native city,
Sienna.

I.—Of these principles, of these particular signs, the first was the *progress of the human intellect*, inevitable in the order of things, and resulting in a two-fold oppugnancy to the established dominion of the Church. The first offspring of the expanding intellect was the long-felt, still growing impatience, intolerance of the oppressions and the abuses of the Papacy, of the Papal Court, and of the Papal religion. This impatience did not of necessity involve the rejection of the doctrines of Latin Christianity. But it would no longer endure the enormous powers still asserted by the Popes over temporal sovereigns, the immunities claimed by the clergy as to their persons and from the common burthens of the State, the exorbitant taxation, the venality of Rome, above all, the Indulgences, with which the Papal power in its decline seemed determined wantonly to insult the moral and religious sense of mankind. Long before Luther this abuse had rankled in the heart of Christendom. It was in vain for the Church to assert that, rightly understood, Indulgences only released from temporal penances; that they were a commutation, a merciful, lawful commutation for such penances. The language of the promulgators and vendors of the Indulgences, even of the Indulgences themselves, was, to the vulgar ear, the broad, plain, direct guarantee from the pains of purgatory, from hell itself, for tens, hundreds, thousands of years; a sweeping pardon for all sins committed, a sweeping licence for sins to be committed: and if this false construction, it might be, was perilous to the irreligious, this even seeming flagrant dissociation of morality from religion was no less revolting to the religious.[b] Nor was there as yet any general improve-

[b] Chaucer's Pardoner is a striking illustration of the popular notion and popular feeling in England.

ment in the lives of the Clergy or of the Monks, which
by its awful sanctity might rebuke the vulgar and
natural interpretation of these Indulgences.[1] The antagonism of the more enlightened intellect to the *doctrines* of the mediæval Church was slower, more timid,
more reluctant. It was as yet but doubt, suspicion,
indifference; the irreligious were content to be quietly
irreligious; the religious had not as yet found in the
plain Biblical doctrines that on which they could calmly
and contentedly rest their faith. Religion had not risen
to a purer spirituality to compensate for the loss of the
materialistic worship of the dominant Church. The
conscience shrunk from the responsibility of taking
cognisance of itself; the soul dared not work out its
own salvation. The clergy slept on the brink of the
precipice. So long as they were not openly opposed
they thought all was safe. So long as unbelief in the
whole of their system lurked quietly in men's hearts,
they cared not to inquire what was brooding in those
inner depths.

II.—The second omen at once and sign of change was
the cultivation of classical learning. Letters
almost at once ceased to be cloistral, hierarchical, before long almost to be Christian. In Italy,
indeed, the Pope had set himself at the head of this
vast movement; yet Florence vied with Rome. Cosmo
de' Medici was the rival of Nicolas V. But, notwithstanding the Pope's position, the clergy rapidly ceased

Revival of
Letters.

---

[1] The irrefragable testimony to the
universal misinterpretation, the natural, inevitable misinterpretation of the
language of the Indulgences, the misinterpretation riveted on the minds of
men by their profligate vendors, is the solemn, reiterated repudiation of those
notions by Councils and by Popes. The
definitions of the Council of Trent and
of Pius V. had not been wanted, if
the Church doctrine had been the belief
of mankind.

to be the solo and almost exclusive depositaries of letters. The scholars might condescend to hold canonries or abbeys as means of maintenance, as honours, or rewards (thus, long before, had Petrarch been endowed), but it was with the tacit understanding, or at least the almost unlimited enjoyment, of perfect freedom from ecclesiastical control, so long as they did not avowedly enter on theological grounds, which they avoided rather from indifference and from growing contempt, than from respect. On every side were expanding new avenues of inquiry, new trains of thought: new models of composition were offering themselves. All tended silently to impair the reverence for the ruling authorities. Men could not labour to write like Cicero and Cæsar without imbibing something of their spirit. The old ecclesiastical Latin began to be repudiated as rude and barbarous. Scholasticism had crushed itself with its own weight. When monks or friars were the only men of letters, and monastic schools the only field in which intellect encountered intellect, the huge tomes of Aquinas, and the more summary axioms of Peter Lombard, might absorb almost the whole active mind of Christendom. But Plato now drove out the Theologic Platonism, Aristotle the Aristotelism of the schools. The Platonism, indeed, of Marsilius Ficinus, taking its interpretation rather from Proclus and Plotinus and the Alexandrians, would hardly have offended Julian himself by any obtrusive display of Christianity. On his deathbed Cosmo de' Medici is attended by Ficinus, who assures him of another life on the authority of Socrates, and teaches him resignation in the words of Plato, Xenocrates, and other Athenian sages. The cultivation of Greek was still more fatal to Latin domination. Even the familiar study of the Greek Fathers (as far as an imposing ritual

and the monastic spirit consistent with those of the
Latin Church) was altogether alien to the scholasticism
dominant in Latin Theology. They knew nothing of
the Latin supremacy, nothing of the rigid form, which
many of its doctrines, as of Transubstantiation, had
assumed. Greek revealed a whole religious world,
extraneous to and in many respects oppugnant to Latin
Christianity. But the most fatal result was the revelation of the Greek Testament, necessarily followed by
that of the Hebrew Scriptures, and the dawn of a wider
Biblical Criticism. The proposal of a new translation
of the Scriptures at once disenthroned the Vulgate
from its absolute exclusive authority. It could not but
admit the Greek, and then the Hebrew, as its rival,
as its superior in antiquity. Biblical Criticism once
begun, the old voluminous authoritative interpreters, De
Lyra, Turrecremata, and the rest, were thrown into
obscurity. Erasmus was sure to come; with Erasmus
a more simple, clear, popular interpretation of the
divine word.[k] The mystic and allegoric comment on
the Scriptures, on which rested wholly some of the
boldest assertions of Latin Christianity, fell away at
once before his closer, more literal, more grammatical
study of the Text. At all events, the Vulgate receded,
and with the Vulgate Latin Christianity began to withdraw into a separate sphere; it ceased to be the sole,
universal religion of Western Christendom.

III.—The growth of the modern languages not merely

Modern
Languages. into vernacular means of communication, but
into the vehicles of letters, of poetry, of oratory,
of history, of preaching, at length of national documents,

---

[k] The Paraphrase and Notes of
Erasmus, in my judgement, was the
most important book even of his day.
We must remember that it was almost
legally adopted by the Church of England.

still later of law and of science, threw back Latin more
and more into a learned dialect. ' It was relegated into
the study of the scholar, into books intended for the
intercommunication only of the learned, and for a certain
time for the negotiations and treaties of remote kingdoms,
who were forced to meet on some common ground. It
is curious that in Italy the revival of classical learning
for a time crushed the native literature, or at least re-
tarded its progress.   From Dante, Petrarch, Boccaccio,
to Ariosto and Machiavelli, excepting some historians,
Malespina, Dino Compagui, Villani, there is almost total
silence : silence, at least, unbroken by any powerful voice.
Nor did the liberal patronage of Nicolas V. call forth
one work of lasting celebrity in the native tongue. The
connexion of the development of the Transalpine, more
especially the Teutonic languages, has been already
examined more at length. Here it may suffice to resume,
that the vernacular translation of the Bible was an
inevitable result of the perfection of those tongues. In
Germany and in England that translation tended most
materially, by fixing a standard in general of vigorous,
noble, poetic, yet idiomatic language, to hasten and to
perpetuate the change. It was natural that as soon as a
nation had any books of its own, it should seek to have
the Book of Books. The Church, indeed, trembling for
the supremacy of her own Vulgate, and having witnessed
the fatal perils of such Translations in the successes of
all the earlier Dissidents, was perplexed and wavered in
her policy. Now she thundered out her awful prohibition;
now endeavoured herself to supply the want which
would not remain unsatisfied, by a safer and a sanctioned
version. But the mind of man could not wait on her
hesitating movements. The free, bold, untrammelled
version had possession of the national mind and national

language; it had become the undeniable patrimony of the people, the standard of the language.

IV.—Just at this period the two great final Reformers, *Printing and Paper.* the inventor of printing and the manufacturer of paper, had not only commenced, but perfected at once their harmonious inventions. Books, from slow, toilsome, costly productions, became cheap, were multiplied with rapidity which seemed like magic, and were accessible to thousands to whom manuscripts were utterly unapproachable. The power, the desire, increased with the facility of reading. Theology, from an abstruse recondite science, the exclusive possession of an Order, became popular; it was, ere long, the general study, the general passion. The Preacher was not sought the less on account of this vast extension of his influence. His eloquent words were no longer limited by the walls of a Church, or the power of a human voice; they were echoed, perpetuated, promulgated over a kingdom, over a continent. The fiery Preacher became a pamphleteer; he addressed a whole realm; he addressed mankind. It was no longer necessary that man should act directly upon man; that the flock should derive their whole knowledge from their Pastor, the individual Christian from his ghostly adviser. The man might find satisfaction for his doubts, guidance for his thoughts, excitement for his piety in his own chamber from the silent pages of the theological treatise. To many the Book became the Preacher, the Instructor, even the Confessor. The conscience began to claim the privilege, the right, of granting absolution to itself. All this, of course, at first timidly, intermittingly, with many compunctious returns to the deserted fold. The Hierarchy endeavoured to seize and bind down to their own service these unruly powers. Their presses at Venice, at Florence, at Rome, displayed the new art in its highest magnificence; but it was not the splendid volume, the bold and majestic type, the industrious editorial care, which worked downwards into the depths of society; it was the coarse, rude, brown sheet; the ill-cut German type; the brief, sententious, plain tract which escaped all vigilance, and so sunk untraced, unanswered, unconfuted, into the eager mind of awakening man. The sternest vigilance might be exercised by the Argus-eyes of the still ubiquitous Clergy. The most solemn condemnations, the most awful prohibitions might be issued; yet from the birthday of printing, their sole exclusive authority over the mind of man was gone. That they rallied and resumed so much power; that they had the wisdom and the skill to seize upon the education of mankind, and to seal up again the outbursting springs of knowledge and free examination, is a mighty marvel. Though from the rivals, the opponents, the foes, the subjugators of the great Temporal Despots, they became, by their yet powerful hold on the conscience, and by their common interests in keeping mankind in slavery, their allies, their ministers, their rulers; yet, from that hour, the Popes must encounter more dangerous, pertinacious, unconquerable antagonists than the Hohenstaufens and Bavarians, the Henrys and Fredericks of old. The sacerdotal caste must recede from authority to influence. Here they would mingle into the general mass of society, assimilate themselves to the bulk of mankind, become citizens, subjects, fathers of families, and fulfilling the common duties and relations of life, work more profoundly beneficial, moral, and religious effects. There they would still stand in a great degree apart, as a separate, unmingling order, yet submit to public opinion, if exercising control, themselves under strong control. This great part of the sacerdotal order

at a much later period was to be stripped with ruder
and more remorseless hands of their power, their rank,
their wealth; they were to be thrust down from their
high places, to become stipendiaries of the state. Their
great strength, Monasticism, in some kingdoms was to
be abolished by law, which they could not resist; or it
was only tolerated as useful to the education, and to the
charitable necessities of mankind; almost everywhere it
sunk into desuetude, or lingered as the last earthly resort
of the world-weary and despondent, the refuge of a rare
fanaticism, which now excites wonder rather than wide-
spread emulation. From Nicolas V., seated, as it were,
on its last summit, the Papal power, the Hierarchical
system, commences its visible decline. Latin Christianity
had to cede a large portion of its realms, which became
the more flourishing, prosperous, intellectual portion of
the world, to Teutonic Christianity. It had hereafter to
undergo more fierce and fiery trials. But whatever may
be its future doom, one thing may be asserted without
fear, it can never again be the universal Christianity of
the West.

I pretend not to foretell the future of Christianity;
but whosoever believes in its perpetuity (and to disbe-
lieve it were treason against its Divine Author, apostacy
from his faith) must suppose that, by some providential
law, it must adapt itself, as it has adapted itself with
such wonderful versatility, but with a faithful conservation of its inner vital spirit, to all vicissitudes and
phases of man's social, moral, intellectual being. There
is no need to discuss a recent theory (of M. Comte) that
man is to become all intellect; and that religion, resid-
ing rather in the imagination, the affections, and the
conscience, is to wither away, and cede the whole
dominion over mankind to what is called "positive

philosophy." I have no more faith in the mathematical
millennium of M. Comte (at all events we have centuries
enough to wait for it) than in the religious millennium
of some Judaising Christians.

Latin Christianity or Papal Christianity (which is
Latin Christianity in its full development), whatever it
may be called with least offence, has not only ceased to
be, it can never again be, the exclusive, the paramount,
assuredly not the universal religion of enlightened men.
The more advanced the civilisation, no doubt, in a certain sense, the more need of Christianity. All restrictive
views, therefore, of Christianity, especially if such
Christianity be at issue with the moral sense and with
the progressive reason of man, are urged with perilous
and fearful responsibility. Better Christianity vague in
creed, defective in polity, than no Christianity. If Latin
Christianity were to be the one perpetual, immutable,
unalterable code, how much of the world would still be
openly, how much secretly without religion ? Even in
what we may call the Latin world, to how large a part
is Latin Christianity what the religion of old Rome was
in the days of Cæsar and Cicero, an object of traditionary
and prudential respect, of vast political importance, an
edifice of which men fear to see the ruin, yet have no
inward sense of its foundation in truth? On more religious minds it will doubtless maintain its hold as a
religion of authority—a religion of outward form—an
objective religion, and so possessing inexhaustible powers
of awakening religious emotion. As a religion of authority, as an objective religion, as an emotional religion, it
may draw within its pale proselytes of congenial minds
from a more vague, more subjective, more rational faith.
As a religion of authority it spares the soul from the
pain of thought, from the harassing doubt, the despond-

ing scruple. Its positive and peremptory assurances not only overawe the weak, but offer an indescribable consolation—a rest, a repose, which seems at least to be peace. Independence of thought, which to some is their holiest birthright, their most glorious privilege, their sternest duty, is to others the profoundest misery, the heaviest burthen, the responsibility from which they would shrink with the deepest awe, which they would plunge into any abyss to avoid. What relief to devolve upon another the oppressive question of our eternal destiny!

As an objective religion, a materialistic religion, a religion which addresses itself to the senses of man, Latin Christianity has no less great and enduring power. To how many is there no reality without bodily form, without at least the outline, the symbol suggestive of bodily form! With the vulgar at least, it does not rebuke the rudest, coarsest superstition; for the more educated, the symbol refines itself almost to spirituality.

With a large part of mankind, a far larger no doubt of womankind, whose sensibilities are in general more quick and intense than the reasoning faculties, Christian emotion will still either be the whole of religion, or the measure, and the test of religion. Doubtless some primary elements of religion seem intuitive, and are anterior to, or rise without the consciousness of any reasoning process, whose office it is to confirm and strengthen them—the existence of God and of the Infinite, Divine Providence, the religious sense of right and wrong, retribution; more or less vaguely the immortality of the soul. Other doctrines will ever be assumed to be as eternal and immutable. With regard to these, the religious sentiment, which lives upon religious emotion, will be as reluctant to appeal to the

slow, cold verdict of the judgement. Their evidence is
their power of awakening, keeping alive, and rendering
more intense the feeling, the passion of reverence, of
adoration, of awe and love. To question them is impiety;
to examine them perilous imprudence; to reject them
misery, the most dreary privation. Emotional religion
—and how large a part of the religion of mankind is
emotional!—refuses any appeal from itself.

Latin Christianity, too, will continue to have a firmer
hold on the nations of Latin descent; of those whose
languages have a dominant affinity with the Latin. It
is not even clear whether it may not have some secret
charm for those instructed in Latin; at all events, with
them the religious language of Latin Christianity being
more intelligible, hardly more than an antiquated and
sacred dialect of their own, will not so peremptorily
demand its transference into the popular and vernacular
tongue.

But that which is the strength of Latin Christianity
in some regions, in some periods, with some races, with
some individual minds, is in other lands, times, nations,
and minds its fatal, irremediable principle of decay and
dissolution; and must become more so with the advancement of mankind in knowledge, especially in historical
knowledge. That authority which is here a sacred,
revered despotism, is there an usurpation, an intolerable
tyranny. The Teutonic mind never entirely threw off
its innate independence. The long feuds of the Empire
and the Papacy were but a rude and premature attempt
at emancipation from a yoke to which Rome had submitted her conqueror. Had the Emperors not striven
for the mastery of the Latin world, had they stood aloof
from Italy, even then the issue might have been different.
A Teutonic Emperor had been a more formidable anta-

gonist. But it is not the authority of the Pope alone,
but that of the sacerdotal order, against which there is
a deep, irresistible insurrection in the Teutonic mind.
Men have begun to doubt, men are under the incapacity
of believing, men have ceased to believe, the absolutely
indispensable necessity of the intervention of any one of
their fellow-creatures between themselves and the mercy
of God. They cannot admit that the secret of their
eternal destination is undeniably confided to another;
that they must walk not by the light of their own conscience, but by foreign guidance; that the Clergy are
more than messengers with a mission to keep up, by
constant reiteration, the truths of the Gospel, to be prepared by special study for the interpretation of the
sacred writings, to minister in the simpler ordinances
of religion; that they have absolute power to release
from sins; without omniscience to act in the place
of the Omniscient. This, which, however disguised or
softened off, is the doctrine of Latin, of mediæval, of
Papal Christianity, has become offensive, presumptuous;
to the less serious, ludicrous. Of course, as the relative
position of the Clergy, once the sole masters of almost
all intellectual knowledge, law, history, philosophy, has
totally changed, their lofty pretensions jar more strongly
against the common sense of man. Even the interpretation of the sacred writings is no secret and esoteric
doctrine, no mystery of which they are the sole and
exclusive hierophants.

    Toleration, in truth—toleration, which is utterly
irreconcileable with the theory of Latin Christianity—
has been forced into the mind and heart of Christendom,
even among many whose so-called immutable creed is
in its irrevocable words as intolerant as ever. What
was proclaimed boldly, nakedly, without reserve, without

limitation, and as implicitly believed by little less than
all mankind, is now, in a large part of the civilised
world, hardly asserted except in the heat of controversy,
or from a gallant resolution not to shrink from logical
consequences. Wherever publicly avowed or maintained,
it is thought but an odious adherence to ignorant bigotry.
It is believed by a still-diminishing few that Priest,
Cardinal, Pope has the power of irrevocably pre-declaring the doom of his fellow men. Though the Latin
Church-language may maintain its unmitigated severity,
it is eluded by some admitted reservation, some implied
condition utterly at variance with the peremptory tone
of the old anathema. Excommunication is obsolete; the
interdict on a nation has not been heard for centuries;
even the proscription of books is an idle protest.

The subjective, more purely internal, less demonstra-
tive character of Teutonic religion is equally impatient
of the more distinct and definite, and rigid objectiveness
of Latin Christianity. That which seems to lead the
Southern up to heaven, the regular intermediate ascending hosts of Saints, Martyrs, Apostles, the Virgin, to the
contemplative Teuton obscures and intercepts his awful,
intuitive sense of the Godhead, unspiritualises his Deity,
whom he can no longer worship as pure Spirit. To him
it is the very vagueness, vastness, incomprehensibility of
his conception of the Godhead which proclaims its reality.
If here God must be seen on the altar in a materialised
form, at once visible and invisible; if God must be
working a perpetual miracle; if the passive spirit must
await the descent of the Godhead in some sensible sign
or symbol;—there, on the other hand (especially as the
laws of nature become better known and more familiar,
and what of old seemed arbitrary variable agencies are
become manifest laws), the Deity as it were recedes into

2 A 2

more unapproachable majesty. It may indeed subtilise
itself into a metaphysical First Cause, may expand into
a dim Pantheism, but with the religious his religion
still rests in a wise and sublime and revered system of
Providential government which implies the Divine Personality.

Latin, the more objective faith, tends to materialism,
to servility, to blind obedience or blind guidance, to the
tacit abrogation, if not the repudiation, of the moral
influence by the undue elevation of the dogmatic and
ritual part. It is prone to become, as it has become,
Paganism with Christian images, symbols, and terms; it
has, in its consummate state, altogether set itself above
and apart from Christian, from universal morality, and
made what are called works of faith the whole of religion;
the religion of the murderer, who, if while he sheathes
his dagger in the heart of his victim, he does homage to
an image of the Virgin, is still religious;[m] the religion
of the tyrant, who, if he retires in Lent to sackcloth and
ashes, may live the rest of the year in promiscuous concubinage, and slaughter his subjects by thousands. So
Teutonic Christianity, more self-depending, more self-
guided, more self-wrought-out, is not without its peculiar
dangers. It may become self-sufficient, unwarrantably
arrogant, impatient not merely of control, but of all
subordination, incapable of just self-estimation. It will
have a tendency to isolate the man, either within himself
or as a member of a narrow sect, with all the evils of
sectarianism, blind zeal, obstinate self-reliance, or rather
self-adoration, hatred, contempt of others, moroseness,
exclusiveness, fanaticism, undue appreciation of small

---

[m] Read what Mr. Coleridge used to call the sublime of Roman Catholic
Antinomianism.   Calderon, Devocion de la Cruz.

things. It will have its own antinomianism, a dissociation of that moral and religious perfection of man which is Christianity; it will appeal to conscious direct influences of Divine Grace with as much confidence, and as little discrimination or judgement, as the Latin to that through the intermediate hierarchy and ritual of the Church.

Its intellectual faith will be more robust; nor will its emotional be less profound and intense. But the strength of its intellectual faith (and herein is at once its glory and its danger) will know no limits to its daring speculation. How far Teutonic Christianity may in some parts already have gone almost or absolutely beyond the pale of Christianity, how far it may have lost itself in its unrebuked wanderings, posterity only will know. What distinctness of conception, what precision of language, may be indispensable to true faith; what part of the ancient dogmatic system may be allowed silently to fall into disuse, as at least superfluous, and as beyond the proper range of human thought and human language; how far the Sacred records may, without real peril to their truth, be subjected to closer investigation; to what wider interpretation, especially of the Semitic portion, those records may submit, and wisely submit, in order to harmonise them with the irrefutable conclusions of science; how far the Eastern veil of allegory which hangs over their truth may be lifted or torn away to show their unshadowed essence; how far the poetic vehicle through which truth is conveyed may be gently severed from the truth;—all this must be left to the future historian of our religion. As it is my own confident belief that the words of Christ, and his words alone (the primal, indefeasible truths of Christianity), shall not pass away; so I cannot presume to say that men may not attain to a clearer, at the same time more full, comprehensive, and balanced sense of those words, than has as yet been generally received in the Christian world. As all else is transient and mutable, these only eternal and universal, assuredly, whatever light may be thrown on the mental constitution of man, even on the constitution of nature, and the laws which govern the world, will be concentered so as to give a more penetrating vision of those undying truths. Teutonic Christianity (and this seems to be its mission and privilege), however nearly in its more perfect form it may already have approximated, may approximate still more closely to the absolute and perfect faith of Christ; it may discover and establish the sublime unison of religion and reason ; keep in tone the triple-chorded harmony of faith, holiness, and charity; assert its own full freedom, know the bounds of that freedom, respect the freedom of others. Christianity may yet have to exercise a far wider, even if more silent and untraceable influence, through its primary, all-pervading principles, on the civilisation of mankind.

(359)

INDEX.

INDEX.

ART.

iii. 184. Reinstates Queen Theatberga, 186. His flight and death, 200.

ART, devotional, ii. 345. Objects of, 393, 394. Conventional, ix. 323. Development of, 329. Cultivated by Mendicant orders, 333. German—Flemish, 338.

ARTAVASDUS, usurps throne of Constantinople, ii. 368. Is defeated and blinded, 370.

ARTHUR, King, legends of, ix. 317.

ARTHUR, Prince, death of, v. 264.

ARUNDEL, Archbishop of Canterbury, viii. 208. Accuses Lord Cobham, 217.

ASPILALTER, Peter, Archbishop of Mentz, vii. 305, 386.

ASIATIC Christianity, feebleness of, ii. 163.

ASSISI, birthplace of St. Francis, vi. 25. Splendour of church at, ix. 334.

ASTOLPH, Lombard king, seizes Ravenna, iii. 15. Threatens Rome, 16. Defeated by Franks—obtains peace—besieges Rome, 21. Yields to Pepin, 24. His death, 35.

ASYLUM, in Barbaric law, ii. 51, 58.

ATHALARIC, son of Theodoric, raised to throne of Italy—his death, i. 426. Laws of, on church matters, ii. 36.

ATHANASIAN creed, i. 78.

ATHANASIUS, i. 75. His ascendency at Rome, 76. Supported by Pope Liberius, 81.

ATHANASIUS, Bishop-Duke of Naples, iii. 222. Unites with the Saracens, 222. Excommunicated by John VIII., his intrigues, 231.

ATTALUS made Emperor by Alaric, i. 128. Deposed by him, 129.

ATTILA, his unbounded power, i. 274. His invasion of Italy, 275. Threatens Rome, 275. Induced to retire by Leo I., 276. Probable causes of this, 276.

BACON.

AVERRHOES, ix. 110, 117.

AUGUSTINE, St., his 'City of God,' i. 138. Opposes Pelagius, 142. The leader of Latin theology, 147. Opinions on infant baptism, 148. Persecutes Pelagians, 163, 164.

AUGUSTINE, his mission to Britain, ii. 124, 229. His meeting with Ethelbert, 230. Bishop of Canterbury, 230. His dispute with British clergy, 233. His establishment at Canterbury, 234.

AUGUSTINIANISM coincides with sacerdotal system, i. 149. On transmission of original sin, 150. Similar to Manicheism, 152. Exalts celibacy, 152.

AUGUSTUS, title of Rienzi, vii. 482.

AVICENNA, ix. 110, 117.

AVIGNON, Pope Clement V. at, vii. 280. Consistory at, 285. Its political situation, 334. Becomes seat of popedom, 339. Court of, under Clement VI., 451. Immorality at, 452. Sold to Pope, 462. Consistory of, viii. 2. Conclave at, its statutes, 4. Papal residence at, concluded, 31. Siege of, 88.

AVITUS, Bishop of Vienne, adheres to Clovis, i. 351. His conference with Gundebald, 354.

AUSITZ, battle of, viii. 143.

AUTHARIS, king of Lombards, his wars with the Franks, ii. 111. Overruns Italy, 111. His death, 114 note.

AUTOCRACY, Papal, growth of, v. 168.

AZEVEDO, Bishop of Osma, vi. 12.

BABYLON, name applied to Rome, vii. 353, 372.

'BABYLONISH captivity' ended, viii. 31.

BACON, Lord, ix. 159.

BACON, Roger, ix. 152. At Oxford, 153. His studies, 154. Persecuted by Nicolas IV., 155. Dedicates work to Clement IV., 156. His astrology, 157. His science and discoveries, 159.

392 INDEX.

2 D 2

THE END.